ECONOMIC CHANGE AND THE NATIONAL QUESTION IN TWENTIETH-CENTURY EUROPE

The authors in this collection of essays address the largely neglected but significant *economic* aspects of the national question in historical context during the course of the twentieth century.

There exists a large gap in our understanding of the historical relationship between the 'national question' and economic change. Above all, there is insufficient knowledge about the economic dimension of the historical experience with regard to the former multinational states, such as the Soviet Union, Yugoslavia or Czechoslovakia; and, equally, too little is known about the economic component of national tensions and conflicts in bilingual Belgium or Finland, or the multilingual Spain or Switzerland. At the same time as emphasis is placed on the complex relationships between the economy and society in individual European countries, questions of state, identity, language, religion and racism as instruments of economic furtherance are at the centre of the contributors' attention.

The overall aim of the volume is to promote a better understanding of the resurgence of the national question in late twentieth-century Europe against the changing economic, social and political background.

ALICE TEICHOVA is Emeritus Professor of Economic History, University of East Anglia and an Honorary Fellow of Girton College, Cambridge.

HERBERT MATIS is Professor of Economic and Social History, Wirtschaftsuniversität, Vienna.

JAROSLAV PÁTEK is Professor of Economic History, Institute of Economic and Social History, Charles University, Prague.

ECONOMIC CHANGE AND THE NATIONAL QUESTION IN TWENTIETH-CENTURY EUROPE

EDITED BY

ALICE TEICHOVA, HERBERT MATIS
AND JAROSLAV PÁTEK

CAMBRIDGE
UNIVERSITY PRESS

#43513340

PUBLISHED BY THE PRESS SYNDICATE OF THE UNIVERSITY OF CAMBRIDGE
The Pitt Building, Trumpington Street, Cambridge, United Kingdom

CAMBRIDGE UNIVERSITY PRESS
The Edinburgh Building, Cambridge CB2 2RU, UK   http://www.cup.cam.ac.uk
40 West 20th Street, New York, NY 10011–4211, USA   http://www.cup.org
10 Stamford Road, Oakleigh, Melbourne 3166, Australia
Ruiz de Alarcón 13, 28014 Madrid, Spain

© Cambridge University Press 2000

First published 2000

Printed in the United Kingdom at the University Press, Cambridge

Typeface Monotype Baskerville 11/12.5pt.   *System* QuarkXPress™   [SE]

A catalogue record for this book is available from the British Library

Library of Congress Cataloguing in Publication data

Economic change and the national question in twentieth-century Europe / edited by Alice
Teichova, Herbert Matis and Jaroslav Pátek
p.   cm.
ISBN 0 521 63037 1 (hbk)
1. Europe – Economic conditions – 20th century.   2. Nationalism – Economic
aspects – Europe – History – 20th century.   I. Teichova, Alice.   II. Matis, Herbert.
III. Pátek, Jaroslav
HC240.C272 2000   330.94′05–dc21   00-024474

ISBN 0 521 63037 1 hardback

Contents

v

Figures

Tables

Notes on contributors

NEVEN BORAK is at the University of Ljubljana, Slovenia. Recent publications include: *Iskanje Guliverja* [Searching for Gulliver], (Ljubljana, 1994); *Denarne reforme* [Monetary reforms], (Ljubljana, 1998).

CHRISTOPH BOYER is a Fellow at the Hannah-Arendt Institut für Totalitarismusforschung, and a Reader in Social and Economic History, Technical University Dresden. Publications include: 'Die deutsch-tschechoslowakischen Wirtschaftsbeziehungen seit 1918. Alte Verbindungen-Neue Ängste' in Niedersächsische Landeszentrale für politische Bildung (ed.), *Tschechen, Slowaken und Deutsche. Nachbarn in Europa* (Hannover, 1996); *Nationale Kontrahenten oder Partner? Studien zu den Beziehungen zwischen Tschechen und Deutschen in der Wirtschaft der ČSR (1918–1938)* (Munich, 1999).

ERIK BUYST is Professor of Economic History at the Centrum voor Economische Studien, Katholieke Universiteit Leuven. Publications include: *An Economic History of Residential Building in Belgium between 1890 and 1961* (Leicester, 1993); 'National accounts for the Low Countries, 1880–1990', *Scandinavian Economic History Review* 43 (1995), 53–76.

LUIGI DE ROSA is Professor of Economic History at the Free International University in Social Sciences (LUISS), Rome. He is editor of the *Journal of European Economic History*, and the author of many books and articles including: 'Economics and nationalism in Italy (1861–1914)', *The Journal of European Economic History* 11(3) (1972), 537–74, *History of the Bank of Naples*, 4 vols. (Naples, 1989–1992); *History of the Bank of Rome* (Rome, 1992–1993); *The Economic Development of Italy from the Second World War to 1996* (Rome, 1997).

MARGARITA DRITSAS is Professor at the Department of History, University of Crete. She is author of books and articles on Greek economic, social and business history. Her publications include: *Industry and Banking in Interwar Greece* (Athens, 1990); *The History of the Greek Paint Industry 1830–1990* (Athens, 1995); 'Swedish capital in Greece', *Scandinavian Economic History Review* (1996), 3–22; editor with Terry Gourvish *European Enterprise Strategies of adaptation and renewal in the Twentieth Century* (Athens, 1997).

BRUNO FRITZSCHE is Professor of History at the University of Zurich. His main field of research is the history of urbanisation in the nineteenth and twentieth centuries. His most recent publications include: 'Grenzen und Grenzverletzungen in sozialen Räumen' in Inst. f. Denkmalpflege an der ETH Zurich (ed.), *Stadt- und Landmauern*, vol. III (Zurich, 1999), pp. 40–8 and (as a coauthor), *Handbuch der Buendner Geschichte* (Chur, 2000).

MONTSERRAT GÁRATE OJANGUREN is Professor of Economic History, Universidad des País Vasco, San Sebastian, Spain. Among her publications are: 'Instituciones financieras en el País Vasco. Articulaciòn y crecimiento del sistema bancario en Gipuzkoa (1899–1930)' in P. Martin Aceňa (ed.), *Economía y empresa en el Norte de España* (1994); 'La ilustraciòn vasca y el sector del País' in *Ilustrazíoa Euskal Herrian* (1998); *La historia de un banco regional. El Banco Guipuzcoano 1899–1999* (1999).

RIITTA HJERPPE is Professor of Economic History, Department of Economic and Social History, University of Helsinki, Finland, and is editor of *Scandinavian Economic History Review*. Among her many publications: *The Economic History of Finland* (Helsinki, 1989).

ROMAN HOLEC is Reader of History, Philosophical Faculty, Comenius University, Bratislava. Among his publications: 'Medzi slovanskou vzájomnosti a podnikatelskou aktivitou. Pražská banka Slávia v Uhorsku v druhej polovici 10. storočia' [Between Slavic mutuality and business activity. The Prague bank Slávia in Hungary in the second half of the nineteenth century], *Economic History* 21 (1995), 145–72.

STEFAN HOUPT is Lecturer at the University of St Louis in Madrid and at the Universidad San Pablo. His dissertation dealt with *Technical Change and Location of the Spanish Integral Iron and Steel Industry, 1882–1998* (Madrid, 1998). He is coeditor of *Astilleros Espanoles. La contrucciòn naval en España, 1872–1998* (Madrid, 1998).

ANU MAI KÖLL is Professor of Baltic History, Culture and Society, Department of Baltic Studies, Stockholm University. Among her publications are: *Peasants and the World Market* (Stockholm, 1993); *Economic Nationalism and Industrial Growth: State and Industry in Estonia 1934–39* (Stockholm, 1998).

EDUARD KUBŮ is a Reader at Charles University, Prague. Among his publications are: *Německo – zahraničně politické dilema Edvarda Beneše* [Germany – foreign policy dilemma of Eduard Beneš] (Prague, 1994); with Antonín Klimek, *Československá zahraniční politika let 1918–1924* [Czechoslovak foreign policy 1918–1924] (Prague, 1995).

JUHA-ANTTI LAMBERG is Researcher of the Finnish Academy Department of History, University of Jyväskylä. Recent publications include: 'Economic interest groups in Finnish foreign trade policy decision-making', *Scandinavian Economic History Review* 2 (1998); doctoral dissertation: *Taloudelliset eturyhmäl neuvolleluprocesseissa – Suomen kauppasoplmuspolitiikka 1918–1938* [Economic interest groups in negotiation processes – Finnish trade agreement policy 1918–1938].

HERBERT MATIS is Professor of Economic History at the Economics University, Vienna. He is author of books and articles including: with D. Stiefel, *'Mit der vereinigten Kraft des Capitals, des Credits und der Technik . . .' Die Geschichte des österreichischen Bauwesens am Beispiel der Allgemeinen Baugesellschaft – A. Porr Aktiengesellschaft*, 2 vols. (Vienna, Cologne and Weimar, 1994); editor with Alice Teichova, *Österreich und die Tschechoslowakei 1918–1938 Die wirtschaftliche Neuordnung in Zentraleuropa der Zwischenkriegszeit* (Vienna, Cologne and Weimar, 1996).

ALAN O'DAY is Professor of Economic History at the University of North London. He is author of many books and articles including: *The Making of Modern Irish History Revisionism and the Revisionist Controversy* (editor with D. George Boyce) (London, 1996).

JAROSLAV PÁTEK is Professor of Economic History at Charles University, Prague. His publications include: *Dějiny hospodářství českých zemí* [The economic history of the Czech Lands], (Prague, 1995).

ÁGNES POGÁNY is a Senior Research Fellow at the Department of Economic History, Budapest University of Economic Sciences. Among her publications are: 'The history of the Hungarian Bank of Issue, 1914–1924', Parts IV and V of *A Magyar Nemzeti Bank Története*

[The history of the Hungarian National Bank] (Budapest, 1993), vol. I, pp. 343–499; 'The liquidation of the Austro-Hungarian Bank' in *Fra Spazio e Tempo Studi in Onore di Luigi De Rosa*, Edizioni Scientifiche Italiane (1995), vol. III.

ALICE TEICHOVA is Emeritus Professor of Economic History at the University of East Anglia in Norwich and Honorary Fellow of Girton College, Cambridge. She received Honorary Doctorates from the University of Uppsala and the University of Vienna. Recently she edited with Eric Bussière and Michel Dumoulin *L'Europe centrales et orientale en recherche d'intégration économique (1900–1950)* (Louvain-la-Neuve, 1998).

JÖRG ROESLER is Professor of Economic History and Fellow of the Leibniz-Societät, Berlin. He is author of numerous publications, including: 'Handelsgeschäfte im Kalten Krieg' in Ch. Buchheim (ed.), *Wirtschaftliche Folgen des Krieges in der SBZ/DDR* (Baden-Baden, 1995); 'Der Einfluss der Aussenwirtschaftspolitik auf die Beziehungen der DDR-Bundesrepublik', *Deutschland Archiv* 5 (1993).

JERZY TOMASZEWSKI is Professor of Economic History and Director of the M. Anielewicz Centre for the Study and Teaching of the History and Culture of Jews in Poland, Warsaw University. Among recent books are: with J. Adelson, T. Prekerowa and P. Wròbel, *Najnowsze dzieje Żidów w Polsce w zrysie (do 1950 roku)* [The most recent history of Jews in Poland (until 1950)], (Warsaw, 1993); and with Zbigniew Landau, *Bank Handłowy w Warszawie S. A. Zarys dziejów 1870–1995* [The Commercial Bank in Warsaw Ltd. The history from 1870 to 1995], (Warsaw, 1995).

GABRIEL TORTELLA is Professor of Economic History, at the Universidad de Alcala, Madrid. He is President of the Academic Committee of the European Association for Banking History. His latest books include: *Una historia de los Bancos Central e Hispano Americano, 1900–2000* with J. L. Garcia Ruiz (forthcoming); editor with R. Sylla and R. Tilly, *The State, the Financial System, and Economic Modernization* (Cambridge, 1999); *El desarrollo de la España contemporánea. Historia econòmica de los siglos XIX y XX* (Madrid, 1994, 1995 and 1998).

NUNO VALÉRIO is Professor of Economic History, Technical University of Lisbon. Among his publications, with Eugénia Mata, *História Económica de Portugal* (Lisbon, 1994).

ANDREI YU. YUDANOV is Professor of Economics at the Financial Academy under the Government of Russia, Moscow. His recent publications include: *Applied Theory of Competition* (Moscow, 1996); 'Unternehmensmanagement unter den Bedingungen der Wiederherstellung des Wettbewerbes in Russland' in Claus Steinle *et al.* (eds.), *Management in Mittel- und Osteuropa* (Frankfurt am Main, 1996).

Acknowledgements

This volume arose out of the preparations for the session on 'Economic change and the national question in twentieth-century Europe' at the Twelfth International Economic History Congress in Madrid, 24 to 28 August 1998. The papers were presented and discussed at a pre-Congress conference in Vienna in June 1997 and at the session in Madrid. We should like to thank the authors of papers, rapporteurs and discussants who made both the Vienna conference and the Madrid session a success. The preparatory period gave authors time to revise their papers and editors the chance to be in close contact with the authors.

We have incurred various debts to institutions: the Institute of Economic and Social History of the Economics University of Vienna, the Austrian Ministry of Science and Transport and the British Academy. For their assistance we are truly grateful. Our warm thanks go to Dr Charlotte Natmeßnig who helped in the organisation of the Vienna conference and special thanks are due to William Davies of Cambridge University Press for his interest and help in the completion of this volume.

Introduction

Alice Teichova, Herbert Matis and Jaroslav Pátek

The twentieth century has been called 'the age of extremes'[1] as well as the cruellest and bloodiest century in the history of mankind. Its course was crucially influenced by nationalism combined with racism. During its history, nationalism, intrinsically connected with the national question, manifested itself in diverse forms in various countries and regions at different times. While there are a good many publications on nationalism, including its political, cultural and religious background, the economic dimension of the national question has been little examined. In the last analysis there lurks the demanding problem of mediation. That is, essentially, the problem of identifying and comprehending the interconnections between political, ideological and economic spheres.

The problem has very rarely been addressed and this volume attempts to draw attention to the need to study it. There can be no doubt about the enduring significance and the immense historical impact of the national question,[2] which, we realise, concerns European as well as non-European populations. But, in order to achieve a feasible geographical scope and timescale, this volume deals with the national question in the light of economic change in European countries in the twentieth century. It contains twenty case studies on nations and nationalities in countries spanning Europe from west to east – Ireland to Russia – and south to north – Greece to Estonia. Applying a multifaceted approach by taking into account such aspects as the state, national identity, language or religion, the authors investigate the relationship between economic activity and the national question in the twentieth century.

The political landscape of Europe does not permit a neat division of countries into those with a nationally homogeneous population and those with nationally mixed populations. Such divisions have, indeed, never existed as states are dispersed throughout Europe either with linguistic and ethnic majorities, or small ethnic minorities, or bilingual, multilingual and/or multiethnic populations.

I

In countries of western Europe the national question has, generally, not been accompanied by frequent eruptions of violence. The exception is Ireland, discussed in Alan O'Day's essay. The changing contours of Irish nationalism are examined in the framework of Britain's capitalist development and its situation as a world empire and centre of international trade and finance to which, as O'Day argues, historically Ireland has belonged – even after Southern Ireland's independence in 1921 – down to the present day. Throughout, the strength and violent features of the national question have not abated.

Beginning with the western countries of continental Europe, Erik Buyst analyses the history of the close interplay of economics and politics in Belgium that affected the seesawing relationship between the two large language groups, the French speakers in Wallonia and the Dutch speakers in Flanders. He convincingly shows how changes in economic performance in both regions profoundly affected power-political issues. That is, until the 1950s the economic performance of French-speaking Wallonia had been more significant; however, since the 1950s Flemish economic growth has strengthened the political influence of Dutch speakers, leading to linguistic, administrative and fiscal equivalence.

In the case study of divided post-Second World War Germany, Jörg Roesler implicitly poses the question of whether Germans living under different socio-economic systems in the Federal Republic of Germany (FRG) and the German Democratic Republic (GDR) developed separate national identities. Taking German–German trade as a touchstone, he examines periods of strong trade links, which tended to strengthen unifying elements against the official policy of political separation, and periods of virtually complete economic and trading separation followed by frozen political relations. Although two separate German national identities had not developed by 1990, when unification occurred differing economic structures in East and West stymied the process of overcoming social and mental differences.

Quite different was the fate of the small Slav enclave of the Sorbs in pre-1945 Germany and in the post-1949 GDR, which is examined by Eduard Kubů. Before 1945, in the setting of the numerically and economically overwhelming power of the German population, the Sorbs were unable to resist relentless Germanisation in the face of urbanisation and industrialisation. After 1945, even with official support during the decades of the GDR regime, a question mark was hanging over the continuing existence of Sorbs as a separate ethnic and language community.

Various authors show that the pressures of the market economy tend to sharpen national conflicts and bring them to the surface where they latently exist. In Switzerland considerations of national issues appear as an act of political pragmatism. Thus Bruno Fritzsche maintains that Switzerland is not a multinational but a multilingual state, whose population has acquired a Swiss identity. Historically decisive was the reality of linguistic and administrative autonomy. While national prejudices and economic reasons for conflict have not been absent and regional economic differentiation has always existed, economic levels on a cantonal basis have been fairly equal, and there has been no concentrated economic backwardness in any linguistic region. This is shown in detail in Fritzsche's chapter. During the twentieth century, differences due to industrialisation and migration more strongly affected social antagonisms than cultural or national conflicts.

Southern European countries of the Mediterranean peninsulas display remarkable parallels of political and economic nationalism in historic perspective but, towards the end of the twentieth century, the European Union played an integrating role. Portugal is one of the few European countries where the population is ethnically almost homogeneous and to which the term 'nation state' can effectively be applied. Nuno Valério distinguishes between two periods in the course of the twentieth century. The first half of the century was dominated by the perception of a threat from Spain, which seems to have been a reaction to Portugal's long-lasting economic decline in the wake of the loss of its empire. However, from the late 1940s this traditional pattern was changing when the Portuguese, turning towards European integration, brought forth economic recovery and growth.

Although the threat from Spain, as perceived in Portugal, never materialised, strong Spanish nationalism is, according to Gabriel Tortella and Stefan Houpt, a twentieth-century phenomenon; it developed almost parallel to Catalan and Basque nationalism, which was brutally suppressed. This was accompanied and supported by Spanish economic nationalism in its extreme forms during the dictatorships of Miguel Primo de Rivera and Francisco Franco. Nationalist interventionist and protectionist policies were slightly loosened during the endphase of Franco's fascist hold on the economy and society and only finally disappeared as late as 1986, with Spain's admission to the European Union.

Spain's membership of the European Union has not solved the Basque national question. As one of Europe's serious violent movements, Basque nationalism has long historical roots. These are traced from its beginnings to the present by Montserrat Gárate Ojanguren, who emphasises the importance of economic factors such as Basque participation in key sectors of the Spanish economy since the late nineteenth century, the dramatic impact of the world economic crisis and the decline of heavy industry, which increased social grievances and fanned the Basque nationalist movement.

As to Italy, it was the legacy of territorial fragmentation and relative economic backwardness that affected the national question there. Luigi De Rosa shows that there existed a strong and unceasing relationship between nationalism and the economy in the course of the twentieth century. Fascist chauvinism was accompanied by extreme economic protectionism and military campaigns aimed at colonial conquest in the first half of the century. Italy's participation in the process of European cooperation in the second half-century was not bereft of nationalist tendencies, eager to assert national interests within the European Community.

In Greece, as in Italy, memories of a glorious ancient past were prone to be misused to foster the irredentist dream of a 'Great Greece', as Margarita Dritsas remarks. But her concern is with the historical process of nation-building, national integration and economic development, in which commerce played a larger role than industry in comparison with Italy or Spain.

Turning to central and south-eastern European states – Austria, Czechoslovakia, Hungary and Yugoslavia – which arose on the ruins of the Habsburg Monarchy, we are confronted with great diversity: such as a west–south-east gradient of relative economic backwardness and ethnic dispersion intensified by wars, national strife and migration.

In nationally largely homogeneous Germany the striving for a common national market, in the nineteenth century, furthered the national unification process culminating in the establishment of a nation state. In nationally heterogeneous Austria-Hungary the existence of a common market did not prevent its demise in the wake of its defeat in the First World War. The unsolved national question in a multinational empire, inhabited as it was by twelve ethnic groups with different languages, various religions and diverse cultures, and at different levels of economic development, proved to have had the explosive force of dynamite. After the dissolution of Austria-Hungary in 1918, the national question reappeared variously in the newly formed small states of central and south-eastern Europe, which had inherited the west–east and, in the case of Yugoslavia, also the north–south gradient of economic development from the former empire.

The German-speaking Austrians living after 1918 in a shrunken state that remained from a large empire in which they had been the dominant national group did not, for a long time, see themselves as a people with a national identity separate from that of the Germans. They also doubted the economic viability of their new state. Herbert Matis pursues these issues through the twentieth century and guides the reader through the stages from 'the state that nobody wanted' to the post-Second World War period when the decisive economic upswing supported a common feeling among Austrians of being 'a distinct Austrian nation'.

At the same time as Austria became nationally a largely homogeneous state, the Czechoslovak Republic, founded on 28 October 1918, remained, as Jaroslav Pátek writes, a kind of miniature Austria-Hungary. His detailed analysis of the national and social composition of the Czechoslovak population leads the reader towards a deeper understanding of the internal and external forces that, in a relatively successful economy, enhanced national strife and brought about the fateful Munich Agreement in 1938, followed by the dismemberment of the only remaining democracy in Central Europe.

Pátek's survey of the geographical and occupational distribution of nationalities provides a necessary background to understanding Christoph Boyer's essay on the complicated issue of competition between indigenous German-speaking and Czech-speaking entrepreneurs in the economy of interwar Czechoslovakia. Contrary to some contemporary assertions, Boyer shows that there existed neither a pure Czech nor a separate German economy within Czechoslovakia. He finds both partnership and rivalry in which nationalistic and chauvinistic arguments were used, influenced strongly by National Socialism since its rise in Germany in the 1930s.

Slovakia's economic development, and particularly the Czech–Slovak relationship through all stages of political changes, from Austro-Hungarian times to the present receives attention from Roman Holec. He elucidates a little-known chapter in the history of the two nations and throws light on the separation of Czechoslovakia into two separate republics in 1992 when, as he says, all differences, including the levelling out of the disparate economic development, were less contentious than at any time during the existence of Czechs and Slovaks in a common state.

Slovaks constituted themselves ethnically within the Hungarian state and politically as a nation during the nineteenth century. They are included in Ágnes Pogány's account of national minorities in Hungary, where the content of the national question rapidly changed with the break-up of Austria-Hungary. Magyars found themselves in a majority accounting for almost 90 per cent of Trianon Hungary's total population. Nevertheless, Magyar nationalism was made use of by Hungary's ruling elite to bolster revisionist demands at the same time as, in an atmosphere of suspicion and aggressive nationalism, ethnic minorities became a weapon in economic competition against neighbouring successor states.

Since its foundation in 1918, multinational Yugoslavia – which, not unlike Czechoslovakia, inherited its uneven economic development from the Habsburg Monarchy – has been a country of economic contrasts, from the relatively industrially advanced Slovenia and Croatia to the poorest and economically most backward Kosovo. Neven Borak presents a historical survey of the changing political scene and an analysis of economic changes. He discusses the causes and consequences of events that led, in the course of the post-1945 decades, to the revival and growth of destructive nationalism and the violent dissolution of Yugoslavia in the 1990s. While the economic situation has been misused as a potent instrument for mutual nationalist accusations about 'exploitation' among federal units, the divergent pace of democratisation in different parts of Yugoslavia and the vacuum left by the dissolution of the communist system played an equally, if not more important, role than economic factors in the country's disintegration. The violent consequences of these dramatic events have been witnessed in the last decade of the twentieth century.

Lastly, the relationship between the economy and nationalities are explored in states that arose on the territory of Wilhelmine Germany after its defeat in the First World War and of tsarist Russia after the victory of the Bolshevik Revolution in 1917 and following upon the disintegration of the Soviet Union after 1989.

Jerzy Tomaszewski deals with the considerable socio-economic, national and regional differences in the post-1918 Polish Republic, whose territory had been divided between the three neighbouring powers – Austria, Prussia and Russia. Within Poland, where the dominant Polish-speaking population held a two-thirds majority, the geographic boundaries between nationalities were, similar to Czechoslovakia, seldom clear-cut. This is shown in Tomaszewski's survey, in which he confronts economic statistics with the regional distribution of nationalities from Poland's population censuses. The author states that, generally, historians stress the political aspects of the national question in Poland; against this opinion he puts forward evidence that backs up his conclusion that national conflicts could only be solved by fundamental changes in the economic and social structure of Poland accompanied by economic growth and diminishing differences between economically advanced and backward regions.

Among the Baltic peoples, Estonians perceived foreign domination, immigration and low demographic growth as the main threats to their survival as a nation. These aspects are addressed by Anu Mai Köll in her discussion of the ethnic division of labour and the economic and ethnic policy of successive governments in Estonia. She details how the social structure of the Estonian population, which came to consist overwhelmingly of workers and employees, was strongly affected by economic change.

Remarkably, Riitta Hjerppe and Juha-Antti Lamberg find, on the basis of analysis of foreign trade, that economic developments seem to have had no significant impact on the national question in Finland. In spite of discontinuities, similar to those in Estonia, Finland was able to withstand Russification and Sovietisation in the course of the twentieth century. Also, the equalisation of Finnish and Swedish as official languages seems to have prevented the rise of national antagonisms on a mass scale. The authors conclude that Finland gained independence not as a result of nationalism but rather because of the chaotic developments in Russia.

Andrei Yudanov introduces a novel approach as he tackles the complicated case of multinational Russia by investigating entrepreneurship during the period of industrialisation in the Soviet Union and during the period of disintegration in post-Soviet Russia. The author's main concern is to approach national issues from the point of view of their impact on the functioning of the community of enterprises. He shows that the break-up of the multinational Soviet state and of the Union-wide web of enterprises that had contributed to unifying it caused a grave crisis in the economy when national conflicts and political power struggles contributed to destroying the centralised macroeconomic superstructure of Soviet enterprises. In conclusion he optimistically finds some evidence of a contemporary trend toward the regeneration of the historically shaped community of enterprises.

The subject-matter approached cannot be exhausted in one volume of essays. As indicated, its aim is to stimulate study and debate. This is essential if we wish to begin to understand, for example, the historical background of terrible events in Yugoslavia we see and read about as the book goes to press.

NOTES

1 Eric Hobsbawm, *Age of Extremes: The Short Twentieth Century 1914–1991* (London, 1994).
2 Cf. Mikuláš Teich and Roy Porter, *The National Question in Europe in Historical Context* (Cambridge, 1993).

CHAPTER ONE

Nationalism and the economic question in twentieth-century Ireland

Alan O'Day

> We believe that Ireland can be made a self-contained unit, pro-
> viding all the necessities of living in adequate quantities for the
> people residing in the island at the moment and probably for a
> much larger number.   (Séan Lemass, 1932)[1]

INTRODUCTION

It is commonly suggested that the white-hot flame of Irish nationalism
has abated gradually since the earlier part of the twentieth century. If
so, this at least fits part of E. J. Hobsbawm's controversial declaration
that nationalism at the close of the twentieth century is on the verge of
redundancy.[2] Certainly it is true that nationalism in Ireland, especially
in economic policy, has different contours now from a generation ago.
Nationalism in Ireland has four significant ingredients: it is shaped by
the archipelago's history, including its political and social structure as
well as economic factors during the great age of capitalist development;
it is contingent upon Britain's position in the pre-1914 era as the centre
of international trade and finance and its continuing role in exercising
these functions since then; it is formed by Britain's situation as a world
empire at least up to the 1960s; and finally England, more specifically
London, remains the hub of a multinational internal economy to which
Ireland belonged even after 1921 and arguably down to the present day.

The experience of the area now incorporated as the Republic of
Ireland – which is less than the island of Ireland, it is maintained – falls
within the contending frameworks of current theories of nationalism.
Because Northern Ireland, the area comprising the north and eastern
part of the island, remained part of the United Kingdom, it did not have
the option of running an economic policy distinct from that of the
British government at Westminster. It is therefore given less attention in
the present analysis. Ireland has gone through four stages: a modified

economic nationalism of a variety inherited from pre-statehood leaders of the national movement from 1922 to 1932; more complete adoption of protectionism within an ideology of self-sufficiency after Eamon de Valera's government assumed power, 1932 to 1958; planned capitalism accompanied by more open trade and foreign investment, 1958 to 1973; and partial protectionism within the capitalist framework of the European Union, post-1973. None of the eras were self-contained, nor were the predominant strategies within any of the time-spans pursued exclusively; opportunities and constraints of a post-colonial economic reality had an impact on the options available. The goal of policy makers at all times is aptly expressed by Séan Lemass, quoted at the beginning of this chapter; the outcome was often different.

A theme examined here is one suggested by Liam Kennedy, who implies that broadly the economic policy of the Republic of Ireland has been consistent since the creation of the new state. He observes, 'mirroring its role in the nineteenth century as part of the British Empire, Ireland today is an integral part of the developed world. Through its involvement in various international treaties and frameworks, it defends its own interests *against* Third World countries.'[3] 'The Irish state', Kennedy insists:

> through its membership of the European Community actively promotes policies of agricultural protectionism which discriminates strongly against Third World imports. It also participates in schemes to dump European surplus output, produced under conditions of EC subsidy, onto world markets, thereby undercutting the prices of Third World producers.[4]

Coming from a younger economic historian, born in the Irish Republic but a member of the faculty at The Queen's University of Belfast, his thesis merits careful consideration for it takes issue with the predominant strain of thinking about Ireland's approach to economic development since 1958, most notably the presumption of a wider perspective and internationalism.

IRELAND: PRECONDITIONS OF ECONOMIC NATIONALISM

Irish nationalism has been a dynamic ideological movement for attaining and maintaining the autonomy, unity and identity of Ireland and her people; it was a vehicle for activating people and creating solidarity among them in the common quest for a cherished goal. Three ideas are fused – the collective self-determination of the people, an expression of national character and individuality, and the vertical division of the world into unique nations, each contributing its special genius to the common fund of humanity.[5] It rests on what Elie Kedourie describes as the assumption that a nation must have a past and, no less fundamentally, a future and, of course, that future must be attractive economically.[6] What constitutes the state, territory, people and culture has various and far from consistent definitions. This semantic and ideological indecision has an economic dimension, leading to a far from clear-cut set of national priorities. John Breuilly points to the way nationalism fudges distinctions between the cultural and political community:

The demand for statehood is rooted in the national spirit, even if inarticulate and repressed, and the nationalist simply speaks for that spirit.

The identity of the nation is provided in arbitrary ways. The leap from culture to politics is made by portraying the nation at one moment as a cultural community and at another as a political community, whilst insisting that in an ideal state the national community will not be split into cultural and political spheres. The nationalist can exploit this perpetual ambiguity. National independence can be portrayed as the freedom of the citizens who make up the (political) nation or as the freedom of the collectivity which makes up the (cultural) nation. Nationalist ideology is a pseudo-solution to the problem of the relationship between state and society but its plausibility derives from its roots in genuine intellectual responses to that problem.[7]

His assessment is amplified in a rephrased form by a sociologist, Liah Greenfeld, who sees structural, cultural and psychological aspects as part of the same nationalist phenomena.[8] If economic identity is added to constructs proposed by Breuilly and Greenfeld, their descriptions fit Irish circumstances. As a popular political ideology concealing complexities of purpose, Irish nationalism succeeded in the necessary simplification, repetition and concreteness of its message in order to appeal to a mass clientele. By reducing complex emotions to simple expressions, it was able not merely to influence Ireland's politics since the eighteenth century but also to shape the frame of reference within which Anglo-Irish affairs are discussed. Nationalism's success in Ireland, though, was achieved at a heavy cost to the dream of uniting all the peoples of Ireland under one sovereign government and the outcome was narrowed, albeit reluctantly, to a relatively homogeneous state for the twenty-six county area of the island, something depreciated in the derisory republicans' ballad:

> God save the southern part of Ireland
> Three quarters of a nation once again.[9]

On a positive note, Kennedy points out, however, that the 'vanishing Protestant' population 'brought ethnic and sectarian confrontation to a close over much of Ireland'.[10]

A second casualty has been an inability to define a coherent and distinctive long-term economic purpose for the community, especially for its relationship to the former colonising power, at least until after 1973 when the European Union provided a partial alternative rationale. Mary Daly comments on the interplay of the Anglo-Irish legacy, nationalist ideas and practical economics:

> The fledgling Irish state [in 1922] therefore inherited a confused baggage of ideals: a desire to protect rural society and its values and to stabilize the rural population; a vision of industrial development minus the evils of capitalism, materialism, and urbanization; a desire to redress previous disadvantages suffered by Irish businesses; an expectation of material progress without the state provisions; the restoration of the Irish language and culture; and, though not explicit until the 1920s, the enshrining of Catholic social teaching. Other issues were not clearly addressed, in particular the nature of future economic relations with Britain, how exporting industries would coexist with a protected sector and how to reconcile cattle farmers and the restoration of tillage. Except for hopes that electricity and motor cars would help to create this economic idyll, no account was taken of the dictates of the market economy.[11]

Her rather jaundiced assessment can be qualified in three respects: it was not fundamentally distinguishable from the inheritance and outlook of most new states in post-1918 Europe; the confusion of the Irish leadership was not so far removed from that of British policy makers faced with the problems of the interwar economy; and there was more consistency in the approach of the new state than she acknowledges.[12] Always there was a reality, as the Fianna Fáil election manifesto stated in 1932, that 'the people of Britain and ourselves are each other's best customers. Our geographical position and other factors make it unlikely that this close trade relationship will rapidly change.'[13] Even in April 1939 an official acknowledged 'we are very largely at the mercy of other countries and particularly of the United Kingdom, in respect of our external trade and the economic activities of this country could in such circumstances be completely paralyzed'.[14] This paralysis, induced by British national needs during the Second World War, did strike hard in Ireland, leading to a substantial overall reduction in the standard of living, economic activity and social welfare provision. Nationalists scored much better in influencing the outlook of posterity about their political efforts than they have over the economic development of the country. Historians and economists generally have been critical of the nation's economic performance and policy until the close of the 1950s. In *Programme for Economic Expansion*, superintended by an Irish official, T. K. Whittaker, published in 1958, it was observed, 'after 35 years of native government people are asking whether we can achieve an acceptable degree of economic progress'.[15]

Ireland was fertile soil for an outburst of nationalism.[16] Progression from people to nation to state is seen as a natural, legitimate and inevitable course of Ireland's history. Nationalists demanded self-determination and statehood as a historic right. In 1907 John Redmond voiced the nationalist postulate:

That national demand, in plain and popular language, is simply this, that the government of every purely Irish affair shall be controlled by the public opinion of Ireland, and by that alone. We demand this self-government as a right . . . The demand for national self-government is therefore, founded by us, first of all, upon right, and we declare that no ameliorative reforms, no number of land acts, or labourers acts, or education acts, no redress of financial grievances, no material improvements or industrial development, can ever satisfy Ireland until Irish laws are made and administered upon Irish soil by Irishmen.[17]

Michael Collins spoke for another vision of the nation: 'I stand for an Irish civilization based on the people and embodying and maintaining the things – their habits, ways of thought, customs – that make them different.'[18] But over the long haul, Irish nationalists devoted far fewer words to questions of abstract rights, to idealised visions of the future, to the historic basis of the nation or the uniqueness of Irish culture – though, to be sure, these ideas feature in their rhetoric – than they did to expressing themselves in the language of 'historical wrongs'. Emphasis upon 'wrongs' had the strategic virtue of offering the widest common denominator, providing a unifying principle capable of binding together peoples, including potentially a significant segment of Protestants. Its limitation was that such appeals were primarily materialistic, focusing heavily on supposed economic deprivation and exploitation. This sense of disadvantage received ample expression in the common rhetoric of the national movement, though the objective basis for these complaints has been subjected to modern criticism. Kennedy, for instance, deflates the tendency of some commentators to compare Ireland with contemporary Third World nations, pointing out that in 1911 the country had much the same living standard as Spain, Norway, Finland and Italy.[19]

A second strand of the deprivation or 'grievance' theme revolved around the sense of a section of Ireland's peoples, namely Protestants, benefiting from the British connection at the expense of Catholics. For the Irish it was not continental communities but Great Britain and

America that was the point of comparison. Irish standards of living might be comparable to Spain but such comparisons were wide of the mark. Yet even the differentials between Great Britain and Ireland narrowed significantly between the mid-nineteenth century and 1914.[20] Additionally, Donald Akensen shows that if income from rentals is excluded, the economic differential between Irish Protestants and Catholics is quite narrow.[21] It is not, however, what the cold statistics demonstrate so much as what Irish Catholics at the time believed. Greenfeld makes the important observation that feelings of resentment polarised around an ethnic or national cause are likely when a people believes that it is equal to the dominant group but is denied equality because of artificial barriers maintained by the state or the ascendant society.[22] Despite limitations in their strategic vision, nationalists proved remarkably capable of mobilising and retaining the loyalty of most Catholics for the patriotic platform. For the reasons outlined by Greenfeld, they were able to override regional, economic, class and cultural distinctions in spite of British concessions that conceded the substance of their material claims.

Several theoretical insights aid understanding of the emerging nationalism and its economic dimension in Ireland. Miroslav Hroch notes that national movements postulate three demands: political aims centring on self-administration; cultural claims in which they try to establish and strengthen an independent culture; and social and economic goals, asking for a just division of national income along with a full social structure, corresponding to the stage of capitalist transformation of the dominant state.[23] Also, Hroch points out that:

conflicts of interest between classes and groups whose members were divided at the same time by the fact that they belonged to different linguistic groups [in Ireland, religious affiliation] had indisputable significance for the intensification of the national movement. The polarity of material contradictions therefore ran parallel to differences of nationality and as a result of this conflicts of interest were articulated not (or not only) at the social and political level appropriate to them but at the level of national categories and demands.[24]

The situation in Ireland in the nineteenth century conforms to cases of peasants belonging to the non-dominant ethnic group and landlords to the dominant nation, of an ethnic differentiation between the 'centre', that is England, and 'province', that is Ireland, and where a substantial section of the new intelligentsia (he uses the term 'academics') belong to the non-dominant group and the old elites stem from the ruling nation.[25] By the same token he notes, 'where the national movement . . . was not capable of introducing into national agitation . . . the interests of specific classes and groups . . . it was not capable of attaining success'.[26] To this Ernest Gellner affirms that 'conflict of interest and cultural difference are politically effective if, and only if, they are *jointly* present'.[27] Michael Hechter and Margaret Levi suggest that ethnic solidarity arises in regions developed as internal colonies where there is a hierarchical cultural division of labour determining life's chances.[28] Solidarity increases when members interact within the boundaries of their own group. The movement's durability, however, depends on the ability to deliver on its promises. They distinguish between regional and ethnoregional movements: the first couches claims solely in terms of material demands; the second bases its case on ethnic distinctiveness. Greenfeld's analogous point has been examined already.

In the battle for 'hearts and minds' in the late nineteenth and early twentieth centuries, national propagandists scored another huge triumph, stigmatising opponents as bigots, reactionaries or at best well-meaning but misguided dubs; and at the same time engaging their critics to a debate within the parameters defined by themselves. Much of that discussion centres on the two traditions within nationalism – the constitutional and revolutionary – both seeking the same ends by different paths. Redmond's statement above is an example of this dichotomy. A difficulty of the literature on Irish nationalism is that it is politically focused; the economic dimension is typically omitted or given a low priority. It is misleading to break it into political or economic segments. More appropriately, following Daly, it must be viewed as a total process. Nevertheless, Irish nationalists themselves, it must be admitted, often did engage in precisely this sort of myopic analysis at the expense of minimising economic factors.

Ireland exhibits characteristics found elsewhere.[29] National movements everywhere had to locate and then persuade people whom they wish to mobilise that distinctions between themselves and the dominant state were fundamental and more important than any common bonds. Also, they needed to pinpoint the dominant state as the enemy. As in other cases, advance of the national movement in Ireland was complicated by a triangular relationship, which in an ethnic phase found the threatened mainly Protestant minority choosing to identify with, and seek the protection of, Britain, associating themselves culturally and, even more completely, economically with it rather than with Ireland. In other respects, the country differed from the European norm where the more economically advanced regions tended to adopt nationalism for, excepting the north-eastern corner, it was an economic periphery to Great Britain. Language played a much weaker role in Ireland; religion, which was frequently less important as a catalyst elsewhere, was a substitute.[30] While the language question was not wholly absent, because Ireland has been integrated into the Atlantic economy since the eighteenth century, nationalist priorities and more fully those of Irish commerce declined to place it above the clear advantages of being part of a transnational economic community.

The Irish national ideal has three fundamental components – a historic territory, a population 'entitled' to live in the historic territory and an aspiration to establish a separate state coterminous with the island and people. It was least effective in devising a satisfactory definition of what constituted the 'Irish people' for, as George Bernard Shaw observed, 'we are a parcel of mongrels'.[31] Despite a language resplendent with the terminology of 'race' nationalists never developed a 'blood' definition of what constitutes being 'Irish'. Religion was a partial and incomplete substitute. Instead, divisions were horizontal between Protestants and Catholics and laterally within the two groups with the first proving easily the more influential. In Europe lateral divisions within ethnic communities were a more typical feature. Early attempts to include all creeds and classes dissolved ultimately in a national movement, focusing on uniting Catholics alone no doubt because forging a common secular identity proved discordant with Irish realities. In the years before 1922 southern Protestants tended to be owners of tenanted land (a declining but still significant feature in 1914), industrialists, professionals, mercantile folk or they were engaged in other occupations that appeared to be vulnerable under a Catholic-dominated regime. Protestants were an endangered economic group; their social and economic stations were eagerly sought by an aspiring Catholic *petite bourgeoisie*, which, as Greenfeld notes, saw their aspirations of equality blocked by artificial constraints.

As in other cases, the Irish were fragmented into numerous localised subcultures. The emergence of national identity owes much to modernising forces. Literacy, education, communication, the centralising bureaucratic state, a more organised and disciplined Catholic Church and the market economy, were factors facilitating the growth of a common culture of which the intelligentsia were its prime agents. This is labelled 'high culture' by Ernest Gellner.[32] The cultural dimension by the twentieth century was reinforced with a modern or modernising economy derived from Britain, which paradoxically gave Catholics a common purpose but, as noted already, tended to alienate the two religious communities on the island who increasingly were competing for the same opportunities. Daly suggests that the primarily agrarian and *petit bourgeois* base of the Catholic community derived the greatest benefit from the economic policies of the 1930s, a reminder that national movements are never neutral concepts in any of their manifestations.[33]

Problems of timing and of who participated remain to be untangled. Nationalist appeals did not meet with unqualified acceptance even from Catholics, who did not fully adopt them before the 1880s. Even then, as the civil war of 1922–3 demonstrated, there was a substantial differentiation along class lines about the content of the national movement as well as economic distinctions between those who supported or opposed the Anglo-Irish Treaty signed in December 1921.[34] As the appeal of one or other variety of national identity increasingly became popular with Catholics, nearly all Protestants took up an oppositional posture. This is hardly surprising as Catholic rhetoric sprouting from all patriotic camps appeared antagonistic to Protestant interests, not least to their economic security. Rational-choice theorists emphasise that individuals identify with a particular community because this serves their interest.[35] Identification may bring returns in the form of employment, physical comfort, or merely emotional satisfaction. Cultural nationalism, as John Hutchinson and Greenfeld note, is complementary, reinforcing objectives and thereby elevating the return on investment in patriotism.

Finally, the question of who benefits from patriotic activism has been receiving considerable attention. There is a recent trend to see in it a bourgeois effort to strengthen a class position against the existing dominant state and also as a means to exert authority over the masses below. Economic theorists provide a means to resolve the question, pointing to psychology and prestige as nationalism's 'value-added' for groups receiving fewer of the direct material compensations. In practice the benefits to individuals cannot be measured in terms of concrete material advantages, a point long articulated by nationalists but the modern formulation of this argument is quite different from theirs.

THE ECONOMIC LEGACY

When the Union of Great Britain and Ireland came into existence on 1 January 1801 the neighbouring islands had already been increasingly linked economically. Previously, Ireland had been under the suzerainty of the British crown and controlled by the government in London. However, prior to incorporation, Ireland was subjected to a number of trade restrictions. Under the Union these limitations were removed gradually and Irish goods obtained free entry into the British market. This should have aided Ireland's economic development but the Union had a reverse effect.

Nineteenth-century nationalists were adept at propagating the idea that Irish economic and especially industrial development had been thwarted by British interests that sought to destroy competition. During the first half of the nineteenth century, agriculture in Ireland responded to the opportunities of the British market. Wheat-growing boomed during the Napoleonic wars but contracted afterwards. During this period and throughout the century there was a move away from tillage towards livestock and dairy production. In the hard times of the post-1815 years, manufacturing outside Ulster stagnated and declined. Ulster's economy moved in another direction. Linen production, ship-building and engineering geared to the British and overseas market boosted the importance of Belfast.[36] These trends were accentuated after the Great Famine (1846–9). In the second half of the nineteenth century the Irish economy was characterised by a highly industrialised north, especially north-east, an east dedicated to livestock and dairying for the British market, a subsistence western region and an excess population that migrated to areas of demand (Britain and overseas) for unskilled labour. By 1914 the agricultural share of the labour force was 43 per cent, while industry had 25 per cent; both were in line with European norms.[37] Regional concentration of economic specialism is also typical. Industry elsewhere tended to be located in certain areas and not distributed evenly, a pattern that applied with equal force to Great Britain. This 'normal' economic pattern disguises crucial ethnoreligious differences. Land ownership and industrial proprietorship were overwhelmingly in Protestant hands, while this group also tended to be dominant in the professions and upper echelons of the state bureaucracy (for example, a cultural division of labour). The skilled workers in northern industry were generally Protestants as well, though Catholics were present in lower remunerated employment.

By 1914 Catholics had made considerable inroads into land ownership (peasant proprietors of their previously tenanted holdings) and had gained an enlarging share of bureaucratic employment, though were still over-represented in the lower grades. They were aided by the growth of a service sector, school teaching and clerical work. Nevertheless, they continued to feel disadvantaged. This perception has been analysed by Hutchinson, who points to 'blocked mobility'.[38] Ireland had a bloated but static state bureaucracy (Gladstone in 1886 argued for Home Rule, in part, as a way to curb this inflated sector) and teaching positions were stagnant due to a decreasing population while the numbers of qualified Catholics seeking these posts rose. Nationalist economic ideas were hammered out on the anvil of perceptions that viewed Ireland and Catholics as the deliberate victims of discrimination. Although the north was industrialised heavily, this was not part of the 'mental' picture that most nationalists (though not Arthur Griffith) held of 'their' Ireland. Greenfeld's observation is germane to the situation. She notes where nationalists seek to emulate a model that makes their own situation appear to themselves as inferior (Great Britain and the Protestant north), the consequence is *resentment*.[39] From this resentment comes an emphasis on elements of indigenous traditions and a rejection of the dominant culture and the original principles of nationalism. This formulation affords context for Daly's estimate of the economic policies of the new state already cited.

Ireland had a number of liabilities in the race for economic development, though these must be kept in perspective. These can be expressed simply as a limited natural resource base, a small domestic market, low incomes for a considerable portion of the population, weak traditions of skills and transport deficiencies due to location disadvantages. Such constraints were not a product of British policy. Manufacturing in the north was able to circumvent these obstacles by producing for an international market. Ireland, at the same time, had an abundance of natural grass along with a mild climate, facilitating livestock rearing. From a Catholic national point of view, the problem with more modest industrialisation in the southern provinces combined with growing dependence on grazing was that pasturage was not labour intensive and there was no alternative employment locally available; therefore the people (Protestants emigrated in only slightly lower proportions) left the country in large numbers. The disappearing Irish were a central theme in national rhetoric and are reflected in the citation from Lemass at the beginning of this chapter. These trends predated the famine. Set against this picture was a rising standard of living that rapidly converged towards the United Kingdom level by 1914. Much of this admittedly is attributable to the decline in labour supply. Between 1861 and 1911 the male labour force fell by 25 per cent; real wages for agricultural workers in the sixty years to 1911 rose 72 per cent while for builders the shift upwards was a remarkable 101 per cent, both considerably higher than the average for the United Kingdom.[40] Also, Ireland experienced a significant growth of productivity as a consequence of improved technology and capital accumulation.[41]

The Union was accomplished for political reasons but it soon had economic repercussions. Isaac Butt in 1846 outlined the case for Irish tariffs as the means to aid his country's economic development. At this juncture he was a Conservative in politics and Butt wrote just when protectionism was being abolished in the United Kingdom. He saw that his country was so seriously in arrears to its industrialised neighbour that it required insulation from competition. Butt's arguments found only a limited audience. Modernisation, however, soon bore out Butt's foreboding. Between the 1850s and the 1870s Ireland was equipped with a comprehensive rail network. The impact was swiftly felt. In the 1860s Joseph Chamberlain, then a Birmingham manufacturer, traversed the country by rail, selling the nails his firm produced. This was multiplied many times over as superior and cheaper goods penetrated local Irish markets, which previously were isolated from competition. Subsequently, the efficiency of the transport and distribution systems would press hard on Irish farmers, driving down incomes and increasing the attraction of the national agenda. The chief radical-national movement of the late 1850s and 1860s, Fenianism, was composed of urban artisans threatened by displacement.[42] Hroch, comparing recent developments in post-Soviet Europe with nineteenth-century national movements, sees the first as a response to short-term depression and decline, the latter as arising from the general trend towards economic growth joined to social improvement.[43] If his view is correct, Irish circumstances in the nineteenth century more accurately approximate to present-day national movements in the former Soviet bloc rather than they do those of the earlier epoch, for the growth of national sentiment was a response to perceived decline not improvement. Greenfeld and others point to the psychological function of national identity because of its utility to solve a crisis, and Ireland was certainly in the midst of economic turmoil.[44]

Two other factors enter into the discussion – capital deficiency and economic theory. The former had a double-barrelled explanation. First, the Irish landowners (and some others) lived in London and/or spent their rentals there (buying goods, etc.), depriving Ireland of much-needed investment. Secondly, from the 1870s nationalists argued vigorously that the country was overtaxed. Both had some substance though there is little objective evidence to suggest that Ireland suffered from a shortage of available capital. The argument conveniently ignores reverse expenditure, repatriated funds from overseas investments, remittances from the Irish overseas and similar sources of capitalisation. That the country was overtaxed may have been true – a Royal Commission reporting in 1896 adopted this view. L. M. Cullen estimates that there was a net out-flow of capital between the 1870s and 1900 but thereafter a huge in-flow caused by improved prices for agricultural produce, more direct government expenditure and social welfare programmes such as old age pensions created under legislation enacted in 1908.[45] While it is doubtful that the argument about capital shortage is strictly applicable to Ireland's case, there is some reason to accept a core–periphery explanation for the thirty years up to the turn of the century.

Irish nationalists were not notably interested in economic theory. Isaac Butt was something of an exception and his views were expressed mainly before he espoused self-government. Another partial exception is Parnell, leader of the national party from 1880 to 1890 and a member of parliament between 1875 and 1891, when he died. Parnell was one of the rare advocates of protectionism in the movement.[46] Like Butt, he reasoned that only through some form of tariffs could Irish manufacturing be developed, overlooking the industries of the north-east. As linen, engineering and ship-building depended on access to overseas markets, protection posed a threat to these industries. Parnell, a Protestant, nevertheless had little sensitivity for the north-east. Curiously, though a landlord, he was not concerned about agricultural tariffs in spite of abundant evidence that Irish farmers were being swamped by cheap American imports. He gave voice to his protectionist views on several occasions in 1885 but his ideas were promptly repudiated by most nationalists. In 1886 the British Liberals, a free trade party, adopted Home Rule for Ireland and Parnell shelved his advocacy of protection. The mainstream of the national movement was hostile to protection for two reasons – most were imbued with liberal economic thinking and identified themselves with the traditions of the Liberal party; also, home rulers were responsive to the tenant-farmer interest, especially after the electoral changes of 1885, which expanded the rural electorate and redistributed parliamentary constituencies to the advantage of farmers. As they would be obliged to pay more for goods, agriculturists saw in tariffs a threat to their own standard of living. Enthusiasm for protection, then, remained confined to a small section of bourgeois home rulers.

An Irish unionist, Sir Horace Plunkett, introduced another vital strand to national economic ideas.[47] He spearheaded the modernisation of agricultural production and the marketing of its output. His impetus had several facets: government-sponsored research and training, improved quality of Irish goods, construction of creameries, and he fostered the co-operative movement. Plunkett's economic approach was professedly non-political, though in Ireland politics inevitably intruded. The underpinning theme was self-help and greater self-sufficiency. Plunkett's economic ideas were in harmony with the cultural revivalism that began to flourish in the last decade of the century. In 1904 Plunkett's *Ireland in the New Century* emphasised the Gaelic League's contribution to promulgating the doctrine of self-reliance, observing:

in the course of my work of agricultural and industrial development I naturally came across this new intellectual force and found that when it began to take effect, so far from diverting the minds of the peasantry from the practical affairs of life, it made them distinctly more amenable to the teachings of the dry economic doctrine of which I was an apostle.[48]

That revival, which had two wings, modernising journalists and professionals and romantic nationalists, stressed the virtue of rural culture and of self-help.

Cultural revivalists were not distinguished for their economic thinking but in the new century protectionism did find a fresh advocate in Arthur Griffith, a moderniser and founder of Sinn Féin. Griffith saw in cultural revivalism a route to induce the rapid economic development of the country.[49] His economic ideas were inspired by the German, Frederick List's, *The National System of Political Economy*, first published in 1842 and available in translation in English in 1885, which advocated national tariffs. Griffith linked economic development with the other aims of nationalism, also making the case for the necessity of a nation fostering both agriculture and industry:

With List I reply: a nation cannot promote and further its civilization, its prosperity, and its social progress equally as well by exchanging agricultural products for manufactured goods as by establishing a manufacturing power of its own. A merely agricultural nation can never develop to any extent a home or foreign commerce, with inland means of transport, and its foreign navigation, increase its population in due proportion to their well-being or make notable progress in its moral, intellectual, social and political development . . . A mere agricultural state is infinitely less powerful than an agricultural-manufacturing state . . . We must offer our producers protection where protection is necessary.[50]

Following List, he believed that civilisation progressed naturally from pastoral economy to agriculture and then onwards to agriculture, industry and commerce. Griffith shared the hostility of traditional nationalist economics to grazing and asserted that it would have to give way in some considerable degree to a restoration of tillage. Under Griffith's influence Sinn Féin advocated protectionism and self-sufficiency as the economic strategy of the nation in waiting. The Sinn Féin constitution in 1917 adopted a number of measures for economic advancement, including 'the introduction of a protective system for Irish industries and commerce'.[51]

Neither Sinn Féin nor cultural revivalism generally made more than modest headway. Irish politics was in the hands of the National Party, which to the extent it considered the future economic course of the nation, remained wedded to liberal orthodoxy. In the normal course of events this leadership would have taken control of Irish government on the creation of Home Rule. However, between 1916 and 1921 the old leaders were displaced by radicalised successors, including Griffith. This new elite was more committed to the aspirations of the cultural revival than to nationalist economics but the second should not be discounted. Moderating the visible triumph of the new order, though, was its realisation that its rapidly widening popular appeal brought in train old home rulers who shared few of the radical pretensions.[52] If the old elite was virtually wiped out politically speaking, at local level the levers of power remained in the hands of a bourgeoisie that had little sympathy for radical notions of property rights, reversal of the trend toward livestock production and any vast application of protectionism.

Finally, the new state founded in 1922 had three important constraints. First, the Anglo-Irish Treaty signed in December 1921 made Ireland a dominion rather than a fully free-standing state; secondly, the most industrialised region, Northern Ireland, was severed from the state, leaving the southern leadership even more politically beholden to a socially conservative *petite bourgeoisie*; and, thirdly, the civil war that erupted between the victors over the terms of settlement, affected the stability of the regime and increased its reliance upon the entrenched respectable classes.

In sum, the new state found that it had to function within perimeters defined by present circumstances and also by the past. These necessitate a pragmatic course, especially on fiscal matters, but it is no more appropriate to label these a jumble of confused ideas than a similar description would fit interwar Britain. The minority views of Butt,

Parnell, Plunkett and Griffith, with the partial exception of the latter, tend to be ignored but, placed in a longer perspective, they, more than the orthodox economics of home rulers generally, have guided future approaches.

IRELAND, 1922–1932

The problem of the interwar Irish economy confirms the observation that the later the industrialisation, the greater the need for state involvement. As noted, the new regime inherited a dual legacy – colonial dependence and associated British economic ideology along with the doctrine of self-reliance. Three other problems were present as well – partition cut off much of the industrial base, the Great War caused substantial dislocation and disruption (5 per cent of Ireland's adult males were killed), and the civil war in 1922 and 1923 exacerbated the task of establishing stability. The years between 1914 and 1920 had seen unprecedented prosperity in Ireland;[53] the new regime would be assessed against this standard. It pursued a strategy that downgraded industrialisation, pinning its policy on a booming livestock and dairy sector.[54] The sagging world economy injured economic expectations. By 1923 the price of arable produce was 57 per cent below 1920 levels; the value of animals fell by 38 per cent, with store cattle declining in value by 40 per cent, whereas the cost of living dipped by merely 10 per cent.[55] Under the Land Purchase Act of 1923 the government signalled an intention to complete the traditional national programme on land ownership. It allowed for compulsory purchase of all remaining leasehold land. In the following year legislation was enacted to raise the quality of agricultural produce, again building on Plunkett's earlier vision. Also, the state fostered economic development. Beet sugar production rose from zero in 1925 to 24,000 tons in 1930, falling again to 5,000 tons the next year.[56] In 1926 an independent Tariff Commission was established; it had a marginal impact, not least because many of the newly protected industries were either owned by British interests or the necessary machinery was used under licence from British firms. In 1928 50 per cent of confectionery was produced by British firms in Ireland, while the manufacture of shoes was dominated by British interests.[57] Economic gains continued in spite of the Currency Act of 1927, attaching Ireland's currency to British sterling, causing it to be overvalued and tied to British monetary policy.[58] Yet Ireland maintained a sound currency and a balanced budget; unlike many of its continental counterparts it did not resort to printing money, enjoying a good credit rating as a consequence. Some customs duties were implemented, which Daly characterises as a 'rag bag'.[59] Between 1925 and 1930 agricultural prices rose in money terms by 12.4 per cent in the south as against only 5.8 per cent in Northern Ireland. David Johnson concludes that probably both parts of Ireland benefited from partition. Northern Ireland received British subsidies while the Free State escaped the costs of supporting the north's high unemployment.[60] The first years of the Free State saw slow economic progress, some efforts to apply nationalist solutions and a general caution in an atmosphere of political discord at home and weak international trade. In 1931 the Customs Duties Act attempted to prevent dumping of foreign goods on the Irish market. Overall, however, the pre-existing Anglo-Irish economic relationship remained largely untouched. The United Kingdom in 1931 absorbed over 96 per cent of Irish exports; Ireland purchased the bulk of its imports from Great Britain.[61]

The regime, though, did not go unchallenged. Eamon de Valera formed a new party in 1926, Fianna Fáil, which offered many of the same economic recipes but, drawing upon a more radical clientele, it called for the redistribution of land 'so as to get the greatest number possible of Irish families rooted in the soil of Ireland' and to make Ireland 'as self-contained and self-sufficient as possible – with a proper balance between agriculture and the other essential industries'.[62] In the following year he linked unemployment to protectionism:

Work can be got if we concentrate on protecting and keeping for ourselves the home market, instead of allowing the foreigner to dump their goods upon us, as at present. To concentrate on the diminishing of imports will more quickly reduce the adverse balance of trade than to concentrate on an increase in exports (though there is no reason why we should not endeavour to increase our exports as well). The difference is that in one case we have to face the intense competition in an outside market which we cannot control. In the other case we have the power of control and exclusion.

I have said repeatedly that our guiding principle will be to make Ireland as self-contained and as self-supporting as possible.[63]

With the sharp downturn in the country's economy, a condition resulting chiefly from external factors, the Cumann na nGaedheal government lost public confidence after 1930. A general election was held in February 1932. Fianna Fáil's election manifesto urged that the country should be made as 'independent of foreign imports as possible' and 'to preserve the home market for our farmers'.[64] De Valera's party won the election, beginning a continuous run in office until 1948. Cumann na nGaedheal had pursued nationalist objectives within the narrow band of possibilities available; its successor would extend this approach.

ECONOMIC NATIONALISM, 1932–58

The new government quickly reinforced the economic nationalist disposition of the state. Erhard Rumpf and A. C. Hepburn note that Fianna Fáil's concern to disassociate Ireland politically and socially from Britain was less pronounced than the efforts to sever the economic links.[65] According to them, the party's main thrust was to drive the economy in a direction that corresponded to nationalist political aspirations, though their assertion should be treated with caution with respect to outcomes if not intention.[66] In May de Valera asserted, 'we saw that the economy of this country had in the past been dictated not for the advantage of the people here, but for the advantage of people across the water'.[67] He promised the introduction of more rigorous tariffs. Fianna Fáil sought to direct balanced growth and push agriculture towards tillage.[68] There was a short-term rise in government spending, expanding from 24 per cent of gross national product in 1932 to over 30 per cent by 1933. This was accompanied by efforts to speed up development of the mixed economy. During the next few years state-owned companies were created for several sectors, including beet sugar, industrial alcohol, credit and some other enterprises. Also, the numbers and levels of tariffs rose considerably. By 1936–7 more than 1,900 articles (against 68 in 1931) attracted impositions and on average these were one third higher than similar duties in Great Britain. Some business, though, such as insurance, remained heavily dominated by foreign, usually British, interests. However, there was a limit to self-sufficiency. It completely failed to reduce dependence on imports from Great Britain; further state control was unacceptable to Irish society; a corporatist movement lacked popular support; and it was not pursued with unrelenting commitment.[69] The perceived fall in imports concealed royalty payments to British firms.[70] Moreover, the advent of the de Valera regime had brought about a dispute with Britain over continued payment of the land-purchase annuities, with the resulting trade war between the two countries. Britain retaliated against the withholding of the annuities with a bevy of restrictions on Irish trade, the most irksome being the controls on coal exports. From 1935 the fuel situation eased with a series of Coal–Cattle Pacts. The trade agreement of 1938 ended the dispute,[71] marking the closure of an attempt to secure pure or nearly complete self-sufficiency, though in theory the state as Séan Lemass reaffirmed that year continued to adhere to it as an ideal. The trade war had a mixed impact on Ireland, resulting in both losses and gains, the latter in the form of lower welfare costs from higher levels of domestic employment.[72] It caused a reduction in gross national product by only 2 to 3 per cent. In the north, however, economic growth during the 1930s comfortably exceeded its southern neighbour's.

Self-sufficiency was replaced by a modified form of economic nationalism acceptable to middle-class Irish opinion until the late 1950s. Settlement of the trade war did not herald an improvement for, ironically, the conflict in Europe enforced a degree of economic self-reliance beyond the wildest nationalist anticipation. Between 1939 and 1945 the economy was virtually isolated from world markets. From the beginning of the war to 1943 there was a 30 per cent drop in real wages and then a slight rise thereafter.[73] Most goods were in very short supply.

After a brief recovery at the close of the 1940s and start of the 1950s, the economy stagnated. Ireland remained tied to Great Britain. In 1946–7 de Valera called for 'a dovetailing of the two economies' but this made little impact on British leaders.[74] Instead of rebuilding industries that had been destroyed in the conflict, he advocated that British firms be transplanted to Ireland where there was a surplus of labour; British leaders preferred that the labour migrate to where the rebuilt industries were in the United Kingdom. As Daly observes, the Anglo-Irish relationship was reshaped by British not Irish politicians, something that remained a reality until the 1970s.[75] By the mid-1950s there was widespread disillusionment with aspects of the traditional economic formula. The balance of payments position fluctuated, reaching crisis point in 1951.[76] Internal competitiveness was so limp that the Restrictive Practices Act in 1953 attempted to foster efficiency. Emigration rose with an average of approximately 40,000 people annually leaving the country. The average annual increase in gross national product was only 1.1 per cent for the five years to 1955, leaving Ireland near the bottom of the league table of the Organisation of Economic Co-operation and Development (OECD). A vigorous debate on the Irish economy took place at official level between 1956 and 1958. In January 1957 the economic and political consequences of closer harmonisation with other western European nations were outlined. This same report suggested, in addition, that:

The setting up of a free trade area in which both the Six Counties [Northern Ireland] and ourselves participated would lead to the removal of such economic barriers to the reunification of the country as are related to the vested interests on both sides of the Border in the trade protection which would be abolished by the free trade area . . . if we should remain outside the free trade area while the Six Counties go in, the economic disparities between the areas would tend to increase, with a likely strengthening of vested interests opposed to reunification . . .[77]

This was a pertinent reminder that economic policy was never wholly detached from the wider nationalist political agenda.

PLANNED CAPITALISM, 1958–73

Coming out of the concerns about economic stagnation, a state-sponsored reassessment emerged in November 1958 as the *Programme for Economic Expansion*. It pointed to the inherent economic defects in Ireland, calling for the application of market principles, an end of strict self-sufficiency, the opening up of the internal economy and encouragement of foreign investment. De Valera's retirement in 1959 brought the succession of Lemass, facilitating the shift in economic approach. During the 1960s the Republic of Ireland moved to forthright capitalist economics, though the continued dependence on agriculture with the prime destination of the nation's goods still being Great Britain left the position looking outwardly similar to what it had been earlier. It was also the case that the volume of agricultural production did not rise, being virtually the same in 1963 as it was in 1957.[78] Moreover, foreign firms investing in the country were to direct their efforts to exports and not compete directly with protected firms producing mainly for the home market.[79] In a sense, nationalist rhetoric was remoulded to conform to an already existing reality, though it would be misleading to say that nothing consequential had changed.[80] Nevertheless, Lee's pithy appraisal that for Lemass by 1959 self-reliance had been transformed into meaning not self-sufficiency but an economy sufficiently viable to enable all the Irish to live in their own country encapsulates the position.[81]

IRELAND AND THE EUROPEAN UNION SINCE 1973

A fourth stage of economic nationalism emerged when Ireland along with the United Kingdom on 1 January 1973 joined the European Community. The price of membership negated certain political precepts of historic nationalism. Redmond's insistence 'that national demand, in plain and popular language, is simply this, that the government of every purely Irish affair shall be controlled by the public opinion of Ireland, and by that alone', was necessarily abrogated by the Treaty of Rome. Subscription to the Community explicitly rejected his assertion that 'no redress of financial grievances, no material improvements or industrial development, can ever satisfy Ireland until Irish laws are made and administered upon Irish soil by Irishmen'. However, it is not far-fetched to suppose that Redmond himself would be an enthusiastic European at the opening of the twenty-first century. A small militant faction of orthodox republicans called for a rejection of Ireland's membership on exactly these traditional grounds, though this force was easily overcome by the dominant sector of modernised bourgeois nationalists at the heart of the political establishment. It is true, of course, that membership of the Community has brought substantial material benefits to the country, especially during the past decade. The point here, however, is not whether the last two and a half decades have seen Ireland's prosperity advance but, rather, is this a negation of economic nationalism or its affirmation. On balance the latter is the more convincing explanation and has the added ingredient that it allowed Ireland to detach itself more thoroughly than overt economic nationalism ever achieved. Though what has emerged is something rather different from traditional economic national doctrine, centring on self-sufficiency, it bears similarities with older objectives by affording an insulated if capitalist solution, a partially open and quasi-internationalist approach, to the age-old problem of how to make a country still substantially linked to agricultural commodities, prosperous. To date the amount of sovereignty conceded is minimal, specially as a ratio to economic benefits. Ireland, then, has emerged as the European nation *par excellence*, if only because the qualified market economy, capitalist ethos and maintenance of national dignity afforded has allowed for a genuine tenable nationalism, an economic nationalism built on a wider regulation of prices, output and market access that suits the Irish environment as well as, if not better than, any other in Europe. This conforms to Liam Kennedy's proposition. But there is, to be sure, some cost. The core–periphery conundrum has not disappeared but been moved. Power has shifted, in part, from London to Brussels. Within southern Ireland Dublin has been more, not less, the economic hub. If the axis and contour of economic nationalism has shifted during the twentieth century, there is little in the Irish example to uphold Hobsbawm's thesis that the force of nationalism is in terminal decline at the close of the millennium.

NOTES

 1 Quoted in Cormac Ó Gráda, *Ireland: A New Economic History 1780–1939*
    (Oxford, 1994), p. 406.
 2 E. J. Hobsbawm, *Nations and Nationalism since 1870* (Cambridge, 1997).
 3 Liam Kennedy, *Colonialism, Religion and Nationalism in Ireland* (Belfast, 1996),
    p. 180; also adumbrated in Paul Bew and Henry Patterson, *Seán Lemass and
    the Making of Modern Ireland 1945–66* (Dublin, 1982), p. 194.
 4 Kennedy, *Colonialism, Religion and Nationalism*, p. 180.
 5 Peter Alter, *Nationalism* (2nd edn, London, 1994), p. 4; Anthony D. Smith,
    National Identity (London, 1991), p. 74; Anthony D. Smith, *Theories of
    Nationalism* (London, 1971), p. 23.
 6 Elie Kedourie, 'Dark gods and their rites' in John Hutchinson and Anthony
    Smith (eds.), *Nationalism* (Oxford, 1994), p. 208.
 7 John Breuilly, 'The sources of nationalist ideology', in Hutchinson and
    Smith, *Nationalism*, pp. 103–13 at p. 111.
 8 Liah Greenfeld, 'Types of European nationalism', in Hutchinson and
    Smith, *Nationalism*, pp. 165–71 at pp. 171–2.
 9 Quoted in D. George Boyce, *Nationalism in Ireland* (3rd edn, London, 1995),
    p. 22.
10 Kennedy, *Colonialism, Religion and Nationalism*, p. 34.
11 Mary E. Daly, *Industrial Development and Irish National Identity 1922–1939*
    (Dublin, 1993), p. 11.
12 Though she implicitly modifies her position in Mary E. Daly, 'Integration
    or diversity? Anglo-Irish economic relations, 1922–39' in S. J. Connolly (ed.),
    Kingdoms United? Great Britain and Ireland since 1500: Integration and Diversity
    (Dublin, 1999), pp. 171–80.
13 Quoted in Maurice Moynihan (ed.), *Speeches and Statements by Eamon de Valera
    1917–73* (Dublin, 1980), p. 190.
14 Quoted in Cormac Ó Gráda, *A Rocky Road: The Irish Economy since 1920*
    (Manchester, 1997), p. 4.
15 Quoted in *ibid.*, p. 25.
16 See Hugh Seton-Watson, 'Old and new nations', in Hutchinson and Smith,
    Nationalism, pp. 134–7 at p. 137.
17 John Redmond, 4 September 1907, reproduced in R. Barry O'Brien (ed.),
    Home Rule Speeches of John Redmond, MP (London, 1910), pp. 337–8.
18 Quoted in Frank O'Connor, *The Big Fellow* (Dublin, 1965), p. 6.
19 Kennedy, *Colonialism, Religion and Nationalism*, p. 170.
20 Ó Gráda, *A Rocky Road*, p. 35.
21 Donald Harman Akensen, *Small Differences: Irish Catholics and Irish Protestants
    1815–1922* (Dublin, 1988), pp. 15–41.
22 Greenfeld, 'Types of European nationalism', pp. 169–70.
23 Miroslav Hroch, 'Nationalism and national movements: comparing the past
    and present of central and eastern Europe', *Nations and Nationalism* 2(1)
    (1996), 35–44 at p. 38.

24 Miroslav Hroch, *Social Preconditions of National Revival in Europe* (Cambridge, 1985), p. 197.

25 Hroch, 'Nationalism and national movements', p. 41.

26 Hroch, *Social Preconditions of National Revival*, pp. 185–6.

27 Ernest Gellner, *Encounters with Nationalism* (Oxford, 1994), p. 198.

28 See Michael Hechter and Margaret Levi, 'Ethno-regional movements in the west', in Hutchinson and Smith, *Nationalism*, pp. 184–95.

29 See John Coakley, 'Typical case or deviant? Nationalism in Ireland in a European perspective' in Myrtle Hist and Sarah Barber (eds.), *Aspects of Irish Studies* (Belfast, 1990), pp. 29–35.

30 Frank Wright, *Two Lands on One Soil* (Dublin, 1996), p. 20.

31 Quoted in D. H. Greene and D. H. Lawrence, *The Matter with Ireland* (London, 1962), p. 294.

32 Ernest Gellner, *Nations and Nationalism* (Oxford, 1993), pp. 35–8.

33 Daly, *Industrial Development*, pp. 171–82.

34 See E. Rumpf and A. C. Hepburn, *Nationalism and Socialism in Twentieth-century Ireland* (Liverpool, 1977); David Fitzpatrick, 'The geography of Irish nationalism 1910–1921' in C. H. E. Philpin (ed.), *Nationalism and Popular Protest in Ireland* (Cambridge, 1987), pp. 403–39.

35 See the stimulating essays in Albert Breton, Gianluigi Galeotti, Pierre Salmon and Ronald Wintrobe (eds.), *Nationalism and Rationality* (Cambridge, 1995).

36 See Liam Kennedy and Philip Ollerenshaw (eds.), *An Economic History of Ulster 1820–1939* (Manchester, 1985).

37 Kennedy, *Colonialism, Religion and Nationalism*, p. 169.

38 John Hutchinson, *The Dynamics of Cultural Nationalism: The Gaelic Revival and the Creation of the Irish Nation State* (London, 1987), pp. 266–82.

39 Greenfeld, 'Types of European nationalism', pp. 169–71.

40 George R. Boyer and Timothy J. Hatton, 'Wage trends in the regions of the United Kingdom, 1860–1913' in Connolly, *Kingdoms United?*, pp. 135–52 at pp. 135, 144.

41 Frank Geary and Tom Stark, 'Comparative output and growth in the four countries of the United Kindom, 1861–1911' in Connolly, *Kingdoms United?*, pp. 153–68 at p. 168.

42 R. V. Comerford, *Fenianism in Context: Irish Politics and Society 1848–82* (Dublin, 1985).

43 Hroch, 'Nationalism and national movements', p. 41.

44 Greenfeld, 'Types of European nationalism', p. 171.

45 L. M. Cullen, *An Economic History of Ireland since 1660* (London, 1972), pp. 167–80.

46 Parnell's outlook is traced in Liam Kennedy, 'The economic thought of the nation's lost leader: Charles Stewart Parnell' in D. George Boyce and Alan O'Day (eds.), *Parnell in Perspective* (London, 1991), pp. 171–200.

47 See Trevor West, *Horace Plunkett, Co-operation and Politics: An Irish Biography* (Gerrards Cross, 1986).

48 Sir Horace Plunkett, *Ireland in the New Century* (reprint, Port Washington, NY, 1971), p. 149.
49 Richard Davis, *Arthur Griffith and Non-violent Sinn Féin* (Dublin, 1974), pp. 127–30.
50 9 December 1905, quoted in Arthur Mitchell and Pádraig Ó Snodaigh, *Irish Political Documents 1869–1916* (Dublin, 1989), p. 122.
51 Quoted in Arthur Mitchell and Pádraig Ó Snodaigh, *Irish Political Documents 1916–1949* (Dublin, 1985), p. 35.
52 See David Fitzpatrick, *Politics and Irish Life 1913–21* (Dublin, 1977).
53 David Johnson, *The Interwar Economy in Ireland* (Dublin, 1985), pp. 2–5.
54 Ó Gráda, *A Rocky Road*, p. 4.
55 Johnson, *The Interwar Economy*, p. 5.
56 *Ibid.*, pp. 11–12.
57 Daly, 'Integration or diversity?', pp. 171–2.
58 Also see Johnson, *The Interwar Economy*, p. 89, for comments on the inheritance of the banking system.
59 Daly, *Industrial Development*, p. 17.
60 Johnson, *The Interwar Economy*, p. 7.
61 Daly, 'Integration or diversity?', p. 175.
62 Quoted in Moynihan, *Speeches and Statements by Eamon de Valera*, p. 131.
63 Quoted in *ibid.*, p. 153.
64 Quoted in *ibid.*, p. 189.
65 Rumpf and Hepburn, *Nationalism and Socialism*, p. 174.
66 *Ibid.*, p. 175.
67 Quoted in *ibid.*, p. 203.
68 J. J. Lee, *Ireland, 1912–85* (Cambridge, 1989), p. 184.
69 Johnson, *The Interwar Economy*, p. 27; Lee, *Ireland, 1912–85*, pp. 185–7.
70 Daly, 'Integration or diversity?', p. 178.
71 See, Deirdre McMahon, *Republicans and Imperialists: Anglo-Irish Relations in the 1930s* (New Haven and London, 1984), pp. 237–84; Paul Canning, *British Policy Towards Ireland 1921–1941* (Oxford, 1983), pp. 121–220.
72 J. Peter Neary and Cormac Ó Gráda, *Protection, Economic War and Structural Change: The 1930s in Ireland* (London, 1986), p. 20.
73 Ó Gráda, *A Rocky Road*, p. 16.
74 Quoted in Daly, 'Integration or diversity?', p. 179.
75 *Ibid.*, p. 180.
76 D. J. Maher, *The Tortuous Path: The Course of Ireland's Entry into the EEC 1948–73* (Dublin, 1986), pp. 34–5.
77 Quoted in *ibid.*, p. 65.
78 Raymond D. Crotty, *Irish Agricultural Production: Its Volume and Structure* (Cork, 1966), p. 210.
79 Lee, *Ireland, 1912–85*, p. 352.
80 Bew and Patterson, *Seán Lemass*, pp. 192–3.
81 Lee, *Ireland, 1912–85*, p. 399.

CHAPTER TWO

Economic aspects of the nationality problem in nineteenth- and twentieth-century Belgium

Erik Buyst

INTRODUCTION

The tensions between Dutch- and French-speakers in Belgium have a long history. Even before the creation of the Belgian state in 1830, we already find traces of linguistic controversies.[1] The political aspects of this conflict have been the subject of much scholarly research and argument.[2] The impact of economic developments on the issue, however, has received far less attention. Economists started a debate in the late 1970s about the magnitude of the financial transfers between Flanders and Wallonia. Most of these analyses take 1975 as a starting point, which is, for a historical economist, a very short time horizon.[3] Moreover, the link between shifts in relative economic performance and its effect on the political bargaining power of the two linguistic groups is rarely taken explicitly into consideration.

The goal of this chapter is to analyse long-term changes in the economic structure of Flanders and Wallonia from the second half of the nineteenth century to the present day. It will be demonstrated that changes in the relative economic performance of both regions affected profoundly their bargaining power in political issues.

THE NINETEENTH CENTURY

The official linguistic census of 1846 indicated clearly that a majority (57 per cent) of the Belgian population used Dutch as its mother tongue. Moreover, the census showed that the two linguistic groups were confined to specific areas: Dutch was spoken in the north of the country (Flanders) and French in the south (Wallonia). Brussels and its suburbs took up a somewhat unusual position. The agglomeration was located north of the linguistic frontier – and was thus in Dutch-speaking territory – but contained a substantial minority (approximately 30 per cent of the population) of French-speakers.[4]

This reality was not reflected in the administrative organisation of the newly created Belgian state. French was the only official language of all central government services, including the army. The *Belgian Law Gazette*, which published the laws and decrees of the realm, only appeared in French. Translations in Dutch and German were provided for, but they had no legal value. The central government's privileging of French had far-reaching consequences for the Flemish part of the country. It led to the virtually exclusive use of French by many provincial and local authorities, law courts and educational institutions, although they were in theory free to choose which language they wanted to use. The only exceptions to this general picture were the municipal administrations of small towns and villages located at a certain distance from Brussels and the linguistic border. They continued to use Dutch until well into the second half of the nineteenth century.[5]

How can the rapid Frenchification of public life in Flanders during the early Belgian period be explained? First, it should be mentioned that from the second half of the eighteenth century, the language of Molière became a symbol of refined, modern cultural life in many European countries. Secondly, French was the language used by the Brussels court and by the central administration of the Austrian Low Countries (1713–94). As a result, large segments of the Flemish nobility and bourgeoisie started to adopt French as their mother tongue in the second half of the eighteenth century. This process gained momentum during the annexation of the southern Low Countries to France (1795–1814) as the French authorities pursued an energetic policy to stamp out all other languages in their empire honouring the principle 'one nation, one language'. In some instances even theatre performances, books and newspapers in Dutch were forbidden. In the 1820s French was so well established among the 'Belgian' upper classes that attempts of King William I (between 1815 and 1830) to restore the use of Dutch in all official and semi-official institutions dealing with Flanders met stiff resistance. The Belgian Revolution in 1830 marked the end of the United Kingdom of the Netherlands and brought the French-speaking bourgeoisie to power. They immediately imposed their language on the rest of the country.[6]

The large-scale privileging of French in the newly created Belgian state soon provoked reactions from Dutch-speaking intellectuals in Belgium. At first, it was mainly a cultural movement promoting the publication of books and journals in Dutch, organising plays in Dutch and so forth. By 1840, however, a political campaign was launched aimed at the restoration of Dutch next to French in Flanders as an official language in public administration, law courts and education: the Flemish Movement was born. Nevertheless, the Belgian government remained deaf to these complaints as it considered a unilingual state as a necessity for enhancing the development of a Belgian nation and maintaining national unity.[7]

In the mid-nineteenth century the Belgian government could easily ignore the Flemish Movement for several reasons. First, the Flemish Movement was politically divided between Catholics and freethinkers. Secondly, it relied on the Flemish middle classes, which lacked political muscle in a period of wealth-based voting. Thirdly, Flanders' political bargaining power was handicapped by disastrous economic conditions. In a period in which Wallonia played a pioneering role by launching the so-called Industrial Revolution on the European continent, important sectors of the Flemish economy collapsed. What went wrong economically in Flanders?

In the early nineteenth century two sectors dominated the Flemish economy: agriculture and the rural linen industry. In the 1830s cheap cotton textiles and products of the mechanised British linen industry increasingly penetrated markets previously dominated by the Flemish rural linen producers. Flemish rural spinners and weavers responded to this challenge by lowering wages. It proved to be a bad strategy as technological improvements enabled Britain to reduce its linen prices continuously. By the 1840s wages of Flemish spinners and weavers had fallen to subsistence level, which impeded further cuts. British linen prices, however, continued to decline, so sales of Flemish linen dropped dramatically. To make matters worse, the collapse of the Flemish rural linen industry in the second half of the 1840s coincided with severe harvest failures (potato blight, etc.). The combination of extremely high food prices and mass unemployment inevitably provoked large-scale starvation and a complete disintegration of the Flemish rural economy.

Unfortunately, Flanders could not offer alternative employment opportunities for its desperate rural population, other than the mechanised cotton industry in Ghent and the flourishing port of Antwerp. Consequently, unemployment and underemployment remained a structural problem for several decades to come, resulting in extremely low wages. Hence, it is not surprising that many Flemings decided to emigrate to Wallonia, northern France, the United States and Canada. Others became commuters or seasonal workers in neighbouring areas.[8] These circumstances were detrimental to the social status of Dutch in

Belgium. As a language it became more and more associated with extreme poverty and poor education. Of course, such a perception stimulated the Frenchification process of the upper middle classes in Flanders.

The ailing Flemish economy contrasted sharply with the thriving Walloon manufacturing sector. Based on modern coal-mining, the iron industry and machine-building Wallonia experienced rapid economic growth.[9] But despite this very divergent economic performance, Flanders continued to pay more taxes than Wallonia during the second half of the nineteenth century. The main reason for this paradox is that Belgium's tax system still referred to an agrarian society, so that income from large-scale manufacturing activities remained largely untaxed.[10]

The almost exclusive use of French by the Belgian administrative and judicial authorities caused many social abuses. In 1860, for instance, two Dutch-speaking workers were erroneously sentenced to death and decapitated. The fact that the trial took place in a language that the accused did not understand was soon identified as the main cause of this dramatic mistake.[11] As a result of such scandals a minimal legal protection was offered in the 1870s to those in Flanders – the large majority – who did not speak French. Although the effects of these first linguistic laws remained very limited, Walloon civil servants posted in Flanders perceived them as a threat for their future careers as they required in some instances some knowledge of Dutch. It was the start of the Walloon Movement, which favoured a monolingual French-speaking Belgium.[12]

By the end of the nineteenth century the Flemish economy showed clear signs of recovery. Based on low wages, the mechanised textile industry showed continuous growth. Antwerp attracted not only port-related industries – food processing, ship-building and ship repair – but also new manufacturing sectors, such as chemicals (photographic paper) and car construction. It also became an important international centre of diamond processing. In addition, Flanders benefited from the gradual exhaustion of Wallonia's coal mines. This necessitated increasing imports of coal from overseas, which encouraged the construction of new coke factories in the neighbourhood of port facilities. Partly for the same reasons the zinc industry moved from Wallonia to the *Kempen* (north-east Belgium). Other producers of non-ferrous metals soon followed this example.[13]

The catching-up movement of Flanders' economy is illustrated by the following figures on employment in manufacturing (domestic industry excluded). The share of the four integral Flemish provinces as a proportion of the total Belgian manufacturing employment rose from 26 per cent in 1896 to 32 per cent in 1910. In the same period the share of the four integral Walloon provinces fell from 57 per cent to 51 per cent. The share of the linguistically mixed province of Brabant remained unchanged at 17 per cent.[14] In 1910 the four integral Flemish provinces accounted for 44 per cent of the Belgian population, so the Flemish economy still had a long way to go.

The revival of the Flemish economy stimulated the self-awareness of the Flemish middle class. They were less and less prepared to accept the hegemony of French in Flemish public life. As a result, the use of Dutch made some progress in provincial and local government, in law courts and in official secondary education. At the national level, a certain move towards bilingualism can be detected. From 1895 the *Belgian Law Gazette* also appeared in Dutch. A couple of years later laws and decrees published in Dutch got legal value. Nevertheless, Dutch-speakers still had a long way to go in their struggle for equal opportunities – Belgium's central administration and army, for instance, remained exclusively French-speaking.[15] Institutions of higher education, including the universities, continued to offer courses only in French. The higher education issue, especially, provoked much discontent in Flanders. As a result, the introduction of Dutch-speaking classes at the State University of Ghent became a top priority for the Flemish Movement in the years just before the First World War.[16]

THE PERIOD 1914–1945

The First World War intensified the tensions between French- and Dutch-speakers in Belgium. On the one hand, the German occupier pursued a policy of preferential treatment of the Dutch language in occupied Belgium (*Flamenpolitik*). An important example of this policy was the reopening of the University of Ghent with Dutch as the language of instruction. It lured a small fraction of the Flemish Movement into political collaboration with the German occupier. At the other side of the IJzer front, much resentment was caused by the fact that French was the only language of command in the Belgian army, although 70 per cent of the infantry consisted of Dutch-speakers. These developments changed the agenda of the mainstream Flemish Movement. Full equality of Flanders and Wallonia based on a monolingual status for each region, reform of the central administration and introduction of separate Flemish and French-speaking units in the army became basic issues.[17]

In the first years after the war the demands of the Flemish Movement were largely ignored. The University of Ghent, for instance, became French-speaking again after the liberation. A decade later, however, things would change dramatically as a new series of important linguistic legislation was passed in parliament. Economic developments played an important role in the reversal. First, in the postwar years the reconstruction issue and related problems – such as large budget deficits, an exploding public debt, inflation and currency depreciation[18] – dominated the political agenda. It was the end of 1926 before the major macroeconomic imbalances in Belgium were corrected. Secondly, the Flemish economy pursued its catching-up process *vis-à-vis* Wallonia. In 1930 the share of the four integral Flemish provinces as a proportion of total Belgian manufacturing employment (domestic industry excluded) reached 38 per cent (up from 32 per cent in 1910). Meanwhile, the share of the four integral Walloon provinces had fallen from 51 per cent in 1910 to 41 per cent in 1930.[19] The relative success of the Flemish economy is explained by the strong growth performance of sectors such as non-ferrous metals, chemicals, car assembly (Ford, General Motors), telecommunications (Bell Telephone), glass production, and the start of coal-mining in Limburg.[20] The picture is completed by the emergence of a modern service sector in Flanders based on banking, insurance and so on.[21] Despite remaining structural weaknesses – low wages, much long-distance commuting to Walloon coal mines and heavy industry – these economic successes again strengthened Flemish self-awareness. Therefore, it is probably no coincidence that politicians from Antwerp – a city that attracted a large share of the new investments – were at the forefront of the Flemish Movement in the 1920s and 1930s.

As Wallonia refused to accept bilingualism throughout the whole country – thus including the Walloon provinces – the call for a monolingual Flanders became louder. In the decade after 1928 this became reality as a series of laws was enacted that converted to Dutch all levels of public administration, of public education (from primary schools to universities), and of law courts in Flanders. Army units were also divided along linguistic lines, so that in principle only officers with a sufficient knowledge of Dutch could command Flemish soldiers. At the same time, territorial integrity became a cornerstone in Belgium's language legislation: Flanders was recognised as being Dutch-speaking, Wallonia as French-speaking, and Brussels and its suburbs as bilingual. The linguistic frontier between these areas could only be adjusted on the basis of population censuses, which explicitly asked about the individual person's language use.

In principle, most demands of the mainstream Flemish Movement were realised by the end of the 1930s. But already during the 1930s disillusionment followed as the language laws were openly violated along the linguistic frontier and in Brussels. Consequently, belief in democratic procedures waned in some circles and radical Flemish nationalists gained popular support. In these circumstances it is not surprising that a substantial part of the Flemish Movement decided to collaborate with Germany during the Second World War – the more so as the German occupier fully enforced the existing language laws and pursued a policy of positive discrimination favouring Dutch-speakers in public life. Soon, however, it became clear that this policy was only intended to facilitate the annexation of Flanders to the German *Reich*. Moreover, the hardship caused by the Nazi occupation regime in Flanders also created much popular hatred *vis-à-vis* collaborators.[22] As a result, large sections of the Flemish population despised the Flemish Movement as a whole by the end of the war.[23]

THE LATE 1940S AND THE 1950S

It was not only the collaboration issue that handicapped the political bargaining power of Flanders in the postwar period. Economic factors also contributed to its weakness. Once the reconstruction phase (1945–7) was over, Flanders became again the victim of relatively high unemployment. Wallonia, on the other hand, faced labour shortages in the early and mid-1950s. How can these striking differences be explained?

First, demographic factors played an important role. In Wallonia the so-called demographic transition occurred much earlier than in Flanders. In the first half of the twentieth century the south of Belgium registered considerably lower birth rates than the north.[24] In the 1940s and 1950s rapid aging of the population caused a decline in the Walloon labour force. Flanders, on the contrary, experienced a substantial increase in its active population due to a much younger age structure. Secondly, the Flemish economy still included many small farmers in the late 1940s. In the following decade intensified mechanisation pushed many of them out of business, thereby further increasing the number of

people looking for a (new) job.[25] Thirdly, Belgium's hard-currency policy
– partly designed to prevent the overheating of the Walloon economy –
was detrimental to new job creation. It hurt export opportunities of
labour-intensive sectors, such as textiles and leather industries, which
were mainly located in the north of the country. As a result, Flanders'
traditional image of being a region of high unemployment, low wages
and mass long-distance commuting to the industrial areas of Wallonia
and northern France and to Brussels, was reinforced.

The weak position of Flanders from various points of view was
immediately reflected in political issues. In the second half of the 1940s
and in the 1950s the language laws were again violated on a large scale
in Brussels and along the linguistic frontier. In these areas much social
pressure was exerted on the local population to declare themselves as
being French-speaking in the 1947 census. Consequently, several Flemish
municipalities were given bilingual or French-speaking status. Other
complaints referred to the striking under-representation of Dutch-
speakers in the Belgian government and at top positions in the central
administration.[26] The most painful defeat for the Flemings, however,
was the neglect of the referendum outcome on King Leopold III's return
to the throne in 1950. Although 58 per cent of the Belgian population
voted in favour of the king's return, he had to abdicate. What had happened? A closer look at the referendum results shows that the king had
only obtained a majority in Flanders (72 per cent). In Wallonia, on the
contrary, a majority had voted against his return (58 per cent).
Consequently, as soon as the king did actually return riots broke out in
the industrial centres of Wallonia. After bloody clashes with the *gen-
darmerie*, Leopold III decided to abdicate in favour of his son, Baudouin.
In Flanders the whole affair was perceived as a defeat of democracy *vis-
à-vis* street violence.

FROM THE LATE 1950S TO THE EARLY 1970S

The late 1950s marked the start of a rapid and fundamental change in
the economic balance of power between Flanders and Wallonia. The
breakthrough of oil as a major supplier of energy in western Europe
caused serious difficulties for many European coal producers. Overproduction and falling prices hit the Walloon coal mines particularly
hard because of their irregular seams and problems of exhaustion. In
a couple of years employment in the Walloon mines more than

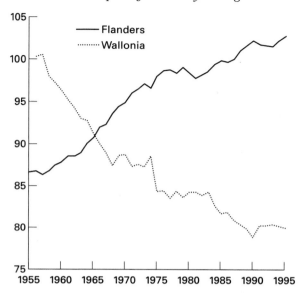

Figure 2.1. *Gross value added at factor cost per inhabitant: relative figures (Belgium's average = 100), 1955–1995*[30]

Source: Calculated from NIS, 'Economische groei van de provincies en de gewesten van 1980 tot 1988' [Economic growth of provinces and regions from 1980 to 1988], *Statistische Studiën* 91 (1991), 76–9 and INR, *Economische groei van de gewesten, provincies en arrondissementen. Periode 1985–1995* [Economic growth of regions, provinces and districts. Period 1985–1995], (Brussels, 1997), p. 39.

halved.[27] It was a blow from which southern Belgium would never really recover.

At the same time, Flemish economic growth started to accelerate again. By the end of the 1950s increasing labour shortage in the economically more developed areas of Europe made Flanders and its large reservoir of cheap labour attractive for American and other multinational enterprises that wanted to take advantage of the European integration process. A wave of new investments centred around the Flemish ports not only absorbed unemployment but also modernised the economic structure of northern Belgium. In particular, chemicals, petrochemicals and metal processing (car assembling) expanded rapidly.[28]

As a result of these divergent economic developments the income gap between Flanders and Wallonia decreased rapidly in the early 1960s (figure 2.1). It helped to restore Flanders' political bargaining power,

Figure 2.2. *Belgium: regions and provinces, 1990*

Source: Theo Hermans *et al.* (eds.), *The Flemish Movement. A Documentary History 1780–1990* (London, 1992), p. x.

which – after a silence of twenty-five years – led to the introduction of new language laws. In 1960 the decennial demarcation of the linguistic border once again provoked mounting tensions between Dutch- and French-speakers. Therefore, the government decided to fix once and for all the linguistic border. At the same time, the monolingual status of Flanders and Wallonia, and the bilingual status of the Brussels urban area, was strengthened (1962–3).[29] Finally, guarantees were given to Dutch-speakers to provide them a fair share of top positions in Belgium's central administration and other public and semi-public institutions.

In the 1960s the content of the discussions between Dutch- and French-speakers changed. The Flemish Movement now focused on *cultural* autonomy, while Wallonia demanded *economic* autonomy and safeguards against possible domination by the Flemish demographic majority.[31] Shifts in the relative economic performance of the two regions help to explain the changes in political agenda. By the mid-1960s Wallonia had clearly lost its position as Belgium's most powerful economic region (figure 2.1). Hence, economic power no longer compensated for its position as a demographic minority in Belgium. Moreover, many Walloons blamed their economic difficulties on the Belgian state's lack of initiative. For that reason, they wanted to take care of their own economic affairs.

In 1970–1 these discussions resulted in constitutional reform. A Dutch- and a French-speaking Community Council were established, each having exclusive authority to issue decrees concerning cultural policy (education excluded) and health policy (social security excluded). French-speakers gained parity in the Council of Ministers, which allayed their fear of being in the minority in Belgium's central government. In 1980 additional reforms created three regions (Flanders, Wallonia and Brussels) with powers in the field of town and country planning, housing, environment and supervision of local authorities (see figure 2.2).

EPILOGUE: THE 1970S AND BEYOND

The oil shocks of the 1970s and their aftermath hit southern Belgium particularly hard. Energy-intensive sectors, such as Wallonia's important steel industry, had to go through a phase of substantial downsizing. As a result, the unemployment rate in Wallonia's old industrial areas reached 25 per cent by the mid-1980s. The relative impoverishment of southern Belgium created large financial flows from Flanders to Wallonia. In the system of social security alone, roughly BEF 80 billion went in 1990 from north to south, which represents approximately 10 per cent of Flanders' social security contributions.[32] The principle of solidarity between the two regions is not put in jeopardy by the mainstream Flemish Movement. Criticism focuses on the non-transparency of the financial flows and the fact that insufficient incentives were built into the system to keep social spending under control.

Another element of controversy deals with the financing of communities and regions. New constitutional reforms in 1988 and 1993 extended considerably the power of these institutions: taken together they now control one quarter of total government expenditure (social security included). Moreover, they obtained separate and directly elected parliaments.[33] Nevertheless, the taxation powers of these legislative assemblies remain extremely limited. The federal government still collects more than 90 per cent of their tax revenues and distributes it among the communities and regions according to a very complex mechanism. Many Flemish politicians and economists consider it as a violation of the so-called fiscal equivalence principle, which maintains that autonomy concerning expenditure should be matched by equivalent fiscal autonomy. Only in such conditions can politicians assume full financial responsibility for their actions.[34] Walloon politicians, however, are very reluctant to change the existing system, as it could lead to higher taxes in Wallonia than in Flanders.

CONCLUSION

From this short overview it is clear that shifts in the relative economic performance of Flanders and Wallonia had a considerable effect on the political bargaining power of the two regions. The deep structural crisis that characterised the Flemish economy during most of the nineteenth century made it relatively easy for the French-speaking bourgeoisie to impose its language on the rest of the Flemish population. From the late nineteenth century the gradual recovery of the Flemish economy helped the Flemish Movement to resist this policy of Frenchification more and more successfully. In the late 1940s and in the 1950s, however, the catching-up process of the Flemish economy stalled. It helps to explain the loss of Flemish political bargaining power during that period. In the late 1950s economic growth in Flanders accelerated again, which led to Flanders overtaking Wallonia in per capita income by the mid-1960s. As a result, important Flemish demands, such as cultural autonomy, could

be realised. From the mid-1970s onwards the economic decline of southern Belgium has given rise to new tensions between Dutch- and French-
speakers. The Flemish Movement's demands have shifted from linguistic
and cultural issues to economic problems, such as a reduction of
financial transfers between the regions, and more fiscal autonomy for the
communities and regions.

NOTES

1 For example, Jan Baptist Chrysostomus Verlooy, *Verhandeling op d'onacht der
   Moederlyke Taal in de Nederlanden* [Treatise on the neglect of the mother tongue
   in the Low Countries], (published anonymously, Maastricht, 1788).
2 To mention just a few of the recent contributions: Martine Goossens,
   Ontstaan en groei van het Vlaams Parlement 1970–1995 [Emergence and growth of
   the Flemish parliament 1970–1995], (Brussels and Kapellen, 1995); Theo
   Hermans *et al.* (eds.), *The Flemish Movement. A Documentary History 1780–1990*
   (London, 1992); Lode Wils, *Van Clovis tot Happart. De lange weg van de naties in
   de Lage Landen* [From Clovis to Happart. The long way of the nations of the
   Low Countries], (Leuven and Apeldoorn, 1995); Els Witte, *Taal en territori-
   aliteit: een overzicht van de ontwikkelingen in België sinds 1830* [Language and
   territoriality: an overview of the developments in Belgium since 1830],
   (Brussels, 1993), pp. 97–120.
3 For example, Philippe Defeyt, *De la régionalisation de la sécurité sociale à la
   communautarisation des soins de santé* (Louvain-la-Neuve, 1991) and Paul Van
   Rompuy and Valentijn Bilsen, *Regionalisering van de sociale zekerheid*
   [Regionalisation of Belgium's social security system], (Leuven, 1993).
4 *Population. Recensement général (15 octobre 1846)* (Brussels, 1849), pp.
   xxxvi–xxxvii and 252–383.
5 Lode Wils, 'A brief history of the Flemish movement' in Hermans *et al.*, *The
   Flemish Movement*, pp. 1–39 at pp. 1–7.
6 Marcel Deneckere, *Histoire de la langue française dans les Flandres (1770–1823)*
   (Ghent, 1954).
7 Renée Doehaerd *et al.*, *Geschiedenis van Vlaanderen. Van de oorsprong tot heden*
   [History of Flanders. From the origins till today], (Brussels, 1983), pp. 237–8.
8 A detailed overview is found in Guillaume Jacquemyns, *Histoire de la crise
   économique des Flandres, 1845–1850* (Brussels, 1929).
9 See Pierre Lebrun *et al.*, *Essai sur la révolution industrielle en Belgique, 1770–1847*
   (*Histoire quantitative et développement de la Belgique*, vol. II(1) (Brussels, 1981), pp.
   78–475 and Joel Mokyr, *Industrialization in the Low Countries, 1795–1850* (New
   Haven, 1976), pp. 41–67.
10 Juul Hannes, 'Met de fiscale bril bekeken. Vlaanderen in België, 1830–1914'
   ['From a fiscal perspective. Flanders in Belgium, 1830–1914'] in Adriaan
   Verhulst and Luc Pareyn (eds.), *Huldeboek Prof. dr. Marcel Bots. Een bundel his-
   torische en wijsgerige opstellen* (Ghent, 1995), pp. 167–94.
11 Theo Luykx and Marc Patel, *Politieke geschiedenis van België* [Political history

of Belgium], 2 vols. (Antwerp, 1985), p. 174. For a comprehensive evaluation of the linguistic situation of the courts in Flanders, see Herman Van Goethem, *De taaltoestanden in het Vlaams-Belgische gerecht, 1795–1935* [The linguistic situation in the Flemish–Belgian courts, 1795–1935], (Brussels, 1990).

12 Wils, 'Brief history', pp. 12–13.

13 Ginette Kurgan-Van Hentenrijk, *Industriële ontwikkeling* [Industrial development] (Haarlem, 1978), pp. 235–6.

14 Paul Olyslaeger, *De localiseering de Belgisch nijverheid* [The localisation of Belgian manufacturing], (Antwerp, 1947), p. 112.

15 Wils, 'Brief history', p. 17.

16 Luykx and Patel, *Politieke geschiedenis*, p. 275.

17 Wils, 'Brief history', pp. 18–22.

18 Erik Buyst *et al.*, 'National accounts for the Low Countries, 1800–1990', *Scandinavian Economic History Review* 43 (1995) 53–76 at pp. 70–2.

19 Statistics from Ministerie van Arbeid en Sociale Voorzorg (MASV: Ministry of Labour and Social Affairs), 'De handels- en nijverheidstelling op 31 december 1930' [The 1930 census of commerce and manufacturing], *Arbeidsblad* 36 (1935), 1353–1521, at pp. 1366–7. The linguistically mixed province of Brabant is not taken into consideration.

20 Karel Veraghtert, *Het economisch leven in België, 1918–1940* [Economic life in Belgium, 1918–1940], (Haarlem, 1979), pp. 98–100.

21 Herman Van der Wee and Monique Verbreyt, *Mensen maken geschiedenis: de Kredietbank en de economische opgang van Vlaanderen, 1935–1985* [People make history: the Kredietbank and the economic rise of Flanders], (Tielt, 1985), pp. 21–60.

22 For more details, see, for example, Bruno De Wever, *Greep naar de macht. Vlaams-Nationalisme en Nieuwe Orde: het VNV, 1933–1945* [Seizing power. Flemish nationalism and the new order: the VNV, 1933–1945] (Tielt, 1994).

23 Wallonia also faced pro-Nazi collaboration (*Rex*) during the war, but it was not rooted in language issues.

24 Ron Lesthaeghe, *The Decline of Belgian Fertility, 1800–1970* (Princeton, NJ, 1977).

25 Jan Blomme, *The Economic Development of Belgian Agriculture, 1880–1980. A Quantitative and Qualitative Analysis* (Brussels, 1992).

26 Josef Smits (ed.), *Gaston Eyskens: De memoires* [Gaston Eyskens: the memoirs], (Tielt, 1993), pp. 428–9.

27 Alan S. Milward, *The European Rescue of the Nation-state* (London, 1995), pp. 46–118.

28 Herman Van der Wee, 'De Belgische economie in de maalstroom van een halve eeuw, 1925–1975' [The Belgian economy during half a century, 1925–1975], in Gaston Eyskens *et al.* (eds.), *Gaston Eyskens 80* (Tielt, 1985), pp. 57–118 at pp. 104–5; André Mommen, *The Belgian Economy in the Twentieth Century* (London and New York, 1994), pp. 127–33.

29 The many exceptions to these general rules in the language legislation of the 1930s, which entailed so many abuses, were now abolished. For more details, see Wils, 'Brief history', pp. 268–70.

30 Figure 2.1 does not show the data for the Brussels urban area.
31 In the 1960s more than 55 per cent of the Belgian population was Dutch-speaking.
32 Van Rompuy and Bilsen, *Regionalisering*, pp. 1–18.
33 For a detailed overview of the constitutional reforms of 1970, 1980, 1988 and 1993, see, for example, Goossens, *Ontstaan en groei*, pp. 45–444.
34 Wim Moesen and Paul Van Rompuy, *De kleine kanten van de grote staatshervorming* (Leuven, 1993), p. 13.

CHAPTER THREE

The economy as a pushing or retarding force in the development of the German question during the second half of the twentieth century

Jörg Roesler

INTRODUCTION

The so-called German question is one of the most important features of German history during the last 200 years.[1] It began to develop in the first half of the nineteenth century, when the Germans became aware that they were lagging behind their neighbours, especially France and Great Britain, in the progress of nation building.[2] For the second half of the twentieth century the German question was about the future of Germany after it had been split up into two states economically and politically after the Second World War.[3] To the solution of the German national question there existed two alternative choices: to re-establish unity or to confirm the separation into two independent states, the Federal Republic of Germany (FRG) in the west and the German Democratic Republic (GDR) in the east. It seemed to be that the latter option had been narrowly avoided,[4] when Germany in 1990 once again had one government and one economic system (the market economy of the Federal Republic). Only later did East and West German politicians and social scientists learn that the so-called 'inner unification' ('innere Wiedervereinigung'),[5] which could be reached only after the 'demolition of the wall in the minds' that separated East and West Germans, was a task that would last up to the end of the century or even longer.

There exist numerous scholarly works about the latest period of Germany's division into (two) different states, its origins, the attempts of both German states and of their main protective powers (USSR and USA) to avoid or to deepen the split, to develop or to hinder the progress of mutual relations and finally the circumstances of reunification. This chapter is limited to the twenty-five experts' reports on the political and psychological problems of German division and unification policy between 1945 and 1990,[6] ordered by the 'Enquete Commission for the research of history and consequences of the SED (Socialistische

Einheitspartei Deutschlands) dictatorship in Germany'[7] and published in volume V of the series. Compared with this flood of publications, analyses of the economic relations between the FRG and GDR are comparatively rare. In the above-mentioned volume V of the Enquete Commission's publications, dedicated to 'intra-German policy and policy toward Germany', economic analyses are restricted to the development of the trade between both countries so-called intra-German trade, and to the financial transfers between the FRG and GDR.[8] Economic change in Germany during the last four decades had been analysed usually separately for West and East Germany, often in relation to their main economic partners in the west or east, seldom with reference to the German counterpart in the other economic system.[9]

The aim of this contribution is to bring together the results of the political and economic research in order to answer the question whether the economic change in the two Germanies has – in comparison with the politics – more favoured the tendency to deepen the separation or whether the economy was a reason to keep the remaining links between both states or even to strengthen them. If we look at the history of Germany between 1945 and 1949 and 1990 and 1998 as the road to division and from division to formal and real (inner) unification, we may define the economic decision-making and the economic changes of the second half of this century in Germany as a pushing or retarding force on the journey along this road in contrast with the efforts made in the fields of politics. Between 1945 and 1997 we will define four periods during which the economy can be characterised as pushing force, and another four periods during which it acted as a retarding force on the solution of the German question. During these eight periods the effect of the economy on the German question has to be analysed and juxtaposed with the contemporaneous role of politics.

THE ROLE OF ECONOMIC POLICY IN PRESERVING ECONOMIC UNITY IN THE FOUR-ZONE POTSDAM GERMANY (1945–1947)

During their meeting in Potsdam in July/August 1945 the leading statesmen of the United States, Britain and the Soviet Union agreed on a four-power occupation of Germany, including France. Though an Allied Control Council for Germany was formed, the political responsibility for the development of each zone was to rest with the particular occupation force. But economically Germany should remain united.[10] The influence of the Allied Control Council as a 'superior government for the whole of Germany' was limited from the beginning and decreased further in 1946 and 1947. In particular, the split in the political treatment of the occupation zones between the Soviet Union and the western Allies became visible as soon as the Cold War became public.[11] Attempts from the German side to bridge the gap that was becoming obvious between the Allies – the most important event of this kind was the meeting of prime ministers of the German states in Munich in June 1947 – were unsuccessful.[12]

In contrast to the political development, the economic links and trade between the four zones remained more or less untouched by the increasing hostilities between east and west. The intra-zone trade was allowed to expand between 1945 and 1947, starting from a very low point. The more war damages could be overcome and the dismantling (which took place, above all, in the Soviet Occupation Zone – SOZ) became restricted, the more the inner German flow of goods increased. In 1946 and 1947 more than two thirds of the whole trade of what would become the GDR was with what would become the FRG. But compared with 1936 it was only 5 per cent in 1946 and 16 per cent in 1947 of the former level of goods exchange. But it was at least imaginable that the streams of goods would be able to reach prewar levels again, once the shortage of goods became less pressing as the result of an economic upswing.[13] One of the main driving forces behind the intra-zone trade was the inner division of labour between big corporations, which had been split up between the different zones. One example of this is the Agfa photo company, an enterprise of the IG Farben Corporation. The largest enterprise of the corporation was situated in the Soviet zone. In order to keep the production in Wolfen going, the enterprise – which was, from 1946, a Soviet joint-stock company – had to trade with the Agfa enterprises in the other zones. Of the deliveries between the end of the Second World War and July 1946, 40.8 per cent went to the British, 39.8 per cent to the Soviet, 18 per cent to the American and 1.4 per cent to the French occupation zone.[14] Economic unity was more than a declaration of the Allies and went further than mutual exchange of deliberately needed goods. This can also be shown by the history of the Zeiss Corporation in the first years after the war. After American troops had taken the management and some of the leading scientists out of Jena, which only was temporarily occupied by American forces, the headquarters of the Zeiss firm was transferred to a small town in Württemberg, Oberkochen. They began to build a second optical

Table 3.1. *Regional structure of SOZ/GDR foreign
trade in 1936 and 1946–1952*

Year	FRG	Eastern Europe	Other countries
1936	65.1	15.5	19.4
1946	72.6	25.9	0.5
1947	68.1	26.9	6.0
1948	39.5	44.6	15.9
1949	32.3	58.4	9.3
1950	23.5	64.8	11.7
1951	6.0	76.2	17.8
1952	5.2	74.9	19.9

Source: Calculations of the author according to Heinz
Kohler, *Economic Integration in the Soviet Bloc* (New York,
1965), pp. 61 and 65; *Statistisches Jahrbuch der DDR 1960/61*
(Berlin, 1961), p. 573.

factory there. By a 'gentlemen's agreement' with Zeiss Jena, now under
Soviet occupation, Oberkochen got from Jena the necessary optical
instruments and other equipment for the start of its plant.[15]

Thus the economy can be identified for the first few postwar years as
an important sphere, linking the eastern with the western zones in a time
when political co-operation between the Allied powers for a common
policy in Germany lost momentum. Intra-zone trade and continuing
exchange of raw material, equipment and know-how were rare indicators that the negative influence of the emerging Cold War could be
limited – at least in the four-zone Potsdam Germany (see table 3.1).

THE MUTUAL ECONOMIC BLOCKADE OF BOTH PARTS OF
GERMANY BY THE GREAT POWERS AND LAST ATTEMPTS TO
PRESERVE GERMAN UNITY IN 1948–1949

The (limited) economic unity of Germany came to a virtual standstill
soon after the currency reforms in June 1948, in the united
US–British–French zone and in the Soviet zone, which created different
currencies for the western and eastern parts of Germany. Economic
blockade and counter-blockade soon followed the currency reform. The
blockades occurred as a result of the political strife between the former
Allies over Berlin. The Berlin Blockade was one of the climaxes of the

early Cold War.[16] While again and again attempts at the political level were made in 1948 and at the beginning of 1949 to prevent a final political division of Germany,[17] the economy was the forerunner of complete separation. The division of Germany was completed in the field of politics only sixteen months later, in autumn 1949, when in September the Federal Republic of Germany and in October the German Democratic Republic were founded.

The evidence that both parts of Germany could survive (with some help from outside) without trading with each other, an idea that politicians in east and west could not imagine prior to the summer of 1948, turned political separation – hitherto unthinkable – into a manageable question in the eyes of the policy makers in east and west.

THE EAST–WEST INTRA-ZONE TRADE AS THE ONLY LINK BETWEEN GOVERNMENT INSTITUTIONS OF FRG AND GDR (1950–1960)

At the end of 1949 the importance of the role of politics and economics in the German question suddenly changed again. Only one day after the second German state, the GDR, was founded and the political division of Germany was completed, representatives of both newly founded states signed an agreement in Frankfurt-am-Main about intra-zone trade. The so-called 'Frankfurt Agreement' was the result of intensive negotiations that had been taking place since May 1949, when the so-called 'Jesup-Malik Agreement' set an end to the Berlin Blockade. The agreement of Frankfurt was the start of trade relations between the two German states. Its main formulae were incorporated into the so-called 'Berlin Agreement' of September 1951, which regulated the trade between the GDR and FRG until 1960 and, with some amendments, until 1989.[18]

The legal requirements of the Berlin Agreement reflected the delicate political situation of the two states that did not recognise each other, each insisting that it was the only 'true' democratic republic of Germany.[19] The Berlin Agreement evaded the official name of both states. It was entitled 'Agreement about trade between the currency regions (Währungsgebiete) of DM-West and DM-East'. Though the partner of the GDR side was the Ministry of 'Inner German and Foreign Trade', the FRG denied official contacts with its Ministry of Economics and created a 'Trustee of Intra-zone Traffic', which officially was not part of the Federal government, but got its instructions from the

Ministry of Economics of the FRG.[20] As a result of the non-recognition of the GDR as a political unit, the Federal government did not impose customs on trade between East and West Germany and asked in 1957, when the Economic Community was founded, for the continuation of the special trade regulations with the SOZ. The other members of the European Community agreed.

Nevertheless, trade between both states developed again. It was heavily regulated, bureaucratically managed and often disturbed by the Cold War, but, after reaching a nadir in 1951 and 1952, it increased sixfold (measured in current prices) by 1960.[21] The share of the Federal Republic as a trading partner of the GDR doubled from 5.2 per cent of the total GDR foreign trade in 1952 to 10.3 per cent in 1960.[22]

During that climax year of Cold War and mutual reproaches between the two German governments, the annual trade arrangements signalled that contacts and negotiations between the two German spearheads of Cold War were still possible. It became apparent that political non-recognition was only a part of the relations between the two Germanies. This was a remarkable contrast with the 'coexistence' of both Koreas after the Korean war. To keep the mutual trade going during the periods of intensive Cold War was far from easy. Not only the German side, but also the former occupation powers, exerted influence on the realisation of the agreements. They did this openly up to 1955, when both German states officially received 'full sovereignty', and also unofficially later on.

To a certain degree, albeit a smaller degree than in the first years after the war, the links between enterprises of the same prewar corporations continued to exist in the 1950s. When the German corporations succeeded in regaining their trade marks, which they had lost as a result of the Second World War, the enterprises in the West mostly got the right to use them. But after negotiations, in some important cases gentlemen's agreements came into being, which also allowed the East German parts of the former corporations to take advantage of the trade mark. Gentlemen's agreements of this kind came into being between, for instance, Agfa Wolfen (East) and Agfa Leverkusen (West) or between the institutions responsible for the enterprises in 1953.[23] Similar gentlemen's agreements also became possible for Zeiss East and Zeiss West, but only for a limited time.[24]

The intra-zone track was the last link that kept the two parts of Germany officially together. But in the autumn of 1960 the ongoing political fight between the FRG and the GDR finally seemed to destroy the trade links between the two states. In any case, the one-sided denouncement of the Berlin Agreement by the Federal government in Bonn put an end to the one decade when the economy was the fore-runner in keeping together what remained of the former German unity.

THE CLIMAX OF ECONOMIC WARFARE BETWEEN THE TWO GERMAN STATES: THE FRG'S CANCELLATION OF THE TRADE AGREEMENTS AND THE GDR'S CAMPAIGN FOR TOTAL ECONOMIC SEPARATION (1961–1964)

Both the cause and the aim of the Federal government's cancellation of the Berlin Trade Agreement of 1951 were completely politically moti-vated: the GDR authorities threatened to restrict the access of a certain group of West Germans to West Berlin. The West German government threatened to cancel the Berlin Trade Agreement in case the East German threat was carried out. When the unimpressed GDR author-ities carried their access restrictions out, the West German government answered with the cancellation of the trade agreement. It looked like the GDR would be the loser, because the inner German trade was much more important for East than West Germany. At the end of the 1950s, 10 per cent of the GDR's foreign trade was with the FRG, while only 2 per cent of the FRG's foreign trade was with the GDR.[25] Probably of even greater importance was that the GDR economy depended to a remarkable degree on certain deliveries from the West, mainly steel and iron, while in the Federal Republic the cancellation of trade with the GDR hit only a very limited number of individual firms.[26] But the Federal government – never very united on this question (the Ministry of Economics was much less eager to wage a trade war with the FRG's eastern neighbour than was the Ministry of Foreign Affairs) – had to learn that East German industry only relied up to 7 per cent on West German hard coal and coke in 1960 and imported only one tenth the amount of steel products from the FRG compared to the amount it had had to import in 1950.[27] The expected collapse of GDR industry thus did not happen. But the most important reason for the defeat that the Federal Republic suffered was the Soviet government's backing of the GDR political position on West Berlin.

At the end of 1960 the cancellation of the Berlin Agreement, which would have come into effect in January 1961, was withdrawn by the Federal government and replaced by a revised version, which included a revocation clause ('Widerrufklausel') that gave the Bonn government the right to stop annual deliveries, but did not force it to do so.[28] The bad experience with the cancellation of the Berlin Agreement of August 1960 was reason enough for the Federal government not to make use of the revocation clause, when the wall around West Berlin was built by the GDR only one year later.[29]

A long-standing result of the short-lived cancellation of the intra-zone trade agreement was the campaign of the GDR government to make the East German economy 'free from intervention' ('Störfreimachung') by the Federal Republic. The 'Störfreimachung' was the result of an evaluation of the economic dependencies of East German industrial branches by the Planning Commission and the ministries of economics in the GDR, undertaken under the threat of the cancellation of the intra-zone trade agreement in autumn 1960. The result worried the East German policy makers. Not only was there a dependence on imports from West Germany for coke and steel, but in nearly all branches of the machine-building industry the situation was no better. A campaign was started, therefore, to replace the existing links to enterprises in the Federal Republic by taking over their production in the GDR or shifting the import to the allied east-European countries. The commitment of the GDR leadership to 'Störfreimachung' was very serious. They sacrificed even the young GDR aircraft industry, the pride of many East Germans,[30] in order to free up investment, engineers and skilled labour for their programme of autarky. With enormous pressure from above, it was possible to reduce the number of enterprises in the heavy-machine-building industry that would be endangered by a possible cancellation of the trade treaty from 60 to 26 per cent, or from 25.4 to 14.8 per cent of the capacity.[31] Similar 'successes' were envisaged and often also realised in other industrial branches.

In the beginning of the 1960s the conflict about trade marks, waged between East and West German firms since the 1950s, escalated. The period of gentlemen's agreements between Agfa Leverkusen and Agfa Wolfen, and between Zeiss East and Zeiss West, ended. Both Agfa firms severed their trade mark links peacefully. Agfa Wolfen developed the trade mark ORWO and was renamed ORWO Wolfen at the beginning of the 1960s. Since the second half of the 1950s both Zeiss firms had been going to the courts in the FRG and abroad in order to prevent the former partner from using the Zeiss trade mark. A climax of the trade-mark war was reached in 1961, when, between Zeiss and Zeiss, seventy-two major cases in twenty-one countries and sixty-nine smaller ones in forty-one countries were pending decisions.[32]

The years of 'trade-mark war' and of 'Störfreimachung' (1961–4) became the climax years of industrial separation of the German economies. Month by month, the East German economic links to the western part of Germany, which had developed since the industrial revolution, were cut. The economy was the clear trendsetter in completing Germany's division during the first half of the 1960s. The amount of mutual trade declined, even in current prices, between 1960 and 1965. The political relations became icy with the creation of the Wall in August 1961. But a thaw began in politics much earlier than in economics. While the mutual trade policy of FRG and GDR was characterised by confrontation, as early as 1963 the first agreement between both German governments in the political field was signed. The agreement allowed West Berliners to visit their East Berlin relatives for the first time since the building of the Wall. Concerning the German question, relations between both German states in the economic field lagged behind that in politics up to 1964, when the policy confrontation in intra-German or 'German–German' trade, as it now became known, ended.

THE IMPROVEMENT OF TRADE LINKS AS A FORERUNNER OF POLITICAL DÉTENTE BETWEEN THE TWO GERMAN STATES (1964–1971)

Between 1965 and 1972 the volume of intra-German trade doubled (in current prices).[33] During this time the share of GDR trade with the Federal Republic rose only slightly from 9.5 to 12.3 per cent.[34] The policy of confrontation between East and West German enterprises that used the same traditional trade mark, came to an end. Even the East and West German Zeiss firms reached an agreement in London, based on the status quo, on how to share out the world market for Zeiss products.[35]

Thus there were many indications during the second half of the 1960s and the beginning of the 1970s that the severing of economic links between both parts of Germany had ended and was to be followed by a period of mutual co-operation and recognition – at least at the level of firms. Indeed, since the reformers in the SED leadership had taken over the command in the economy and introduced the 'New economic system of planning and management' (NES) they recognised that a complete severing of the economic links with the Federal Republic would be adverse for the new goals of raising productivity and the technological level of GDR industry. During the first year of the NES, when the reformer Apel became head of the commanding body of the GDR economy, the State Planning Commission, the policy of 'Störfreimachung' ended. To increase trade with the West in order to benefit from West–East technology transfer became one of the main goals of the NES.[36]

But the new attitude to reconstructing and expanding economic links between both German states in the second half of the 1960s was not only felt among GDR policy makers. On the part of the Federal Republic of Germany there was also a readiness to end its policy of confrontation in the trade sector. The revocation clause of the revised Berlin Agreement, which made trade between the FRG and the GDR insecure, was lifted in 1967. Numerous smaller improvements followed during the same year and in 1968.[37]

Economic relations between both German states not only became more intensive, but took the lead in keeping the relations between both German states going, leaving politics behind again.

There was a move in the Federal government, after Konrad Adenauer's chancellorship had ended in 1963, to come to mutual agreements with the other German state. But this move was blocked by a conservative majority in parliament and in the Federal government, which denied the GDR – as in the 1950s – the right to exist or, at least, to be internationally recognised. While these forces were able to block entente during the chancellorships of Ludwig Erhard and Georg Kiesinger and the first chancellorship of Willi Brandt (1964–72),[38] the field of the economy, where (camouflaged) relations between both German states already existed, was chosen by successive West German governments as a training ground for political negotiations, which they were convinced would happen in the near future. The 200 rounds of negotiations in 1967–8, aimed at introducing improvements in intra-German trade agreements, were thus not only of importance for the expansion of the trade between both German states, but had a political function as well. They demonstrated the possibility of establishing a dialogue with the other German state and of reaching agreements in the interests of both partners. The economy had again become the forerunner of closer relations between both Germanies. In this sense, developments in the economic relations between the two German states helped keep the 'German question' open.

POLITICAL PROGRESS AND ECONOMIC STAGNATION IN GERMAN–GERMAN RELATIONS (1972–1982)

At the end of the 1960s and the beginning of the 1970s, the political situation that had created a deadlock in the relations between the two German states changed in the Federal Republic of Germany. Those forces that wished officially to recognise the GDR as the second German state became ascendant. Nevertheless, the pledge for the eventual unification of Germany was not given up. This was in accordance with what had been written in the West German Constitution of 1949. A new formula was found: 'Two states – one nation.' In autumn 1969 the CDU (Christlich demokratische Union) lost control of the government for the first time in the history of the FRG. Social Democrats and Free Democrats, now forming the government, began to realise their aims of 'Ostpolitik', which included the recognition of the GDR. But it took until 1972 before the resistance of the CDU and – even more so – the CSU (Christlich soziale Union) against the political recognition of the GDR could be overcome and treaties about access to Berlin, improved relations with the GDR ('Grundlagenvertrag'), the USSR and Poland could be ratified by the Federal parliament. As a consequence, in 1973 both German states became members of the United Nations and signed the final documents of the Helsinki Agreement in 1975.[39] The new political relations between the two German states created the conditions for non-trade or non-commercial flows of goods and money between the FRG and GDR. Measures taken by the GDR government to improve access from West Germany to West Berlin and the freeing of political prisoners (for hard currency!) in the GDR were the main reasons, while the Federal Republic decided in favour of the West–East intra-German flow of money, which had only a limited positive impact on the East German currency balance.

While the political relations between both German states were put on a new basis, the economic links between the FRG and the GDR remained unchanged. The Berlin Agreement of 1951 in its updated version of 1960 remained valid throughout the 1970s and 1980s. That intra-German trade was not put on the level of the new 'Two states – one nation' level of political relations was a political setback for the GDR, which accepted the fact only hesitantly,[40] but it was forced to do so by adverse economic circumstances. Nevertheless, the Federal Republic had become the second most important trading partner of the GDR and its main source of technology imports.[41]

It was not only the framework of trading between the FRG and the GDR that remained unchanged. Trade itself more or less stagnated, after a period of fast growth in the second half of the 1960s. 'Intra-German trade has been in a phase of stagnation for a long time,' wrote Horst Lambrecht, analyst of the West Berlin-based Deutsches Institut für Wirtschaftsforschung (DIW) in 1982. 'There had only been real growth twice since 1972 – in 1976 and 1980 . . . During the period between 1972 and 1981 the real trade increase was only 0.6 or 0.7% per annum.'[42]

One of the reasons for stagnation in intra-German trade was the increasing difficulty experienced by the GDR processing industry in selling their products on western markets. In the West, competition intensified after the oil-price shock, the 1973/4 world economic crises and the forceful appearance of the Asian new industrialised countries on western markets.[43] As a result of the GDR being less able to compete in the innovation drive, the share of the GDR's machine-building industry in total exports to the FRG fell from 5.8 per cent in the period 1966–70 to 3.5 per cent in 1971–6 and finally to 3.1 per cent in 1976–80.[44]

The treaties of 1970–2 also allowed both German states to propagate détente publicly on the political level. This was not without consequences for the conditions of economic co-operation. It was no longer necessary for the FRG to demonstrate its willingness for détente indirectly by creating favourable conditions for intra-German trade. Some conditions, such as the lowering of Deutschmark interest rates for East Germany, which were subsequently reduced on a fixed, step-by-step basis, were conducive to a dynamic trade upswing.[45] The share of intra-German trade in East Germany's total foreign trade subsequently remained nearly unchanged.[46]

THE ECONOMY AGAIN AS FORERUNNER OF CLOSER RELATIONS BETWEEN BOTH GERMANIES (1983–1989)

In December 1981 a climax in the improvement of the political relations had been reached, when the political leaders of the two German states, the SED party boss Erich Honecker and the chancellor of the Federal Republic, Helmut Schmidt, met in the Schorfheide, north of Berlin. Honecker was invited by Schmidt for an official visit to the Federal Republic in the near future. But the political improvement of German–German relations was met with increasing distrust from several quarters. First there was opposition to the 'appeasement policy' of Honecker, who was 'born in western Germany',[47] by hard-liners within the SED politburo.[48] Secondly, there was growing distrust of the Soviet leadership under Brezhnev and Chernenko in the policy of developing 'special political relations' between the FRG and the GDR leadership.[49] Thirdly, there was a political change in the FRG, which was expected to disturb relations between both German states, as they had been developed between Schmidt and Honecker. The SPD-led coalition, which had initiated political détente with the GDR at the beginning of the 1970s, was overthrown by a vote of no confidence. The head of the opposition, Helmut Kohl, became chancellor of a CDU-led government. He underlined the necessity of reunification in his first speeches. This had not been a topic of the Social Democrats in previous years. Honecker was forced to cancel his visit to the Federal Republic.[50] It looked like the beginning of a period of stagnation in the political relations between both German states. The main field of German–German relations in 1983 shifted again from the more frosty – officially, at least – political scene to the economic field, which up to the end of the GDR became the main field of co-operation between the two German states.

But the changed political situation was not the only reason why the economy again became more important for German–German relations. In 1983 East Germany's economy was in trouble because of its growing hard-currency debt. The causes of this indebtedness went back to the beginning of the 1970s, when the GDR policy makers launched a scheme for the development of foreign economic relations with West Germany, which relied on credit-financed imports for the modernisation of the industrial capital stock. The credits were to be paid back in the second half of the 1970s by the goods produced in the new factories, which were supposed to have been completed by then. This scheme involved several risks: it was assumed that the West Germans would build most of the modern factories, that the same technique could be performed identically in the environment of another economic system and, lastly, that the situation of the markets could be predicted five to ten years ahead. At the end of the 1970s the politburo of the SED became aware of the complete failure of this scheme.

The answer was not very innovative: import restrictions and forced export of GDR goods at dumping prices. The results were modest. The hope of getting out of the mess finally had to be given up, when a failure of confidence on the part of the international banking community was sparked off by the insolvency crisis in Poland and Romania. The GDR was also drawn into the crisis.[51] East Germany was in the same situation as Poland, Romania or Hungary, which had also got into financial trouble because of their hard-currency deficit. These countries had relations with the IMF (International Monetary Fund) and the World Bank, which the GDR did not have. Honecker's intermediary, Alexander Schalck-Golodkowsky, therefore unofficially turned to the influential West German politician and prime minister of the state of Bavaria, Franz-Josef Strauss, asking for the help of the Federal Republic. The GDR got this help. In 1983 the Federal government organised and guaranteed a loan by West German banks to the East German regime worth 1,000 million deutschmarks. Another West German loan, again of 1,000 million deutschmarks, was forthcoming in 1984. This deal[52] allowed East Germany to fulfil its financial obligations and ended the distrust of the international banks towards the GDR.[53]

The Deutschmark loans were the beginning of closer co-operation between the two German states in the economic field. The Kohl government improved the financial framework for trade in order to make intra-German relations more flexible. But for the first time in the history of economic relations between the German states, trade was no longer the main field of co-operation. There was no upswing in intra-German trade. Trade between the FRG and GDR continued to suffer from the same difficulties as in the 1970s: the competitive weakness of East German processing industries.[54] Real progress was made in the development of different versions of contracts between GDR and FRG firms. A GDR government framework for 'Kompensationsgeschäfte' made the establishment of factories by West German firms politically possible. The attraction for West German firms was cheap labour. The GDR authorities envisaged that the investments would be paid back with the products of the newly built enterprises. Other than in the 1970s, the West German firms this time organised market access for the products in West Germany and got the right to intervene in the marketing process and also, indirectly, in other sections of the management of the East German factories. The best known of the Kompensationsgeschäfte was the construction of an automobile factory according to Volkswagen (VW) specifications. A second form of co-operation was termed 'Gestattungsproduktion'. Products were made in the GDR under West German licence and according to West German quality standards directly for the West German market. The best known of the Gestattungsproduktion deals was with the West German shoe producer 'Salamander'.[55] This co-operation came close to being a joint venture. But despite some attempts from the most influential economic leader of the SED, Günther Mittag, joint ventures remained a taboo in the GDR till 1989. Politburo hard-liners resisted any schemes that would, in their view, increase the dependence of the GDR's economy on West Germany.[56] (For development of West–East trade, see table 3.2.)

During 1989, when the political crisis of the SED regime was looming, and even when the Wall came down in November 1989, the progress in economic co-operation that had been attained seemed to be the firm base for the new political goal of creating a German confederation.[57]

Table 3.2. *Trade between GDR and FRG between 1952 and 1990 (in million DM, current prices)*

Year	GDR export	GDR import	Turnover	Balance
1952	220.3	178.4	398.7	+41.9
1953	306.9	271.3	578.2	+35.6
1954	449.7	454.4	904.1	−4.7
1955	587.9	562.6	1,150.5	+25.3
1956	653.4	699.2	1,150.5	−45.8
1957	817.3	845.9	1,663.2	−28.6
1958	858.2	800.4	1,658.6	+53.8
1959	891.7	1,078.6	1,970.3	−186.9
1960	1,122.4	959.5	2,081.9	+162.9
1961	940.9	872.9	1,813.8	+68.0
1962	914.0	853.0	1,767.0	+62.0
1963	1,022.0	860.0	1,822.0	+163.0
1964	1,017.0	1,151.0	2,178.0	−124.0
1965	1,260.0	1,206.0	2,167.0	+54.0
1966	1,345.0	1,625.0	2,971.0	−280.0
1967	1,264.0	1,483.0	2,747.0	−219.0
1968	1,440.0	1,432.0	2,872.0	+8.0
1969	1,656.0	2,272.0	3,928.0	−616.0
1970	1,996.0	2,416.0	4,412.0	−420.0
1971	2,319.0	2,499.0	4,817.0	−180.0
1972	2,381.0	2,927.0	5,308.0	−546.0
1973	2,660.0	2,998.0	5,568.0	−338.0
1974	3,252.0	3,671.0	5,923.0	−418.0
1975	3,342.0	3,922.0	7,264.0	−579.0
1976	3,877.0	4,269.0	8,145.0	−392.0
1977	3,961.0	4,409.0	8.370.0	−448.0
1978	3,900.0	4,575.0	8,475.0	−675.0
1979	4,589.0	4,720.0	9,309.0	−131.0
1980	5,580.0	5,293.0	10,873.0	+286.0
1981	6,051.0	5,575.0	11,626.0	+476.0
1982	6,639.0	6,382.0	13,022.0	+257.0
1983	6,878.0	6,947.0	13,825.0	−69.0
1984	7,744.0	6,408.0	14,152.0	+1,336.0
1985	7,636.0	7,901.0	15,537.0	−265.0
1986	6,844.0	7,454.0	14,298.0	−611.0
1987	6,650.0	7,406.0	14,056.0	−756.0
1988	6,790.0	7.230.0	14,020.0	−440.0
1989	7,205.4	8,103.5	15,038.9	−898.1
1990	8,274.1	21,325.7	29,599.0	−13,051.6

Source: Statistisches Bundesamt Wiesbaden: Warenverkehr mit der DDR und Berlin (Ost), Fachserie 6, Reihe 6.

But at the end of 1989 and the beginning of 1990 the demands of the demonstrators turned from democratic socialism with a mixed economy to unification with the market economy of West Germany.[58] During this time the main focus of German–German relations again turned away from economics to politics.

SLOW PROGRESS IN ECONOMIC UNIFICATION ENDANGERS THE ACHIEVEMENTS OF FAST POLITICAL UNIFICATION (1990–1997)

The political situation of the GDR changed in the first quarter of 1990 dramatically from a scene dominated by the SED/PDS (Party of Democratic Socialism) and other 'revolutionary' movements, to a political landscape like that in the Federal Republic.

With the first free elections in March 1990 the CDU (Christlich Demokratische Union) and the SPD (Sozialdemokratische Partei Deutschlands) became the main parties in the GDR, too. The PDS, the successor of the SED, got only 16 per cent, the revolutionary parties, successors of the revolutionary movements, only 5 per cent of the vote.[59] These political decisions of the GDR population were confirmed by the elections to the five provincial parliaments in the East in October. The first all-German election was held in December 1990, when the PDS, the remaining 'Eastern party', got only 11 per cent of the votes in the former GDR and 0.3 per cent in the old Federal Republic of Germany.[60] In 1991 the post-communists were in a deep crisis. Generally it was expected that they would be completely marginalised[61] as had been the Communists in the West of Germany some decades before. Political analysts were convinced that with the 1994 federal elections the political unification would be completed.

But beginning with the Berlin state elections in June 1992 the downturn of the post-communists was stopped. During the 'super election year' of 1994, when there was not only the federal election, but also elections for the European parliament and elections in several provinces and local elections, the PDS was able to increase its share of the vote in the East, compared with the December 1990 federal election and even with the last GDR elections of March 1990. In the East it got 19.8 per cent of the vote. These elections, which took place at the local and province levels in East Germany, confirmed this result as did the elections for the European parliament.[62] After the 1994 super election year there again emerged in Germany two different political landscapes: one in the West, where the post-communists remained marginalised (1 per cent of the

vote) and the four parties that were able to override the 5 per cent hurdle
– the Christian Democrats, the Social Democrats, the Free Democrats
and the Greens – and one in the East, where only three parties got above
the 5 per cent hurdle: the Christian Democrats, the Social Democrats
and the post-communists.

The clear backlash that political unification had suffered in 1994 was
to a remarkable degree the result of the deficits in economic unification,
which have become more and more visible for the East Germans since
1992. While the institutional framework of the West German 'social
market economy' was introduced on the day of the 'currency union', 1
July 1990, with great haste,[63] privatisation and marketisation did not
create an East German economy similar to that in the West. The newly
emerging economic structures in the new Bundesländer differed sharply
from those in the old ones. Deindustrialisation did not come to a halt
before the most industrialised state of the East (Saxony) had a lower
share of industry in GNP than the least industrialised state in the West
(Schleswig-Holstein). On average, the industrial level in the East in 1995
reached only 60 per cent of that of West Germany, the capital intensity
56 per cent.[64] The efforts to reduce the size of the former big state-
owned enterprises, the Kombinate, called the 'dinosaurs', did not stop
before the average enterprise in the East was minimised to such a level
that it lacked the capital for marketing, research and development and
other 'extra' costs. Only investment in these areas could have prepared
these enterprises to face the future.[65] Opening the way for an influx of
West German management methods by selling off the East German
enterprises to West German private firms – 95 per cent of the capacity
of former East German industry was privatised this way – did not stop
until these enterprises had been turned into pure subsidiaries.[66] In 1994
it became known that there was only one remaining large enterprise –
with a workforce of more than 1,000 and including all the functions of
a modern enterprise – in the former East Germany.[67]

The dysfunction in the economy can be pursued to the enterprise level
of the 'reference' firms of this chapter, Zeiss and ORWO (formerly Agfa)
Wolfen. Though a basic agreement about close co-operation between
Zeiss East (Jena) and Zeiss West (Oberkochen) was signed as early as
November 1990 and the Oberkochen manager got access to all production secrets of Zeiss Jena, the former offspring hesitated to buy the
former 'mother' company when it was offered to Zeiss West by the
Treuhand privatisation agency. Only when Treuhand threatened to sell
the Jena plant to Japanese competitors was Oberkochen ready to take
over the traditional optical production of Zeiss Jena. That occurred in

June 1991. It soon renounced its financial help for the Jena plant and turned the former 'mother' into a subsidiary, denying Zeiss Jena its own responsibility for marketing. The chief manager of the Jena plant (a West German), resigned. Only in 1995/6 did Oberkochen accept Jena as a core enterprise of the Zeiss firm and give it responsibility for special aspects of optical production and greater autonomy.[68] For Agfa Leverkusen, the East German ORWO Wolfen was of no interest, even though ORWO managers and Treuhandanstalt tried to come to terms with the West German firm, which had been a co-operation partner of ORWO for decades, even during the first ten years of separate political development in East and West Germany. ORWO was scaled down by the Treuhandanstalt again and again, in order to make a suitable package out of the former giant that could be sold to a western investor. But for a long time nobody came. Only in 1995 did the owner of a medium-sized camera factory from West Germany take over the remnants of the former ORWO giant and begin to deliver films from Wolfen with the famous ORWO trade mark. At the beginning of 1997 the workforce of the plant was 100 people, compared with 21,000 in 1989. One year later the last firm with the name ORWO was closed.[69]

The differences in the economic structure of East and West Germany have consequences for its social structure. Mainly as a result of high-speed deindustrialisation, unemployment in the new federal provinces is considerably higher than in western Germany. Though unemployment has been relatively high in the whole of Germany since the 1992/3 economic crises, differences between old and new federal provinces are remarkable. The average official unemployment in 1998 reached 19.3 per cent in the east and 9.4 per cent in the west of Germany. Unemployment in the most affected state of eastern Germany, Sachsen-Anhalt, is three times higher than in the state with the lowest level of unemployment in the west, Bavaria.[70] While in the west the real unemployment figures are not far from the official ones, in the east real unemployment is much higher than officially admitted – around 30 per cent.[71] Thanks to huge transfers of Deutschmarks from the west to the east after currency union,[72] the disparity in the standard of living is not as big as could be expected from the economic situation. The net income in the new Länder reached around 85 per cent of that of the west in 1997.[73] If one considers the property of east and west German households instead of current income, the figure for east Germans is 14.6 per cent of that of west Germans. Particularly alarming is the fact that – in contrast to the current income development – the east German private wealth level has, in relation to that of the west, not increased but

Table 3.3. *Monthly net income per employed person in the new and the old German Bundesländer in DM, 1991–1997*

Year	New Länder	Old Länder	New Länder (old Länder = 100)	Increase (%)
1991	1,367	2,248	54.7	
1992	1,754	2,511	69.9	15.2
1993	2,032	2,689	75.6	5.7
1994	1,108	2,691	78.4	2.8
1995	2,221	2,695	82.4	4.0
1996	2,352	2,788	84.4	2.0
1997	2,362	2,776	85.0	0.6

Source: Calculated from data of Statistisches Bundesamt Wiesbaden, *Der Tagesspiegel*, 15 August 1998.

decreased (see table 3.3). The forecasts of economists who think that equality in economic performance and income will be reached envisage this happening in the first or second decade of the new century. Taking these estimates into consideration, the period when the economy acts as a brake to the unification process will last much longer than in any other of the earlier periods between 1945 and 1989.

CONCLUSION: THE IMPACT OF THE ECONOMY ON THE GERMAN QUESTION FROM 1945 TO THE PRESENT AND ITS RELATIONSHIP TO POLITICS

As has been shown, the economy served during the last five decades as either a pushing or a retarding force in the development of the German question. On the one hand the economy played a pushing role in the solution of the German question. It did this either by keeping Germany at least partially together or by providing the basis for co-operation under the aegis of a special relationship. 'Special' is understood here to mean 'not usual for other neighbouring "capitalist" and "socialist" countries'. The economy was the main link that kept together the eastern and the western zones, which were drifting in different directions politically, during the first years after the war (1945–7). The economy also acted as the only bridge between the two German governments when the political dialogue broke down (1950–60). Later on, the economy was again the field of intensive negotiations. It was important for the development of trust between the representatives of both German governments, when it was not possible to co-operate more closely in the political field due to hostility towards the superpowers or internal opposition to a continuation of political negotiations. (1983–9).

On the other hand the economy also acted as a retarding force in the development of the German question, which deepened the division of Germany or prevented closer co-operation between both Germanies. In 1948–9 and in 1961–4 the economy took the lead in the final division of Germany. In the 1970s and beginning of the 1980s, no signals for the improvement of relations between the FRG and the GDR came from the economy. Since unification, the economy has become the main retarding force in the process of what is referred to by politicians and the media as 'real unification', by providing the 'material base' for ongoing social and mental differences.

But a look at the history of the German question in the last five decades also reveals that economic activities, directed either towards reunification or separation, have often been connected with political attempts to keep the east and west of Germany separate or together.

The Cold War policy in 1948 jeopardised efforts to keep Germany economically together. In 1960, existing economic links between the GDR and the FRG were almost completely sacrificed to the demands of the Cold War. During the second half of the 1960s and the beginning of the 1970s, the economy acted as a proxy for détente, which, due to internal pressure in the FRG and the GDR, could not take place politically. In the second half of the 1980s, economic co-operation between the two German states had its own logic and momentum. But it was the (partially secret) negotiations in the economic field that created the necessary degree of trust between Honecker and the CDU/CSU-led Kohl government of the Federal Republic, for the long-delayed 1987 Honecker visit to Bonn to have been possible. In the 1990s the slow progress of economic unification – the broken promise of a flourishing landscape – seems to have jeopardised progress in political and mental unification, which had been reached initially in 1990 and 1991.

NOTES

1 The origins of the 'German question' are often dated back to the late middle ages, when the Reformation and the Thirty Years War confirmed religious and cultural diversity and political decentralisation in Germany for more than 200 years: Mary Fulbrook, *Germany 1918–1990. The Divided Nation* (London, 1991), pp. 1–3.

2 William Carr, *The Origins of the Wars of German Unification* (New York, 1991),

pp. 25–33; Mary Fulbrook, *A Concise History of Germany* (Cambridge, 1990), pp. 114–15 and 123.

3 Christoph Klessmann and Georg Wagner (eds.), *Das gespaltene Land. Leben in Deutschland 1945–1990* (Munich, 1993), p. 13.

4 Peter Bender, *Episode oder Epoche? Zur Geschichte des geteilten Deutschland* (Munich, 1996), pp. 255–6.

5 Werner Weidenfeld and Karl Rudolf Korte (eds.), *Handbuch zur deutschen Einheit* (Bonn, 1996), pp. 385–96.

6 Enquete-Kommission (ed.), *Aufarbeitung von Geschichte und Folgen der SED-Diktatur in Deutschland im Deutschen Bundestag* (Baden-Baden, 1995), vol. V, pp. 1108–542 and 1572–2600.

7 For more details see Weidenfeld and Korte, *Handbuch*, pp. 264–75.

8 Enquete-Kommission, *Aufarbeitung von Geschichte*, pp. 1543–71 and 2761–97.

9 *Ibid.*, pp. 1579–647 and 2889–940; Rainer Klump, *Wirtschaftsgeschichte der Bundesrepublik Deutschland* (Wiesbaden, 1985); Wolfgang Mühlfriedel and Klaus Wiessner, *Die Geschichte der Industrie der DDR bis 1965* (Berlin, 1989). A look at the other German economy is included to a certain degree in Werner Abelshauser, *Wirtschaftsgeschichte der Bundesrepublik Deutschland 1945–1980* (Frankfurt am Main, 1983), pp. 94–8.

10 Karl Bittel (ed.), *Das Potsdamer Abkommen und andere Dokumente* (Berlin, 1957), pp. 71–2, 75.

11 Fulbrook, *Concise History of Germany*, pp. 133–4.

12 Manfred Overesch, *Die Deutschen und die Deutsche Frage 1945–1955* (Hanover, 1985), p. 25.

13 Heinz Kohler, *Economic Integration in the Soviet Bloc* (New York, 1965), pp. 61 and 65.

14 Christoph Buchheim (ed.), *Wirtschaftliche Folgelasten des Kriegs in der SBZ/DDR* (Baden-Baden, 1995), p. 195.

15 Wolfgang Schumann, *Carl Zeiss Jena. Einst und jetzt* (Berlin, 1962), pp. 660–5.

16 Gerhard Keiderling, *Die Berliner Krise 1948/49* (Berlin, 1982).

17 In spring 1948 the prime ministers of the West German Länder – in a first reaction to the demand of the western Allies – refused to take part in the elaboration of a separate constitution for the western zones, because they did not wish to risk the split of Germany. In the Soviet Occupation Zone at the end of 1947 the 'German Peoples Congress for Unity and a Just Peace' began to resume work: Christoph Klessmann, *Die doppelte Staatsgründung. Deutsche Geschichte 1945–1955* (Bonn, 1986), pp. 199 and 203.

18 Detlef Nakath, *Zur Geschichte der deutsch-deutschen Handelsbeziehungen. Die besondere Bedeutung der Krisenjahre 1960/61 für die Entwicklung des innerdeutschen Handels* (Berlin, 1993), p. 10.

19 Bender, *Episode*, pp. 36–46.

20 Nakath, *Zur Geschichte*, pp. 9–10; Renate Hrzan and Walter Kupferschmidt, 'Zur historischen Entwicklung der Aussenhandelsorganisation der DDR', *Wissenschaftliche Zeitschrift der Hochschule für Ökonomie 'Bruno Leuschner'* 4 (1987), 3–5.

21 *Statistisches Jahrbuch der Deutschen Demokratischen Republik 1960/61* (Berlin, 1961), p. 573.

22 *Ibid.*

23 Rainer Karlsch, *Von Agfa zu ORWO. Die Folgen der deutschen Teilung für die Filmfabrik Wolfen* (Wolfen, 1992), pp. 13–17.

24 Federal State Archives (Bundesarchiv), files of the former GDR central state authorities (Abteilung DDR); DE-4, 6128, without folio numbers. In the following: B Arch DDR.

25 B Arch DB102, 108.149, without folio numbers.

26 *Ibid.*

27 *Ibid.*

28 For details, see Nakath, *Zur Geschichte*, pp. 22–35.

29 Hans Georg Lehmann, *Deutschland-Chronik 1945–1995* (Berlin, 1995), p. 191.

30 In a contemporary East German publication the re-establishment of the aircraft industry was called 'the true German economic miracle': Rolf Kindscher, *Entwicklungstendenzen im Luftverkehr* (Berlin, 1960), p. 114.

31 B Arch DDR, DE-4, 4471, without folio numbers.

32 B Arch DDR, DE-4, 6128, without folio numbers.

33 *Ibid.*

34 *Statistisches Jahrbuch der DDR 1970* (Berlin, 1970), pp. 294–5; *Statistisches Jahrbuch der DDR 1976* (Berlin, 1976), pp. 265–6.

35 Zeiss West (situated in Oberkochen), for example, got the exclusive rights to sell under the Zeiss trade mark in West Germany, Italy, Scandinavia and the United States. In the Comecon countries only Zeiss East (Jena) had the right to sell products under the Zeiss trade mark. In a third group of countries both Zeiss Corporations were allowed to sell their products. These 'countries of coexistence' included, for example, Great Britain and the British Commonwealth, Spain and some African states: Gustav Neumann, 'Es waren einmal zwei Brüder. Werden Zeiss-Ost und Zeiss-West der erste gesamtdeutsche Konzern?', *Neues Deutschland*, 6–7 October 1990.

36 B Arch DDR, DE-4, 26678, without folio numbers. See also Gerd Leptin and Manfred Melzer, *Economic Reforms in East German Industry* (Oxford, 1978), pp. 55–6.

37 Nakath, *Zur Geschichte*, p. 16.

38 Christoph Klessmann, *Zwei Staaten, eine Nation. Deutsche Geschichte 1955–1970* (Göttingen, 1988), pp. 82–98; Lehmann, *Deutschland-Chronik*, pp. 216–17.

39 Lehmann, *Deutschland-Chronik*, pp. 239–44.

40 Erich Honecker in an interview with the U.S. journalist Sulzberger, *Neues Deutschland*, 25 November 1971.

41 Werner Weidenfeld and Hartmut Zimmermann, *Deutschland-Handbuch. Eine doppelte Bilanz 1949–1989* (Bonn, 1989), pp. 647–8. The specialist on the intra-German trade history, Nakath, speaks about a 'compromise between extreme different positions. The FRG was able to realise most of her political interests' during the negotiations for the 'Grundlagenvertrag': Nakath, *Zur Geschichte*, p. 18.

42 Horst Lambrecht, 'Innerdeutscher Handel weiterhin ohne Dynamik', *DIW* (Deutsches Institut für Wirtschaftsforschung) *–Wochenbericht* 22 (1982), 285.

43 US Congress: Joint Economic Committee (ed.), *East European Economies: Slow Growth in the 1980s* (Washington, 1986), vol. II, pp. 12–13.

44 Lambrecht, 'Innerdeutscher Handel', p. 287.

45 The swing was normally fixed in trade agreements between the two German states as a certain sum of money. The dynamic swing was fixed as percentage of intra-German trade. In the case of growth in trade the volume of the swing grew automatically.

46 Statistisches Bundesamt (ed.), *Sonderreihe mit Beiträgen für das Gebiet der ehemaligen DDR* (Wiesbaden, 1993), vol. IX, pp. 16–17.

47 Peter Przybylski, *Tatort Politbüro. Die Akte Honecker* (Berlin, 1991), p. 352. Honecker was born in 1912 in the Saarland, near the French–German border.

48 Detlef Nakath and Gerd-Rüdiger Stephan, *Von Hubertusstock nach Bonn* (Berlin, 1995), pp. 21–4.

49 Brigitte Zimmermann and Hans-Dieter Schütt (eds.), *ohnMacht. DDR-Funktionäre sagen aus* (Berlin, 1992), pp. 224–5.

50 Lehmann, *Deutschland-Chronik*, pp. 303–5, and 332.

51 US Congress: Joint Economic Committee, *East European Economies*, vol. II, pp. 153–4 and 169–70.

52 Officially there did not exist any condition on the side of the Federal government for its help in arranging the credits. But unofficially the GDR government agreed to make the border and the border controls between East and West Germany more humane. It also allowed a wider circle of GDR citizens to emigrate to the West (Lehmann, *Deutschland-Handbuch*, p. 332). As for the reasons for the credit deal, Strauss, in his memoires, gives another argument: when East Germany, because of the consequences of its indebtedness, seemed likely to get into severe economic and political trouble, the leading circles in the FRG foresaw and feared another intervention of Soviet forces as had happened on 17 June 1953. Strauss and other West German politicians tried to avoid another round of bloodshed, or at least additional hardship, for the population of East Germany: Franz-Josef Strauss, *Memoiren* (Berlin, 1989), p. 475.

53 Strauss, *Memoiren*, pp. 471–3.

54 Horst Lambrecht, 'Innerdeutscher Handel: Kontinuität erforderlich', *DIW-Wochenbericht* 10 (1986), 120; Horst Lambrecht, 'Innerdeutscher Handel. Expansionsmöglichkeiten wirklich nutzen!', *DIW-Wochenbericht* 9–10 (1989), 100.

55 Günter Mittag, *Um jeden Preis. Im Spannungsfeld zweier Systeme* (Berlin, 1991), p. 104.

56 *Ibid.*, pp. 105–7.

57 Detlev Nakath and Gerd-Rüdiger Stephan, *Countdown zur deutschen Einheit* (Berlin, 1996), pp. 30–2.

58 Konrad H. Jarausch and Volker Granzow (eds.), *Uniting Germany. Documents and Debates 1944–1993* (Providence, RI, 1994), pp. 64–102.

59 *Ibid.*, p. 128.
60 Gero Neugebauer and Richard Stöss, *Die PDS. Geschichte, Organisation, Wähler, Konkurrenten* (Opladen, 1996), pp. 174–5 and 184.
61 *Ibid.*, pp. 43–53.
62 *Ibid.*, pp. 206–26.
63 Bernd Rebe and Franz Peter Lang (eds.), *Die unvollendete Einheit. Bestandsaufnahme und Perspektiven für die Wirtschaft* (Cloppenburg, 1996), pp. 94–5.
64 Manfred Wegner, 'Die deutsche Einigung oder das Ausbleiben des Wunders', *Aus Politik und Zeitgeschichte*, B 40 (1996), 18; Wolfgang Dümcke and Fritz Vilmar (eds.), *Kolonialisierung der DDR* (Münster, 1995), pp. 127–9; *Der Tagesspiegel*, 13 August 1998.
65 Jörg Roesler, 'Privatisation in East Germany – experience with the Treuhand', *Europe–Asia Studien* 3 (1994), 510–11; Wegner, 'Die deutsche Einigung', pp. 19–20.
66 Jörg Roesler, 'Privatisation of East German industry: its economic and social implications', *Labour Focus on Eastern Europe* 51 (1995), 63. Wegner writes: 'In East Germany mainly subsidiaries emerged ("verlängerte Werkbänke") of West German and foreign enterprises. The headquarters of nearly all larger enterprises are situated outside of the new federal states': Wegner, 'Die deutsche Einigung', p. 19.
67 Ralf Neubauer, 'Gewinne in weiter Ferne', *Die Zeit* 33 (1994), 17.
68 Peter Liebers, 'Personalkosten belasten die Zeiss-Bilanzen', *Neues Deutschland*, 12 April 1996.
69 Peter Christ and Ralf Neubauer, *Kolonie im eigenen Land* (Berlin, 1991), p. 158; Martin Flug, *Treuhandpoker. Die Mechanismen des Ausverkaufs* (Berlin, 1992), p. 107; Hans-Dieter Vater, 'ORWO: Nach der Rettung Start zu neuer Fahrt', *Neues Deutschland*, 18 March 1997.
70 *Neues Deutschland*, 7 May 1997.
71 Dümcke and Vilmar, *Kolonialisierung*, pp. 125–7.
72 The net transfer sum from 1991 to 1996 was 898.4 billion DM. In 1996 the net transfer amount of 137 billion DM was as large as 34.7 per cent of the east German GDP and 4.3 per cent of the west German GDP: Wegner, 'Die deutsche Einigung', p. 20.
73 Ulrich Busch, 'Vermögensdifferenzierung und Disparität der Lebensverhältnisse im vereinigten Deutschland', *Berliner Debatte Initial* 5 (1996), 105; *Der Tagesspiegel*, 15 August 1998.

CHAPTER 4

Lusatian Sorbs in Germany before the Second World War: the influence of the economy on the national question

Eduard Kubů

Geographical position, climatic conditions and natural wealth, together with the economic and social development closely related to these factors, have always played a fundamental role in the life of states, peoples or sub-communities. These factors were of particular importance in the case of the smallest distinct Slavonic ethnic group still in existence – the Lusatian Sorbs. In the medieval and early-modern periods the geographic–economic factor tended to promote the survival of the Sorbs' language and specific social characteristics, hemmed in on all sides by Germans. The Slav areas of Lusatia were mainly poor and sparsely settled and had an incomparably smaller share of towns and town populations than the German-speaking areas that surrounded them. For this reason the Sorbs could live in a degree of isolation from the German environment and were able to develop in their own way, with a significant degree of autonomy. Hartmut Zwahr even goes so far as to speak of the Sorbs' insular existence, citing Jakub Lorenc-Zalěsky's characterisation of the group as 'an island of the forgotten'.[1]

This situation may be convincingly demonstrated using the example of the later Saxon Lusatia as described by Karlheinz Blaschke.[2] In 1835, for instance, in the Saxon territory populated by Sorbs, there was only one town with more than 10,000 inhabitants (Budyšin (German: Bautzen)), and two towns with a population of between 1,000 and 5,000 (Lubij (German: Löbau) and Mužakow (German: Muskau)). Population density essentially varied between three categories – up to 50 inhabitants per km^2, up to 100 per km^2 and, in a smaller area, up to only 20 per km^2. In central Lusatia quite large areas of territory were not settled at all. In contrast, in the southern part of Lusatia, rapidly industrialising and inhabited by a German population spreading out along the Czech border, population density was in most areas up to 200 or up to 500 per km^2, and where less then at least up to 100 per km^2. These significantly smaller territories could also boast a larger number of urban areas and, in the same ratio, a larger number of more affluent inhabitants.

In the later nineteenth and twentieth centuries, however, economic development and modernisation encouraged the ever-deeper integration of the Lusatian areas settled by Sorbs into German areas. This had a major impact on the formation of modern Lusatian Sorb ethnic society and helped to strengthen Germanising influences that soon raised a series of crucial questions, especially that of the preservation and future development of the Lusatian Sorb language and ethnic life.

Germanisation was not simply a consequence of economic development. It was the effect of a constellation of factors, including major international and political questions, and socio-economic change, but also involving developments in administration, military service, culture, education and religion. Scholars are, however, generally agreed that the negative effects of economic and social change were more of a burden on the Lusatian Sorbs than the Germanising policies of the Saxon and Prussian states (between which the Sorb areas of Lusatia were divided), and therefore contributed more to their Germanisation.[3]

Both in Prussian and Saxon Lusatia it was the Prussian model of transition from feudal to capitalist agriculture that was applied. In Prussian Lusatia the new agrarian legislation was introduced in 1821, and in Saxon Lusatia, in modified form, a decade later. The abolition of serfdom and the corvée led to the transformation of the feudal estate into a capitalist enterprise. In practice the reform meant the impoverishment of the freed peasant, who in Prussia usually had to compensate the former lord with a third of the land in his ownership and a monetary purchase payment, undertake to pay an annual monetary rent for several years and, not infrequently, to provide services as well. In Saxony the conditions of agricultural reform were less burdensome for the serfs; redemption was secured by a single payment or yearly monetary rent, but there was no obligation to give up part of the land.[4]

Many poor peasants were forced to work as hired labour in order to pay their dues on their own land. As a result of this heavy burden only a small proportion of the peasantry could enjoy the prospect of becoming substantial landowners. On the contrary, at the end of the agrarian reforms in the 1860s, the multiplication of the village poor meant the relative overpopulation of the Lusatian countryside, creating the conditions for the subsequent migration of the population in search of work. Increasing industrialisation then logically attracted a wave of migrants to the manufacturing centres. Since the nobility in both Lusatias had been, for centuries, purely German, the result of the agrarian reforms was the weakening of the position of the Slav population to the advantage of the German-speaking element, which consolidated its superior economic position even in the areas dominated by Sorb inhabitants. The 'small peasant' character of Sorb economic activity was reinforced.

In the following decades the position of the Sorb rural population deteriorated more slowly, but still inexorably. This was because the major landowners retained rights of first refusal on any land that the freed peasants might wish to acquire. Various German associations with important political and, above all, economic backing were also working quietly to promote Germanisation. The Bund 'Deutscher Osten' operated with a fund 'for the economic protection of border areas', which at the time of Weimar Germany had 22 million marks at its disposal for the purposes of Germanisation. Newly organised waves of German farmer colonists were given systematic advantages, with ten-year periods of tax relief, cheap credit and assistance in getting a good price for their corn. The Sorb element, however, enjoyed none of these benefits, and was placed at a significant disadvantage.[5]

The development of industry dramatically increased the rate at which the Lusatian Sorbs were being Germanised and assimilated. In the Žitawa (German: Zittau) region, textile manufacture had been developing from the eighteenth century, with ironworks, machine-tool enterprises and others following. In Lower Lusatia industrialisation started much later, not before the mid-nineteenth century, when textile production began to develop in Chocebuz (German: Cottbus) – cloth and carpet manufacture. In these phases industrialisation was principally an urban phenomenon. In the last third of the nineteenth century, however, it was penetrating into the Lusatian countryside. Brown coal-mining was introduced and rapidly developed between Chocebuz and the Upper Lusatian border country, as was the mining of high-quality sands, which allowed the development of glass manufactures. In central Lusatia the wood-processing industry developed. At the same time industrialisation also started in the western part of the Upper Lusatian district of Wojerecy (German: Hoyerswerda). Infrastructures were built to serve the needs of manufactures, especially railways, first from the later 1840s in Upper Lusatia and then in Lower Lusatia in the 1870s.

Major industrial enterprises included the brown coal industry (in the Seftenberger Revier), the aluminium works in Luty (German: Lauta), which as late as the 1920s were still among the largest works of their kind in Germany, the Mitteldeutsche Stahlwerke in Kalawa (German: Calau), the synthetic benzine factory in Rólany (German: Ruhland), the factory for the manufacture of electrotechnical porcelain in Wulka Dubrawa (German: Groß Dubrau), the locomotive works, ironworks and paper factory in Budyšín (German: Bautzen) and the glassworks in Běla Woda (German: Weisswasser).

Industrialisation proceeded, without exception, on an ethnically German basis. As the Saxon government asserted in 1919, not a single medium-sized or large industrial concern on the territory that it administered was in Sorb hands,[6] and the economic situation of the Sorb population in Upper Lusatia was, in fact, better than in Lower Lusatia. Jiří Kapitán, who was very well acquainted with Lusatian conditions, wrote that 'The concept of a Sorb industrialist, an owner of a large factory, or indeed of any Sorb capitalist whatsoever, simply does not exist. I have known only one Sorb family that owned some quarries before the First World War (after the war they naturally lost them), and a doctor, who inherited a small spa facility.' He went on to mention a few small building contractors and sawmill owners and ended with the assertion that 'the Lusatian Sorbs are a proletarian nation'.[7]

The German entrepreneurs used German as the language of communication at work, and so employment in a German enterprise almost automatically involved the gradual Germanisation of employees and their families, where the absence of Sorb schooling also had a negative impact. Nor should we forget the fact that membership of the Sorb ethnic group was, in practice, a barrier to significant upward social and economic mobility. This problem, too, was a driving force for the voluntary 'economic' Germanisation of the Sorb population. The lifestyle of the urban population, and the use of German in other areas where Sorbs were employed, such as transport and trade, as well as in public administration, should also be borne in mind.

Social confrontation between the workers and employers also tended to undermine the Sorb language, as trade unions and political movements brought their own Germanising pressures. As Kapitán notes, 'The German comrades made fun of the Sorbs, saying that they obeyed their teachers and priests, and they directly challenged them to abandon their language', arguing that it 'split proletarian forces unnecessarily' and saying that German would open up greater 'cultural possibilities'.[8]

Life in the large communities and agglomerations therefore led inevitably to bilingualism in the first generation followed by a gradual transfer to German as the only language of communication. The wave of industrialisation that started in the later nineteenth century created new work opportunities and these meant an influx not just of German, but also of Polish and other non-Lusatian, immigrants to the towns and even to the countryside. The population rose, with Sorbs representing an ever smaller percentage, as is clear from statistical data and estimates from the end of the nineteenth century and first half of the twentieth century. In both the Lusatias, Lusatian Sorbs were already clearly in a minority. The only exceptions were in the districts of Kamenz, Bautzen, Löbau, Rothenburg, Hoyerswerda, Spremberg, Calau and Cottbus (Sorbian denotations: Kamjenc, Budyšin, Lubij, Rózbork, Wojerecy, Grodk, Kalawa and Chocebuz), or their main constituents – in other words, in the territory that the Sorb National Committee wanted annexed to Czechoslovakia, or, when this suggestion was turned down by the Allies after the First World War, at least to be given autonomy.[9]

The most important, massive and also most characteristic branch of industry in Lusatia deserves special attention. This was the brown coal industry, which had the greatest negative impact on the Sorb ethnic group. The first expansion of the Senftenberger Revier came in the years 1871–89. The later 1880s then saw the establishment of the two largest joint-stock companies, which set the pattern for future development. These were Braunkohlenwerke und Brikettfabriken AG, which was under the influence of the Czech 'brown coal king', Ignaz Petschek, and Ilse Bergbau-AG, as the daughter company of the Berlin firm Kunheim & Co., which grew into one of the biggest chemical firms in Wilhelmine Germany. At first the exploitation of the coal required only the seasonal labour of local peasants without enough land to be self-sufficient, but soon a large part of the population was engaged in the industry, which was originally open cast, but came also to include deep mining. Work in the mines provided better opportunities for earnings than work on the Junker estates.[10]

Coal-mining grew rapidly: 2.5 million tons were mined in 1890 but this figure had jumped to 19.5 million tons by 1913.[11] Despite the increasing mechanisation of mining, especially the introduction of excavators, the number of employees rose. The local, mainly Sorb workforce was augmented, to an ever greater degree, by workers coming longer distances, from Saxony and Prussia and also Congress Poland and Galicia. The ethnic composition of the coal region acquired a new face. The Sorb population dropped both as a percentage of employees in the coal industry and in the region as a whole. While the Sorbs who had transferred entirely from agriculture to industry assimilated quickly, the 'half-peasant' miners, who continued to cultivate their small farms as well as working in the mines, continued to preserve their mother tongue and customs.[12]

The establishment of new mines brought about a significant weakening of the Sorb element, because this was usually accomplished through the forced purchase of land and resettlement of the population. As many as seventy-seven villages and small settlements were destroyed as a result of mining. In the years 1924–93 more than 25,000 people were resettled.[13] Mined-out land could not be returned to agricultural production and the process of recultivation was long and demanding. Mining also advanced inexorably across the territory. It spread from the original mining centre near Senftenberg, where the coal lay close to the surface, to the deep levels towards the east into the vicinity of the towns of Wojerecy, Grodk and Běla Woda, to the north-west (Lübbenau) and to the north-east (Peitz). Lusatian coal production secured roughly half of the electrical energy of the territory of the former German Democratic Republic.

As early as the beginning of the 1870s the strong supporter of German nationalism, Richard Andree, in his 'Wendische Wanderstudien', expressed the hope that coal-mining and industrialisation would be a useful adjunct to the anti-Sorb state policy of the Hohenzollern empire. His words were very soon to become reality.[14] A comparison between Arnošt Muka's Sorb language map of 1886 and the language map published in 1956 by Arnošt Černík shows how strikingly Sorb language territory shrank as a result of the development of coal mining. Foreign language islands have emerged at the boundary between Lower and Upper Lusatia. The whole area between Kalawa, Chocebuz, Grodk and Zly Komorow (German: Calau, Cottbus, Spremberg and Senftenberg) has essentially, and rapidly, succumbed to Germanisation. The Sorb population in Upper Lusatia and that of Lower Lusatia have come to form two language islands, and are no longer contiguous.[15]

The Lusatian Sorb ethnic group entered the twentieth century with a very unfavourable social structure. The Sorb population was essentially a rural one. The overwhelming majority supported themselves by agriculture, and most were small farmers. Richer farmers lived only in two regions – between Budyšin and Kamjenc in Upper Lusatia and in the Chocebuz district of Lower Lusatia. Very few Sorbs owned large landed estates. Briefly put, Lusatian Sorb settlement essentially corresponded to the agrarian areas of Lusatia. The number of manufacturing concerns inside Lusatian Sorb language territory was very small, and the businesses themselves were usually very limited in size. It is worth mentioning that the Adolfshütte by Chróst-Lomske (German: Crosta-Lomske) and

Margarethenhütte at Wulka Dubrava (Groß Dubrau) were in German hands, and represented only a minimal source of employment.

The class of rural artisans and small tradesmen was very narrow and largely tied to agriculture, animal production and small-scale construction, as were the owners of rural inns, as well as potters and the Lower Lusatian charcoal-burners. Most of the soil in Lusatian Sorb territory was of low fertility, and therefore small farms were frequently unable to yield enough to secure a livelihood for their owners. The lack of land and work opportunities, which, as has been mentioned, caused relative overpopulation in the countryside, drove the Sorb population to migrate to the towns, and often further afield outside Lusatia, or even overseas.[16] In the large neighbouring conurbations such as Berlin and Dresden, the Sorb element soon dispersed and vanished.

In the urban agglomerations of both Lusatias, which were traditionally German despite the Slav settlement of the territory overall, the Sorbs represented a minority, albeit often a large minority. In the 1890s the Sorbs represented roughly 17 per cent of Budyšin's population of 18,000, 25 per cent of Wojerecy's population of almost 3,000, and 13 per cent of the slightly larger town of Mužakow (German: Muskau). The single exception was Kulow (German: Wittichenau), with Sorbs making up 60 per cent of its population of 2,000. This selection of the most important centres in Saxon Lusatia indicated that we are speaking about very small towns. With the passage of time the size of towns increased, but the number of Sorb inhabitants fell both absolutely and as a percentage. Unfortunately, precise figures are not available in a wide range of cases, but a quarter-century later (1910) Sorbs represented only approximately 10 per cent of the population of Budyšin.[17]

The Sorb population in the towns was principally made up of artisans and small tradesmen (carpenters, smiths, locksmiths, cobblers, tailors, bakers, butchers, innkeepers), and also wage-labourers. The Sorb group lacked economically successful urban strata. For this reason Sorbs did not have the preconditions for the formation of economic elites growing into a strong national bourgeoisie that would be able to formulate and push through a programme of ethnic political and economic emancipation.

In the interwar period there was a certain shift in the socio-professional profile of ethnic Sorbs, but this was not enough to consolidate a more affluent nationally conscious entrepreneurial element of the population. In the census of 1925, people who gave Lusatian Sorb as their mother tongue (a total of 71,000, although in fact the real number was obviously higher) fell into the following categories in relation to employment: 66.24 per cent agricultural, 20.36 per cent industrial workers, 4.45 per cent tradesmen and 8.95 per cent other.[18] In the first half of the twentieth century nothing occurred to change this negative state in any substantial way. The building of a strong middle class and economic elite remained a mere desideratum even in 1945.[19]

The banner of national revival and the hope for building a modern nation was thus carried by a narrow group of minor clerics and intelligentsia, very limited in terms of real resources and linked to a not particularly numerous group of Sorb peasants in the medium to small farm range.[20] The Lusatian Sorb emancipation movement, which reached its highest point immediately after the end of the First World War, was strikingly *petit bourgeois* and peasant in character.

In 1918–19, after the defeat of the central powers, it appeared that conditions had been created for the emergence of a Lusatian Sorb emancipation movement. The Sorb National Committee (Serbski narodny wuběrk), founded on 16 November 1918 in Budyšin, demanded the unification of Upper and Lower Lusatia and the right of national self-determination. On 21 November the committee then sent a memorandum to the peace conference, requesting that it recognise the Lusatian Sorbs as a free and independent nation and admit its representatives to the peace negotiations.

The original demands for independence or a somewhat hazy linkage to the Czechoslovak state as an autonomous unit (see the Czechoslovak memoranda presented to the peace conference[21]) proved to be unrealistic. Czechoslovak foreign policy had essentially abandoned the idea of incorporating the Lusatian Sorbs as early as March 1918 in the face of the opposition of the Allies. The territory of Sorbian Lusatia, which would have had to be joined to Czechoslovakia by a narrow six-kilometre corridor, would not only have raised the numbers of Czechoslovak Germans but also have created a wedge of land reaching almost as far as Berlin that would have cut through a series of important German communication links. The territory would have been militarily indefensible and a permanent source of discontent and tension. The peace conference and its results did not bring the Lusatian Sorbs the desired fundamental improvement in their situation.

Czech policy, influenced by the small but energetic group of friends of Lusatia around Sorb specialists Adolf Černý and Josef Páta (the 'Adolf Černý' of the Czecho-Lusatian Association), nevertheless kept the Lusatian question alive. This was not just the result of a feeling of moral responsibility for the support of a related Slavonic ethnic group that for centuries had been a part of the old Bohemian Crown Lands, but also reflected the political attempt to make the Lusatian Sorbs a counterargument against the Czech Germans' agitation for change in the legal position of minorities. However, in the course of time and with growing foreign-policy problems, Czech interest in Lusatia declined.

The programme of the Lusatian emancipation movement as represented by the Sorb National Committee headed by Arnošt Bart (a deputy in the Saxon assembly and originally a small peasant and innkeeper) consisted at first of the demand for incorporation into the Czechoslovak Republic, and later for autonomy within the framework of the German Reich. It also involved a range of other demands that could be described as radical left-wing. It demanded the break-up of all estates larger than 300 korces (German: Scheffel), i.e. approximately 80 hectares. The large estate-owners would be compensated and the land divided between small and medium-sized peasants at appropriate prices. Large capitalist enterprises 'which have destroyed the small trades and agricultural businesses of the middle ranks' would be prohibited. Tax was to be paid principally by those who had made money during the war. Wartime gains of more than 100,000 marks would be confiscated. Tax would be removed from foodstuffs and objects of daily consumption.[22]

The origin of these demands was not so much ideological as conditioned by the specific overall unfavourable socio-economic development described above and the social composition of the Lusatian Sorb community. It was based on the interests of small and middle-sized peasants, artisans and tradesmen. In the social environment represented by the National Committee, large-scale capital, industry and trade were perceived as German-language institutions hostile to Lusatian Sorbs. This attitude was also expressed in the documents drawn up by Adolf Černý in Prague to communicate Sorb aspirations on an international stage. The Seventh Memorandum for the peace conferences speaks of how German capital, trade and industry, with their businesses, railways and factories run by German colonists, were robbing the Sorb people of land and forcing it to become Germanised.[23] A draft of a memorandum for the American President Wilson of 17 March 1919 states: 'German capital has seized the natural wealth of Lusatia . . . it has taken the soil from under the feet of the Sorb people, proletarianised them and colonised their land with German workers.'[24]

After the failure and political defeat of the emancipation movement, Sorbs turned to the idea of strengthening their economic position and closing ranks as a starting-point for a new campaign. This found expression above all in building up economic and financial self-help mechanisms. The initial impulse came from Czech sources and was carried through by a group of people around the National Committee. Small Sorb deposit and savings banks had existed since the previous century, linked to German-language banking and its unions and serving as collecting points for minor investments in German banks. These Sorbs savings banks, it was considered, should instead serve national goals and have their own Sorb central institution. The opportunities for launching major initiatives in this area were, however, limited by a lack of available funds. Oldřich Heidrich, who visited Lusatia at the beginning of September 1920 with his colleague from the Ministry of Foreign Affairs, Josef Pitterman, wrote in his report that 'the Lusatian Sorbs require both moral and financial help'.[25]

The Sorb People's Bank (Serbska ludowa banka; German: Wendische Volksbank), founded in November 1919 with a basic capital of 300,000 marks, was undoubtedly the most important institution designed to assist in the economic integration of the Sorb population. It was established by the National Committee with a crucial share provided by Czech banking capital. Stocks to a value of 125,000 marks were taken by the Prague Credit Bank (Czech: Pražská úvěrní banka), which also appointed its own representative, Blažej Posedel, as director. The bank's headquarters were in Sorb House in Budyšin, and it had branches in Chocebuz and Wojerecy as well as eight local agencies. The founding of the bank did not, however, meet with the Sorb Lusatian enthusiasm that had been anticipated, and the bank itself, after no more than a year's existence, escaped from the direct influence of individuals close to the National Committee, veered away from support for the Lusatian Sorb political movement and devoted itself mainly to trading activity, to some extent even oriented to a German clientele.[26] Its fumbling business activities and risky credits already foreshadowed future difficulties. In the great economic crisis in 1932, it collapsed after prolonged rescue attempts.[27]

In the long term, no greater success awaited the Sorb Economic Association (Serbske hospodarske towarstwo) in Budyšin, the Association Lusatia (Towarstwo Lužica) in Běla Woda, the Smoljer's printworks in Budyšin and the Sorb Economic Association (Serbske hospodarske towarstwo) in Chocebuz. Of the few business or agricultural co-operatives that survived the crisis, the most important was Sorb Farmer (Serbski hospodar).

The economic pressure of the later 1930s, the ensuing Nazi persecution, and later the transfers of German population approved at Potsdam, caused further deterioration in the base-line situation of Sorbs in their struggle to preserve their independent existence after the Second World War. Attempts to strengthen the Sorb Lusatians economically and give them cohesion essentially failed. The Sorbs never achieved a fully developed social structure, and a clearly defined national bourgeoisie never emerged. The chances for a successful outcome of the emancipatory process were therefore severely limited by the absence of one of the fundamental factors in such developments. The statistical parameters reflecting the ethnic composition of the Lusation region in the course of the twentieth century have provided ever less favourable indicators.

The Czech historian Miroslav Hroch has devoted many decades to the comparative study of the formation of modern European nations. In his most recent book, in which he considers changes in the social division of labour and their influence on the development of ethnic relations, he notes two theories which, although contradictory, are still relevant in different environments.[28] The so-called functionalist theory speaks of the way in which ethnic relations are weakened by the onset of modernisation and industrialisation, which may therefore lead to assimilation. According to the reactive theory, on the other hand, industrialisation can strengthen consciousness of ethnic identity, enhance the solidarity between members of an ethnic group and help to transform it into a modern nation. In the case of the Lusatian Sorbs it is the first theory that seems to apply. The negative effects of industrialisation were amplified by the demographic processes arising from them, and especially the influx of ethnically different populations into what were economically the most rapidly developing areas of Sorb territory. This increasingly diluted the Sorb population and, in concert with a whole range of other negative factors, led to its Germanisation.

NOTES

1 Hartmut Zwahr, *Revolutionen in Sachsen. Beiträge zur Sozial- und Kulturgeschichte* (Weimar, Cologne and Vienna, 1996), p. 344.
2 Karlheinz Blaschke, *Bevölkerungsgeschichte von Sachsen bis zur industriellen Revolution* (Weimar, 1967), pp. 58–9, 73–4, 85–6, 104–5 and 130–58.
3 For example, Jan Šolta, *Abriss der sorbischen Geschichte* (Bautzen, 1976); cf. Blaschke, *Bevölkerungsgeschichte*, pp. 214–16; Friedrich W. Remes, *Die*

Sorbenfrage 1918/19. Untersuchung einer gescheiterten Autonomiebewegung (Bautzen, 1993), p. 53.

4 In Prussian Lower Lusatia alone, by 1848 the peasants had been forced to hand over 95,000 *morgen* of land, pay 710,000 tolars in one-off compensation payments, 60,000 tolars in annual payments and, individually, fourteen scheffels of rye as rent.

5 Jiří Kapitán, *Srbská Lužice* [The Sorb Lusatia], (Prague, 1945), p. 75.

6 Draft memorandum of the Saxon government, drawn up for the peace conference in Paris (February–March 1919), Anlage 11 'Wirtschaftliches im wendischen Sprachgebiet', Sächsisches Landeshauptarchiv Dresden, Sächsische Staatskanzlei, vol. 150, fol. 245.

7 Kapitán, *Srbská Lužice*, p. 75.

8 *Ibid.*, p. 76; Šolta, *Abriss der sorbischen Geschichte*, p. 93.

9 Cf. Zdeněk Boháč, *České země a Lužice*, cást: *Národnostní poměry v Lužici od konce 19. století do současnosti* [Czech Lands and Lusatia, part: National situation in Lusatia since the end of the nineteenth century to the present]. (Tišnov-Budyšín, 1993), pp. 78–88; cást: *Srbská katolická Lužice ve světle statistik* [part: Sorb Catholic Lusatia in the light of statistics]; Remes, *Die Sorbenfrage*, pp. 42–52.

10 Frank Förster, *Senftenberger Revier 1890–1914. Zur Geschichte der Niederlausitzer Braunkohlenindustrie vom Fall des Sozialistengesetzes bis zum Ausbruch des Ersten Weltkrieges* (Bautzen, 1968), pp. 21–3.

11 *Ibid.*, p. 60.

12 *Ibid.*, p. 87.

13 Frank Förster, *Verschwundene Dörfer. Die Ortsabbrüche des Lausitzer Braunkohlenreviers bis 1993* (2nd edn, Bautzen, 1996), pp. 18–19.

14 Förster, *Senftenberger Revier*, p. 86.

15 Förster, *Verschwundene Dörfer*, pp. 20–2; Jan Petr, *Nástin politických a kulturních dějin Lužických Srbů* [Political and cultural history of Lusatian Sorbs in outline], (Prague, 1972), pp. 248–9; Antonín Frinta, *Lužičtí Srbové a jejich písemnictví* [Lusatian Sorbs and their literature] (Prague, 1955), Map 2.

16 The number of Sorbs who emigrated overseas in the period from 1815 to 1914 has been estimated at 4 per cent of the entire people: Trudla Malinkowa, *Ufer der Hoffnung. Sorbische Auswanderer nach Übersee* (Bautzen, 1995), p. 7.

17 See *Historisches Ortsverzeichnis von Sachsen*, bearbeitet von Karlheinz Blaschke, part 4, *Oberlausitz* (Leipzig, 1957), pp. 1, 43, 49 and 84.

18 Petr, *Nástin politiských*, p. 249.

19 Kapitán, *Srbská Lužice*, pp. 74–5; Šolta, *Abriss der sorbischen Geschichte*, p. 93.

20 Z. Boháč has attempted to produce a statistical picture of the Sorb cultural elite over the last three centuries. This suggests that the key element was the clergy, i.e. 53 per cent from the 1840s, followed by teachers, 26 per cent. The other levels, obviously mainly peasants, represent 21 per cent. Boháč, *České země a Lužice*, cást: Studie o původu lužickosrbských kulturních pracovníků

(part: Essay on the origin of Lusatian Sorbs cultural activists), p. 110; see also Zwahr, *Revolutionen*, pp. 354–5.

21 See Hermann Raschhofer, *Die tschechoslowakischen Denkschriften für die Friedenskonferenz von Paris 1919/1920* (Berlin, 1937), Memoires II and VII, pp. 79–81 and 225–55.

22 Remes, *Die Sorbenfrage*, Appendix of Documents No. 2, Zehn-Punkte-Programm des Wendischen Nationalausschusses, p. 209.

23 Raschhofer, *Die tschechoslowakischen Denkschriften*, p. 239.

24 Archiv ministerstva zahraničních věcí (Archive of Ministry of Foreign Affairs of the Czech Republic), Paris Archives, No. 5056.

25 Archiv Památníku Národního písemnictví [Archive of National Literature Memorial], fond Josef Páta, referát dr. O. Heidricha o cestě do Lužice [Message of Dr O. Heidrich about his Lusatian tour], 4–11 September 1920, p. 7.

26 *Ibid.*, Memorandum of B. Posedel, 'Několik poznámek o hospodářském stavu lužicko-srbské větve' [Some remarks about the economic situation of Lusatian Sorbs], 23 September 1920.

27 Kapitán, *Srbská Lužice*, p. 77; Alfred Simon, 'Zum Zusammenbruch der "Serbska Ludowa Banka – Wendische Volksbank AG" in der Weltwirtschaftskrise 1929/1932', *Lětopis* B, 9(1), 3–16.

28 Miroslav Hroch, *V národním zájmu. Požadavky a cíle evropských národních hnutí devatenáctého století v komparativní perspektivě* [In the national interest. Requirements and goals of European national movements in the nineteenth century in comparative perspective], (Prague, 1996), p. 18.

CHAPTER FIVE

Unequal regional development in Switzerland: a question of nationality?

Bruno Fritzsche

In summer 1996 the privately owned 'national' airline Swissair made it known that most of its intercontinental flights starting from Geneva were to be discontinued, and that instead there was a shuttle service to be established between the airports of Geneva–Cointrin and Zurich–Kloten. This measure provoked an enormous outcry in the French-speaking part of Switzerland (the 'Romandie'). Such a concentration of the long-distance flights on the airport situated in the German-Swiss part of the country and lying, incidentally, no more than some 200 kilometres from Geneva, passed for one further proof that the French-Swiss minority was and continued to be dominated – or even colonised – by the German-Swiss majority.

In actual fact the great economic crisis setting in after 1990, hitting the French-speaking part of Switzerland rather harder than the rest of the country, only served to accentuate a latent uneasiness of quite a few years' standing. A first peak of tension had been reached on the occasion of the plebiscite of 2 December 1992, when the issue was whether or not Switzerland was to become a member of the EEA (European Economic Area). As a whole the Swiss rejected membership by a very slim majority (50.3 per cent of noes), while the French-speaking cantons quite distinctly voted in favour of membership, the portions of ayes lying between 56 per cent (in the Valais) and 80 per cent (in the canton of Neuchâtel).[1] Ever since, the relationship between the French- and the German-speaking parts of Switzerland, at all times precariously harmonious at best, has remained quite openly and obviously strained. A public opinion poll of July 1996 put the slightly captious question whether the Swiss nation was going to disintegrate. In the Romandie 27 per cent of those replying answered in the affirmative, in the rest of Switzerland distinctly less: 13 per cent in the German-speaking part of the country and 14 per cent in the Italian-speaking Ticino. Among those who predicted the dissolution of the nation, a quarter expected this to happen within the next ten years.[2] But of course it has to be borne in mind that results like these reflect a mood much more than any trustworthy and concrete prognosis.

The following is intended to outline the history of the origins of multilingual Switzerland in the nineteenth century, to delineate the political and institutional settings involved, and to show up the fields of tension operating between the different regions of the country; the chapter will then look at the question of their varying economic development and try to explain the causes thereof.

HISTORICAL BACKGROUND

Up to 1798 the Swiss Confederation consisted of thirteen sovereign states ('Orte') and, additionally, of a number of subject territories. Of these latter some belonged to one or another of these thirteen states, others were under the joint rule of several or all of them and, consequently, were under joint administration. All of the thirteen sovereign states were German-speaking; French or Italian was spoken in some of the subject territories.

In 1798 this ancient and all too brittle Confederacy was dealt its death blow by Revolutionary France. Subsequently some of the former subject territories emancipated into separate independent states or cantons, while others remained within their old federation, but claiming equality of status with their former masters, the hitherto-privileged full citizens ('Vollbürger'). This process of emancipation, however, took some time and was not fully completed until after 1830.

At the end of the Napoleonic Wars the Congress of Vienna made it its business to define anew the borderlines of the Swiss Confederacy that by now consisted of twenty-two individual cantons (see figures 5.1 and 5.4). This newly established political structure contained among others the exclusively French-speaking former 'associated republics' of Geneva and Neuchâtel. Similarly, the population of the newly constituted canton of Vaud, emerging from a former subject territory of Berne, was of French tongue exclusively. Yet another former subject territory was the Italian-speaking new canton of Ticino. Cantons with partly French- and partly German-speaking populations emerged in those instances where former subject territories had not defected from their old masters – that is, in the cantons of Valais and Fribourg. The canton of Berne counted among these as well, since for the loss of its former subject territory of the Vaud it had been compensated with what had previously

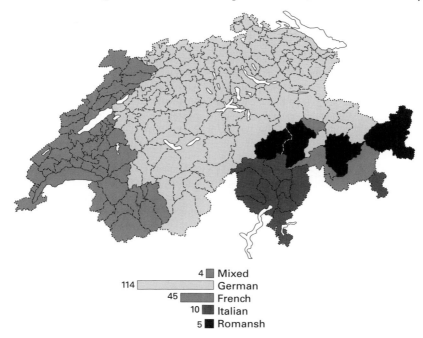

Figure 5.1. *Languages by districts*[3]

been the 'Fürsterzbistum Basel', a small prince-bishopric, left over from the Reformation, and situated in the Jura mountains. The Grisons, before 1798 one of the 'associated' republics, make for a special case of further complexity. In accordance with the decisions of the Congress of Vienna, the Grisons were obliged to relinquish their Italian-speaking subject territory of Valtellina. Conversely they retained the remaining three southern Italian-speaking valleys – the Poschiavo, Mesocco and Bregaglia. These had always been sovereign communities within the loosely knit political structure of the so-called 'Three Leagues'. Thus, together with the valleys of Rhaeto-Romanic tongue, the population of the new canton came to be composed of people speaking three different idioms, namely German, Italian and Romansh. Moreover, the Romansh idiom in its turn was split up into a number of clearly distinct dialects, which, up to a very few years ago, did not share any common standard or literary language.

The Federal Constitution of 1848 formed the conclusion of a long process of transformation; it defined the new political structures of the transformed state that have, broadly speaking, remained valid ever since. The individual cantons have remained autonomous to a high degree: of particular interest in the present context is the fact that the cantons continued – and continue – to retain their independence in cultural as well as in educational matters. This means that they are free to cultivate their ancestral language in school as well as in their cantonal administrations.

On a federal level, German, French and Italian count as official languages ('Amtssprachen') of equal status. In accordance with unwritten customary law, however – and this rule has been observed from the very beginning – out of the total of seven members of the Executive Federal Council at least two have to be provided by either the French-speaking Romandie or the Italian-speaking Ticino.[4] The extensive autonomy allowed to the individual cantons, together with the pronounced protection of linguistic minorities, may help to explain why the former subject territories of Vaud and Ticino, once released from the rule of their former German-Swiss masters, did not display any desire to unite politically with their respective culture areas. In 1798 the population of the territory of Vaud did indeed hail the French invasion army as their liberators; also, the newly constituted canton subsequently inscribed the revolutionary motto 'Liberté et Patrie' on its flag. Freedom from the hands of their French brethren: yes, of course! But when it came to give meaning to the second term, to that of 'homeland': that could certainly not mean the 'Grande Nation', that could only mean their own native soil, their own, modest little 'Pays de Vaud'! Quite naturally this vision met with far less opposition within the loosely knit Swiss Confederacy than within the definitely centralist, and very soon afterwards once again monarchic, political structure of France.

No more was the Ticino hankering for secession. The Irredenta movement, aiming, after the establishment of the Kingdom of Italy in 1861, at liberating the still 'unredeemed' Italian-speaking regions, did indeed achieve the incorporation into Italy of both Istria and South Tyrol after the end of the First World War, but it met with nothing even approaching serious response in the Ticino.

It was natural that in the course of time the Confederate government attempted to appropriate a number of domains originally lying within the competence of the cantonal governments. These centralist tendencies, increasingly gathering strength, began with the total revision of the Federal Constitution in 1874 and are still well underway today. On the other hand there are two essential items of cantonal sovereignty never touched by the Union, namely the right of the cantons to raise taxes at their own discretion and their exclusive competence in matters of culture and education.

In the face of so strong a position of the cantonal governments, the strengthening of the federal government at the expense of cantonal sovereignty would, of necessity, have to proceed only sluggishly and laboriously: attempts had – and have – quite often to be made several times for the central government to succeed. The French-Swiss cantons as well as quite a number of other minorities, in constant fear of losing their independence, were and continue to be highly distrustful of 'Berne', that is, of the seat of the Swiss federal government. One of the outstanding characteristics of the Swiss political system consists in the possibility for even relatively small minorities to avail themselves of use of the referendum, one of their chartered rights, which allows them to obstruct what they consider to be undesirable trends or developments. At times, very strange bedfellows thereby happen to join forces: as in 1872, for instance, when French-Swiss Protestants and German-Swiss Catholics jointly brought to nought the revision of the Constitution, which, in their view, seemed to be of an all-too-centralist bent.[5] Or, to cite a more recent instance, in 1978 ultra-conservative federalists from the Romandie united with the German-Swiss left-wing in order to forestall the establishment of a federal security police.[6]

Showing consideration for minorities is therefore in the very first place an act of political pragmatism since, on the one side, united minorities may easily grow into a majority and since, on the other side, practically every single Swiss citizen may well belong sometime or other to one minority or another, be it religious, political, social or whatever else: this fact makes for the consciousness that, sooner or later and according to circumstances, everyone may depend on the goodwill of other minorities. Seeing that, generally speaking, the confessional, ideological and social distinctions do not follow the linguistic boundaries, the differences of linguistic culture do not usually pose any serious problems in the business of politics. It is only when the Romandie finds itself standing opposed in a solid block to the German-Swiss majority that cries of protest are to be heard and reference is made to a cultural minority being oppressed: and such was the case on the occasion of the plebiscite mentioned above, namely the vote of 1992 with respect to Switzerland joining the EEA.

While of necessity at the political level there exists constant and lively contact between all parts of the country, on the level of individual or social intercourse the relationship between the various cultural areas tends to remain rather cool and reserved. It is true that, predominantly in the nineteenth century, but continuing until quite recently, upper middle-class families made a point of sending their daughters to one of the many finishing schools in the Romandie for a period of time, to be taught, in addition to the French language, the French way of life. Until recently it was customary for daughters of less well-to-do German-Swiss families to spend some time (usually one year) in French Switzerland after completing school or apprenticeship, almost always living with a family and working as domestic helps or nursery-maids, less frequently as shopgirls, waitresses or some such.[7] Conversely, young people from the Romandie were – and are – hardly ever known to spend their 'year of apprenticeship' in the German-speaking part of Switzerland. This may well have to do with the fact that, worldwide, French was considered to be the fashionable language and that, worldwide, the refinement of the French way of life was seen as an example to be imitated and lived up to. On the other hand it may well have appeared less than worthwhile to young French-Swiss girls to undergo part of their education in the comparative 'barbarism' of Alamannic Switzerland.

Broadly speaking, population exchange between the various linguistic areas has always been relatively slight. As everywhere else, industrialisation in Switzerland triggered a huge internal migration. In connection with the population census of 1910 the inquiry with respect to the place of birth has been analysed. It thereby emerged that in 1910 somewhat more than half of the Swiss population no longer lived in their respective birthplaces (51.6 per cent): at least once in the course of their lives, therefore, they had changed their place of residence. It is to be noted, however, that it was predominantly a matter of migrating to nearby areas. The crossing of language boundaries, changing from one confessional area to another or, less obviously, even migrating from one canton to another, occurred to a markedly lesser degree (see figure 5.2).[8]

In terms of absolute numbers migration was considerably greater from the German-speaking regions to the Romandie than the other way round, whereas, in terms of percentage and relative to the sum total of the native population, migration from the Romandie to German-speaking Switzerland was more important than vice versa.

As is shown in table 5.1, the percentage shares of the different language groups have, in the long run, remained relatively stable. Nevertheless, and even though on the whole percentage shares remained more or less unchanged, there occurred irritations along the language boundaries because even minute shifts in the make-up of the population shares

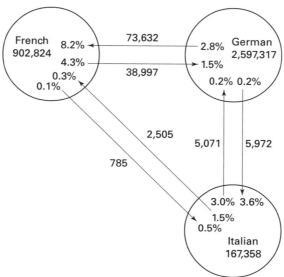

How to use this figure:

Taking the uppermost arrow as an example:
73,632 persons migrated from German-speaking to French-speaking districts. This number corresponds to 2.8% of the inhabitants of German-speaking districts (2,597,317 persons) and 8.2% of French-speaking districts (902,824 persons).

Figure 5.2. *Migratory balance 1910*[9]

led to grave worries that the respective area might become wholly Frenchified or Germanised, as the case might be.[10]

A conflict of some gravity brewed round the turn of the century, produced, however, much more by economic and international than by internal political problems. The great economic growth after 1885, the era of the so-called 'second industrial revolution', provoked a series of fundamental changes leading to the loss of previous identity and to a general sense of insecurity. The old and established elites in French Switzerland, in particular, felt that their position was in jeopardy. The aggressive economic powers of the newly established German Reich were particularly accused of and blamed for disturbing the former balance. These, in conjunction with the German-speaking part of Switzerland which they were supposed to be dominating already, were accused of being on the point of colonising the Romandie as well.[11]

As a matter of fact, German large-scale enterprise had indeed expanded to German-Switzerland in the first place and, starting from

Table 5.1. *Native language of the Swiss population in percentage share, 1880–1990*[12]

Year	German	French	Italian	Romansh	Others
1880	71.3	21.4	5.7	1.4	0.2
1910	72.7	22.1	3.9	1.2	0.1
1950	74.2	20.6	4.0	1.1	0.2
1990	73.4	20.5	4.1	0.7	1.3

there, had set up branch establishments in the Romandie. Also, the Germans were the most numerous group of foreigners living in Switzerland: in 1910 they made up 5.8 per cent of the total population, while the French percentage share amounted to a mere 1.7 per cent. Italian workers in more important numbers did not migrate to Switzerland before 1880, but their percentage share, growing very rapidly in the course of the following decades, had by 1910 increased to 5.4 per cent. At the same time the sum total of foreigners living in Switzerland reached 14.7 per cent.[13] Furthermore, Swiss foreign trade was increasingly concentrating on Germany while at the same time foreign trade with France showed a definite downward tendency (see table 5.2).

What is referred to as the 'Gotthard Agreement' ('Gotthard-Vertrag') gave the formal grounds for large-scale protest against German economic expansion. In 1898 the Confederation had decided to transfer to state ownership the hitherto privately owned Swiss railway network. Both Italy and Germany held an interest in the Gotthard railways, the repurchase of which proved particularly difficult. Thus the Gotthard Agreement of 1909 had to make considerable concessions to these two foreign co-possessors. As a consequence, one of the foremost exponents of Swiss conservatism, a prominent lawyer otherwise well known for his unbiased judgement, completely lost his sense of proportion in this instance, denouncing the agreement as 'the beginning of a collective protectorate' and as 'something similar to the international Suez Convention with respect to Egypt'.[14] Even though there were harsh voices of protest to be heard from the German-speaking part of Switzerland, coming predominantly from conservative-national circles, the agreement met with far more violent resistance in the Romandie, since there it was rated as one further proof of the impending threat of Germanisation. But in fact it was not the agreement as such that provoked this outraged French-Swiss outcry: rather, it was a matter of

Table 5.2. *Foreign trade in percentage shares of total value, 1892–1913*[15]

	Importation		Exportation	
Year	Germany	France	Germany	France
1892	26.1	20.6	24.8	15.7
1913	32.6	18.7	22.4	10.4

giving vent to the ever-latent resentment against Germany and the German-Swiss, for even though Italy had extorted exactly the same terms as Germany, at no time did the Italians come within the firing line of the French-Swiss opponents. Moreover, the French-Swiss storm of protest led to a mass rally in Lausanne in 1913, some four years after the actual conclusion of the agreement.[16]

This French-Swiss eruption may therefore be interpreted as a reaction against the widespread German-Swiss enthusiasm for the German Reich. The extent of this enthusiasm had become quite apparent in 1912, when the German emperor had visited Zurich, on which occasion he had not only been paid all due honour but had also been given an exuberant welcome. In fact, the increasing tensions between German-speaking Switzerland and the Romandie reflect the increasing rivalry between Germany and France. During the second Moroccan crisis (in 1912), the sympathies of the various Swiss areas lay with their respective linguistic kins. But the peak of the crisis was reached during the First World War. The 'gap' between eastern Switzerland, where the German victories were being acclaimed, and the Romandie, where the people were commiserating with France – had become such that the very existence of the multilingual nation seemed in jeopardy.

At the end of the war, linguistic-cultural differences were overlaid by social antagonism. The general strike of 1918 made apparent the abyss existing between the bourgeoisie and the working class. If the strike movement was hardly paid any attention to in the French part of Switzerland, this was principally because the strike committee consisted of German-Swiss members exclusively.[17]

In Alamannic Switzerland, the sympathies for Germany were still quite tangible even after the German defeat in 1918, as was clear on the occasion of the plebiscite where the Swiss entry to the League of Nations was at stake. The League of Nations was the organ of the victorious powers from which Germany was to be excluded for the time being. This caused the Latin cantons, in unison, to vote quite massively in favour of joining while a plurality of German-Swiss cantons voted against, which resulted in an accordingly narrow margin of ayes.[18]

Not before the world economic crisis of the 1930s did the various parts of the country again find themselves acting in harmony, then, however, joining forces in strong unity and in unanimous opposition to National Socialism. Certainly there did exist German-Swiss supporters of the Nazis, just as there existed in the Romandie admirers of fascism (and Mussolini, who, incidentally, was awarded an honorary doctorate by the University of Lausanne); but their political influence was always quite negligible. After the seizure of power by Hitler in 1933 the danger emanating from the Third Reich became increasingly obvious. In order to disassociate from and form a distinct contrast to the various fascist ideologies of the surrounding countries, there emerged in Switzerland a strange and somewhat contradictory sort of national ideology. On the one hand, this definitely admitted fascistic ideas that were by no means free from the 'blood and soil' myth and were also suggestive of racial prejudice, rejecting everything 'foreign', but also on the other hand and at the same time, laid considerable stress on Switzerland as a nation created by free will ('Willensnation'), a nation embracing a plurality of cultures, a country displaying 'unity in diversity'. To give just one pertinent example in the present context of linguistic minorities: the Romansh, a language spoken by a mere 1 per cent of the sum total of the Swiss population, was in 1938 by constitution formally declared to be one of the four Swiss national languages ('Nationalsprache').[19]

This curious ideology, known as 'Geistige Landesverteidigung' ('spiritual home defence'), rendered good service during the Second World War. Also it was quite smoothly taken over into the postwar years. Then, in the era of the Cold War, it was the Soviet Union that was designated the role of the new enemy. Any (political) opinion diverging from the national consensus was apt to be stigmatised as communist and therefore denounced as traitorous to the country. Even though the newly defined internal enemy, said to be 'steered by Moscow', failed to put in an appearance in any appreciable number, it was – just because of that fact – supposed to be particularly dangerous since it was imagined to perform its work of subversive agitation surreptitiously and in the dark. At any rate, this to a wide extent fictitious enemy whom the nation had agreed upon proved an excellent device to sustain the extensive national consensus of the 1950s and 1960s; it very materially helped to achieve

Table 5.3. *Occupational structure by districts, 1910 (as
a percentage of labour force)*[20]

Sector	German	French	Italian
I	27	28	44
II	51	43	33
III	22	29	24

the social unanimity and stability that in turn made possible the
unprecedented economic growth of the postwar era as well as the rapid
development of the welfare state. But on the other hand the suppression
of well-nigh all attempts at criticism tended to engender spiritual narrowing and political stagnation. It thus happened, for instance, that historians taking upon themselves the task of critically evaluating the role
of Switzerland during the Second World War, if they were taken
account of at all, were quite likely to be pooh-poohed and dismissed as
communists. All the more painful and distressing is the awakening going
on at present. For, simultaneously with the breakdown of the eastern
bloc states, the long-cherished enemy threat dissolved into nothingness.
In its stead, problems that had been dammed up, repressed and stowed
away for a long time now keep arising with sudden vehemence. It is certainly not merely accidental that the latent tensions between German-
speaking Switzerland and the Romandie have been flaring up again
soon after the end of the Cold War.

To sum up: on the political level the sensitivities of minority groups in
questions of language were – and still are – invariably treated with due
consideration. But on the other hand, conflicts arose in the economic
context, that is, in a field traditionally ruthless and inconsiderate in socio-
political matters. Divergencies as well as convergencies occurred in particular with regard to the evaluation of international phenomena that
were heavily ideological.

ECONOMIC DEVELOPMENT IN THE TWENTIETH CENTURY

Not much is known about the economic performance of individual
cantons or districts around the turn of the twentieth century, but the
occupational structures of the various regions may at least serve as a
pointer with regard to their respective levels of technical-industrial
development (see table 5.3). The very considerable share held by the

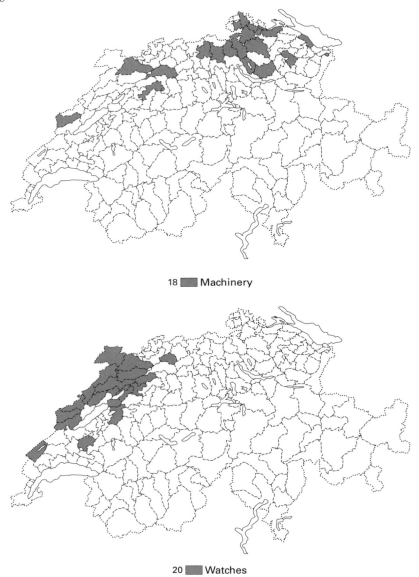

18 ■ Machinery

20 ■ Watches

Figure 5.3. *Distribution of major branches, 1910*[21]

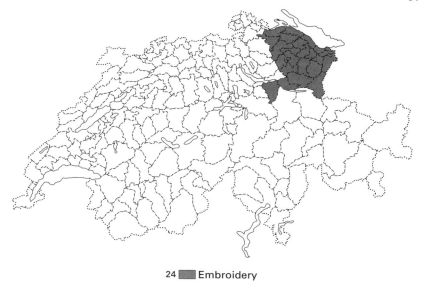

24 ▓ Embroidery

The shaded areas show where more than 15 per cent of the labour force of the secondary sector are employed in the corresponding branch.

Figure 5.3. (*cont.*)

agricultural sector (sector I) in the Italian-speaking regions points towards their comparative backwardness, which is not very surprising, since the southern Alpine valleys of the Grisons are quite secluded and do not naturally lend themselves easily to the establishment of industrial enterprise (sector II). Also the Gotthard railway did not link up the Ticino to the international or even the national Swiss traffic network until 1882. Within this same period the agricultural sectors in Alamannic Switzerland and the Romandie dwindled to about a quarter. Noteworthy is the prominence of the services sector (sector III) in the Romandie, caused by the flourishing tourism in the region of Montreux during the 'Belle Epoque' on the one hand and the numerous finishing schools established between Neuchâtel and Geneva on the other.

The various branches of the secondary sector are distributed quite unevenly among the different districts. We shall here discuss only the few industrial branches displaying the most important growth potential (see figure 5.3). The watch- and clock-making industry concentrated – and still concentrates – on the western part of Switzerland. The reasons for this are mainly historical. The art of watchmaking was brought to Geneva in the seventeenth century by a number of Huguenot families driven out of France after the revocation of the Edict of Nantes in 1685. From thence it spread northward to the upper regions of the Jura mountains belonging to the cantons of Vaud (Vallée de Joux), Neuchâtel (La Chaux-de-Fonds, Le Locle) and Berne (Moutier). After the crisis of the 1870s new and modern factories were increasingly set up at the foot of the Jura mountains and, therefore, within the boundaries of the German-Swiss canton of Solothurn.

The machine-building industry originated from the repair workshops of the textile industry, which was in the greatest part located in the eastern part of Switzerland. As well as spinning frames and weaving machines these engineering workshops manufactured turbines and steam engines, chiefly employed in the textile industry. In addition, they started, later on, to manufacture railway locomotives, coaches and goods trucks. The rapidly expanding enterprises in the new field of electro-technology contributed their fair share to the great economic upswing in the years after 1885. Swiss firms such as the Maschinenfabrik Oerlikon and Brown, Boveri & Co. moved to the very top of technological development on an international level, whether with respect to the production, transmission or the application of hydroelectric energy, thus acquiring a leading position in the manufacture of turbines and generators, as well as in the construction of whole power plants, the development of transformers and high-voltage transmission lines and the electrification of the railways. Analogously to the textile industry the Swiss electrical industries preferred to set themselves up in the German part of Switzerland, and there again by preference in the vicinity of Zurich. This choice of location suggested itself for more than one reason: there was, of course, the nearness to the earlier-established engineering industry; but being in the vicinity of Zurich also granted easy access to the main Swiss centre of research, the Swiss Federal Institute of Technology, and to the Swiss capital market, which was increasingly concentrating on the city of Zurich as well. This concentration of both the engineering and the electrical industries in the region around Zurich is very clear when exclusively large-scale business is taken into consideration: in 1905 out of a total of fourteen large-size enterprises with more than 500 employees, eleven were situated within a radius of forty kilometres from the city of Zurich.[22]

Equally resting on scientific research, both the aniline dyes and pharmaceutical industries had increasingly gained importance up to the turn of the century. These were predominantly domiciled in Basle and were thus also in the German-speaking part of the country. Since the production process in the chemical industry was automated at a very early date, its importance for the Swiss national economy is not accurately reflected by the number of people employed. But in actual fact the dyestuffs manufacture of Basle contributed in the years around 1895 some 15 per cent of total world production.[23]

The textile industry, which was the industrial branch instrumental in introducing the Industrial Revolution to Switzerland in the first half of the nineteenth century, had by the end of the century lost much of its relative importance – with one single exception, however, for the embroidery works, set up in the eastern part of Switzerland, had by then achieved worldwide fame. Responsible for the great prosperity of the whole region, they continued to export their fashionable articles to the four corners of the world. But the branch broke down altogether in the years of the First World War, never to recover from its disastrous collapse: the fashionable lady of the 1920s liked to pass herself off as emancipated, sporty and tomboyish, therefore no longer having any use for any kind of embroidery work. The city of St Gall, centre of the Swiss embroidery business, failed to recover from the crisis throughout the whole period between the two world wars: its population, running to 76,000 persons in 1910, shrank to some 63,000 by 1941.

To sum up: around 1910 the economic power between the Romandie and German-Switzerland was fairly evenly balanced while, on the other hand, the economic development in the Italian-speaking districts was somewhat lagging behind. In comparison to the German-speaking part of Switzerland the industrial sector in the Romandie was admittedly less prominent, but the deficiency was almost made up for by the important role played by tourism. Tourism being what may be termed a 'soft' branch of industry, its relative significance and importance is often and easily underrated, though in fact it contributed substantially to the balance of payment and thus ranked among the most important elements of Swiss foreign trade. Its contribution to the national income was quite on a level with that of the watch- and clock-making or the machine-building industries. Thus, allowing for the fact that the different branches of industry were unevenly distributed among the various regions of the country, the trumps in the hands of the different regions were still fairly equal in terms of value. The 'new' trend-setting industries, such as electrotechnology and the chemical industry, were indeed concentrated in German-speaking Switzerland, but conversely

Table 5.4. *Occupational structure, 1880–1941 (in %)*[25]

Sector	1880	1910	1941
I	42	27	21
II	42	46	44
III	16	28	36

the old-established watch- and clock-making industry was monopolised by the Romandie for all practical purposes, its economic weight still unimpaired and continuing to dominate the world market. In 1913 Switzerland exported about 13.8 million clocks and watches, covering much more than half of the whole world market.[24] An impressive achievement but, of course, just because the watch- and clock-making industry was – and is – so extremely dependent on exportation, it was – and remains – extremely subject to crises.

As anywhere else in the industrialised world the decades between the two world wars in Switzerland were stamped with a heavy postwar crisis in the years following 1918, then a few years of boom and prosperity in the 'roaring Twenties', and then with the great worldwide depression of the 1930s, from which Switzerland did not extricate itself until 1936, thus somewhat lagging behind the rest of the industrialised countries. Broadly speaking the time between the wars must be put down as a period of economic stagnation during which the occupational structures of the country changed but slowly and with pronounced reluctance (see table 5.4).

Unlike most European countries, Switzerland survived the Second World War unscathed: it did not hesitate to make the very best of this competitive advantage. Never before had the economic growth been greater or more constant than between the 'Korea boom' in 1950 and the 'oil crisis' in 1974. But on the other hand the conspicuously comfortable economic situation of the country largely failed to stimulate any spirit of innovation. Thus, Switzerland to a great extent neglected to link up in good time with, for example, the revolution in microelectronics, thereby losing the opportunities this might have offered. This seems a pity, especially so because the watch- and clock-making industry commanded the know-how as well as a labour force used to working with great precision and to dealing competently with diminutive units. The easy import of a cheap labour force, however, permitted an expansive economic growth within the existing economic structures. This in turn,

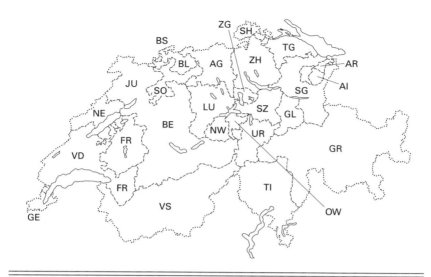

		Per capita income		Pop. (in 1,000s)
Cantons		1950	1980	1990
German-speaking				
Aargau	AG	3,540	22,479	508
Appenzell-Innerrhoden	AI	2,575	16,506	14
Appenzell-Ausserrhoden	AR	2,915	19,050	52
Bern	BE	3,525	21,470	958
Basel-Land	BL	3,845	22,905	233
Basel-Stadt	BS	5,080	34,485	199
Glarus	GL	3,640	26,064	39
Luzern	LU	3,135	19,939	326
Nidwalden	NW	2,945	21,945	33
Obwalden	OW	2,855	18,326	29
St Gallen	SG	3,380	20,809	428
Schaffhausen	SH	3,690	22,892	72
Solothurn	SO	3,780	21,261	232
Schwyz	SZ	2,915	18,993	112
Thurgau	TG	3,440	19,772	209
Uri	UR	2,865	20,423	34
Zug	ZG	3,545	31,648	86
Zürich	ZH	4,305	29,567	1179
French-speaking				
Genève	GE	4,635	29,538	379
Jura*	JU	0	17,296	66
Neuchâtel	NE	4,360	19,947	164
Vaud	VD	3,670	21,608	602
Italian-speaking				
Ticino	TI	3,035	19,022	282
Mixed				
Graubünden	GR	2,850	23,566	174
Fribourg	FR	2,725	18,608	214
Valais	VS	2,355	19,378	250

*Established 1979. Formerly part of the canton Bern.

Figure 5.4. *The Swiss cantons*

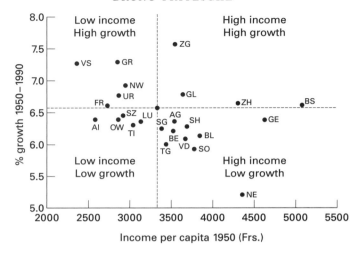

Figure 5.5. *Economic performance, 1950–1980*

and relative to the total Swiss population, resulted in a percentage share of 17.2 per cent of foreigners living in Switzerland by 1970.[26]

Covering the period after 1950 we possess calculations not only of the national but of the cantonal incomes as well.[27] We are thus able to give more accurate and detailed information with regard to the development of the various regions in the more recent past. In evaluating the available data, however, one must bear in mind that the Swiss cantons are of greatly varying dimensions: the most populous canton, Zurich, has about eighty-five times more inhabitants than the smallest, Appenzell-Innerrhoden. In order to obtain valid comparisons therefore, the following data will invariably apply to the per capita income (see figure 5.4).

In only three cantons is the native language of the whole population French – the cantons of Geneva, Neuchâtel and Vaud. Three further cantons possess no distinct majorities: in the cantons of Fribourg and Valais more than half but less than two thirds of the inhabitants are French-speaking; similarly, in the Grisons something between a half and two thirds of the population is German-speaking, the native language of the rest being either Italian or Romansh. The canton of Berne is a special case: after a long and rather troublesome period of political conflict the greater part of its French-speaking areas have separated, constituting an additional canton of their own since 1979 – the canton of Jura. But owing to the fact that the French-speaking minority has at no time run to more than a mere 10 per cent, the canton of Berne has always been numbered among the German-speaking cantons.

Condensed information regarding the economic performance of individual cantons may be gathered from figure 5.5, where per capita incomes are combined with the economic growth between 1950 and 1980. The graph clearly reveals that the three exclusively French-speaking cantons rank among the wealthy ones: Geneva and Neuchâtel are placed at the very top, together with the two German-speaking cantons of Zurich and Basle City. But it is also true that their economic growth is less than average, which has resulted in their losing ground in the course of time. This is especially striking in the case of Neuchâtel. The canton of Neuchâtel displays the lowest absolute growth rate. This is a faithful reflection of the whole watch- and clock-making industry, which, helping the region to great prosperity in the first place, appears to have at the same time induced a spirit of self-complacent laziness. As a result the industry reacted with excessive tardiness to the electronic revolution in horology, which in turn led to a serious and protracted crisis of the whole watch- and clock-making industry.

The predominantly French-speaking Valais, though the least prosperous canton in 1950, has tolerably good prospects because of its above-average economic growth. Among the Romanic cantons the Ticino alone remains below average with respect to both its income and its growth rate. In the present context, however, the salient point lies in the fact that the graph fails to reveal any kind of cluster formed by the Romanic cantons. Quite the reverse is true: they find themselves dispersed over the whole of the spectrum. This proves that any idea of economic backwardness of the French- or Italian-speaking cantons in general is clearly fictitious.

The determining factor of economic performance of the various cantons therefore is by no means a question of language. In order to explain differences in economic performance there must be a number of other factors taken into consideration, such as the topography or the geographic situation of individual regions, their accessibility by way of the existing traffic system, or, again, the historical background of industrial locations. The cantons of Valais and Ticino, together with other Alpine and prealpine cantons, form a group of low-income regions. Again, the graph places the French-speaking canton of Vaud in a very similar position to that of the German-speaking canton of Berne: here the similarity of economic performance is matched by a similarity of

BRUNO FRITZSCHE

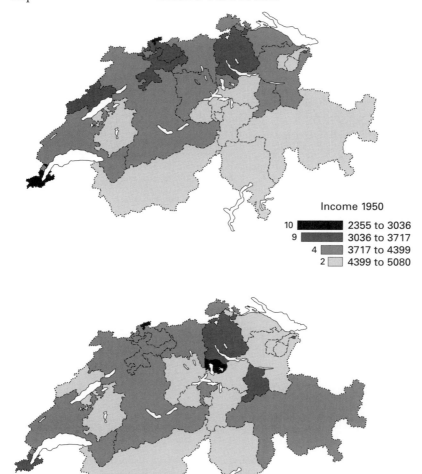

Figure 5.6. *Cantons: income per capita*

their respective topographical and industrial structure. The French-speaking canton of Geneva shares its top position in the graph with the German-speaking Basle City: in their case the similarity in economic performance is matched by and largely due to the fact that both these cantons are made up of a city and nothing else, to the virtual exclusion of any kind of additional rural areas.

Our cartographical representation in figure 5.6 elucidates these circumstances, indicating at the same time the shift of incomes between 1950 and 1980. By 1980 Geneva had lost its position of second place but still manages to retain a respectable placing of third. Meanwhile, the canton of Neuchâtel, painfully weakened, shares its economic downfall with the German-Swiss canton of Solothurn, both of them being heavily dependent on the watch- and clock-making industry.

CONCLUSIONS

Does all this suggest that the postulated economic discrimination of the French-Swiss cantons is not more than idle talk? To answer this question, some problems of long-range tendency defying any direct description by means of tables, diagrams and numbers must be touched upon. Two contradictory developments must thereby be noted. On the one hand, Swiss politics has for the last few decades been trying to level out disparities by way of purposely furthering or supporting the economic structures of backward regions. The cantonal data presented here, for instance, are derived from an extensive scientific research work in aid of regional economic development and are meant to form a solid foundation for future political decisions. It appears that the attempt has borne fruit to a certain extent: the cantonal incomes of 1980 diverge perceptibly less than those of 1950, the coefficient of variation being 28.5 per cent in 1950 as compared with 20.0 per cent in 1980. But on the other hand, and in blatant contradiction to the overall pattern encouraged by political effort, one specific metropolitan area is increasingly, and ever more plainly, standing out against the rest of the country.

Figure 5.7 is an attempt to visualise this state of affairs. The large majority of cantons form one fairly compact cluster while the few remaining ones are split off from the rest in an almost offensive way. In three instances these 'outsiders' are easily identifiable as those cantons where the large cities are located – that is, Zurich, Basle and Geneva. Of these three the canton of Zurich, with respect to per capita incomes,

BRUNO FRITZSCHE

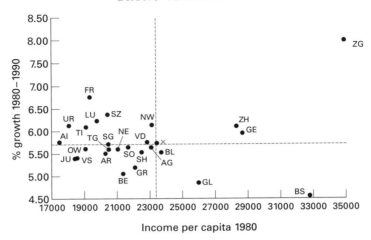

Figure 5.7. *Economic performance, 1980–1990*

forms the tail-end. This is not especially astonishing since, unlike Geneva and Basle, the canton of Zurich consists of the city and also quite an extensive rural district. Conversely, and with respect to economic growth, Zurich in the 1980s ran rings around both Basle and Geneva. But none of the cantons can even begin to compete with the canton of Zug, neither with regard to per capita income nor with regard to economic growth. This very small canton boasting no more than 86,000 inhabitants in 1990 and still forming the absolute peak, represents a unique case in the Swiss economic landscape. Situated a mere thirty kilometres south of the city of Zurich, Zug has succeeded in turning this happy vicinity greatly to its own advantage by turning into a kind of 'free rider', capitalising on the infrastructure of the neighbouring economic centre of Zurich. At the same time, by way of special and uncommonly advantageous tax legislation laws, it managed to attract a number of important international investment and holding companies. In this way Zug, politically speaking an autonomous unity, is still – seen from the economic point of view – to be categorised as part of the agglomeration belonging to the city of Zurich.

Around the beginning of the nineteenth century the economic significance of the city of Zurich was still considerably lagging behind that of Geneva or Basle. Since then it has overtaken them both, in the course of the twentieth century turning into the unchallenged principal centre of Swiss finance and, quite generally, of Swiss economic life. Today more than 15 per cent of the total Swiss population live in the agglomeration of Zurich, producing about a quarter of the sum total of the Swiss national income. Such a predominance is ominous in a country that is proud of its linguistic and cultural diversity and that cherishes the extensive rights of self-determination of its local communities. As a consequence there exist grave misgivings about the dominating position of Zurich in the rest of Switzerland. Complaints are, indeed, to be heard from all parts of the country, clamouring against the economic centre snatching ever more greedily ever larger bits of the economic 'cake'. But it is true enough that lamentations coming from Basle or St Gall enjoy far less publicity than those expounded in the Romandie, where they blurt out their protest against what they refer to as 'Alamannic predominance' while, in reality, they essentially mean to pillory the city of Zurich.

To conclude: uneven economic growth of the various cantons is not to be attributed to language problems. A 'centre versus periphery' model (in the sense of G. Myrdal) is far likelier to account accurately for the existing irritations between the various regions of the country.

But why was it Zurich that achieved its present dominating position? Why not Geneva, a city that began the nineteenth century in a position decidedly superior to that of Zurich? If one attempts to argue the point on the basis of the dissimilarities of mentalities, before long a host of difficulties will present themselves. Then the nebulous notion of the so-called 'Teutonic efficiency' would have to be played off against the almost as nebulous concept of the particularly Calvinist affinity to the spirit of capitalism originally forwarded by Max Weber. It is preferable to offer instead a few hard facts easily submitting to verification.

Geneva is situated at the periphery of the Swiss market area emerging after 1848. In sharp contrast to Geneva and unquestionably enjoying a much more central geographical location to begin with, Zurich by means of a consistent and aggressive traffic policy has succeeded in improving continuously – and decisively – upon its initial advantage: an undeviating course of action easily to be traced from the laying of the very first track of the Swiss railway network in the middle of the nineteenth century to the construction of the first Swiss intercontinental airport in the immediate vicinity of the city of Zurich shortly after the Second World War.

Geneva, headquarters of the International Committee of the Red Cross as well as the League of Nations, has for a long time remained the most distinguished Swiss city. Not so very long ago, on the occasion of the first summit conference in 1955, Geneva still offered itself quite naturally as the meeting place for Eisenhower and Khrushchev. It is only in recent years that the international reputation of Geneva has lost prestige to some extent, not least because reorientation in matters of foreign policy and in relationships with international organisations appear not to come easily to the nation. To wit: Switzerland to this day has not brought itself to apply for membership of the United Nations; also, the nation has only recently declined to become part of the European Economic Area (EEA), and it is still putting up resolute resistance to a proposed entry into the European Union. It is therefore no longer a matter of course that newly founded organisations of the United Nations establish their headquarters in Geneva, nor indeed that the old-established ones choose to remain there. Zurich, on the other hand, is not confronted with any such problems. Its rank as the absolute Swiss economic centre recommends the city – as it were automatically – as the first-class address for international economic contact of all kinds. With a view to the economic 'globalisation'; so constantly referred to in recent years, the international aspects of the economic life of Zurich have increasingly gained significance for the further development of the city and its hinterland (including Zug).

Considering the steadily progressing development of industrial society towards a postindustrial 'services society', the advantages of easy accessibility as well as the possibility of quick and intensive communication will be of ever greater consequence. It must therefore be conceded that the vigorous French-Swiss remonstrances referred to at the outset of this paper are well founded, beyond a doubt: on an international level the retrenchment of the international air service proposed for Geneva airport will indeed impair the competitive capacities of the Romandie. On the other hand, however, the notion of this being just one further measure of German-speaking Switzerland calculated to oppress the French-speaking minority has no rational foundation whatever. But we are here faced with well-known resentments of old standing: resentments that have required constant and careful consideration in the past and will continue to require no less careful consideration in the days to come.

NOTES

1 *Bundesblatt der Schweizerischen Eidgenossenschaft* (Bern, 1993), vol. I, p. 168.
2 COOP-Zeitung 31 (31 July 1996), pp. 6–9.
3 From data in *Schweizerische Statistik 195* (Bern, 1915), pp. 18–29.

4 Only once, namely from 1876 to 1880, was there just one single representative from Romanic Switzerland on the Executive Federal Council.

5 William E. Rappard, *Die Bundesverfassung der Schweizerischen Eidgenossenschaft 1848–1948* (Zurich, 1948), pp. 318–21.

6 *Bundesblatt der Schweizerischen Eidgenossenschaft* (Bern, 1979), vol. I, p. 213.

7 For a fuller account, see Ueli Gyr, *Lektion fürs Leben. Welschlandaufenthalte als traditionelle Bildungs- Erziehungs- und Uebergangsmuster* (Zurich, 1989).

8 Urs Rey, *Demographische Strukturveränderungen und Binnenwanderung in der Schweiz 1859–1910* (unpublished Master's thesis, University of Zurich, 1990).

9 From data in *Schweizerische Statistik 195*, pp. 420–89.

10 *Statistisches Jahrbuch der Schweiz 1979* (Basel, 1979), p. 27 and *Statistisches Jahrbuch der Schweiz 1997* (Zurich, 1998), p. 440.

11 For an in-depth analysis of the language question, see Hans-Peter Müller, *Die schweizerische Sprachenfrage vor 1914* (Wiesbaden, 1977).

12 Georg Kreis, 'Krisenreaktionen in der französischen Schweiz vor 1914' in Andreas Ernst and Erich Wigger (eds.), *Die neue Schweiz? Eine Gesellschaft zwischen Integration und Polarisierung* (Zurich, 1996), pp. 21–39 at pp. 25–7.

13 *Statistisches Jahrbuch der Schweiz 1979*, p. 24.

14 Alfred Bosshardt, 'Die schweizerische Aussenwirtschaft im Wandel der Zeiten' in Schweizerische Gesellschaft für Statistik und Volkswirtschaft (ed.), *Ein Jahrhundert schweizerischer Wirtschaftsentwicklung* (Bern, 1964), pp. 302–27 at p. 326.

15 Carl Hilty, *Politisches Jahrbuch der schweizerischen Eidgenossenschaft* (Bern, 1909), p. 375.

16 Kreis, 'Krisenreaktionen', pp. 32–5.

17 Willi Gautschi, *Der Landesstreik 1918* (Zurich, Einsiedeln and Cologne, 1968), p. 94.

18 *Bundesblatt der Schweizerischen Eidgenossenschaft* (Bern, 1920), vol. III, p. 800.

19 Rappard, *Die Bundersverfassung*, p. 406.

20 From data in *Schweizerische Statistik 212* (Bern, 1919), pp. 204, 208, 292, 336 and 380.

21 From data in *ibid.*, pp. 204, 208, 292, 336 and 380.

22 Bruno Fritzsche, 'Die Spinne im Netz' in *Geschichte des Kantons Zürich* (Zurich, 1994), vol. III, pp. 164–80 at p. 169.

23 David S. Landes, 'Technological change and development in western Europe, 1750–1914' in H. J. Habakuk and M. Postan (eds.), *The Cambridge Economic History of Europe* (Cambridge, 1966), vol. VI, pp. 274–603 at p. 503.

24 David S. Landes, 'Swatch! ou l'horlogerie suisse dans le contexte mondial' in Paul Bairoch and Martin Körner (eds.), *Die Schweiz in der Weltwirtschaft* (Zurich, 1990), pp. 227–36 at p. 232.

25 From data in Francesco Kneschaurek, 'Wandlungen der schweizerischen Industriestruktur seit 1800' in Schweizerische Gesellschaft für Statistik und Volkswirtschaft, *Ein Jahrhundert schweizerischer Wirtschaftsentwicklung*, pp. 133–66 at p. 139.

26 *Statistisches Jahrbuch der Schweiz 1979*, p. 24.

27 All data with regard to the cantonal incomes are taken from Georges
   Fischer, *Räumliche Disparitäten in der Schweiz* (Bern, 1985) (especially from the
   table on p. 82) and from Bundesamt für Statistik, Volkswirtschaftliche
   Gesamtrechnung, electronic file STATINF.

CHAPTER 6

The Portuguese national question in the twentieth century: from Spanish threat to European bliss

Nuno Valério

INTRODUCTION

In spite of its small size, the Portuguese territory has great geographical diversity.[1] Yet, in spite of this geographical diversity, the Portuguese population has great cultural homogeneity.[2] These two facts ensure that there has never been any internal Portuguese national question during the twentieth century.

From an external point of view, however, the situation is rather different. Since at least the eighteenth century, Portuguese society had perceived a Spanish threat to Portuguese independence, and such a problem was still predominant in the first half of the twentieth century. As a matter of fact, this Spanish threat never materialised into aggression, or even significant interference in Portuguese affairs. Anyway, the absence of any conflict between the two countries should perhaps be explained as a consequence of the three steps Portugal took to protect the country against the Spanish threat: the alliance with Britain, the African adventure, and the efforts to promote modern economic growth. The roots of this perception of a Spanish threat, the relations between the two countries during the first half of the twentieth century, and the measures taken to protect Portugal against the Spanish threat will be dealt with in the first half of this chapter.

From the late 1940s until the mid-1980s, the Portuguese national question gradually moved from the traditional pattern summarised above to a full commitment to European integration. European integration seems to have afforded Portugal economic prosperity and national security. Portuguese steps towards European integration, and the main consequences of European integration for Portuguese society, will be the subject of the second half of this chapter. This inquiry will then consider an important question that still remains unanswered as the century ends: will this European bliss last?

THE SPANISH THREAT

A prelude

First of all, why is Portugal separated from Spain? This is a complex question, which is beyond the scope of this chapter, but its main aspects must be summarised here, so that the roots of the perception by Portuguese society of a Spanish threat may be understood.

Medieval Iberian Christendom was a frontier society, faced directly with hostile Islamic societies. The need for a local supply of public goods, especially defence, implied an extreme feudalisation, in which local lords not only exercised *de facto* state power, but even usurped *de jure* royal functions.[3] This generated a political fragmentation that Iberian royal houses tried to undo by means of royal marriages. They finally succeeded in 1580 in gathering all Iberian kingdoms under the rule of the same king, but four different nationalities – Basque, Castilian, Catalan and Portuguese – had already laid their own deep roots. This situation was translated into three distinct kingdoms – Castile (dominating the Basques), Aragon (centred upon Catalonia) and Portugal. Moreover, two of the three kingdoms had sizable colonial empires – Castile in America and the Philippines; Portugal around the Indian Ocean, in the Far East and in Brazil. At the same time, the Iberian kings (of the House of Austria) were also sovereigns of several other European states – Sardinia, Sicily, Naples, Milan, Burgundy and the Low Countries (in revolt since 1572) – forming what may be called the Western Habsburg Empire. As a consequence, the peaceful formation of a unified Iberian nation proved impossible. In 1640, both Catalonia and Portugal broke out in revolt. The Western Habsburg Empire was able to subdue Catalonia, but not Portugal.[4] Thus, when the War of Spanish Succession (1701–14) created the Kingdom of Spain (plus Castilian colonies), without any further European territories, Catalonia was integrated, but Portugal remained outside.

The coexistence of a small Portugal (slightly less than 100,000 km^2 and around 10 million inhabitants today) and a large Spain (slightly over 500,000 km^2 and around 40 million inhabitants today) proved to be a stable pattern for the Iberian political map. However, fears of a Spanish attempt to rebuild Iberian unity were a constant feature of Portuguese life after the early eighteenth century.

A danger that never materialised

This does not mean that formal relations between the two countries were usually bad. In fact, the peaceful settlement of disputes (the most complex ones being those on the definition of the colonial border in South America during the eighteenth century) was the general rule, and war only broke out on three occasions in the eighteenth and nineteenth centuries, making a total of around three years of war.[5]

During the twentieth century, acute friction between the two countries has occurred only twice. In 1911–12, the Spanish monarchic government helped Portuguese monarchic refugees to organise military actions against the recently established (1910) Portuguese republican government, but this attitude was abandoned as soon as it became clear that success was improbable. In 1936, the Portuguese authoritarian government helped the military revolt against the Spanish republican government, and then supported the right-wing side during the 1936–9 Civil War. This means that the Spanish threat was a danger that never materialised.[6]

Insurance against the Spanish threat

The alliance with Britain

It may, however, be argued that the absence of Spanish aggression, or even any really significant actual pressure on Portugal, was simply the consequence of several protective measures taken by Portugal to insure against the Spanish threat.

From a strategic point of view, Portugal's main insurance against the Spanish threat was the alliance with Britain. This alliance had medieval roots, and was definitively established in 1654, after a war between Portugal and England that had been triggered by Portuguese support for King Charles I and his son in their fight against parliament. In 1899, the alliance was strengthened, when Britain agreed to give formal guarantees to protect the Portuguese colonial empire (and implicitly Portugal proper – that is, the mother country) in exchange for Portuguese help (through its colony of Mozambique) in the war against the South African Boer states.

During the twentieth century, the Portuguese–British alliance was formally invoked on three different occasions. In 1916, Britain asked Portugal to impound German ships harboured in Portuguese ports, and to lend some of them to Britain. Portugal agreed, and Germany declared war on Portugal, leading the country to a formal intervention in the First World War. In 1943, Britain asked Portugal to permit it to use military bases in the Azores (actually the bases were mainly used by the American air force). Germany protested, but did not declare war; thus, Portugal was able to remain non-belligerent during the Second World War. In 1961, Portugal asked Britain to protect Portuguese possessions in India against an attack from India. Britain declined to act, invoking its compromises with India, as a member of the Commonwealth.[7]

This summary does not mean that the invoking of the Portuguese–British alliance during the twentieth century was a one-sided affair that always favoured Britain. Its deterrent effect was certainly effective in the general evolution of Iberian and colonial affairs, favouring the more-or-less peaceful survival of the Portuguese colonial empire until the second half of the twentieth century, and the protection of Portugal proper against the perceived Spanish threat.

The post-Second World War years saw a decline in the British influence on international affairs, and this meant that the alliance with Britain no longer provided reliable protection against the Spanish threat (nor against the various dangers that threatened the Portuguese colonial empire). Somewhat reluctantly, Portugal turned to the new hegemonic maritime power, the United States of America, for alternative protection. This meant accepting the presence of an American military base in the Azores (which prolonged the Second World War arrangements) and becoming a member of the North Atlantic Treaty Organisation (NATO) from its beginnings in 1949. American protection functioned quite well in the European context, but worked poorly (from the Portuguese point of view) in colonial affairs, because the United States favoured decolonisation and was unwilling to support the Portuguese colonial empire.[8]

The African adventure

The lesson that Portuguese strategists learned from the historical experience of wars against Spain (or previous Iberian neighbours) was that, when Spanish commitment went beyond border attrition, Spanish invasions could not be stopped by border garrisons, but had to be fought by fortifying the main Portuguese cities, resisting along these shorter defensive lines, whilst attacking Spanish communication lines. If this strategy failed, only the Atlantic extension of the Portuguese territory (Azores and Madeira) could save the country.[9] Such an extension could be

increased by further colonial possessions. Given the popularity of imperial endeavours, and allied to the hope that these possessions might
provide a positive contribution to economic growth (a subject which will
be dealt with in more detail below), this led Portugal to the building of
its fourth colonial empire, in Africa, in the late nineteenth century.[10]

The fourth colonial empire was the cause of two periods of war: one
from the 1880s until the First World War years, to ensure the submission
of the previously existing societies in what was to become Angola,
Portuguese Guinea (Guinea-Bissau) and Mozambique; another from
1961 until 1974, to resist independence movements in the same territories. The first one was not very demanding for Portuguese society,
because the small size and technological backwardness of African tribal
societies permitted rather easy victories by the Portuguese armies.[11] The
second one put heavy pressure on Portuguese society, because the co-
ordinated action of the independence movements and the help they
received from African, communist, and even western countries prevented any possibility of a Portuguese victory. Attempts were made to
mobilise support from Portugal's NATO allies by invoking the anti-
communist significance of the Portuguese colonial wars, but they met
with only limited success. Exhaustion finally dampened popular support
for the colonial policy, and Portugal abandoned its colonial empire in
1974–5, as soon as the deterioration of the economic situation made the
cost of the war prohibitive.[12]

Economic growth

Real insurance against the Spanish threat could, however, only come
from the Portuguese capacity to stem any Spanish attempt to take action
against the country. This meant the capacity to command enough military resources; and this, in turn, meant the capacity to command enough
economic resources.

Modern economic growth was a difficult goal for Portugal to achieve.
Between the 1850s and the 1880s there was a first spurt of growth, but
this proved to be a false start. This first spurt of growth was based on
private exploitation of the resources of Portugal proper, with the stimu-
lative support of public investment in infrastructures, within a mildly
free-trade framework. The breakdown of the Portuguese economy in
the early 1890s was mainly due to financial causes, but it led to the
suspension of the gold standard and to a partial bankruptcy of the
Portuguese government, and called for new ideas to foster economic
prosperity. Protectionism, colonial expansion and investment in human

capital were the solutions chosen. Protectionism and colonial expansion became the main elements of a nationalist economic policy that would dominate the first half of the twentieth century and survive until the 1980s, in spite of the gradual drive towards European integration from the 1940s onwards. This nationalist development strategy was initiated by the last governments of the constitutional monarchy (from the 1890s until 1910) and maintained by the governments of the liberal First Republic (1910–26), the military dictatorship (1926–33) and the constitutional authoritarian republican regime (1933–74) that followed, in spite of their political differences.

Protectionism was designed to achieve industrialisation and a higher degree of self-sufficiency in agricultural activities. It certainly contributed to its first goal, although it may be argued that it went far beyond what would be reasonable according to the infant-industry argument, supporting many inefficiencies and introducing many distortions in resource allocation. It failed completely in terms of achieving its second goal, although the supply problems created by the two world wars meant that agricultural protectionism continued to be favourably regarded until late into the second half of the twentieth century. Twice during the twentieth century, additional efforts were made to promote a more intensive use of the land and to introduce some technological improvements, so that dependence upon foreign food supplies could be reduced. However, both the 'wheat campaign' of the military dictatorship and the authoritarian regime in the late 1920s and early 1930s, based on the support of large landowners, and the 'Portuguese bread' campaign of the transitional governments between authoritarian and democratic regimes in the mid-1970s, based on the support of rural wage-earners and the Communist party, met with complete failure. In the long run, it is possible to say that protectionism spread to too many sectors and lasted for a longer period than was necessary to fulfil its potentially useful role in fostering industrial development.[13]

Besides its political goals, colonial expansion aimed at creating a set of economies dependent upon Portugal and acting as providers of raw materials, buyers of final products, and destinations for Portuguese emigration and investment. There is no real agreement about the effects of colonial expansion upon Portuguese economic evolution.[14] It is difficult to believe that they acted as an engine of economic growth for Portugal for two reasons. First, they were usually minor economic partners for the Portuguese economy, in spite of the various schemes of imperial preference and economic integration between Portugal and its colonies implemented between the late nineteenth century and the 1970s. As for their role as providers of raw materials, it was often possible for Portugal to find tropical products in international markets at better prices than in Portuguese colonies. Concerning their role as buyers of final products, in spite of their large area (more than 2 million km²), Portuguese colonies did not have a very large population (around 14 million inhabitants, as against 9 million in Portugal proper, in 1960), and their per capita gross domestic product was, by that time, already almost ten times lower than the Portuguese.[15] Thus, they were unable to compete with Portugal proper, let alone with developed economies, as outlets for Portuguese products. As for their role as destinations for emigration, Portuguese emigrants continued to prefer other destinations: Brazil until the Second World War and Europe (especially France) after the Second World War. Thus, the population of European origin in Portuguese colonies was still less than 200,000 in 1960.[16] The second reason for believing that colonial endeavours were not beneficial for Portuguese economic growth is the fact that they absorbed significant resources, from both private and government origins. Although it is possible to argue that significant profits compensated for private investment, no revenue ever compensated for the public expenditure needed for economic and military purposes, let alone the human losses caused by the colonial wars.[17]

A summary of the main financial flows between Portugal and its colonies provides an interesting perspective on the perceived and actual costs and benefits of nineteenth- and twentieth-century colonial expansion for Portugal (see table 6.1).

The figures for the period 1875–90 show that the colonial empire played a negligible role in Portuguese economic life before the building of the fourth Portuguese colonial empire started. The formative phase of the fourth Portuguese colonial empire, until the First World War, was characterised by a rise of government expenditure and trade flows, with a trade balance favourable to Portugal. The stable existence of the fourth Portuguese colonial empire witnessed further increases of trade flows. Until the Second World War the trade balance was usually unfavourable to Portugal, but it became usually favourable to Portugal after the Second World War. As for the government expenditure, it fell until the Second World War, and rose slightly after it, because of the early threats to the empire during the 1950s. During the period of the colonial war, government expenditure boomed, exports fell, imports rose, and the trade balance became unfavourable to Portugal again. As

Table 6.1. *Main financial flows between Portugal and its colonies, 1875–1974*

Period	Government expenditure (as % of GDP)	Exports (as % of GDP)	Imports (as % of GDP)
1875–90	0.1	0.1	0.1
1891–1918	0.4	0.5	0.3
1919–45	0.3	1.0	1.4
1946–60	0.6	3.4	2.8
1961–74	3.6	3.1	3.2

Source: Nuno Valério, 'O significado económico do império colonial para um pequeno poder – o caso de Portugal (de finais do século 19 ao terceiro quartel do século 20)' in António Telo and Hipolito Torre Gomez (eds.), *Portugal y España en el sistema internacional* (Zamora, 1998), pp. 53–69 at pp. 62–7.

government expenditure began to exceed trade flows and the trade relations seemed to become deleterious for the Portuguese economy, at the same time that the human commitment to the war began to be felt as unbearable, it was impossible to keep the Portuguese society ready to sacrifice to defend the colonial empire.

Investment in human capital, something that the mid-nineteenth-century development blueprint had relegated to a non-priority position, was certainly a good option in the late nineteenth-century blueprint, but it proved slow to implement and slow to bear fruit. Only in the 1920s were any significant efforts made to improve a rather poor situation in terms of literacy and technical education, and only after the Second World War did any significant results begin to be seen in terms of modern economic growth. Anyway, any judgement should be cautious, because other factors interfered with improvements in education and its impact on economic growth.[18]

EUROPEAN INTEGRATION

Towards European bliss

The third quarter of the twentieth century heralded a few significant structural changes in Portuguese society. First of all, there was the definitive take-off of modern economic growth. By the early 1970s, Portugal was already a middle–high income economy. It is impossible to discuss the roots of this success here, but it may be suggested that its main factors were the favourable international background of the golden years of economic growth in western Europe, North America and Japan, the overcoming of the traditional problems of a lack of resources – mainly a qualitative lack of human resources and a quantitative lack of savings – and gains in efficiency resulting from improved technology and freer intercourse with Europe in general.[19]

At the same time, the colonial empire crumbled under the pressure of the 'winds of change'. The traditional British protection was rendered ineffectual as Great Britain lost its importance as a significant world power and proved incapable even of defending its own empire, and Portugal's new privileged ally, the United States of America, did not support European colonial empires, as already mentioned above. Portugal tried to resist, both militarily and economically. Military resistance led to the outbreak of the colonial wars mentioned above, and to military defeat as Portuguese society lost its traditional enthusiasm for colonial endeavours. Economic resistance took the form of an attempt to build a free-trade zone and a monetary union between Portugal and its colonies, and this was a failure as well. Balance of payments problems in the two main Portuguese colonies – Angola and Mozambique – and the unwillingness of Portugal to provide enough financial support for them to overcome their short-term problems led to the (formally temporary) suspension of the free-trade zone and monetary union schemes in 1971. Political decolonisation in 1974–5 ensured that no attempts were made to restore them.[20]

Europe provided an alternative as a preferential economic partner. As a matter of fact, the main European national economies had never ceased to be Portugal's main economic partners. Portugal was involved from the beginning in the process of European integration: it was one of the (moderate) beneficiaries of the Marshall Plan and one of the founding members of the European Organisation of Economic Co-operation (EOEC – 1948); it participated in the European Payments Union (1950), and subscribed to the European Monetary Agreement (1955); when the EOEC split into two trading blocks – the European Economic Community (EEC) and the European Free Trade Association (EFTA) – Portugal chose to become a member of the EFTA, so that the economic integration with its colonies would not be disturbed; and, when Great Britain abandoned the EFTA to become an EEC member, Portugal negotiated an association agreement with the EEC (1973).

For a while (from the late 1940s until the early 1970s), there was an attempt to enjoy simultaneously the advantages of the old nationalist (that is, protectionist and colonialist) development strategy, and those of a new export-led and European-biased development strategy. The mix was clearly contradictory and collapsed in 1974 under the pressure of the first oil shock. The authoritarian political regime was swept away so that the decolonisation process could be carried out, and political democrat-isation followed in 1976, after two years of uneasy transition.

Cutting its links with its former African colonies and building a demo-cratic republican regime led to a deepening of Portugal's relations with the EEC. The association treaty was revised (1976), and an application presented for full membership (1977). Although negotiations proved difficult (mainly because the Portuguese case had to be dealt with at the same time as the much more difficult Spanish case), an agreement was reached and Portugal became a member of the EEC in 1986. In the meantime, it had received significant pre-membership aid, and the influx of European funds increased during the late 1980s and the 1990s, under the scope of European structural funds.[21]

Of course, the deepening of Portuguese relations with the EEC (now the European Union) meant the inevitable adoption of the new export-led and European-biased development strategy, which had been devel-oped since the Second World War. This was not an easy process, because short-term difficulties linked to the first (1973–5) and second (1981–3) oil shocks led to temporary revivals of the old protectionist ideas (and practices, as temporary increases of import duties were implemented). However, the new development strategy triumphed in the long run, as the deepening of European integration brought economic prosperity and national security to Portugal.

Economic prosperity means that modern economic growth has been consolidated and Portugal has been able to attain what is currently considered a high level of development during the 1990s. Of course, Portugal suffered from European and world recessions, as would be expected for a small and open economy, but even the 1991–4 difficulties did not prevent full participation in all economic and monetary union schemes (namely in the single market for commodities, labour and capital from 1993 onwards, and in the first group of countries to adopt the euro as their monetary unit from 1999 onwards).

A look at the rates of growth of the Portuguese economy since the mid-nineteenth century helps to explain why European integration is perceived as very positive from an economic point of view (see table 6.2).

First, it is clear that until the mid-1850s and between the 1890s and

Table 6.2. *Average rates of growth of Portuguese per capita gross domestic product, 1837–1995*

Period	Rate of growth (%)
1837–55	+1.0
1856–90	+2.1
1891–1913	+0.3
1913–28	+0.4
1929–46	+0.8
1947–59	+3.3
1960–73	+6.2
1974–85	+2.9
1985–95	+5.1

Source: Nuno Valério, 'Recent developments on Portuguese retrospective national accounts', Gabinete de História Económica e Social do Instituto Superior de Economia et Gestão da Universidade Técnica de Lisboa, Working Paper 12 (1998).

the mid-1940s, Portuguese economic growth was either sluggish or non-existent, while between the mid-1850s and the 1880s and from the mid-1940s onwards, Portuguese economic growth was either respectable or even exceptional. The positive relationship between the degree of openness of the Portuguese economy and its growth performance is undoubted. Secondly, considering in more detail the post-Second World War period, it is clear that periods of very significant deepening of European integration (the EFTA period between 1960 and 1973, and the EEC/E.C./E.U. period from 1986 onwards) witnessed higher growth rates than periods of less significant deepening of European integration (the EOEC period from 1947 until 1959 and the pre-membership period of association to the EEC between 1974 and 1985). Of course, the evolution of the international economy was as important as the degree of European integration in shaping Portuguese economic performance, but the perception of a positive relationship between the degree of European integration of the Portuguese economy and its growth performance was nevertheless reinforced. Together with net transfers from the European Communities, which remained below 1 per cent of gross domestic product during the association period, but grew after Portugal became a member towards a peak above 3.5 per cent of gross domestic product in the mid-1990s, this perception helps to explain the popularity of the European option within Portuguese society.

National security means that European integration has become a surrogate for the traditional British protection against the old Spanish threat. From the 1940s until the 1970s, as Spain remained outside the main European organisations,[22] Portugal was able to underline its specificity in relation to its Iberian neighbour. From the late 1970s onwards, as Spain became a partner in the process, the good relationship between the two countries was actually deepened. At the same time, their economic relations were significantly intensified – Spain surged from a modest sixth place to become Portugal's leading trade partner, and also became one of the main sources of foreign investment in the country; the Portuguese role in Spain is, of course, relatively more modest, but there has been a boom there as well. Moreover, the development of collective European security schemes has helped to overcome traditional suspicion.[23]

To sum up: European integration has so far proved a source of true bliss for Portuguese society.

How long will European bliss last?

It is, however, impossible to avoid the question: how long will this European bliss last? This may be considered to be a two-sided question. First, will Europe keep on providing a context of economic prosperity and national security for Portugal, at least in the long run? Secondly, will Portugal remain a distinct society within the European framework? These are likely to be the main issues in relation to the Portuguese national question in the early decades of the twenty-first century.

Of course, the future is uncertain. However, two rather optimistic reflections may be made regarding these matters.

First, as the European Union will remain prosperous and stable itself, it will provide a context of economic prosperity and national security for Portugal. Portugal may contribute to the favourable evolution of the Union, but to guarantee this is certainly beyond the capacity of intervention of Portuguese society. In any case, it is of the utmost interest for all European nations that the European Union should remain prosperous and stable. Of course, this does not mean that they will make the right choices, but it increases the likelihood that they will do so.

Secondly, Portuguese society has always been and will continue to remain subject to economic, political and cultural influences from abroad regardless of its participation in the European Union. Past experience shows that these influences from abroad have had a positive effect on the evolution of Portuguese society. It is to be expected that this situation will continue in the future.

NOTES

1 The classic study on the geographical diversity of the Portuguese territory – with Mediterranean, Atlantic and semi-continental regions – is Orlando Ribeiro, *Portugal, o Mediterrâneo e o Atlântico* (4th edn, Lisbon, 1986).

2 According to the nineteenth- and twentieth-century population censuses, the percentage of the population that is of foreign origin, or has a mother tongue other than Portuguese, has always been less than 0.5 per cent of the total Portuguese population, and the percentage of the population with a religious background other than Catholicism has always been less than 2 per cent of the total Portuguese population (although explicit religious indifference and agnosticism extend to some 20 per cent of the population nowadays and practical religious indifference is certainly much more widespread). There is no reason to believe that things have ever been different at any time since the sixteenth century, after the medieval Muslim community had been peacefully converted, and the Jewish community either forcibly converted or expelled (although social discrimination against ex-Jews and their descendants continued until the eighteenth century).

3 The feudal character of medieval Iberian Christendom has been a subject of much controversy. For two contrasting views, see Marc Bloch, *La société féodale* (Paris, 1939) and Pierre Bonassie, 'Du Rhône à la Galice: génèse et modalités du régime féodal' in Pierre Toubert *et al.*, *Structures féodales et féodalisme dans l'Occident Méditerranéen (Xe–XIIIe siècles)* (Paris, 1980), pp. 17–56.

4 The discussion of the reasons for the Portuguese success as against the Catalonian failure to become independent from the Western Habsburg Empire in the mid-seventeenth century is beyond the scope of this chapter. I would suggest that the main reason for the difference was the Portuguese capacity to obtain resources from its (mainly Brazilian) colonial empire as against the inability of Catalonia to obtain resources on the same scale from its (mainly Mediterranean) trade connections.

5 In 1761–3, there was border attrition, linked to the Seven Years War. In 1801, there was a Spanish invasion of southern Portugal, linked to the War of the Second Coalition against France, leading to the cession by Portugal of a small piece of its territory (the municipality of Olivença). In 1807–8, Spain joined with France in occupying the continental part of Portugal, in retaliation for the Portuguese refusal to participate in the so-called Continental Blockade against Great Britain, but Spanish troops withdrew when a revolt against French intervention in internal Spanish affairs broke out on 2 May 1808.

6 For general surveys of the relations between Portugal and Spain during the
   twentieth century, see J. M. Ferreira, *Um século de problemas. As relações luso-
   espanholas da União Ibérica à Comunidade Europeia* (Lisbon, 1989) and César
   Oliveira, *Cem anos nas relações luso-espanholas. Política e economia* (Lisbon, 1995).
7 There is no recent general study on the Portuguese–British alliance. The last
   work that can be quoted is José Almada, *A aliança inglesa*, 2 vols. (Lisbon,
   1946).
8 On the subject of Portuguese participation in NATO during the early years
   of the organisation, see António Telo, *Portugal e a NATO o reencontro da tradição
   atlântica* (Lisbon, 1996).
9 After Portugal became an autonomous state in the twelfth century, there
   were eighteen wars between Portugal and its Iberian neighbour (Leon,
   Castile or Spain). Two of these wars were fought to impose the recognition
   of Portuguese autonomy (1128–43 and 1640–68). Five were fought to solve
   border disputes (1169, 1196–9, 1252–3, 1295–7 and 1336–9). Two were
   Castilian or Habsburg interventions in Portuguese dynastic problems
   (1383–7 and 1580–3). Six were Portuguese interventions in Castilian or
   Habsburg dynastic problems (1369–71, 1372–3, 1381–2, 1396–1400, 1474–9
   and 1703–13). Three were part of broader European conflicts in which both
   countries happened to be in opposite camps (1761–3, 1801 and 1807–8). In
   eleven cases, the Leonese, Castilian, or Spanish armies did not penetrate
   deep into Portuguese territory. In seven cases, they penetrated deep into
   Portuguese territory. In five cases, they were rebuffed. In two cases they were
   able to take the Portuguese capital. In 1580, this confirmed that Portugal
   was to become part of the Western Habsburg Empire. In 1807, the French
   and Spanish occupation of the Portuguese mainland forced the Portuguese
   king to establish the country's capital in Rio de Janeiro, in the colony of
   Brazil. Plans for a similar withdrawal of the Portuguese government (to the
   Azores) in the case of a German or Spanish attack were made during the
   Second World War. For a summary of Portuguese wars, see Eugénia Mata
   and Nuno Valério, *História económica de Portugal – uma perspectiva global* (Lisbon,
   1993). For a detailed analysis of the Portuguese situation during the Second
   World War, see António Telo, *Portugal na Segunda Guerra (1941–1945)*, 2 vols.
   (Lisbon, 1990–1).
10 On the subject of the fourth Portuguese colonial empire, see Gervase
   Clarence-Smith, *The Third Portuguese Empire 1825–1975. A Study in Economic
   Imperialism* (Manchester, 1985). I call the African empire of the late nineteenth and twentieth centuries the fourth Portuguese empire, because it was
   preceded by a North Atlantic empire during the fifteenth century, by an
   empire located mainly around the Indian Ocean and in the Far East during
   the sixteenth century, and by a mainly Brazilian empire from the seventeenth until the early nineteenth century. Clarence-Smith speaks only of a
   third Portuguese empire, because he does not count the first one separately.
11 For an analysis of these late-nineteenth-century and early-twentieth-

century colonial wars, see António Telo, *Economia e império no Portugal contemporâneo* (Lisbon, 1994).

12 As yet, there is no general study on the colonial wars of the 1960s and early 1970s.

13 A discussion of the effects of protectionism on Portuguese economic growth may be found in Paula Fontoura and Nuno Valério, 'Protection, foreign trade and economic growth in Portugal 1840s–1980s' in Jean-Michel Chevet, Peter Lindert and John Vincent Nye (eds.), *Political Economy of Protectionism and Commerce, 18th–20th Centuries* (Milan, 1994), pp. 77–86.

14 For a defence of the view that the fourth colonial empire was beneficial to the Portuguese economic evolution, see Pedro Lains, 'An account of the Portuguese African empire, 1885–1975' in Patrick O'Brien and Leandro Pradros (eds.), *The Costs and Benefits of European Imperialism from the Conquest of Ceuta, 1415, to the Treaty of Lusaka, 1974* (Madrid, 1998), pp. 235–63.

15 As the rate of growth of the Portuguese economy has usually been higher than the rate of growth of the economies of its former colonies, the ratio of Portugal's gross domestic product to the gross domestic product of its former colonial empire has tended to increase in the long run.

16 V. M. Godinho, 'L'émigration portugaise (XVe–XXe siècles)', *Revista de História Económica e Social* 1 (1978), 5–32 is the classical study on Portuguese emigration. Stanley Engerman and J. C. Neves, *The Bricks of an Empire 1415–1999. 585 Years of Portuguese Emigration* (Lisbon, 1996) provides a more recent synthesis.

17 For a discussion of the financial and human costs of the fourth Portuguese colonial empire see Nuno Valério, 'O significado económico do império colonial para um pequeno poder – o caso de Portugal (de finais do século 19 ao terceiro quartel do século 20)' in António Telo and Hipolito Torre Gomez (eds.), *Portugal y España en el sistema internacional* (Zamora, 1998), pp. 53–69.

18 For a discussion of the relationship between education and economic growth in Portugal, see A. B. Nunes, 'Education and economic growth in Portugal: a simple regression approach', *Estudos de Economia* 8(2) (1993), 181–205.

19 For a discussion of the roots of Portuguese modern economic growth, see Mata and Valério, *História económica de Portugal.*

20 All ex-Portuguese African colonies eventually became members of the group of African, Caribbean and Pacific countries subscribing to the Lomé Convention. Thus they became indirectly linked to Portugal again through the mediation of the European Union. In the 1990s, Cape Verde pegged its currency to the Portuguese escudo, and it remained linked to the new European currency after 1999.

21 For a discussion of Portuguese relations with Europe during the integration process, see Nuno Valério, 'Portugal e a integração européia', *Revista ANPEC* 3 (1998), 103–24.

22 It should be recalled that the same thing happened with NATO.

23 Of course, this does not mean that all problems have disappeared in terms of the relations between Portugal and Spain. Nowadays, the main problem in these relations is probably related to the management of Iberian water resources, as around half of Portugal's water resources come from three rivers – the Douro, the Tagus and the Guadiana – that have their sources in Spanish territory. The planning of land routes connecting mainland Portugal to non-Iberian Europe and disputes over the use of maritime resources may become important sources of friction as well.

CHAPTER SEVEN

From autarky to the European Union: nationalist economic policies in twentieth-century Spain

Gabriel Tortella and Stefan Houpt

INTRODUCTION

Discussions related to the concept of nationalism have given rise to a great deal of recent academic work not only in Spain but also in most of Europe. Part of this is due to the fall of the Iron Curtain, which has led to the kindling of nationalist cinders still alive in former eastern European countries. A second element has been the growing federalism in western Europe. More and more decision-making power has been delegated either to a supranational or to a municipal level, thereby putting national policies into jeopardy. The different formulae of nationalism that have evolved in the past have led to additional confusion relating to the concept itself. A minimal definition of nationalism includes at least four overlapping meanings: patriotism, a world order based on the right of each nation to determine its policies unhindered by others, a struggle for national independence, and a system demanding national conduct of all industries. Each of the above phenomena is present to some extent in the recent history of Spain, although it is perhaps the latter one which best defines the most determinant of the four: 'economic nationalism' – a strain that went hand in hand with economic backwardness in Spain throughout part of the nineteenth and most of the twentieth century.

The concept of nationalism has evolved considerably in the last two centuries. Originally, the French revolutionaries put the nation before the patrimonial state of the absolute monarchy. The *nation* therefore was the embodiment of popular sovereignty, the set of free, equal and fraternal citizens. From this a new ideology was created during the nineteenth century, to promote the political and social cohesion of newer nation states such as Italy and Germany or to contribute to the socio-economic unification and integration of peripheral states such as Poland, Hungary or Spain. In both cases it had a common function –

detracting attention from internal conflicts, be they of an ethnic, social, political, regional or economic nature. The driving force behind nationalism aimed at establishing a common identity with which to overcome the antagonisms of opposing forces such as traditionalism and modernism, capitalists and proletarians, centralism and regionalism, and other centripetal and centrifugal struggles that arose in the absence of absolutism and with the rise of reason.

Spanish nationalism can be characterised in this sense, although over time Spain has also developed a secondary strain of nationalism – regional in nature – located in the Basque country, in Catalonia and more recently in Galicia and Valencia. These are autonomist, separatist or independentist movements of geographic regions of the peninsula limited to those areas. Such regionalisms have contributed and may still contribute to reinforcing central economic nationalism.

THE SHAPING OF NATIONALISM

The more immediate origins of Spanish nationalism can be situated at the end of the eighteenth century. Geographical proximity and political affinity generated a great interest for the social and political happenings in France, which in turn were bound to shake the fundamental pillars of the *ancien régime*: the monarchy, the Church and the existing social ties. Joseph Bonaparte's assumption of the Spanish crown and the occupation of Spain by the French army led to a 'war of independence' against France, which united the geographical area of Spain under the common goals of freedom and sovereignty. The struggle against the common enemy united forces – those in favour of simple restoration with those in favour of a more liberal political system with sovereignty placed in the hands of the people. This unanimous and spontaneous expression of sovereignty in defiance of French occupation was the first declaration of national unity for a geographical area that had been – until then – the centre of an empire ruled by a sovereign king.

A decade later, with the loss of its colonies, Spain had evolved *de facto* from an empire to a nation but with elements of social and political discord increasing throughout the century. Feudalism had been dissolved, freedom from *mortmain* both in ecclesiastic and common land could have left a reserve army of industrial labour – a precondition for industrialisation and modern agrarian production. Unfortunately, agrarian modernisation remained strongly limited by low soil quality, exiguous average rainfall, transhumant institutions; all these factors made technologies developed in northern and central Europe inappropriate for Mediterranean agriculture, and agriculture remained stagnant.[1]

The unification of Spain had not been a product of economic integration and the natural formation of a national market but rather the result of a century of administrative centralism, the war against France and the creation of an army. The railway network, public education, conversion to the metric system, common law, and monetary and fiscal reform were steps taken throughout the nineteenth century towards the gradual integration of markets while avoiding radical reform.

THE ORIGINS OF PROTECTIONISM

This process of nation-building was tied to that of constructing a high wall of protectionism. The seed of tariff protection flourished under liberals and absolutists during the first half of the nineteenth century. Liberal, free-trade economic policies in Spain between 1869 and 1891, however, followed the well-beaten path of similar policies in Europe. The liberal two-tier tariff system introduced by the Tariff Law of 1869 (usually known by the name of its sponsor, the then Finance Minister Laureano Figuerola) combined a lower tariff system – no prohibitions and an average protection of between 20 and 35 per cent – with a mechanism of bilateral trade agreements which allowed Spain twenty-two years of trade expansion and substantial foreign investment. Article 5 of the Figuerola Tariff Law established a gradual reduction of tariff protection to a maximum 15 per cent level to be reached by 1881.

In the early 1860s French entrepreneurs contributed to the development of the nascent Spanish banking system, while channelling foreign funds into railway construction.[2] A ten-year exemption on railway material and rolling stock established by the Railway Law of 1855 provoked an outcry about lost opportunities for the Spanish iron industry. The 'millions made by foreigners' thesis was to become one of the keystones of nationalism and of putting the blame for backwardness on others.

Even so, a few Spaniards had amassed fortunes during this period. The iron-ore mining elite in Biscay fed the Bessemer boom in Europe and the United States, wine merchants quenched phylloxera-stricken markets in France, and Catalan textile producers wove a tight net on colonial markets. But by the late 1880s the period of export-led growth was seen as coming to an end as the protectionist tide swept over Europe and foreign markets closed to Spanish products. The Great Depression (1873–95), the massive imports of overseas grains and rearmament had led Europe to a return to protectionism. Germany, Austria-Hungary, Italy, Switzerland, Sweden, Portugal, Belgium, Russia and France raised barriers before Spain tardily set out to follow their example. The renewal of tariff protectionism in Spain was initiated with the Royal Decree of 31 December 1891. This new regulation increased the general level of tariffs substantially but maintained two important exceptions: low tariffs on the imports of railway materials and debenture of duties paid on ship-building materials.

THE QUESTION OF NATIONAL DEFENCE

In the world arena liberalism was losing its momentum and the ghosts of self-sufficiency, expansionism and state intervention took flesh anew in the last decades of the nineteenth century. Modern imperialism and revolutionary changes in arms technology were upsetting the balance of power.

Rising political unrest in Cuba reinforced these rearmament policies in Spain. In 1887, a plan was drawn up for constructing a modern naval force; the navy asked for the construction of three cruisers by the national industry. A new shipyard was built to this end in Bilbao, the centre of Spain's iron and steel industry. Astilleros del Nervión was the first attempt at creating a modern shipyard to diminish the need for imports from France, Germany and Great Britain. And even though its overdimensional installations and undercapitalisation doomed it to failure, it none the less established a precedent that was followed in the future.

The ties between the bourgeois 'triumvirate' – Catalan textile production, Castilian agriculture and Biscayan heavy industry – tightened as foreign products threatened to invade their terrain and political and social unrest made them reconsider the differences amongst them. Reserving home markets for Spanish producers should provide a guarantee for income, employment and benefits, and so it became the battle cry of industrialists and landowners. Clientelism and the remnants of other more traditional forms of political control (such as *caciquismo*, the Spanish version of the rotten boroughs and the spoils system) exerted on behalf of landowners, the commercial bourgeoisie and the *nouveau riche* industrialists all converged into more centralised forms of corporatist organisation. The Fomento del Trabajo Nacional (Promotion of National Work, an association of Catalan textile industrialists that widened their field of political influence to the national arena in 1889) and the Liga Nacional de Productores (National League of Manufacturers, formed around iron and steel industrialists in 1893) were the main regional employer associations early on and created a common platform for their new economic policy. Other intra-regional associations were soon to follow: the Spanish Maritime League (1900), the National Coal Mine Association (1906) and the Iron and Steel Syndicate (1907).

Profit maximising was attained by political lobbying. First, infant-industry protection was requested in order to overcome initial technological backwardness and to compensate for the difficulties of first establishment; little by little, increases in the coverage and scope of these measures were asked for to defend newly gained market positions or situations in which foreign competition threatened. These policies included tariff barriers, direct benefits, tax cuts or subsidies, preferential interest rates, collaterals for loans, and administrative favours. When these turned out to be insufficient, the state mandated consumption quotas for home production and subjected industry to a system of regulations, authorisations and record-keeping. Thus, tariff protection, administrative intervention and corporatist organisation overlapped in a crescendo of nationalist economic policies.

The loss of Spain's last colonial possessions – Cuba and the Philippines – in 1898 entailed a minor economic loss and a major political impetus to economic nationalism in Spain. 'Defeat at the hands of a foreign army becomes a powerful excuse and a basic reference for identifying the enemy and setting the limits of national image. This helps not only to sanctify the nation and the national project, but also to enhance the nationalistic sentiments and to cement the State's central place as the project leader.'[3] Political, economic and military regeneration was placed foremost on the political agenda. Rebuilding a modern navy fleet, and Spain's imperialist incursion into Morocco between 1909 and 1925, were both endeavours intended to increase Spain's standing on the European stage.

THE CONSOLIDATION OF PROTECTIONISM

Spain never came round to applying Article 5 of the 1869 Figuerola Tariff Law whereby the maximum level of tariff duties would be 15 per cent. It was suspended on numerous occasions and finally revoked in 1890. In December of the following year, Spain took a firm step on the road to autarky with the Tariff of 1891 and the revocation of most of its bilateral trade agreements. When the draft for a new trade agreement being negotiated between Spain and Germany was anticipated as becoming a precedent for tariff reduction via bilateral agreements and the most-favoured nation clause, the pressure group of the industrial north called for support. Before its approval in the Cortes in 1894, a lobby of more than thirty parliamentarians conducted press campaigns, rallies and continuous political agitation, which led to abandoning this or any further treaty that might threaten what a German contemporary observer called the 'Chinese Wall' of Spanish tariff protection,[4] at least for the time being. Two years later, metalworking industrialists obtained the abolition of the special duties on railway equipment in practice since 1855.[5] A new tariff hike in 1898, a higher and new tariff in 1906 and the reduction of the last bastion of tariff-free trade – debenture on duties paid for raw materials and equipment used in ship-building – in 1909 consolidated the 'necessary and sufficient' level of protectionism in Spain.[6]

Both the 1891 and 1906 tariffs were nominally high tariffs – the highest in Europe in 1906. But they must be considered moderate in terms of effective protection; Spain's weak position in trade agreement negotiations forced it to concede partial reductions for the large majority of the products it exchanged with its primary trade partners. Few alterations affected this trade policy framework up to the Civil War, with only one further increase in duties in 1922, which made Spanish tariffs come to be regarded as the highest in the world in nominal terms by 1926.

INDUSTRIAL POLICY

The Villaverde stabilisation plan of 1899 was intended to put an end to inflation, budget deficits and large increases in banknote circulation, all of which were due to the Cuban war (1895–8). The plan imposed the principle of a balanced budget, the reduction of public debt and tax reform, which were combined with a restrictive monetary policy and put a halt to inflation and peseta depreciation. It was totally successful. In the atmosphere of price stability that ensued, the agricultural and industrial lobbies kept up mounting pressure for higher degrees of state intervention.

In 1907 a Law for the Protection of Industry reserved public contracts to Spanish producers. The Commission for the Protection of National

Production was created as a watchdog of this new regulation and it soon evolved into a back-seat driver of nationalist industrial policy. Two years later, in 1909, a law was passed for promoting maritime communications and ship construction. This included an important renewal of the system of subsidies for shipping and ship-building linked to a step-by-step reduction of foreign capital and foreign technicians as a precondition. That same year an industrial giant was born. The Sociedad Española de Construcción Naval – future monopolist of Spanish naval constructions and dominant firm in merchant ship-building up to the Civil War – was a joint venture between British armament firms (Vickers, Brown and Armstrong) and several Spanish industrialists and bankers. It was intended to carry out the reconstruction of the Spanish fleet (after its destruction in Santiago de Cuba and Manila in 1898), a 200 million peseta (some £7.4 million) project that had defeated the plans for an integrated system of irrigation and water supply for Spanish agriculture in the Cortes.

Perhaps the need for foreign technical assistance dictated the status of pseudo-public enterprise that the Sociedad Española de Construcción Naval acquired. After the original contract had been completed it received numerous new orders, although these were increasingly conditional on it being able to replace imports. The company invested 267 million pesetas in twenty years in order to comply with the navy's goals of self-sufficiency and the 'nationalisation' of naval defence material – from submarines to ammunition – in exchange for a constant backlog of orders.[7]

The First World War provided a favourable series of circumstances for furthering the process of economic nationalisation. As Spain remained neutral in the conflict, its economy prospered thanks to high international prices, underproduction in Europe and lack of competitors. The process of import substitution received a strong boost from shortages due to the war. During these years legislation promoted the nationalisation of foreign assets; as a consequence most of Spanish public debt bonds abroad, which drew interest paid in gold, were bought up by Spanish citizens who thereby found a refuge against war inflation. Tax exemptions also facilitated the purchase of Spanish firms' equity by Spanish nationals.[8]

Industrialisation by import substitution also received a boost with the new Law for the Protection of National Industry, approved in March of 1917, whose general aim was to protect industries which had been established during the war and which felt threatened with the return to normalcy. The protection of the law was actuated through tax exemptions, postponement of tax payments, tax and tariff reductions, preferential interest rates and guaranteed dividends. A new official bank – Banco de Crédito Industrial (BCI) – was established in 1920 as the main agent of the 1917 Law. The new bank's mission was to channel credit at favourable conditions to industrial firms. In June of 1918 another law decreed that all defence material purchased by the state should be produced by Spanish firms; and in June of 1921 the mining industry was 'nationalised', in the sense that mining companies had to be registered in Spain, their foreign employees limited to one third of the total and all their equipment had to be manufactured in Spain. All this was less earthshaking than it sounds, as Río Tinto, Tharsis and many other large foreign concerns went on with business as usual, but it shows the obsession with 'nationalisation' in government circles.

The exposure to postwar European competition threatened the survival of many of the companies created during the war. Shallow markets and lack of experience originated low economies of scale, scope and speed so that the majority of these firms were not able to compete even under the umbrella of the 1906 tariff. Inflation, shortages and speculative hoarding, combined with growing labour unrest, had driven wages and other costs up during the war. Price and wage stickiness increased the problem of competitiveness, so that additional tariff protection was required and provided by the new tariff law of 1922 to guarantee the survival of the nationalist economy.

The Primo de Rivera dictatorship (1923–9), far from complying with what Wicksell termed as the Pareto-optimum 'benevolent dictatorship', provided some degree of political stability, increased the extent of state intervention in economic matters, and pursued nationalist economic policies further. One of its novelties was an extensive public works programme. Road construction and maintenance picked up strongly, tripling the amounts spent the decade before. Railway investment quadrupled with respect to the previous decade (the 1910s) with 31 per cent of that investment being financed by public institutions and instruments. The construction of dams and harbour installations surpassed all previous levels.[9] In an attempt to replace the monarchy's economic and political corruption, the dictator strove to create a new corporatist structure to substitute for the old order. By July of 1926, Miguel Primo de Rivera had initiated a process of industrial modernisation and concentration with growing regulation of enterprises. In September a regulatory board for national industry had been created. Concern was growing among policy makers about whether private initiative alone could foster growth and development in Spain.[10]

Another distinctive trait of economic policy under the Primo de Rivera dictatorship was the expansion of the state banking system. To the Bank of Spain (1782) and the Banco Hipotecario (1872), the Banco de Crédito Industrial had been added in 1920 and reformed in 1926 and 1927. This was considered insufficient, and several other credit institutions were created. The Banco de Crédito Local was founded in May of 1925 and was oriented towards financing local and municipal administrations; the Banco Exterior de España was created in August of 1928 and designed to service Spanish firms dealing in foreign markets; other minor sectorial credit institutions were created for fishing and for agriculture.

Some of the state monopolies, such as postal communication, salt, tobacco, gunpowder and matches, dated back to the seventeenth century. During the first third of the twentieth century, income from the traditional monopolies followed a downward trend and their weight in total revenues was declining at the same time. In order to compensate for this decline a new monopoly was created: that for the distribution and refining of petroleum. This puzzling monopoly (Spain did not itself produce a drop of petroleum) was the pet project of José Calvo Sotelo, finance minister under Primo de Rivera and one of the most remarkable economic nationalists in Spanish history. The monopoly, decreed in 1927, was a tax-farming device: the farmer was a newly created company, the Compañía Arrendataria del Monopolio de Petróleos S.A., (CAMPSA, or Company for the Leasing of the Petrol Monopoly). CAMPSA, whose life extended until Spain's entry into the European Union, was a quintessential nationalist creation, explicitly intended to prevent Standard Oil and Shell from making profits in Spain and, if possible, to find petrol in Spain and develop a refining and petrochemical industry, a distribution network and so on. In his memoirs, Calvo Sotelo relates with relish his cavalier treatment of Sir Henry Deterding, then head of Royal Dutch-Shell, when Deterding paid him a visit to try to dissuade him from establishing the oil monopoly. Calvo Sotelo saw himself as the representative of a small but proud nation teaching a lesson to an international plutocrat. All in all, it can be shown that the oil monopoly was not a good idea. It did not yield as much revenue as ordinary taxes could have, the service CAMPSA gave consumers was dismal, and it also produced exactly the opposite effects of those intended by Calvo Sotelo; as a monopolist, CAMPSA was not interested in prospection or in risking its capital in petrochemicals or even in refining, and so not only did it drag its feet on all these endeavours, but it did all it could to prevent other companies from doing it.[11]

The Second Republic (1931–6) did not bring about a radical swing back to *laissez-faire* free-market economics but rather continuity in the growing interventionism in economic affairs. The priority of the new governing groups was to reform the socio-political and economic life of Spain but this affected the existing degree of economic intervention to a very small degree. It definitely increased the amount of regulation – especially for labour markets, banking, foreign trade, armaments and to some extent railway transportation. The public works programmes were maintained or increased. Even the oil monopoly was retained, after considerable discussion.

In order to face the growing tensions – the economic tensions of the Great Depression, the social tensions of inequality and the political tensions of polarisation – Spain was to follow the same path as other nations in the first decades of the twentieth century. Russia, Italy, Germany and even the United States (the New Deal) had assumed more authoritarian systems of economic governance. There was a mounting demand for economic and political dirigism and in this the Spanish Republic clearly followed the general trend.

ECONOMIC POLICIES IN THE EARLY FRANQUIST PERIOD

Nationalist economic policies reached a paroxysm in Franco's Spain. Even during the Civil War (18 July 1936–1 April 1939) the Franco side, who called themselves the nationalists (*nacionales*), inaugurated economic policies of strong state intervention in the economy, consciously and purposefully imitating those of their Nazi and fascist allies in Germany and Italy. These policies were qualitatively different from those followed by prior regimes, also quite interventionist, in that the Franco government proclaimed total self-sufficiency – autarky – and the development of a powerful military industry as its avowed aims.

Agriculture was the area where these comprehensive nationalistic policies were first implemented. The body entrusted with the carrying out of these policies was the Servicio Nacional del Trigo (National Wheat Agency, SNT). The SNT was created by the Franquist junta during the war, in August 1937, just when the first harvest was about to be collected in nationalist Spain. Originally it was designed to exercise its control only over the wheat market (hence its name) but it soon extended its purview to all grains and legumes, thereby extending its scope over the largest share of agricultural output.

The basic idea behind the SNT was that Spain could and should be self-sufficient in wheat. The main worry of Franquist officials was that there could be a wheat glut. In the early 1930s there had been serious fluctuations in the wheat market due to a number of miscalculations under the Primo de Rivera dictatorship and under the republic. After the shortages of 1931 two bumper harvests in 1932 and 1934 depressed prices even further in a domestic market already depressed by international conditions. This alarmed farmers and increased their discontent and their opposition to the republic. In this context the nationalists championed state intervention in order to sustain prices, with the twin aims of proving the superiority of their methods and of consolidating the support of farmers to the Franco side. The SNT, therefore, was charged with purchasing the whole wheat crop at prices fixed by the Ministry of Agriculture, of which the SNT was a branch, albeit with a considerable degree of autonomy. The SNT then resold wheat to the milling industry at prices also established by the government, and which the millers had to accept, since the SNT was the only legal seller of wheat.

The wheat prices established by the government were on the low side, for two reasons: first, they did not want the main staple in the diet, bread, to be expensive, secondly, since they were afraid of overproduction, they did not want to stimulate it with high prices. Their forecast turned out to be mistaken: shortages ensued. In order not to sell at low official prices (inflation was high during the war, and it continued during the 1940s), farmers started sowing other crops that they could sell freely. The SNT then tried to gain control over new products in order to prevent farmers from evading the agency's control. Soon it was fixing prices even for birdseed. The consequence was a general decline of agricultural output (at least of officially declared production). Those years were remembered in Spain as the 'hungry years' (*los años del hambre*).

Wheat and corn (maize) harvests remained below their prewar level until well into the 1950s. Wheat output in particular remained at two thirds of the prewar per capita volume. Franco's government attributed the desperate situation to a 'pertinacious drought' and resorted to food rationing. The shortages were partially remedied by food imports and by the black market; food rationing and the black market remained active until the mid-1950s. Imports were expensive and difficult during the Second World War, especially since Spain was viewed as an ally of the

Axis powers. The isolation of the Franco regime after the war and its chronic commercial deficit aggravated the food situation, which was palliated by a commercial agreement with Argentina (1947–8), whose dictator, Juan Perón, sympathised ideologically with Franco. The pervasiveness of the black market during those years has made some historians think that the real agricultural output was larger than official figures indicate. In any case, the black market was in fact tolerated by the authorities, as it was a way of contenting both buyers and sellers. This toleration, however, was a tacit recognition of the failure of the regime's agricultural policies.

A question comes to mind: why were these obviously mistaken price policies not rectified? In fact they were, but not until the mid-1950s. If rectification did not come earlier this was probably for several reasons. First, these policies were ideologically motivated, and the winners of the war were not inclined to recognise their errors – all the more so since, in a dictatorship, popular discontent finds few channels of expression. Secondly, the authorities were afraid that letting agricultural prices rise would worsen the inflationary situation. And thirdly, the black market arrangement was, in the end, agreeable to large landowners, who were among the staunchest supporters of Franco; they benefited by selling at higher than official prices, and they were the ones who had the means to buy the co-operation of the officials and to operate semi-clandestine transportation and distribution networks.

Industrial policies were even more imbued by principles of state intervention, economic isolation and autarky. The man who inspired and put into practice these policies was Juan Antonio Suanzes, a naval engineer of extreme views: his radical nationalism had xenophobic overtones, he mistrusted economic liberalism, favoured state intervention and considered industrialisation as being the only way to nation-building and real national sovereignty in the world arena. During his professional life he had occasion to work at the orders of foreign, especially British, engineers, and developed a strong dislike of them, blaming them for the ills of Spain as intruders and agents of hostile interests.[12] Suanzes joined Franco's first cabinet and became Minister of Industry and Commerce in the early years of the Franco regime and at other times. He remained one of the most influential figures in government circles until the early 1960s.

Industrial policies and legislation after the Civil War were directly inspired by Suanzes, who at that time enjoyed the full support of Franco. The twin preoccupations of Suanzes in the immediate post-civil war period were national economic – and hence political – independence, and reconstruction after the ravages of the war. It has been remarked by several historians that the Civil War damaged more dwellings than factories. In fact, in many areas and sectors factories survived the war in a better state than they had before the hostilities, because forced idleness permitted repairs that were not undertaken in busier times. One could safely say that Spanish industry was more affected by obsolescence and lack of imported parts than by material destruction during the Civil War. At any rate, the obsession after the war was reconstruction and production at any price, while the ultimate aim was political independence from more advanced nations. Of course, a requisite for national independence was thought to be the development of the military industry and the exclusion, or at least a strong limitation, of foreign enterprise. Early industrial legislation in post-civil-war Spain was intended to stimulate the private sector to rebuild and develop while investing in sectors that were considered as preferred by the government and keeping foreigners away from posts of control.

These were the aims of two laws issued on 24 October and 24 November 1939, which were accompanied by some other ancillary measures. The first of these laws (for 'protection and development of new industries') proclaimed in its preamble the need 'to redeem Spain from the importation of exotic products which can be made or manufactured within the realm of our Nation'. Its main thrust was the establishment of a new category of industries of 'national interest'. When a firm or a sector was so declared by the state it automatically obtained access to a series of considerable advantages, such as the right to expropriate land, to obtain substantial tax reductions and import facilities, to receive soft loans, and even to have a minimum guaranteed profit. The possibility also existed that the state might declare compulsory the consumption by other firms of the products that had been declared 'of national interest'. The second law (for 'regulation and defence of industry') divided industries according to their military value and established rigid state controls over the sector: permits were needed to establish an industrial firm, to expand it or to change its location. No more than 25 per cent of the capital of an industrial firm could be owned by non-nationals. The law again gave the state the power to enforce the use of certain industrial products in the market; it also empowered the state to fix prices, and to make it compulsory for government agencies to purchase only Spanish products. These laws, accompanied by a dense network of ancillary measures, met with total failure. What the legislator thought was encouragement of 'national' industry turned out to be the kiss of death. Combined with an iron grip upon foreign trade, these policies left little margin for entrepreneurial discretion. Several other factors explain the lack of industrial response: the population was impoverished, savings – and hence loanable funds – were scarce, and so were petroleum and other power sources; on top of all this, the onset of the Second World War introduced an element of uncertainty and aggravated the difficulties of provisioning.

The Spanish authorities, however, blamed the private sector for industrial stagnation. The decision was taken to create another state agency, the Institute of National Industry (Instituto Nacional de Industria, INI),[13] which was established by a law of 25 September 1941. INI was modelled upon the Italian IRI (Istituto per la Ricostruzione Industriale), which had been created in 1933 in order to acquire a large share of Italian industrial firms so as to avoid a banking crash, and thereafter became a gigantic public holding of industrial companies.

The basic ideas behind INI were the following. First, the industrialisation of Spain was indispensable and therefore had to be attained *at any price*. Secondly, the private sector was unable to achieve the desirable level of industrialisation because it was short of the 'spirit of initiative' and also because it was only moved by a myopic profit motive and lacked the requisite means of long-term investment. Thirdly, reliance upon capital and technology imports had to be rejected because they implied 'submission to the will of others, foreign intervention . . . Hence the need for firm state action, embodied in this case by the Institute [of National Industry].'[14] The president of INI from its creation until 1963 was, naturally enough, Juan Antonio Suanzes.

Like IRI, INI became a large holding company: its main activity was the promotion of, or participation in, industries that its directors deemed worthy of support. From the mid-1940s one could speak of an 'INI group' of industrial firms in which the Institute owned a substantial share of equity, or all of it. INI specialised in basic industries, especially the power (petrol and electricity) and iron and steel sectors. It also had a strong presence in transport industries (automobiles, aircraft, ship-building, aviation), mining, chemicals, metalworking and mechanical manufacturing. Probably the INI firm that was best known abroad was the aviation carrier IBERIA, but many INI firms were well known within Spain because they were huge by Spanish standards and employed thousands of workers; such was the case of the iron and steel firm Ensidesa, the automotive manufacturer SEAT, the petrochemical ENCASO, and the electricity giant ENDESA, among others. Later on, especially during the 1960s and thereafter, INI acquired a series of private firms that were on the verge of bankruptcy, such as Altos Hornos del Mediterráneo and Altos Hornos de Vizcaya (iron and steel) or Hunosa (coal), which added to its smokestack giants, giving employment to tens of thousands and saddling the holding with staggering losses.

INI's effort was gigantic, but it must be asked whether it was not also misguided and wasteful. As has been pointed out,[15] Suanzes had 'the mind of an engineer', for whom production was an end in itself regardless of cost (comparative, opportunity, or otherwise). Martín Aceña and Comín point out that it was an 'outstanding agent of import substitution' during the 1950s but that its 'strategy of autarkic and state-directed development led to inefficient resource allocation'.[16] It is worth noting that in spite of INI's role of import substitution, and in spite of the xenophobia of its president, its propensity to import was also very high; this is logical, since autarky was largely a myth. All in all, although INI contributed decisively to the development of Spain's basic industries, the output of these industries was uncompetitive in international markets, and this was INI's Achilles' heel. As Donges[17] put it:

product costs and prices tended to be high when compared with international levels. Therefore state firms who sold their basic outputs to other industries saddled the economic system with a relatively high level of cost . . . This turned . . . in detriment of the international competitiveness of Spanish industry . . . In the last analysis, it does not appear that INI may have contributed . . . to an efficient functioning of private industry or that it may have combated efficaciously the existence of monopolies.

The fight against monopoly was another role that INI could have played and never seems to have undertaken seriously. There are several studies showing that during the 1940s and 1950s there was a considerable degree of monopolisation in Spanish industry.[18] The Spanish state contributed to this with its protectionism and with many laws which, on the pretext of economic nationalism, in fact restricted competition. There are three ways in which a state can fight monopoly: it may legislate against it; it may strike down those laws and regulations that favour it; and it may use public-sector firms to compete in monopolised sectors. Slowly and weakly the Spanish state, from the 1960s on, has employed the first two means, with some results. INI could have been the instrument for the third way, and at some times it was touted to be, such as when Ensidesa was founded, supposedly to break the monopoly of the Altos Hornos companies. In effect, INI has not only not been an effective competitor in monopolistic sectors, but has often allied itself with its would-be rivals to maintain high prices or to obtain government support and in several cases it has played the role of a lifeboat for obsolete firms which were in trouble after protection had been lifted, by acquiring their assets at prices clearly above those of the market or by channelling funds to them. Such was the case with Hunosa, which grouped a number of uncompetitive coal-mining firms acquired in 1967, and of Altos Hornos del Mediterráneo and Altos Hornos de Vizcaya, the largest iron and steel private firms, which were in fact bought by INI in 1978 and 1981 respectively, after having been supported by the state through INI for many years (this was called the 'clandestine INI' by journalists).[19] Thus, in fact, in this field INI has been doing exactly the reverse of what it was expected to do: not only not fighting monopolists, but aiding them in prosperity and in distress. It has thereby contributed to keeping prices high and Spanish industry non-competitive.

The policy of deep state involvement in industry and in agriculture required heavy outlays; hence the need for wide discretionary spending powers for the state and, therefore, for a very weak and subordinate central bank. The trend towards limiting the independence of the Bank of Spain had started with the Banking Law of 1931, and it belonged to a general international current generated by the Great Depression and the Second World War. The Banking Law of 1931 had greatly increased the control the government had over the Bank of Spain. This was achieved by the appointment by the Ministry of Finance of three board members, and by increasing the power the ministry had over the Bank's policies, especially the setting of interest rates. Banking legislation after the Spanish Civil War followed this same interventionist trend. It was consecrated in the Banking Law of 31 December 1946.[20] There were a series of features in this law that made monetary policy subordinate to nationalist agrarian and industrial policies. Spain was one of the few European countries that had never been subjected to the discipline of the gold standard, and this was confirmed in 1946, when the link between fiduciary circulation and the metallic reserves in the Bank of Spain was definitively broken. The bank's monopoly of note issuing was renewed and the control of the state over the bank reinforced through the direct nomination by the cabinet of the bank's governor, deputy governor and five members of the bank's council, plus an extension of the means of control that the Ministry of Finance had over the bank's policies (veto power, amongst others). The 1946 law also subjected the private banks to strict control (similar to that applied to industrial firms) as relates to the establishment of new firms, expansion, and relocation (this is commonly called the '*statu quo* bancario'), and to the setting of interest rates. One of the openly stated aims of interest-rate controls was to ensure that they remained low, so as to encourage private investment and to allow the state to borrow at inexpensive prices.

The banking law also took exchange-rate policies out of the hands of the Bank of Spain and into those of a Foreign Currency Institute (Instituto Español de Moneda Extranjera, IEME), which in fact was a dependency of the Ministry of Industry and Commerce. This permitted the government to exercise strict control over exchange rates, which became a key policy instrument. Combined with quantitative controls over foreign trade (tariff rates became redundant), exchange-rate controls and multiple exchange-rate systems almost totally sealed the Spanish economy from international markets at the government's will. Insulation from foreign market 'contamination', of course, was essential for the autarkic policies of the early years of Francoism.

NATIONALISATION OF FOREIGN COMPANIES

Two interesting examples of nationalism in action were the 'nationalisations' of two foreign firms of long standing, the Barcelona Traction, Light and Power Company and the Río Tinto Company. The Barcelona Traction, familiarly known as 'La Canadiense', had been created in 1911 by the American engineer Frank B. Pearson; it was the main electricity supplier in Catalonia, and the owner of a substantial tramway and railroad network in Barcelona and its periphery. The distribution of its equity was extremely complex, as was the case with other electrical firms organised by Pearson.[21] Although its seat was in Toronto, Canada (hence its popular name), most of its shareholders were British, German and, above all, Belgian. Its controlling packet soon fell into the hands of SOFINA, a German–Belgian holding company whose head was Daniel Heineman, an American financier with German origins. Due to war problems (the Spanish Civil War and its aftermath, then the Second World War), 'La Canadiense' was unable to pay interest on its debentures in the early 1940s, not for lack of cash-flow but due to problems in converting pesetas into other currencies. 'La Canadiense', whose public relations policies left something to be desired and whose accounting was extremely arcane, found itself pitted against the hostility of the Minister of Industry and Commerce in the late 1940s, none other than Juan Antonio Suanzes, whose feelings about submission to the will of others and foreign intervention were, as we know, anything but friendly. Suanzes' ideas were known to Juan March, a colourful and astute Spanish financier, whose shrewdness and lack of scruples were by then legendary. March managed to harp on Suanzes' (and Franco's) extreme nationalist convictions to harass 'La Canadiense' and prevent it from paying its creditors. While doing this March was carrying on negotiations with Heineman trying to buy SOFINA's shares at a reduced price. In December 1946 Suanzes had made a speech in the Franquist Cortes about 'La Canadiense', where he had referred to the 'possible concomitancies of the [Spanish] red [i.e. republican] leaders, directly responsible of enormous crimes and of the injuries suffered by our country', with the directors of SOFINA and even with Paul-Henri Spaak, a Belgian politician who at the time was the secretary-general of the United Nations.

In spite of all this truculent language Heineman stood fast. March then put into practice his alternative plan. Some of his associates, owners of a relatively small number of Barcelona Traction's debentures, sued the company for bankruptcy on the grounds that it had not paid its debt for years. The suit was submitted in a small town, Reus, to make things more difficult to their opponents. A few months afterwards, bankruptcy was declared and an administrator was appointed, thereby depriving the company's managers of access to its premises, documents and so on. Some time afterwards, 'La Canadiense' was declared extinct and its assets sold in auction. They were bought at bargain prices by FECSA (Fuerzas Eléctricas de Cataluña, Sociedad Anónima), a recently created corporation whose main shareholder was none other than Juan March himself. The president of FECSA was Juan March's son and namesake.[22] The case dragged in the courts for twenty years and in the end the International Court at The Hague was unable to produce a substantive verdict. Meanwhile, FECSA's profits had been accruing to its shareholders, largely Juan March and his heirs.

The Río Tinto Company had been exploiting one of the richest copper pyrite lodes in Europe since it acquired it from the Spanish government in 1873. Río Tinto made enormous profits in the period from 1884 to the First World War. Thereafter, with the fall in the price of ores in the 1920s, the world depression in the 1930s, plus the gradual exhaustion of the best veins, the profitability of the company was limited to rather exceptional moments of high copper and sulphur prices. After the Spanish Civil War, with Suanzes' extreme nationalist principles and dislike of Britons on the ascendant, Río Tinto was viewed in Spain as an 'economic Gibraltar', a phrase that was often used in the press and in government circles. The British company was rather unpopular in Spain due to the exclusive Britishness of its managers, and to the toughness of its labour relations. During the 1940s the Río Tinto company was submitted to undisguised pressure by the Spanish government in an attempt to 'nationalise' it. The government control of prices, foreign exchange rates, and production and export quotas was used to coerce the company and induce it to sell.

There were serious problems in the government approach, however. First, by harassing the main producer and exporter of copper and sulphur in Spain, it was hurting the country's economy. Secondly, in the dire circumstances of the 1940s, the Spanish government lacked the wherewithal to purchase Río Tinto outright, and, while it tried to induce private companies to help INI in making an offer, nothing could be achieved. Río Tinto was not as profitable as it used to be, and its future depended largely on government policies, a fact which no doubt discouraged potential private investors. No Juan March appeared on Río Tinto's horizon. The possibility of expropriation was also contemplated, but British retaliation and international outrage were feared. Franco, who very much wanted to rescue Río Tinto, was characteristically slow in making a decision, in this case because he thought that delay played in his favour, as the company's value was bound to decline in time. In this, as in many other things, he was wrong. After long and tortuous negotiations, Río Tinto was acquired in 1954 by a group of the top Spanish banks, who, induced by the Spanish government and co-ordinated by the Governor of the Bank of Spain, purchased two thirds of its capital for a rather high price. The reasons for this deal were that earlier that same year an offer to purchase Río Tinto had been made by an American company (Texas Gulf Sulphur), and also that the Spanish government was afraid that a hard-nosed approach on its part would have provoked a second uproar after that caused by the rough treatment meted out to the Barcelona Traction Company. Thus the nationalist approach to 'nationalisation' of foreign companies was far from successful: due to the high-handed methods used in the case of Barcelona Traction, the prestige of the country was seriously hurt abroad; and in order to obtain a political victory, the purchase of Río Tinto was made in disadvantageous conditions.[23]

EVOLUTION

The resounding failure of nationalist policies was apparent in the economic stagnation of the 1940s. Compared to the per capita income of other European countries, Spanish income hardly grew during this period. The recovery of Italy, France and Germany after the Second World War was swift, whereas in Spain the per capita levels of 1935 (the last year before the Civil War) were not reached again until the mid-1950s. Ten years after the end of the Second World War, the Italian index of industrial output nearly doubled its 1940 value; ten years after the end of the Civil War, the Spanish index was below the 1935 level. The performances of France and Great Britain were closer to that of Italy: Spain's failure was the exception.[24]

Spain started to grow in the 1950s. This was due to several factors: first, the pull of Europe's growth; secondly, a gradual loosening of the most extreme autarkist policies; thirdly, the onset of Spanish–American co-operation, which started in 1951 and was made firm with the Military Base Agreements of 1953. The dismantling of the most restrictive economic policies was initiated by a new cabinet in 1951, which did not include Suanzes who was replaced by two more flexible men (the Industry and Commerce Ministry was split into two); a better manager also became Minister of Agriculture. From then on the SNT started paying more realistic prices, and soon the problems were of overproduction of grains. But in essence, although somewhat mitigated, the nationalistic policies remained and their incompatibility with economic growth became obvious. Inflation shot up, worker unrest reappeared after more than ten years of quiescence, and balance of payments deficits became recurrent and menacing. After years of hesitation, autarky was officially abandoned as an objective in 1959, when a stabilisation plan, drawn up in agreement with the International Monetary Fund and the OECD, was put into effect. Most quantitative restrictions to international trade were abolished, together with multiple exchange rates. A new and very protectionist tariff was installed in 1961, however. A new Banking Law in 1962 partially removed some of the strongest controls over banking. Suanzes angrily abandoned INI in 1963, complaining in a letter to Franco about 'fundamental discrepancies'.[25] Thus, slow, cautious and partial liberalisation proceeded haltingly during the final fifteen years of the Franco dictatorship. The definitive abandonment of nationalist economic policies arrived with the democratic reforms after Franco's death in 1975 and the accession of Spain to the European Economic Community in 1986.

CONCLUSIONS

The balance of nationalist economic policies in Spanish twentieth-century history is an actively debated topic. Tariff protectionism has been defended by some authors and criticised by others.[26] The same is true of the interventionist economic policies of the Primo de Rivera dictatorship. The extreme nationalist policies of the first twenty years of Franco's long rule (1939–75) have few defenders now, although a number of Franquist economists extolled them in their time. The issues are extremely complex. There is no doubt that the twentieth century has witnessed not only the highest levels of economic growth in Spanish history (this is true of many European countries) but also Spain's transition from backwardness to economic modernity. It is also true that this is the period when economic nationalism reached its highest levels in the country. Some will think that this coincidence implies causation. The opposite view is also possible: that nationalist economic policies were a hindrance rather than an agent of growth. There is some evidence in favour of this latter view, which seems the most plausible to us: growth was fastest in the periods after the relaxation of the most extreme nationalist measures: during the 1960s, after the liberalising policies following the stabilisation plan of 1959, and in the 1980s, after further liberalisation during the transition to democracy and in the early democratic years. It could even be argued that the recent (1997–8) high rates of growth are the consequence of the further liberalisation that followed the arrival of the Popular (centre-right) Party to power in March of 1996. Of course the subject requires and warrants further study. A careful comparison with other countries in similar circumstances (Italy, Portugal and Greece come readily to mind) could yield more positive conclusions.

NOTES

1 J. Simpson, *Spanish Agriculture: The Long Siesta, 1765–1965* (Cambridge, 1995).
2 R. Cameron, *France and the Economic Development of Europe, 1800–1914. Conquest of Peace and Seeds of War* (Princeton, 1961); G. Tortella, *Banking, Railroads, and Industry in Spain 1829–1874* (New York, 1977).
3 P. Fraile and A. Escribano, 'The Spanish 1898 disaster: the drift towards national protectionism', Working Paper 98–03, Universidad Carlos III, Madrid, 1998, p. 17.
4 A. Gwinner, 'La política comercial de España en los últimos decenios' in F. Estapé (ed.), *Textos olvidados* (Madrid, 1973), pp. 253–333 at p. 333.
5 M. Montero, *Mineros, banqueros y navieros* (Leioa, 1990), pp. 255–6.
6 See J. M. Serrano Sanz, *El viraje proteccionista en la Restauración. La política comercial española, 1875–1895* (Madrid, 1987) and 'El proteccionismo y el desarrollo económico en la Restauración. Reflexiones para un debate', *Revista de Historia Económica* 7 (1989), 133–56.
7 S. Houpt and J. M. Ortiz-Villajos (eds.), *Astilleros Españoles, 1872–1998. La construcción naval en España* (Madrid, 1998).

8 José Luis Garcia Delgado (ed.), *España, 1898–1936: Estructuras y cambio. Coloquio de la Universidad Complutense sobre la España Contemporánea* (Madrid, 1984), p. 212.

9 A. Gómez Mendoza, 'Las obras públicas (1850–1935)' in F. Comín and P. Martín Aceña (eds.), *Historia de la empresa pública en España* (Madrid, 1991), pp. 177–204 at pp. 192, 196–8 and 200–1. On the general economic policies of the dictatorship, see J. Velarde Fuertes, *Política económica de la dictadura* (Madrid, 1968).

10 M. Cabrera, *La patronal ante la II República. Organizaciones y estrategia (1931–1936)* (Madrid, 1983); M. Cabrera et al., *Europa en crisis. 1919–1939* (Madrid, 1991), pp. 62–4.

11 Gabriel Tortella, 'CAMPSA y el monopolio de petróleos, 1927–1947' in P. Martín Aceña and F. Comín (eds.), *Empresa pública e industrialización en España* (Madrid, 1990), pp. 81–116; Gabriel Tortella, 'El monopolio de petróleos y CAMPSA, 1927–1947', Hacienda Pública Española' Núm. Homenaje a D. Felipe Ruiz Martín, coordinado por F. Comin y J. Zafra; Gabriel Tortella, Mercedes Cabrera and Sebastián Coll, 'Historia de CAMPSA. Los primeros veinte años, 1927–1947' (1986, unpublished); J. Calvo Sotelo, *Mis servicios al Estado. Seis años de gestión. Apuntes para la Historia* (2nd edn, Madrid, 1974).

12 A. Ballestero, *Juan Antonio Suanzes, 1891–1977. 'La política industrial de la postguerra'* (León, 1993), chs. 3–4.

13 The initial plan was to call it the 'Instituto Nacional de Autarquía': see P. Martín Aceña and F. Comín, *INI. 30 años de industrialización de España* (Madrid, 1991), p. 78.

14 Cited in *ibid.*, pp. 81 and 82.

15 P. Schwarz and M. J. Gonzalez, *Una historia del Instituto Nacional de Industria (1941–1976)* (Madrid, 1978).

16 Martín Aceña and Comín, *INI*, p. 605.

17 J. B. Donges, *La industrialización en España. Políticas, logros, perspectivas* (Barcelona, 1976), pp. 42–3.

18 F. de la Sierra, *La concentración económica en las industrias básicas españolas* (Madrid, 1953); J. Velarde Fuertes, 'Consideraciones sobre algunas actividades monopolísticas en el mercado papelero español', *Revista de Economía Política* 3(3) (1955), 29–125; C. Muñoz Linares, 'El pliopolio en algunos sectores del sistema económico español', *Revista de Economía Política* 6(1) (1955), 3–66; R. Tamames, *La lucha contra los monopolios* (Madrid, 1961); R. Tamames, *Los monopolios en España* (Madrid, 1967).

19 Martín Aceña and Comín, *INI*, pp. 507–9; R. Tamames, *Estructura económica de España* (19th edn, Madrid, 1990), pp. 234–5 and 331–2.

20 For a summary of the 1946 law, see P. Martín Aceña and M. A. Pons, 'Spanish banking after the Civil War, 1940–1962', *Financial History Review* 1 (1994), 121–38 at pp. 123–4. For a longer description, J. Sardá, 'El Banco de España (1931–1962)' in Felipe Ruiz Martín et al., *El Banco de España. Una historia económica* (Madrid, 1970), pp. 455–60. On the 1931 law, see G. Tortella

and J. Palafox, 'Banking and industry in Spain, 1918–1936', *Journal of European Economic History* 13 (1984), 81–111 at pp. 101–3.

21 C. Armstrong and H. V. Nelles, 'Corporate enterprise in the public service sector: the performance of Canadian firms in Mexico and Brazil, 1896–1930' in C. Marichal (ed.), *Foreign Investment in Latin America: Impact on Economic Development, 1850–1930* (Milan, 1994), pp. 69–92.

22 Ballestero, *Juan Antonio Suanzes*, pp. 250–68 and A. Adany and J. Larraz, *La quiebra de la Barcelona Traction, Light and Power Company, Limited. A propósito de un dictamen. Cartas cruzadas entre* (Barcelona, 1957), Annex 3. See also B. Díaz Nosty, *La irresistible ascensión de Juan March* (Madrid, 1977), pp. 366–90; A.Dixon, *Señor monopolio. La asombrosa vida de Juan March* (Barcelona, 1985), ch. XIX; and H. Capel (ed.), *Las tres chimeneas. Implantación industrial, cambio tecnológico y transformación de un espacio urbano barcelonés*, 3 vols. (Barcelona, 1994), vol. III, pp. 15–20.

23 D. Avery, *Not on Queen Victoria's Birthday. The Story of the Río Tinto Mines* (London, 1974); C. E. Harvey, *The Río Tinto Company. An Economic History of a Leading International Mining Concern, 1873–1954* (Penzance, 1981); A. Gómez Mendoza, *El 'Gibraltar económico': Franco y Riotinto, 1936–1954* (Madrid, 1994). Some glimpses of how the negotiations proceeded can be culled from the board meetings of the Banco Central and Banco Hispano Americano (among the purchasers of Río Tinto in 1954) of 23 June, 31 August and 24 November, and 30 June, 30 September and 28 October 1954 respectively.

24 G. Tortella, *El desarrollo de la España contemporánea. Historia económica de los siglos XIX y XX* (Madrid, 1994), pp. 197–9 and 273–4; see L. Prados de la Escosura and J. C. Sanz, 'Growth and macroeconomic performance in Spain, 1939–93' in N. F. R. Crafts and G. Toniolo (eds.), *Economic Growth in Europe since 1945* (Cambridge, 1996), pp. 355–87 for a stylised economic history of the Franco and post-Franco period.

25 Ballestero, *Juan Antonio Suanzes*, pp. 415–16.

26 Richard Sylla, Richard Tilly and Gabriel Tortella (eds.), *The State, the Financial System and Economic Modernization* (Cambridge, 1999), pp. 159–60.

CHAPTER EIGHT

The economic background to the Basque question in Spain

Montserrat Gárate Ojanguren

> Perhaps more than any other one in the Peninsula, the Basque people has had to endure, from opposing factions, distorted inter-pretations of its history.
>
> Julio Caro Baroja

INTRODUCTION

The Basque autonomous community occupies an area of 7,235 square kilometres, which represents 1.43 per cent of the Spanish territory and its population, of slightly more than 2,100,000 inhabitants, comprises 5.41 per cent of the Spanish total. The Basque autonomous community is made up of three provinces, Alava, Guipúzcoa and Vizcaya, the first of which being historically the least densely inhabited – even today its population amounts to barely 13 per cent of the community's and it is far behind Vizcaya in industrial development.

The so-called 'Basque question' is generally understood abroad as the reflection of radical nationalism. An important manifestation of this nationalism is seen to be violence – the latter being the way to attain the Basque country's independence from Spain. Nevertheless, thus under-stood the phenomenon does not correspond with reality. The Basque question is something entirely different and far more complex, and its roots are to be found in the Basque people's own history.

Many scholars who have studied the different nationalist movements in Europe at the close of the nineteenth century and the early twentieth century have pointed out the importance of economic factors in the development of nationalist feeling. Some of these authors have gone so far as to propose that economic changes stimulate the awakening of national feeling in certain countries. In the Basque case the economy has a further significance, since the Basque economic model shows special traits within the Spanish general model, both legally as well as in its structure and development process.

All this considered, and in order to appraise the economic framework in the Basque country and its own particular traits within the Spanish framework, this chapter is divided into two parts: first, a brief analysis of the Basque country's history and characteristics, with special attention to its ruling system and the changes undergone since the middle of the twentieth century, and secondly a concise study of the basic economic changes undergone during the twentieth century and their relation to the Basque fiscal system.

THE BASQUE *FUEROS* IN THEIR HISTORICAL PERSPECTIVE

The ruling system of the provinces actually comprising the Basque autonomous community – Alava, Guipúzcoa and Vizcaya[1] – is encoded in a legal corpus known for a long time as '*fueros*', which can easily be defined as the consuetudinary law in force in the Basque country. These *fueros*, or the Basque common law, have shaped a specific ruling system throughout the centuries. When the Basque provinces freely joined the Kingdom of Castille – all three did not do so at the same time – each one of them brought along its own laws and customs that the king of Castille, and later the king of Spain, was bound to keep. Therefore, the *fueros* have never been – and are still not – privileges bestowed graciously by the king. Besides, it is important to note that if the *fueros* have doubtless framed the relationships between the Basque provinces and the crown, they have also, and foremost, defined Basque society's social and institutional relationships throughout the centuries. This double dimension explains that the loss of the *fueros* had very complex consequences in the Basque country.

The *fueros*'s legal scope is ample, though there are four aspects that ought to be emphasised in view of their importance: political organisation; the '*Pase foral*'; tax exemptions; and military service.

(a) Political organisation. The main trait of the Basques' political organisation are the 'juntas' or provincial assemblies, democratically elected by those who had a right to vote due primarily to their being Basque-born, which accounts for the idea of the Basques' general noble status. These provincial assemblies were legislative chambers, and they met at least once a year to elect in turn a junta or governing assembly commissioned to deal with provincial government matters throughout the year. The executive scope of these assemblies was ample, comprising budget, public health, police, schooling system, public works, agriculture and so on. The juntas of Alava and Guipúzcoa also had judicial powers.[2]

(b) The '*Pase foral*'. *Foral* approval has to be understood in line with the medieval idea of the king sharing the power to the extent that neither of the parties – king or Basque provinces – could take decisions without the agreement of the other.[3] Therefore, the juntas or assemblies had the right to give or withhold their consent to any law or measure decreed by the central power, which would be in force only once the junta had judged it was not contrary to its *fueros*.

(c) Tax exemptions. The Basque provinces were never included in the Castillian tax system – the only exception being the 'Alcabala' tax – on account of which they were called 'exempted provinces'.[4] This circumstance does not mean that they did not contribute to the state's expenses, but whenever they did so it was of their own free will.

In addition, there were no customs posts on the Basque provinces' border with France or along its coastline. Therefore, continental goods imported into the Basque country for 'the sole consumption of its inhabitants' were duty free. However, there did exist customs posts on the Basque provinces' border with Castille and Aragon.

(d) Military service. In peacetime the Basques were also exempted from military service.[5] When Spain entered into war all able men aged from eighteen to sixty were compulsorily drafted into the army, though in the Basque country the juntas had to give their approval beforehand. Likewise, it was the juntas' prerogative to appoint the officers in charge of the Basque forces, who had to be natives of the Basque country. Finally, as long as they served within the Basque country's boundaries the Basques engaged in military service received no wages; otherwise, the king was obliged to pay army wages.

What was the central power's attitude towards Basque *fueros*? Throughout the centuries there have been many attempts to limit the legal scope of the *fueros*, particularly its tax system.

Already as early as the reign of King Henry IV (1454–74) the Castillian Monarchy tried to enforce new taxes on the Basque country. During the Austrian dynasty, Philip II (1556–98), Philip III (1598–1621) and Philip IV (1621–65) continuously attempted to tax salt, as well as to introduce other taxes in the Basque provinces. As these attempts went on, the Basque people's reaction became stronger.

The arrival of the first Bourbon king at the Spanish throne in 1700 meant the reinforcement of a policy of administrative uniformity for all Spanish territories. The central power's pressure over the different Spanish regions was increased. This new policy led King Philip V to the abolition of the *fueros* in Catalonia and in the Kingdom of Valencia. As for the Basque provinces, Philip V ordered the establishment of customs posts on the French frontier, thus altering the *foral* system. The reaction in the Basque country to such a one-sided measure was so immediate and unanimous that, in 1722, the king was obliged to remove the customs posts from the French frontier.

The same policy explains how in 1776 Guipúzcoa was deprived of its *fueros*. On this occasion, four years of negotiations were required so that Guipúzcoa could recover its old rights.

The offensive against the Basque *foral* system increased at the beginning of the nineteenth century. The Cadiz Constitution of 1812 was clearly biased about the *fueros*, as it proclaimed unequivocally the unity of the Spanish nation. From then on, the attempts to abolish the *fueros* would be continuous. In 1820, the Liberals succeeded in applying various common norms in the Basque provinces, which primarily affected customs duties and military service, which then became obligatory for all Basques. Although King Ferdinand VII swore to respect the *fueros* in 1823, as he had previously done in 1814, the fact remains that his tax policy concerning the Basque provinces contravened his sworn promises.[6] Furthermore, the Bourbon policy represented an even greater danger for the significance of the *fueros*, as it declared that the *fueros* were nothing but a privilege conceded by the crown.

The dynastic troubles that followed the death of King Ferdinand VII encouraged the outbreak in 1836 of the first of the three civil wars that would be known as Carlist wars. Besides the dynastic issue, this war was also fought to preserve the *fueros*. The Carlists struggled to uphold the *fueros* while the reformist Liberals wanted to do away with them. According to the former, the *fueros* represented ancestral ways and laws inherited from a long historical experience; on the other hand, what the Liberals pursued in their attempt to reduce the legal scope of the *fueros* – if not their abolition – was to question the lifestyle and indigenous ruling system of the Basque country.

Throughout the first civil war (1833–9), the central government that had aligned itself with the Liberals brought about a series of measures contrary to the *fueros*. In 1835 it tried to introduce in the Basque country the officially stamped paper and the salt tax. A year after, in 1836, the judicial system in force in the rest of Spain was established in the Basque provinces. Finally, in 1837, the *foral* governments or 'diputaciones' were replaced by uncompromising provincial governments organised along lines similar to those in other Spanish provinces.

The first civil war ended in August 1839, with a Liberal triumph over the Carlist party. Its consequences would be felt very soon. In November of that same year it was determined that the representatives of the Basque provinces and Navarre in the Congress and Senate should be elected according to the electoral laws in operation for the rest of Spain, and not according to their own system. In January 1841, the *Pase foral* was abolished in Alava, Guipúzcoa and Vizcaya. The Basque local administrative organisation was to be replaced by the Spanish one, while the Basque country's own judicial organisation was replaced by that of the Spanish state. Customs posts were finally established along the Basque coastline and the French frontier.

Social uneasiness in the Basque country grew worse, as the war had breached the defences that had hitherto sheltered Basque society. To meet the challenge, businessmen and industrialists founded new manufacturing enterprises, which needed the Spanish market to sell the goods that they were potentially capable of producing. In this sense, the establishment of customs posts on the French frontier meant welcome protection from competitive foreign manufactured goods, as well as free access to the Spanish market.[7]

Social unrest in the Basque country following the loss of the main historical rights consequent on the demise of the *fueros* was partially reduced with some of the compensations offered in 1844, when the *foral* governments recovered most of their old rights. However, these were never to include judicial powers.

The outbreak of the second civil or Carlist war in 1870 was partly caused by the weakening of the *foral* system, which had now lost much of its main substance. During the previous decades the *fueros* had been reduced to only three – nevertheless important – elements. These were autonomous organisation of the Basque provinces, exemption from military service and tax privileges.

But the prolonged consequences of the first civil war had given birth to a radical social background that became the background for the outbreak of the second war. From the Carlist party's point of view, the only link between the Basque provinces and Spain was none other than the king. In line with this thesis, the historical agreement between the Spanish sovereign and the Basque provinces could never imply that the Basques had to renounce their laws, ways and own ruling system. And because the Basque country enjoyed an indubitable status of historical freedom, the Liberal forces fighting the Carlist party in the Basque country were considered an army of occupation. In the first place, the Carlists defended not only their own ways of government, they also stressed the value and uniqueness of their country's ancient language: the Basque language.

The triumph of the Liberal forces that ended the second civil war in 1876 once more had immediate consequences for the Basque provinces. A law passed in July 1876 put an end to the traditional *foral* regime, or of what was left of it, forcing the Basques to accept compulsory military service and to share the fiscal burden of the state's expenses.[8] Likewise, it determined that since the *fueros* had been finally suppressed, the Basque provinces had to join the 'Economic Concert' system (see below) common to the remaining Spanish provinces. At the same time, the *foral* governments as such disappeared, though not without first putting up tough resistance to this measure.[9]

All of these measures aggravated the already strained relations between the central government and the Basque provinces, so that the former feared a Basque revolt. After various negotiations with the Basque provincial authorities – already deprived of their *foral* powers – the Spanish government came to an agreement that, notwithstanding its purely economic nature, would attain historical significance. Thus in November 1877 it became established that the Basque provinces' share or 'quota' in the payment of the state's expenses would be provided by the government or 'diputación' of each province, which, in their role as institutions authorised to collect taxes, 'were empowered to establish the way they considered most harmonious with the Basque country's own circumstances'.[10] Accordingly, the *diputación* of each Basque province could decide the amount of tax pressure to be applied to the different economic sectors. Hardly a month later, the *diputación* of Vizcaya decided that its quota to the Spanish Central Treasury would be collected from taxing goods and expenses. Thus began the economic policy to be developed in the Basque provinces: no overtaxing of industrial activity, with special care to be taken to promote manufacturing.

A Royal Decree passed by the central government on 28 February 1878 ratified the system's validity for both parties involved – the Spanish state and the Basque provinces – thus establishing the basis of what came to be called the 'Economic Concert' (Concierto Económico). As was expressed by the July 1876 law, originally the term 'Concert' did not exactly imply the acknowledgement of taxation sovereignty for the Basque country. Nevertheless, the means devised by the Basque provinces for raising taxes with which to satisfy their quota at the Spanish Treasury, acknowledged the *de facto* existence of fiscal sovereignty in the Basque country. Therefore, the February 1878 decree may well be considered to be the birth certificate of the Economic Concert,[11] even though strictly speaking the Economic Concert is but a consequence of the Basque country's history.

Despite some brief interruptions, the Economic Concert has stayed alive throughout the years up to the present day. Its meaning is well explained by what a remarkable non-nationalist Spanish politician said in 1935: 'The Economic Concert must be respected, and not because it is a privilege, but rather because of historical reasons rooted in our oldest historical past and because they have a long secular tradition in History.'[12]

What has been the Economic Concert's consolidating process in the twentieth century? It has evolved around three main principles: fiscal proportionality, quota evaluation with successive updating revisions[13] and the agreement system.

(a) Fiscal proportionality. If the Economic Concert implies that the Basque provinces are compelled to share the payment of the state's expenses, it means that there exists a fiscal proportionality basis; that is, the Basque provinces' share is proportional to that of the other Spanish provinces.

(b) Quota evaluation. The amount of the share or quota provided by the Basque provinces has to be evaluated anew in accordance with economic changes. That is why the quota's duration is temporary.

(c) Agreement system. The Economic Concert is agreed upon by law, which means that it is established by an agreement between the Spanish state and the Basque country, and that therefore it cannot be altered unilaterally. The principle underlying the agreement system was historically the essence of the *foral* philosophy in the Basque country.

Born following the end of the second civil or Carlist war, the First Economic Concert lasted until 1887. The law of 29 June 1887 introduced the Second Economic Concert, which contained some innovations. For example, the quota could henceforth only be modified after *hearing* the opinion of the Basque *diputaciones*. The lives of later Economic Concerts were to be increasingly long. The Fourth Economic Concert lasted from 1906 to 1925, and the Fifth Economic Concert lasted even longer, from 1925 to 1951.[14]

During the Spanish Civil War (1936–9), General Franco abolished *foral* rights in 1937 and with them the Economic Concert in two of the Basque provinces – Guipúzcoa and Vizcaya – as a punishment for their siding with the Republican Party.

The social tension that prevailed in the Basque country throughout the regime of General Franco (1939–75) increased nationalist feeling among many Basques. In 1959 ETA (Euskadi ta Askatasuna[15]) was born, a leftist military organisation that soon led the radical nationalist movement.[16] Franco's state policy favoured the rise of radical nationalism, the develoment and historical significance of which would have been unthinkable, if not impossible, had Basque nationalism not been compelled to engage in resistance activity in the face of extreme political conditions marked by social conflict and unbearable cultural repression.[17]

The new political regime that followed the death of General Franco in 1975 meant a turning point in the history of Spain, and also in that of the Basque country. Basque society was divided between those who supported political reform and those who embraced a radical rupturist position. The Spanish Constitution, which was approved in 1978, acknowledged the historical identity, or 'differential fact', of the three Basque provinces, which comprise the Basque autonomous community; Basque historical rights, such as autonomous government and a separate tax system based on the Economic Concert, were thus finally acknowledged as constitutional rights. Only a year later, in 1979, came the approval of the Basque Country Autonomy Statute, also known as the Guernica Statute. For those who had supported political reform, the new political framework of the Guernica Statute meant the beginning of the long-desired reforms. From the radicals' viewpoint, however, the Guernica Statute was far from satisfactory, thus causing the radical movement flatly to reject the changes and the new political and economic structural processes undergone in the Basque country throughout the past decades.

The Guernica Statute conferred political and public competences upon the Basque country. A step forward was taken in 1981 with the Economic Concert Law, which outlined the policy that henceforth would mould the Economic Concert agreed between central government and the Basque autonomous community until 2001.[18]

The public finance competences with which the *diputaciones* of the Basque provinces were empowered strengthened local manufacturing development. It is thus that twentieth-century economic development in the Basque country, so different from Spanish economic experiences, may be partially understood. Additionally, the new legal status of the Economic Concert has implied the recovery of some of the historical Basque rights.

THE STAGES OF THE BASQUE ECONOMY'S DEVELOPMENT DURING THE TWENTIETH CENTURY

A comparative analysis

The historic development of the Basque economy has been determined to a great extent by the legal–economic peculiarities referred to above. With the establishment of customs authorities along the frontier with France in 1841 (despite the protests of some sectors), Basque production became protected against foreign competition. Thus, most entrepreneurs became the protagonists of an industrialisation process in the Basque country. It was the paper mills, textile factories, ironworks and metallurgy industries which, in a broad sense, led the Industrial Revolution. Moreover, the new customs arrangements allowed direct access for the products of the above-mentioned industries into the Spanish domestic market. Upon the establishment of the Economic Concerts after 1876, the Basque economy displayed considerable growth. The new system allowed Basque institutions to decide upon the sectors that were to bear greater or lesser fiscal pressure. In this period industrial activity was clearly favoured if compared with other parts of Spain. The immediate spin-off was the establishment of a considerable number of industrial companies in the Basque country. Since the late nineteenth century, under the system of the Economic Concert, there had been sectors that had been outstanding in their large volume of production and which brought forth a high degree of industrial specialisation – for example, sectors such as metallurgy, paper mills or ship-building. At the same time, some other traditional industries, such as arms manufacturing, also grew. The Basque economy evolved towards a level of industrialisation that was well above the average of the rest of Spanish society. This degree of industrialisation has been a characteristic feature of the Basque economy throughout the twentieth century.

However, the economic indicators of the Basque economy, considerably above the Spanish average until the 1970s, have been converging with those of the rest of Spain in recent years. The economic crisis of 1973 was particularly serious for the most developed industrial sectors in the Basque country. This added to the problems of national identity that arose after the 1936–9 Civil War and which only became more accentuated in the course of the 1960s and 1970s. In that period, even with the Economic Concert abolished, the Basque national issue and the claim of Basque historic rights were strongly represented. From the 1970s onwards, the crisis of Basque identity was accompanied by the general economic crisis.

Bearing the above changes in mind, the different stages that the Basque economy went through in the twentieth century can also be understood. The first third of the century was marked, in general terms, by considerable growth of the industrial sector, which strengthened the relative position of the Basque economy in the modernisation process of Spain. A second stage can be discerned in the 1930s. The international crisis overlapped with the crisis of the Spanish economy itself and the Civil War between 1936 and 1939.

With the conclusion of the war, the Spanish economy was to start an autarkic phase, which extended throughout the 1940s. The Basque economy continued to grow, until 1973, in the sectors that had already been outstanding in the first third of the century.

From 1973 onwards, the crisis especially affected the most characteristic sectors of the Basque economy. Industrial rationalisation has had a high social and economic cost. Moreover, the crisis coincided with political changes that have had particularly critical results in the Basque country.

The first third of the twentieth century in the Basque country

Even though the Economic Concerts did favour the Basque industrial sector, there were other factors, both endogenous and exogenous, which also contributed to the great economic expansion. Along the endogenous causes was the protectionism of the Spanish market. Among the exogenous causes, there was Spanish neutrality in the 1914–18 war, which opened up exceptional opportunities for the Basque economy; for instance: the profit of the largest Basque iron and steel company in 1917 amounted to 110 per cent of the capital stock and, at the same time, this company was able to increase its capital stock from 32.75 million pesetas to 98.25 million; in 1918 some shipping companies had earnings exceeding 200 per cent of their paid-up capital.[19]

There are some features that explain this growth. In the first place, there was the great polarisation that took place in the Basque country towards specific industrial sectors. Outstanding among these were steelworks and the mechanical-engineering industry (machine tools, shipbuilding, firearms, railroad supplies and so on), along with paper and cement manufacture. Secondly, Basque financial institutions had great stature on the map of the Spanish economy. Thirdly, the proportion of the working population employed in the manufacturing sector – a result of the modernisation of the Basque economy – was well ahead of other areas of Spain.

The concentration of Basque industry in specific sectors had already started at the end of the nineteenth century. Thus, by 1884, a single Basque establishment manufactured 45.4 per cent of the total Spanish production of cast iron.[20] Such leadership on the part of Basque iron and steel plants was to be confirmed in successive years. In 1886–90, production of cast iron in Biscay amounted to 77 per cent of total Spanish production. The rise in production was accompanied by fusions of iron and steel plants. In 1902 a large company, Altos Hornos de Vizcaya, was set up in Biscay, as the result of the merger of three big iron and steel plants (Altos Hornos de Bilbao, La Vizcaya and La Iberia). The capital stock of the new company exceeded 32 million pesetas. This concern was to become the leader in its sector, with iron and steel production of around 60 per cent of total Spanish production. For example, in 1905, the production of Altos Hornos de Vizcaya alone was very high when compared with total Spanish production (see table 8.1).

Some years later, in 1929, pig-iron production in Biscay amounted to 60.9 per cent of total Spanish output. As regards steel, Biscay produced 56 per cent of the Spanish total.[22] The growth of the metallurgical sector in Biscay was mainly due to the existence of ore deposits; adequate capital to finance new plant, thanks – among other things – to the profit obtained from the sale of iron ore to England, and easy access of English coal to the port of Bilbao.[23]

Under the shelter of the growth of the iron and steel industry in the Basque country, ship-building, the production of railroad supplies, armaments, machine tools and bicycles flourished. They were all favoured by the higher protectionist policy enforced in Spain in the early part of the twentieth century. Such industries took up part of the iron produced in Basque ironworks. These new concerns were primarily located in the two most industrialised provinces in the Basque country, namely Biscay and Guipúzcoa, even though their economic structures differed greatly. Thus in Biscay, thanks to the large capital accumulation, the ship-building industries that were established in the early part of the twentieth century were large scale and, through their shareholders, they were connected to the iron and steel plants. On the other hand, in the neighbouring province of Guipúzcoa the firms were smaller and they were scattered over almost the whole province. At the same time, production was more diversified. However, while Biscay became the great-

Table 8.1. *AHV's production expressed as a percentage of total Spanish production for the year 1905*[21]

Production	% of total
Pig iron	55
Bessemer steel	100
Siemens steel	44
Rolled and hammered iron	60

est manufacturer of iron in Spain, Guipúzcoa was to become the greatest paper manufacturer. This sector began its modernisation in the Basque country after 1841, with the starting up, in Guipúzcoa, of the first web paper[24] factory in Spain. In the last third of the nineteenth century, the output of Basque paper mills almost trebled. In 1902, also in the province of Guipúzcoa, the firm La Papelera Española was set up, which made the Basque country the foremost producer of paper and allied products. In 1920 Guipúzcoa's output amounted to 60 per cent of total Spanish paper production. The concentration in metallurgy, shipping and paper manufacture compelled Basque entrepreneurs to resort to forming limited companies. In 1922, almost one fourth of all Spanish joint-stock companies with limited liability had their registered offices in the Basque country.[25]

Industrial growth in the Basque country was accompanied by a great expansion of the financial sector. The extent of the financial boom can be judged both through the founding of new concerns and through the development of existing ones. Apart from the Banco de Bilbao, founded in 1857, other banks were set up in the Basque country in the late nineteenth and early twentieth centuries. Some of them were incorporated thanks basically to Basque capital funds: among them were Banco de Comercio (1891), Banco Guipuzcoano (1899), Banco de Biscay (1901), Crédito de la Unión Minera (1901) and Banco de San Sebastián (1909). Some financial institutes were also set up abroad in the first third of the twentieth century, including Union Bank of Spain and England, Banco Internacional and Sindicato Hispano-Inglés.

As a consequence of such an expansion, the Basque country displayed a high degree of concentration both in the number of financial concerns and in the volume of resources. In 1920, out of the 126 companies and credit banks existing in Spain, Biscay and Guipúzcoa respectively ranked second and fourth as to the paid-up capital.[26] In 1922, the banks

Table 8.2. *Working population by sector*

	Basque country			Spain		
Year	Primary (%)	Secondary (%)	Tertiary (%)	Primary (%)	Secondary (%)	Tertiary (%)
1910	34.7	37.2	28.1	66.00	15.82	18.18

in Bilbao accounted for 22.2 per cent of the registered capital of all Spanish banks. Their situation was even stronger if the legal bank reserves are taken into account. In fact, Bilbao banks held 42.1 per cent of total Spanish legal bank reserves.[27] The boost given by Basque banks to some industrial sectors was remarkable. Thus, the Banco de Bilbao acquired shares in the metallurgical and railroad sector; the Banco Guipuzcoano and Banco de Vizcaya invested in electrical, mining, insurance and other sectors.

Industrial development and modernisation of company structures made the Basque country the most industrialised and developed area in the whole Spanish territory. The distribution of the working population serves to confirm the modern nature of its economy. At the same time, such economic growth fostered the creation of new jobs, which is why the Basque country experienced strong immigration from various Spanish regions. By the year 1910, there was a greater proportion of the working population engaged in the manufacturing sector than in any other. In this respect, the contrast with the Spanish average is striking (see table 8.2).

Even in 1950, the structure of the Spanish working population was far from the position reached by the Basque country at the beginning of the twentieth century.[28] Thus in 1950, in Guipúzcoa, the sectoral distribution of its working population was as follows: primary sector: 21 per cent; secondary sector: 46.3 per cent; services (tertiary) sector: 32.7 per cent.

The 1930s: international crisis, political crisis and Civil War

The economic growth experienced in the previous period gave way to a time of stagnation in the early 1930s. The Basque economy, linked to the domestic market, bore the brunt of changes in Spanish economic policy. The problems arose in the basic sectors affected by the international crisis. To these problems were added those posed, after 1936, by the

Spanish Civil War. In 1937, the two most industrialised Basque territories – Guipúzcoa and Biscay – were deprived of their Economic Concert. When the civil war ended in 1939, the economic situation was considerably worse than it had been in the early 1930s.

The period from 1939 to 1973

Devoid of Economic Concerts, the period between 1939 and 1973 was still to be one of growth for the Basque country, even though growth was slower than during the first third of the century. The autarkic policy in the early part of the period was to mould some of the features of Spanish industries in the future.

In the industrial sector, 1939 saw the birth of a highly protectionist policy coupled with direct state intervention. Protectionism was determined by two factors: the need to boost national industry coinciding with the weakness of foreign competition due to the war and a lack of trade relations with foreign countries. State intervention took the form of the establishment, in September 1941, of the Instituto Nacional de Industria (INI). Through this organisation, the state sought to promote the creation and resurgence of native industries. Another aim seemingly pursued by INI was to overcome the monopolistic character of some sectors, such as electricity, metallurgy, cement, paper manufacture and ship-building. Some of these, as already mentioned, were both basic features of the Basque economy and were leaders as far as total Spanish production was concerned.

The industrial concentration achieved in the Basque country in the first third of the century and the supremacy reached by some sectors still persisted in the 1950s. The Basque company Altos Hornos de Vizcaya alone produced 68 per cent of total cast-iron and 31.52 per cent of total steel production in Spain in 1957.[29] However, the Basque ship-building industry, which was tightly linked to the steel and iron industries, was, at the same time, gradually losing its position relative to ship-builders in other parts of Spain. The relative decline of Basque production was even sharper at the beginning of the 1970s. At that time, ship-building in the Basque country only amounted to 20 per cent of total Spanish production. With regard to paper manufacturing, the Basque country was still at the head of Spanish production, even though its relative position had declined. Between 1951 and 1955, 43 per cent of paper manufactured in Spain came from the Basque country – well ahead of Catalonia, for which the corresponding figure was 29.5 per cent.

The Basque country, on the other hand, kept a considerable level of activity in the fields of processed metal goods: railroad goods, machine tools, bicycles, armaments and household appliances – the latter subsector having sprung up vigorously. Some figures to illustrate the importance of these subsectors, both within the Basque economy and in Spain as a whole, follow. For instance, in the field of machine tools, one single Basque province – Guipúzcoa – contributed more than 50 per cent of Spanish total output between 1939 and 1973. In general, with the exception of some railroad goods manufacturers, the structure of such enterprises was still small, just as it had been at the turn of the century. Guipúzcoa boasted an important number of machine-tool manufacturers, ancillary industries, armaments, bicycles, sewing machines and household appliance companies, which spread all over the province's territory. It displayed a high degree of industrialisation, even though its entrepreneurial structure consisted of small production units. Even the iron and steel works operating in Guipúzcoa, unlike those in Biscay, were based on small companies manufacturing special iron that was used as raw material for the metal goods industry of the province.

The financial sector in the Basque country, which had experienced a great development in the first third of the twentieth century, was to retain an outstanding position in the 1939–73 period. Banking policy regarding private banks kept its restrictive features – a heritage of the Civil War – until the 1960s. As the creation of new banks was banned, existing ones consolidated, while small banks were taken over by large ones. Thus, in 1958, there were twelve national banks in Spain (operating all over the country's territory), plus ninety-seven banks of regional, local or foreign character.[30]

The Basque economy continued to grow and held its leading position in industrial production, per capita income and the modernity of the structure of its working population. Its high degree of industrialisation kept acting as a magnet for a great number of immigrants from other Spanish regions. A clear indicator of the Basque economic position is per capita income. In 1957 in Spain, it ranged – depending on differences between individual provinces – from 30,230 to 7,893 pesetas. The Spanish average in 1957 was 9,862 pesetas. The five leading provinces were Biscay (30,230), Guipúzcoa (30,229), Madrid (24,858), Barcelona (22,453) and Alava (21,294). In short, the three provinces that make up the current Basque community were in first, second and fifth position.[31] As has been shown, their incomes by far exceeded the Spanish average.

Spain's working population structure also illustrates the backwardness of the rest of Spain compared to the Basque country. In 1970, the national average for the sectoral distribution of the Spanish workforce was 30.1 per cent (primary), 36.3 per cent (secondary) and 33.6 per cent (tertiary).[32] Such figures had been surpassed by Basque industry long before (see table 8.2).

THE 1973 CRISIS AND ITS EFFECTS ON A SPECIALISED ECONOMY: FROM INDUSTRIAL RATIONALISATION TO THE RE-ESTABLISHMENT OF ECONOMIC CONCERTS

After the 1973 crisis, the new international economic order has had a negative impact on sectors such as metallurgy and ship-building. It has compelled industrialised countries to undertake a profound restructuring of such sectors. The Basque economy, traditionally oriented toward the above industries, has been more severely stricken than the Spanish economy as a whole.

The consequences of the 1973 crisis were evident at once. Economic indicators between 1973 and 1976 give a clear picture of a general crisis. Unemployment and inflation soared. The economic policies applied in various countries softened the effects, but in the short term they were no solution whatsoever. Only from 1976 could certain symptoms of an economic upswing be discerned in the OECD countries. The rise of average OECD GDP was 5 per cent; in the United States it was 6.25 per cent. Inflation started to fall below 10 per cent (even though it was 21.8 per cent in Italy and 15 per cent in the United Kingdom). An increase in foreign trade was also noticeable; however, unemployment was still very high.

Analysing the performance of the Spanish economy in the period 1973–6, there are big differences compared with the trends conveyed by the above figures. Spain showed little economic dynamism, unemployment was very high and inflation, even in 1976, was 19.77 per cent.[33] At the same time, a serious trade deficit arose. As these facts show, the Spanish economy was in a worse situation than most other industrialised economies. The indicators were no better for the Basque economy. In addition to the structural crisis of Basque production (as a consequence of the Basque economy's heavy dependence on the sectors most affected by the crisis), there was a great dependency of the Basque economy on Spanish and international markets. This dependency was noticeably higher than was the case with other regional economies. In fact, at the time, the Basque country sold 78 per cent of its industrial output on the

Table 8.3. *Unemployment rates 1982–1999 (%)*

Region	Year					
	1982	1983	1984	1992	1993	1999
Alava	14.9	4.4	17.8	18.3	21.4	13.2
Guipúzcoa	18.0	18.6	21.3	18.7	22.1	12.6
Biscay	21.0	22.5	25.1	20.9	25.6	18.0
Basque Com. (average)	19.0	20.2	23.0	18.7	23.9	15.5
Spain (average)	17.0	18.4	21.7	18.4	22.7	15.5
European Union (average)				10.0	11.1	10.0

Source: Author's own computation based on data from the Instituto Español de Estadística (INE), OECD, Boletín Estadística del Banco de España.

Spanish market and 13 per cent on international markets. If the Basque economy's dependency on foreign markets is compared to what happened in Catalonia, which was also an industrialised area, the result is quite different. Catalonia exported 44 per cent of its industrial production to the other Spanish regions and 5 per cent to the international market. The lack of foreign demand could not be easily replaced in the Basque market itself. Confronted with the need to find outlets for their products, the efforts made by Basque companies to promote exports can be understood. In 1976, despite the crisis, the Basque country increased exports by 15 per cent against 12 per cent for the whole of Spain.

All the same, the negative effects of the crisis were more severe in the Basque country than in other Spanish regions. Thus unemployment exceeded the Spanish average; migratory movements started to be negative; industrial rationalisation was necessary, although costly, due to the Basque economic structure and, as a result, per capita income in the Basque country lost its lead relative to other Spanish regions. Such negative effects coincided with political changes. The claim of Basque historic rights was reasserted. Among these, the re-enactment of the Economic Concert was a landmark.

Whereas the effects of the 1973 crisis were subsiding elsewhere, unemployment figures in the Basque Country still rose in the 1980s. The negative evolution of this indicator can be understood by considering the character of the crisis, which was basically industrial and severely affected the metallurgy and ship-building. That is why unemployment figures in the Basque country surpassed the Spanish average in the 1980s and 1990s. Industrial rationalisation did not generate new jobs in the short term. Within the Basque country, the figures were highest in

Table 8.4. *Evolution of migratory balances*

Year	Basque country	Year	Basque country
1962	25,336	1977	−511
1963	32,257	1978	−6,750
1964	36,537	1979	−10,246
1965	31,329	1980	−10,887
1966	17,765	1981	−5,275
1967	16,462	1982	−6,466
1968	11,762	1983	−5,513
1969	12,436	1984	−5,884
1970	12,835	1985	−5,351
1971	5,849	1986	−3,789
1972	11,050	1987	−8,609
1973	14,178	1988	−11,025
1974	16,257	1989	−9,622
1975	10,546	1990	−6,553
1976	492	1991	−4,759
	(inclusive of Navarre up to this year)	1992	−5,907
		1993	−5,299
		1994	−4,882
		1995	−4,446
		1996	−3,651

Source: Author's own computation from data from the Instituto Español de Estadística (INE).

Biscay, this province being more closely linked to the iron and steel and ship-building industries (see table 8.3).

As a result of the industrial crisis the Basque country, traditionally a recipient of people from other regions, started to show negative migratory balances. An additional circumstance should be noted: whereas Alava showed positive balances, Guipúzcoa and Biscay – more industrialised and crisis-stricken – had been losing population since the 1970s (see table 8.4).

Faced with persistent crisis conditions, especially in the metallurgy sector, from 1973 onwards, the EEC started a quota policy with the aim of restricting output. As a result Spain had to limit iron and steel exports, which exacerbated the problems confronting the Basque economy. The iron and steel sector was forced to restructure. This restructuring commenced in the 1970s and was completed in the 1980s.[34] It was then that the Economic Concert was handed over to the government of the Basque autonomous community.

Restructuring of the Basque metallurgical industry – at high social and economic cost – resulted in the closure of Altos Hornos de Vizcaya. Its overstaffing, together with its high production costs, rendered this symbolic concern non-competitive. To replace it, a new company was founded: the Acería Compacta, an electrical steel plant feeding an automatic system, which can turn out a finished product in three hours. Both public and private capital acquired stakes in this new concern. The latest data confirm the new situation in Basque steel production: in 1994, 45 per cent of Spanish output came from Basque factories. In a way, this new technology has allowed the Basque country to set off along the track to the future. The tradition of old foundries and nineteenth-century blast furnaces, exporting their products to Europe and America, has been updated.

Household appliance manufacture, which experienced a sharp rise in the Basque country in the 1960s, was also affected by the crisis. Its industrial rationalisation has followed European patterns. Thus, in the European Union, the number of manufacturers has decreased, while concentration occurred. This entrepreneurial concentration also occurred in the rest of Spain. The Spanish market is currently led by four big groups: the Basque group Fagor, the German Bosch-Siemens, the Swedish Electrolux and Whirlpool (the Dutch branch of the American multinational concern). With the exception of the Basque group, they are funded with foreign capital. For its part, the Basque group trades several brand names (including Westinghouse). The adoption of new technologies has rendered the group's production competitive. The share of Basque production of household appliances in the Spanish market amounted to 20.6 per cent in 1994, an important figure bearing in mind the competition of the other foreign economic groups. In 1993 more than half the export of household appliances manufactured in Spain came from Basque companies.

Although per capita income in the Basque country is still above the Spanish average, it is no longer in first position, as was formerly the case. If figures for 1991 and 1995 are compared, the rate of growth in the Basque country has been lower than in the leading Spanish regions (except for Madrid) (see table 8.5).

CONCLUSIONS

When summing up the Basque country's history throughout the last two centuries, some features deserve special mention. The *fueros* or Basque common law have a long history of their own, which the Basque people has always wished to keep in force. The policy of administrative uni-

Table 8.5. *Family income per inhabitant (base average = 100)*

Autonomous community	Year	
	1991	1995
Baleares	138.21	156.29
Catalonia	120.34	118.38
Madrid	115.72	110.95
Navarre	115.38	118.92
La Rioja	109.95	114.51
Basque country	107.41	108.27
Aragon	106.54	107.68
Extremadura	75.43	75.48

Source: *Economía Vasca. Informe 1996*, Caja Laboral-Euskadiko Kuxta, Bilbao.

formity, pursued by the Bourbons since the eighteenth century, thus met with firm resistance in the Basque country because it meant the loss of many of the basic principles of the *fueros*. Attempts to abolish the *fueros* increased throughout the nineteenth century. The rupture of the traditional social regime was to have special significance for the Basque country, where the sense of traditional values was rooted far deeper than in other Spanish regions. The loss of the *fueros* in the late nineteenth century was the outcome of two civil wars, which resulted in the division of Basque society. Therefore, to claim that the loss of the *fueros* gave birth to a national grievance among the Basques is a logical proposition.

It is equally true to say that if society's 'modernisation' through industrialisation represented a break with the traditional way of life, then the Basque country entered the industrial era faster and more intensely than any other Spanish region. Changes in the way of life were patently obvious. Industrial development brought to the Basque country working people from different parts of Spain, adding a further disruptive factor to Basque society's traditional way of life. From the ideological standpoint, the birth of Basque nationalism at the end of the nineteenth and the beginning of the twentieth centuries took place at a time marked by contradictions arising from a traditional society's crisis and the rise of a liberal bourgeoisie. The loss of the *fueros* did not by any means make the situation easier.

Economic growth and the development of the Economic Concert proved to be not enough to satisfy the great number of Basques who kept demanding their full historical rights. The abolition of the Economic Concert in 1937 during the Spanish Civil War (1936–9), and General Franco's regime (1939–75) favoured the flourishing of a radical branch of Basque nationalism. The Spanish political reform that followed Franco's regime has not been accepted by the Basque radical faction, thus deepening the existing social division in the Basque country.

As far as the economic evolution of the Basque country is concerned, its main periods since the end of the nineteenth century till today have already been described in this chapter. To summarise, the first period, ending in 1930, shows rapid economic growth, at least since 1876. During the second period, covering the 1930s, Basque economic growth suffered a major slowdown due to outside factors. The third period lasted from 1939 to 1973 and showed moderate economic growth. Lastly, the 1973 crisis opened a new period during which the Basque economy has been severely damaged by the changes in its industrial structure.

Economic evolution has also been accompanied by endless political disputes over historical rights. These are so deeply rooted in the Basque people's consciousness that, at least as far as the economy is concerned, they were legally acknowledged through the Economic Concert agreed upon in 1878. Economic growth, industrial concentration, high per capita incomes, modern social structure and the outstanding role of financial institutions are some of the traits that have characterised the Basque economy throughout the twentieth century. High economic growth experienced by the Basque country until 1930 placed the region ahead of the other industrial areas of Spain, where it remained until the 1970s.

Furthermore, as its production rates were so high, Basque industry became dependent on markets outside the Basque territory. Being – as it was – a protected market, the Spanish market was to become vital for the maintenance of Basque industrial production.

Despite the abolition of the Economic Concert in 1937 the Basque provinces' per capita income was the highest in Spain until the 1960s. After nearly 100 years of industrial growth, manufacturing structures had hardly changed: iron, ship-building, paper, metallurgy and hardware still comprised the bulk of industrial production. Likewise, Basque industry continued to be dependent on Spanish and foreign markets. But the abolition of the Economic Concert together with the political situation surrounding the issue of historical rights created increasing tensions in the Basque country that were to explode during the latter years of General Franco's regime. The 1973 crisis inflicted severe damage upon

Basque industrial activity. Among the Spanish provinces the Basque provinces bore by far the most costly burden of industrial reorganisation and suffered the heaviest unemployment rates. The result was a relative decline in Basque incomes. However, the structural reorganisation soon began to bear fruit; indeed there is evidence of a 'new industrial revolution' in the Basque economy.

As far as market movement is concerned, the Basque economy will most probably continue to exhibit its traditional open attitude. Moreover, industrial reorganisation in the Basque country coincided with Spain's entry into the European Economic Community. The Basque economy, even more so than the economies of other Spanish regions, was reorganised with the need to be competitive in a worldwide market being borne in mind.

Finally, it must be pointed out that this important industrial reorganisation has taken place as the Basque country recovered in full its Economic Concert. As has already been said, the Economic Concert has proven most positive for the Basque economy – both in the past as a vehicle for economic development and today as a facilitator of industrial reorganisation. Furthermore, since being fully reinstated almost fifteen years ago, the Economic Concert has gone some way towards satisfying one of the most enduring demands of the Basque people – the demand for the return of their historic rights.

NOTES

1   The Basque country proper is *Euskalherria*, which comprises the three Basque–Spanish provinces – that is, Alava, Guipúzcoa and Vizcaya, plus Navarre or 'High Navarre' – and the three Basque–French Provinces – that is, Labourd, Soule and Navarre or 'Low Navarre' – thus totalling seven provinces of the Basque Nation on both sides of the western Pyrenees.

2   V. Garmendia, *La ideología carlista (1868–1876). Los orígenes del nacionalismo vasco* (San Sebastián, 1985), pp. 365–6.

3   *Ibid.*, pp. 366–7.

4   *Ibid.*

5   *Ibid.*, pp. 368–9. In Spanish Navarre or 'High Navarre', only one member of each family was to pay military service.

6   J. M. Angulo, *La abolición de los Fueros e Instituciones Vascas* (San Sebastián, 1976).

7   Garmendia, *La ideología carlista*, pp. 390–3.

8   M. Herrero y Ridríguez de Miñón, 'Fundamentos históricos y políticos del Concierto Económico Vasco' in *El Concierto Económico Vasco Actas V Semana Delegación en Corte de la RSBAP* (Madrid, 1997), p. 25.

9   J. Real Cuesta, *El carlismo vasco 1876–1900* (Madrid, 1985), pp. 33–40.

10 Royal Decree, 13 November 1877.

11 Some historians see its birthdate with the Law of 21 July 1876, while others see it in the November 1877 Decree.

12 The non-nationalist politician was José Calvo Sotelo. The sentence is quoted by M. Fernández Pelaz in 'Características del Concierto Económico en su dimensión tributaria' in *El Concierto Económico* (1997), p. 57.

13 J. L. Larrea, 'El sistema de cupo dentro del Concierto Económico' in *El Concierto Económico* (1997), pp. 103–12 at pp. 103 and 112.

14 J. Trebolle, 'Sobre el concepto de cupo como sistema de financiación: principios históricos y significación actual' in *El Concierto Económico*, pp. 132–3.

15 'Basque State and Independence'.

16 J. M. Mata López, *El nacionalismo vasco radical* (Bilbao, 1995), pp. 23–4.

17 *Ibid.*, p. 25.

18 I. Zubiri Oria and M. Vallejo Escudero, *Un análisis metodológico y empírico del sistema de cupo* (Madrid, 1995).

19 M. González Portilla (ed.), *Bilbao en la formación del País Vasco contemporáneo* (Bilbao, 1996), pp. 164–5.

20 San Francisco factory, located near Bilbao: J. Nadal, *El fracaso de la revolución industrial en España* (Barcelona, 1975), p. 178.

21 M. González Portilla, 'Mecanismos de producción y reproducción social de las élites económicas ye del capitalismo en la Restauración', *Revista de Historia Contemporánea*, 6 (1992), pp. 143–76.

22 A. Carreras, *Industrialización española: estudios de historia cuantitativa* (Madrid, 1990), pp. 56–7.

23 R. Tamames, *Estructura económica de España* (Madrid, 1960), p. 291. Foreign capital was also a factor contributing to industrial development: González Portilla, *Bilbao*, pp. 126–8.

24 M. Gárate Ojanguren, 'De los catalanes en Guipúzcoa' in A. Segura and Gonzáles Portilla (eds.), *Acta del Congreso els catalans a Espanya 1760–1914* (Barcelona, 1996).

25 González Portilla, *Bilbao*, p. 155.

26 M. Martínez Cuadrado, *La burguesía conservadora* (Madrid, 1979).

27 González Portilla, *Bilbao*, p. 154.

28 In 1950, the Spanish population employed in the primary sector amounted to 47.5 per cent, whereas the secondary sector only occupied 26.5 per cent of the active population.

29 Tamames, *Estructura*, pp. 158–61.

30 G. Tortella, *Modern Financial Institutions in the 20th Century: Spain and Portugal. A Report on Recent Research* (Milan, 1994), 10th International Economic History Congress.

31 *Anuario Estadístico de España* (Madrid, 1962). Figures are in pesetas of 1953.

32 *Informe Económico del Banco de Bilbao* (Bilbao, 1972).

33 *Situación y perspectivas de la economía vasca* (San Sebastián, 1977).

34 J. Imaz, 'Perspectivas de la siderurgia vasca. Proyectos y realidades' in *Actas de la V Semana de la RSBAP* (Madrid, 1997).

CHAPTER NINE

Economic change and nationalism in Italy in the twentieth century

Luigi De Rosa

For most of the nineteenth century the pressure on the Italian government and parliament to abandon liberalism and to pursue a policy that protected and promoted the country's economic interests did not come from any political movement as such but from newspapers, cultural and economic societies, industrial and worker associations and similar organisations. The Chambers of Commerce, in particular, showed themselves to be increasingly in favour of state intervention in the economy, especially in towns where industrial centres had grown up, demanding that contracts to provide the weapons and ships needed for the country's defence be awarded to Italian and not to foreign companies, as had happened in the past, as well as a revision of trade and navigation treaties with foreign powers. It was at the end of the century and the beginning of the new that such forces found a political counterpart – that is, a movement of opinion and action that sought to increase the country's economic and political prestige among the concert of nations.

It is no coincidence that the movement emerged towards the end of the century, stimulated as it was by two circumstances. One was of a political nature: the reaction to the Italian army's defeat at Adua in 1896 in the war against Ras Menelik to conquer the Eritrean Plateau. The other was economic: the awareness that the country was undergoing rapid industrialisation and was no longer the country emerging from the long and difficult period of the Risorgimento. In the forty years since the creation of the Kingdom of Italy, the country had undergone profound change. Overcoming great difficulties and complex problems, it had achieved considerable agricultural progress. The marshland and malaria that infested large coastal areas had been partly reduced. Much uncultivated land was put under the plough. Although many areas of the country, especially in the south, still appeared to be in a worrying state of backwardness, the agrarian crisis that had overcome Italy in the 1880s seemed to be coming to an end. The corn duty, introduced in 1887, had saved the country's cereal growing, while the spread of chemical fertilisers had raised land productivity; at the same time, the increasing employment of agricultural machinery (ploughs, seeders, threshers and huskers), especially in the Po Valley and in some areas of central Italy, testified to the modernisation process that was underway.

Even taking account of the uncertainties connected to the agricultural cycle, the gross marketable production of crop farming and animal husbandry was higher than that of 1861, showing an increase of just under 50 per cent. Moreover, although the population had risen from over 26 million in 1861 to around 33 million in 1896, the number of workers employed in agriculture was falling sharply. This was mainly due to emigration both within the country and abroad. Internal emigration was directed largely at the towns that were industrialising; the destinations of overseas emigration included a number of countries, especially the more distant territories of Argentina, Brazil, the United States and Canada.

In some urban centres, as a result of the flow of workers from the countryside, considerable progress had been made in the industrial sector. Between 1861 and 1900 manufacturing output almost doubled. Progress was made in all areas to varying degrees, even in the mining sector. The production of metal-bearing minerals, for example, tripled.[1] There were also substantial increases in the output of liquid and gas fossil fuels[2] and of various non-metal-bearing minerals.[3] In the metallurgical industry, steel production – which did not exist in 1861 – was introduced and while pig-iron output had been halved, iron production had risen seven times.[4] In short, great progress had been made in nearly all sectors of industry, including those which barely existed or did not exist at all in the early years of unification, such as the construction of boilers and steam engines, machinery for farming, textiles, the paper and wood industry and printing, the construction of iron bridges, roofs and revolving platforms, iron ship-building, the manufacture of marine engines, the railway industry and the chemical industry.

Such a major transformation also had an impact on the service sector. Considerable changes had been made to the banking system, which at the close of the century was structured around three issuing banks (Banca d'Italia, Banco di Napoli, Banco di Sicilia), three large mixed banks (Banca Commerciale, Credito Italiano and Banco di Roma, the first two of which had Italo-German capital and management), a large number of saving and co-operative banks, several land credit institutions, numerous private banks and rural banks. Although it was still incomplete, a better-organised economy was emerging from the travails of a backward country which, over a period of forty years, had: completed geographical unification with the annexing of Venice and the Veneto following the war with Austria-Hungary; taken advantage of the Franco-Prussian war to free Rome from papal rule and raise it to the status of capital; and embarked on an African war to assert its presence among colonial powers.

All this was achieved through the adoption of diverse economic and monetary policies at a time when the economic situation was often unfavourable. The average growth rate of industrial output in this period was neither stable nor continuous. According to Gershenkron, it stood at 4.6 per cent in the period 1881–8, 0.3 per cent in the period 1888–96, and 6.7 per cent in 1896–1908.[5] It is fairly easy to see why, as a result of this increase in the growth rate – which was quite extraordinary, overall – sections of public opinion were convinced that Italy had at last found the path that would lead to its becoming a great power, even though the process still needed encouragement and support.

Progress not only affected the real economy but also applied to public finance and the balance of payments. By the end of the century the amount of government stock in the hands of foreigners had gradually fallen. Taking advantage of a fall in interest rates on the international capital market, the government was able to start a process of refunding, as a result of which the weight of payable interest on public spending was reduced. Since agricultural and industrial development had brought an increase in tax revenue, at the end of the century the government budget showed a surplus that continued from one year to the next and gave rise to a debate about how to spend it: should it be used to reduce taxation or to improve physical and human infrastructure?

The situation regarding the balance of payments had likewise improved considerably. The slow but continuous development of the hydroelectric industry reduced coal imports while industrial progress brought a gradual increase in exports and at the same time led to a fall in imports. Alongside this fall in the trade deficit there was an increase in the flow of emigrant remittances, which, on account of the enormous scale of Italian emigration, continued to grow. The improvement in the balance of payments was also partly due to the revenue from freight as a result of the progress made by the merchant navy, and from tourism, which was enjoying particularly favourable circumstances. The balance of payments thus showed a surplus; this was borne out by the currency situation with the ending of the regime of fiat money that had been introduced in 1866 and with a premium on paper lire in relation to gold lire.

Awareness of such economic progress had aroused the nationalistic enthusiasm of periodicals such as the *Marzocco*, and the *Regno*, which used it to vindicate Italy's expansionist vocation: owing to its geography, history and needs Italy could not avoid the impulse to extend its interests beyond the Mediterranean[6] and to reach areas in the east and far east.[7] Since progress had been achieved through the action of private citizens, the hoped-for colonial expansion was not, at the start, to be managed by the government (which was only to provide the necessary military and customs facilities) but by private citizens. It was pointed out that in the Eritrean colony the Italian government had given a demonstration of 'ineptitude and wretchedness' 'for many years' and so if Italy wanted to conquer Somalia this could only be done by a commercial company,[8] that is to say the company that was already engaged in commercial activity in Somalia, the Compagnia Filonardi.[9]

The supporters of colonial expansionism were also convinced that industrial growth was necessary and indispensable for the country's further economic development and that the government had to use every means to promote it. Of significance in this respect was the political clash over the iron and steel works at Terni in central Italy, which the government had helped to set up with the aim of producing steel armour, mainly for defence. The production costs of such steel were far above those established by the international market and so there was lively opposition against keeping the Terni works in operation. In particular, free-traders launched vehement attacks in the press and in the political clubs and in parliament, to the point of denouncing a collusion of interests between politics and industry.

While admitting that steel armour would have cost less in French and British plants, the nationalists argued that the greater competitiveness of foreign prices masked a political strategy that aimed to damage Italy. 'The aim of foreign governments', they explained, 'is crystal clear: to place [their] plants in a position to conquer foreign markets and defeat foreign plants. And the countries that pursue such an objective', they continued, 'are neither Turkey nor Colombia, but Britain, the United States, France and Germany, the four giants of the world economy.' It was thus in Italy's interests to support production at Terni, even if it was necessary to pay higher prices, rather than to allow it to be swallowed up by foreign competition. None the less, from a theoretical point of view, the nationalists did not admit to being in favour of either protectionism or free trade. They argued 'that the pursuit of a customs policy might in some cases be to the advantage of industry and [was] therefore to be adopted', and 'that in other cases free trade [was] preferable': in other words, they considered themselves to be 'above all, pragmatic in real life'.[10] It was because of such pragmatism and the fact that similar policies had been implemented by foreign governments to defend their industries, that they accepted, albeit with reservations, the setting up of trusts, such as those for shipyards and sugar refineries.[11]

Central to their thinking was the assumption that 'every injury to industry or agriculture [was] an obstacle to progress and every obstacle [was] an advantage handed over to foreign industry and a delay in the development of the economic, intellectual, sanitary conditions of [Italy's] proletariat'.[12]

Colonial expansionism as a way of acceding to new markets in the wake of industrial growth gained currency even outside the nationalist movement. This was a sign that the idea reflected a common aspiration. According to the reputable scholar Marco Fanno, the world market was divided not between developed and undeveloped countries, but between 'industrial capitalism' – concentrated in western Europe and on the Atlantic coast – and 'agrarian capitalism', which, after the previous favourable period in the second half of the nineteenth century, was now showing increasingly declining terms of trade.[13] Italian imperialism was in search not only of agrarian and industrial outlets, but above all in search of farmland; that is, Italian imperialism was 'the imperialism of poor people', as it used to be called, or again 'proletarian imperialism'.[14] In fact those were the outstanding years of Italian emigration.[15] Hundreds of thousands of southern Italians, mostly peasants, set sail from the ports of Naples and Palermo, mostly bound for North America. And since this diaspora was depopulating regions such as Basilicata, Calabria and Sicily, the nationalists stressed the great benefits that would derive for the mass of emigrants from Italian colonisation of north Africa.[16]

Apart from demographic vitality as an impulse for expansion and the settlement of colonial lands, another recurring theme in Italian nationalist thinking was, as has already been mentioned, the insistence on the need to speed up the country's industrialisation. Against positivist theories that did not attribute southern Italians with an aptitude for industrial work, nationalists and others argued that there was no antinomy between industrialisation and the Latin race. The industrial progress recorded in north Italy showed indisputably that the country had an aptitude for industrial activity. Indeed, was not *Magna Graecia* an

industrialised area when northern Europe, including north Italy, lagged
far behind as regards the range and the sophistication of its industrial
products? Therefore, in order to promote industrialisation it was important to adopt measures that facilitated industrial growth in south Italy.
All the more so since industrialisation was 'the great educator of the
poor and the wondrous propagator of civilisation'; 'the dynamometer of
their expansion forces'.[17]

After the 1907–8 recession, which had curbed Italian emigration and
increased repatriation, Italy also benefited from the general improvement in the economic situation. The rate of industrial growth began to
rise again, although not to the same extent as the previous period: from
1908–13 the average annual increase in industrial production was 2.4 per
cent. The main increases were recorded in the metallurgical, engineering and chemical industries between 1881 and 1913. According to
Gershenkron's figures, metallurgical industries showed an annual
growth rate of 9.3 per cent, engineering industries 4.7 per cent and
chemical industries 11.3 per cent. But annual increases were also
recorded in the textile and food sectors,[18] and especially in the electrical
industry where output rose considerably.

Industrial development was accompanied by the consolidation of the
banking system with the entry of a fourth large mixed bank into the
capital market, Società Bancaria Italiana. In addition, several Italian
banks opened subsidiaries in France, Britain, the United States and other
countries,[19] while various mergers were taking place, especially among
co-operative banks and savings banks. Progress was also recorded by
joint-stock companies, which increased in number as well as in the
capital and reserves they possessed.

According to the figures of the National Statistics Institute, there was
a significant increase in the accumulation of savings,[20] which was stimulated by the increasing flow of emigrant remittances; with the ending of
the 1907–8 crisis, migration had started to grow again, especially towards
the United States. At the same time, investment in housing continued to
grow, a sign of the persistent movement of peasant masses towards
industrial centres, as did investment in installations and equipment,
while investment in public works more than doubled.[21] In concomitance
with population growth the number of people employed in public works
and factories also increased. Trade unions and workers' political organisations were also strengthened with the emergence of two opposing currents of opinion: one reformist and one revolutionary, of Sorelian origin.

Such a flurry of activity gave further impetus to the nationalist movement. Between 1908 and 1911 the number of nationalist periodicals mushroomed with *Il Carroccio* (1909), *La Grande Italia* (1909), *Il Tricolore* (1909) and *L'Idea Nazionale* (1911).[22] At the same time a plethora of nationalist articles appeared in various newspapers. Towards the end of 1910, the first Nationalist Congress addressed the economic problem and the speech on 'Great Italy's economic policy' was given by Filippo Carli, then professor at the University of Padua. For Carli, Italy's industrial development had hitherto been financed by foreign capital. On the one hand this was a positive factor because it had reduced the time needed for Italy's industrial take-off; on the other hand it was negative because it had led to a dependence on foreign machinery and a delay in the development of the engineering industry and the training of engineers. This delay emerged from a comparison between the production and commercial systems in Germany and Italy, which saw Germany performing far better than Italy not only in the production and commercialisation of goods but also as regards education; in Germany education responded to the needs of industrial development while in Italy the emphasis continued to be on general culture, even in the field of technology. Therefore Italy had to aim at the creation of a powerful engineering industry, the industrialisation of agriculture, the setting-up of industrialists' associations with the purpose of training staff entrusted with the task of selling industrial products in foreign markets, the creation of a large merchant navy and the adoption of simple and practical transport tariffs like those of the *Schnittfrachtsätze*. As for Italy's trade expansion, Carli argued that this should be directed towards the Levant with the aid of a sound banking system.[23]

Protectionism was to be the basis of this policy but on this point there was no convergence at the Congress. Mainly interested in gaining power, the nationalists did not wish to make a commitment and since some participants argued that protectionism had been the main impediment to Italy's industrial development the Congress concluded that the time was not yet ripe to choose between free trade and protectionism. None the less, the Congress gave birth to the Associazione Nazionalista Italiana,[24] which was organised into sections in all the chief towns throughout the country, where the movement sought to gain widespread support among the population. The speech given by E. Corradini, one of the movement's main theorists, in January 1911 in Naples was thus repeated in Florence, Venice, Padua, Verona and Arezzo.[25]

In these speeches, which were held in towns up and down the country, it was argued that 'nationalism was something quite different from "patriotism"': while patriotism was *selfless*, nationalism meant *selfishness*; that is, 'the development of the sense of power enclosed in the word "nation"'. In particular 'the nation [had to be] power; the army, the force, the means'.[26] In order for this to happen, Italy had to shrug off the state of economic and moral dependence in which it lived in the same way as it had shrugged off political dependence.

Despite this, the events that took place in Italy in 1911 and 1912 (the landing at Tripoli to conquer Libya, and the exclusion of foreign insurance companies from the insurance market with the creation of the National Insurance Institute (INA Instituto Nazionale delle Assicurazioni)) resulted not from the action of nationalists but from their opponents. Both as regards the conquest of Libya and the measures against foreign insurance companies, the nationalists were beaten in their timing. The government, they wrote, 'has taken away the bread from the mouths of the nationalists'[27] even though the nationalists sought to use the Libyan campaign to gain wider consensus. It should also be added that regarding the nationalisation of life-insurance companies, several eminent nationalists took a stand against government monopoly; they viewed it as a political manifestation of state socialism that was advocated by the trade unionists and not as the assertion of national interests.[28]

It was only in 1914 that a discourse on the economy appeared that was clearly and openly nationalist in its inspiration. The author was an illustrious university professor, Alfredo Rocco, recently converted to nationalism, who was later to become Minister of Justice in Mussolini's government. For Alfredo Rocco, 'Italy's economic problem was a production problem and not a problem of wealth distribution' given – as 'statistics show – Italy's enormous economic inferiority compared to nearly all the major European countries'. In other words, as far as wealth was concerned, there was an enormous gap between Italy and the main western countries. Italy's private wealth – estimated at around 50–5 billion lire in the 1880s – had risen to 80–5 billion lire in 1914. In the same year the figure for Britain was 350–400 billion, for France 280–300 billion, for Germany 400–50 billion and for Austria-Hungary 120–30 billion lire. It was calculated, therefore, that if Italy had managed to bring her wealth to French or German levels, the income of workers would have increased by 300 per cent and not the 14–15 per cent hoped for in the nationalists' political programme.[29]

With the aim of increasing production, Rocco's economic programme envisaged the reclamation and irrigation of marshland in south

Italy and on the islands, the valorisation of a large area of uncultivated or scarcely productive land and at the same time a better use of hydraulic forces for the production of electricity. And yet the central point of Italy's economic development in his opinion continued to be the country's territorial expansion. Italy's economic dilemma lay in the binomial poor land/fertile population. Italians had to get used to viewing pacific emigration, such as the huge migratory movement that was taking place towards the United States, as unsuitable and realise the need 'to turn to another form of emigration, armed emigration, which is tantamount to war'. But this was a task for the future. 'The task of the present,' he urged, 'other than the preparation of souls, is the intensification of production at home and pacific expansion abroad.'

The increase in domestic output had to be achieved not only by government action as regards public works, the diffusion of popular and professional culture and scientific and technological progress, but also through private action and initiative with the government providing careful and valuable co-operation. Most of Rocco's discourse was concerned with illustrating the social action of the Nationalist Party, which saw the need for a better distribution of income on behalf of workers and accepted class conflict. 'Only', he specified, 'class conflict must not be denied nor forbidden but disciplined and restrained so that in a contest between two parties, a third party who is not involved in the struggle and whose interests are above any party – that is to say, the Nation – is not damaged or injured.' In this respect the nation was to be viewed as one single unity with specific interests to safeguard and bodies to protect them. Thus 'a national party should not [have] hesitate[d] to support the workers since their demands coincided with national interests'; therefore alongside an 'anti-national and anti-state trade unionism' and a 'Catholic trade unionism', a 'national trade unionism' was advocated.

About three months after the announcement of these views, in a broader and more complex essay entitled 'Economia liberale, Economia socialista ed Economia nazionale' published in the *Rivista delle Società Commerciali*, Rocco gave proof of his historical, legal and economic training and of the sophistication of his analyses, as well as his great debating skills.

First he presented a eulogy of Frederick List, who had set out to revise the basic concepts of the individualist economy in 1841 and to whom Germany was indebted for its own school of economics and for its consciousness of national needs in relation to the economy. According to Rocco, in the space of fifty years these factors had made Germany 'the feared and often victorious rival of Great Britain in the sphere of trade and industry'.[30] Then he pointed out that individuals who at a particular moment in time form a particular society, 'are not this society, which lives through the centuries, and includes all the generations that have been and are yet to come'. Therefore individuals are merely the bodies and instruments of its aims. 'And as long as individuals keep within the limits of their function, as often happens when the obscure instinct of the species is working within them, societies progress.' Against a 'presentist' view Rocco advanced a view based on future benefits according to which costs and sacrifices were justified when they brought national benefits; that is, when they produced benefits for the future. Naturally Rocco justified a policy of protectionism when a country was poor and unfavourably endowed as regards production, when a particular industry was undergoing a crisis, or when an industry was considered to be of national strategic importance 'for reasons of state security'.[31]

It is well known that this essay formed a large part of the address that Rocco gave to the Nationalist Congress in Milan in May 1914 together with Filippo Carli. This was an important congress since the debate on economic policy led to a second schism within the movement, the first having been that of the democratic nationalists. Those who were more in favour of free trade left the movement since the majority espoused most of Rocco's ideas and opted for a policy of state intervention in industry and protectionism.[32]

This move towards a stricter policy of intervention and protectionism and away from a position which up till then had been marked by a deliberate pragmatism, was dictated by developments in the international economy. New countries were industrialising. The market was shrinking and in some cases large industrial plants in Italy, such as those of heavy industry (iron and steel), had managed to survive only through the large-scale intervention of banks and by reducing production. In order to defend themselves from foreign competition, cartels and consortiums had been set up in various sectors of industry in Italy as they had been in other parts of the world. The danger of excessive indebtedness with banks had not been dispelled and thus protectionism and state intervention appeared to be an indispensable means of defence, especially in the eyes of the nationalists who, despite declarations calling for action on behalf of agriculture, were basically tied to the town and big industry.

For a country like Italy, which had not yet fully industrialised and which was still far from reaching the levels attained by other western countries, it was not a question of comparing itself with other countries but rather of protecting itself from other countries' vigour and aggressiveness.

Anti-Austrian in its foreign policy through fear of Austrian domination of the Adriatic, the nationalists were in favour of Italy's going to war from the very outbreak of hostilities, and considered the country's initial neutrality 'as a necessary waiting period before taking its place in battle in a resolute way'.[33] Indeed, in May 1915 Italy entered the war against Austria-Hungary and therefore against Germany.

The war gave a considerable boost to Italian industry. Apart from the need for textiles, clothing, leather goods and foodstuffs, there was a continuous and relentless need for armaments, ammunition, ships and trucks, which stimulated the metallurgical and engineering industries. These were all sectors mainly belonging to heavy industry and therefore wartime demand gave rise to indisputable technological progress, innovation and increases in scale.[34] However, such progress was obtained in a disorganised and hurried way and without the possibility of deriving the benefits that such a process usually engenders in terms of costs and volume. The indifference towards problems of cost and company efficiency was also partly linked to the fact that government orders – which increased considerably and which all demanded urgent consignment – were placed without sparing any expense.

The funding needed to finance the increase in production and the expansion of these industries, with the growth in the number of factory plants, mostly came from the four mixed banks that have already been referred to, including Società Bancaria Italiana, which in 1914 became Banca Italiana di Sconto following mergers with other banks. For the duration of the war these banks performed an essential role in speeding up the process of vertical and horizontal industrial combination, which was a completely new experience for Italian industry.[35] The most outstanding examples of this process of combination were to be found in the iron and steel industry, where two large companies, Ilva and Ansaldo, reached very high levels of production and went on to become the pillars of Italian industry. The war also provided Italy's aircraft, chemical and electricity industries with an opportunity for development.

Apart from the war, the considerable growth in industry was also made possible by a series of government measures. The government gave industries that were directly or indirectly linked to the war effort various forms of incentive. These ranged from substantial advances in the payment of government contracts to large contributions for paying off new installations, and customs exemptions on machinery and materials purchased for installations in new factories.[36]

This policy and another policy in favour of government ownership and control of the war industry in particular and of industry in general, which emerged in the debates of those years, showed that nationalist thought had pervaded much of public opinion, converting even eminent liberals who up till then had been staunch supporters of government non-intervention in the economy, especially in industry.[37]

The disbanding of the army and the dismantling of industry after the war threw the country into a terrible crisis, which was accompanied by rising inflation. Some sectors were affected by total paralysis through the lack of raw materials, uncompetitiveness, the difficulty in converting wartime production to peacetime production, and currency scarcity. All this was happening at a time when socialists were stirring up revolutionary ferment throughout the country, which became increasingly threatening and aggressive in 1919 and 1920 especially considering the serious economic crisis the country was undergoing. The socialists viewed the nationalists as their worst enemies because the latter had always been in favour of Italy's going to war while the socialists had opposed it very strongly.

Since the nationalists had wanted Italy to take part in the war as a means of speeding up imperial expansion, the failure to achieve the aims of expansion in Asia Minor at the end of the war gave rise to their insistence on the myth of a 'mutilated victory' and their blaming the liberal and democratic groups who were then in power for responsibility of the failure. As most historians have concurred, it was the nationalists' continual and vehement attacks that drove the Fascist movement to adopt an anti-system stance (the Fascist movement had risen in 1919, and in 1921 its actions had not yet overshot the bounds of legality[38]).

At the same time, to counter the government formulae advanced by the socialists, the nationalists advocated what was afterwards to become the basis of Fascist corporativism. In 1919, stressing that the main economic objective had to be an increase in production, the nationalists argued that industrialists had to form part of a regime that was made up of 'bodies [having] the utmost sensitivity towards their particular interests'; that is, in 'an organisation . . . made up of the direct representatives of all trade unions, both industrialist and worker' in order to replace the conflict between parties by a conflict between unions; a conflict which would find, in the end, 'that unity among particular interests which is commonly known as general interest', and from which 'capital and labour' could not recoil without destroying one another.[39] Still more explicitly, in the words added by Rocco to the nationalist programme of 1919, they declared that 'the common principle that necessarily governs and must govern the Nation is the corporative principle',[40] meaning it not in a narrow sense as a synonym for worker trade unionism, since the trade union organisation also had to 'include entrepreneurs, industry's chiefs and engineers' and embrace agriculture and the professions. 'When we have created the large trade unions of production,' Rocco carries on, 'which will also be bodies of government interest, we can expect the State to intervene in the country's economy with the necessary means and institutions.'[41] Such an approach affected the whole structure of government, the functioning of institutions and thus the survival of political parties as well as their political role.

It is no accident that this programme of economic and political restructuring of the Italian state was carried out after the fall of the Liberal, Catholic and Fascist Coalition government in 1924 following the assassination of Matteotti that had brought Mussolini to power, with the inception of Mussolini's dictatorship in January 1925. At the beginning, relations between the nationalist and the Fascist movements were not totally void of conflict, but in February 1923 they merged and henceforth nationalism, an elite movement, which had always sought to influence the doctrine and policies of the Fascist movement suggesting plans for government action, prevailed. Mussolini's full assuming of power enabled the movement to display all its strength. In 1925 the Fascist trade unions were given the monopoly over worker and peasant representation; on 2 October of the same year a special labour authority was set up to decide over disputes between workers and management; on 3 April 1926 a single trade union for each category of workers was created; on 10 July 1926 the number of worker trade union confederations allowed was limited to six, one for each branch of production (industry, agriculture, trade, sea and air transport, land transport and communications, banking and insurance), against which there was to be an identical number of corresponding organisations representing management. The twelve confederations formed the corporations, with the addition of a thirteenth confederation representing professional people and artists.

This restructuring was completed on 2 July 1926 with the setting up of the Ministry of Corporations.[42] It is significant that all these measures were promoted and/or signed by Alfredo Rocco, the Minister of Justice, one of the nationalist movement's most influential spokesmen, as we have already seen. Rocco was also responsible for drafting the final text of the Labour Charter, which, with the text presented by the Fascist Bottai, sanctioned 'the superiority of the values of capital and technology over the values of labour'.[43] Without dwelling on the actual functioning of the corporations, it should be pointed out that corporations only began to operate in 1934 – that is, in the aftermath of the 1929 Great Depression.

The other goal of the nationalist programme that was looked favourably upon by Mussolini – a more active and incisive policy of overseas expansion – started to materialise in July 1923 when the Italian government managed to obtain the concession of the Aegean Islands (the *Dodecanneso*) at the Conference of Lausanne. This gave rise to a dispute with the Greek government involving military intervention and the occupation of Corfu by the Italian naval squadron. In the end, under pressure from Britain, Mussolini abandoned the island, accepting the partial apologies of the Greek government.

In the following years, the dynamism of Mussolini's foreign policy grew. In 1926, at the height of an economic crisis due to the bad grain harvests of 1924/5, Mussolini publicly proclaimed his ambition to expand Italy's influence in the Mediterranean. In 1927 he stipulated a series of treaties with countries in eastern and central Europe, which caused tension in Italy's relations with France. And although the 1929 crisis put a brake on Mussolini's foreign policy activism, after 1934 – when the crisis was over – political and military events succeeded one another, all bearing the stamp of expansionism and nationalism. These were: in 1935 the invasion of Ethiopia and the consequent founding of the empire; in 1936 the non-declared intervention in the Spanish Civil War; in 1939 the invasion and occupation of Albania; finally, in June 1940, Italy's siding with Germany in the war against France and Great Britain. Nationalist ideology had succeeded in driving Italian foreign policy towards colonial expansion and war. But what results did it obtain as far as the economy was concerned?

Above, reference was made to the institutional revolution carried out by the government in the country's productive structure. Nothing has been said about the economic conditions out of which the revolution arose and about the changes it engendered. It should be remembered at this point that when Mussolini assumed power for the first time, at the end of October 1922, the grave postwar economic, monetary and financial crisis was virtually over, although it had brought numerous bankruptcies in its wake, including the collapse of the two giant engineering companies, ILVA and Ansaldo, and the close of Banca Italiana di Sconto, one of Italy's four largest mixed banks. Moreover, after the United States had closed its doors to free immigration, unemployment spread considerably. As an American historian has remarked, it is understandable why government policy in the period 1922–6, especially industrial policy, gave 'economic development priority over social reform';[44] and, indeed, during this period industrial growth was continuous and significant.[45] The situation changed in 1926 and 1927 when Mussolini sought to curb the fall of the lire, which had been devalued by at least 30 per cent following the bad harvests from 1924 to 1926, bringing its value to the pre-1922 level.

Deflation had disastrous repercussions for industry, with a marked fall in production, and closures and company bankruptcies, at a time when the economic situation was euphoric in the western world, especially in the United States. The agricultural crisis was followed by an industrial crisis. Under the pressure of continuous demographic growth, which the government itself sought to encourage through various measures, unemployment worsened during the 1930s crisis. In order to curb it, the government took measures to create employment both in the public sector and in agriculture.

From the end of the 1920s to the mid-1930s, there was a gradual increase in direct and indirect employment in the large number of public works undertaken to modernise the main towns (roads, water supply, sewers and schools) and in the work to reclaim land in various regions, including the reclamation of the Pontine Marshes, near to Rome, and their settlement and conversion to farmland. Both on reclaimed land and, more generally, on already cultivated land there was a great effort to increase productivity through the newly created government incentives with a wider use of artificial fertilisers, great mechanisation and knowledge about agricultural technology as well as improved credit facilities and various incentives and prizes. In this way, agricultural production made substantial progress. Yet it was in industry that the results were the most notable, particularly considering the crisis that had long overrun the manufacturing sector in Italy. In 1929, just when Italian industry was emerging from the depression caused by deflation, the world recession set in and struck not only industry but also agriculture following the collapse in grain prices. With the shrinking of the domestic market and the difficulty in acceding to the international market as a result of the protectionist customs policies adopted by various countries, Italian industry went through one of the most dramatic periods in its history. It should be added that the industrial immobilisation that had been adopted since the end of the war had become enormous and was stifling the banks that had financed it, above all Banca Commerciale and Credito Italiano.

In addition to the measures taken to control the situation, such as the creation of compulsory consortia among companies in the same line of business, the need for government authorisation to enlarge or set up new plants, and checks on internal emigration, in 1933 Istituto Mobiliare Italiano (IMI) was set up, although the situation did not improve very much. Recovery began only in 1933 with the creation of Istituto per la Ricostruzione Industriale (IRI), which availed itself of a substantial loan issued on the home market and took over the three mixed banks, freeing them from industrial immobilisation.

While allowing each company to continue to be administered according to private-sector criteria, IRI set up a central holding for each sector (IRI-ferro, IRI-mare, IRI-STET (telephones), Fin-Meccanica, Fin-elettrica, etc.), and got ready to carry out a programme of company reorganisation with the aim of selling businesses to the private sector after they had been reorganised.

These plans were interrupted by the events of 1935–6, that is the sanctions imposed on Italy by the United Nations following the war against Abyssinia, which fully revealed Italy's dependence on foreign powers. Mussolini became convinced that if Italy wanted to have an independent and effective foreign policy and obtain economic independence, IRI could be one of the means of achieving this aim.

Thus, created initially as the pivot of a rescue operation, IRI went on to become the means for managing the industries that had been saved and a major instrument in the government's policy of economic intervention. Through IRI, 'national industry' came into being, controlling 90 per cent of the country's merchant navy, 75 per cent of the country's pig- and cast-iron output, 45 per cent of its raw steel output, major building sites and numerous other sectors.

As regards the banks, whose parcel of stock had been cut owing to the huge concentration of shares in the hands of IRI, their powers as mixed banks were taken away by a law of 1936; henceforth they were authorised only to perform ordinary credit services. The same law reorganised the entire banking system, with Banca d'Italia – which became the sole issuing bank in 1926 – at the centre. The two former south Italian banks of issue – Banco di Napoli and Banco di Sicilia – were defined as public-sector banks, as were several banks that had begun as public banks such as Istituto San Paolo di Torino, Monte dei Paschi di Siena and Banca Nazionale di Lavoro, while Banca Commerciale, Banco di Roma and Credito Italiano became banks of national interest. These banks were authorised to operate on a nationwide basis and to open overseas branches; after them came the local banks, the savings banks, the co-operative banks and rural banks, on whose behalf the government sought to promote mergers.

Thus, the whole banking system, which had become specialised and organised according to different functions, was no longer under private but government control, even though a small number of actions could be traded on the stock exchange. As well as taking over industry, the government had also taken over banking; at the beginning of the century it had taken over the railways.

In 1937 IRI was authorised to become a shareholder in 'major industrial enterprises concerned with national defence, autarky and the defence of the Empire' (that is, Libya, Eritrea, Abyssinia and Somalia). Autarky arose from the government's economic policy, subordinating the whole economy to 'government discipline and control'. Offices and bodies were set up to centralise and control the prices of imported raw materials and other indispensable products. Various measures were adopted to foster the domestic production of the raw materials needed by industry or their surrogates, even at the cost of heavy sacrifices and expense. The mining sector was given an unexpected boost and was one of the sectors that showed the greatest progress. Similar efforts were made to increase the country's supply of electricity and reduce coal imports. IRI undertook to rationalise the industries that had come under its control and to transform them into concerns producing mainly military goods. The policy of autarky and armaments led to an increased demand for all kinds of industrial machinery, especially energy-generating machinery, tools and precision instruments, and agricultural machinery. Consequently, the country's engineering industry recorded great progress, even in areas that were completely new to Italian industry, aided by the improvement in know-how and skills and the results of technological and scientific study. Progress was made by the chemical industry in sectors connected to armaments production and in those geared to the manufacture of synthetic products, in order to cut down on imports. The production of synthetic nitrogenous fertilisers, dyes, pharmaceuticals, synthetic resins and artificial fibres was increased or started up completely afresh. Most progress was achieved by the mining, chemical and electrical industries, by industries producing instrumental goods and all those industries influenced by the policy of autarky or engaged in rearmament programmes.[46]

The industrial system was developing in very exceptional circumstances, and therefore its development, while significant, was incomplete, unbalanced, technologically backward in some sectors, and burdened by costs that could never have borne international competition.[47] What is more important, progress was achieved at the cost of sacrificing private per capita consumption, which returned to the level of 1929 only in 1949.[48]

Industrial development received a heavy blow during the war, owing to the scarcity of raw materials, aerial bombings, and the damage to industrial and agricultural organisation and infrastructure caused by the fighting on national territory. The rate of industrial production (1938 = 100), which had risen from 80 in 1935 to 103 in 1941, plummeted in the subsequent years, falling to 69 in 1943, 42 in 1944 and 29 in 1945. At the end of the Second World War the rate of production had returned to its 1884 level.[49]

The end of the war and the fall of Mussolini did not bring about a major turnaround in policy. Although autarky was abandoned and there was no more talk of colonial expansion, the statist edifice that derived from nationalism was not dismantled. There were two conflicting schools of thought in the country. One school, which consciously or unconsciously cultivated nationalism and which survived among certain social groups and was propagated by various parties both right- and left-wing, was ill disposed to restore to the private sector not only the railways, which had been nationalised since 1905, and the banking system, which had been under government control from 1926 to 1936, but also a number of industrial sectors and companies that had formed part of IRI since 1933. Indeed, IRI continued to take over ailing industries after 1945 and later brought together all state-owned industries under a single ministry, the Ministry for State Ownership, which was especially set up for the purpose. The other school of thought favoured a complete opening up to the market and private initiative. However, although its supporters overcame considerable opposition and managed to bring the country into a wider market, freeing it from customs restraints, firstly with Italy's entry into the European Coal and Steel Community in 1953 and later its outright membership of the European Economic Community in 1957, they had to relinquish plans to restore to private initiative all the industrial activity controlled by the state through government agencies. Indeed, the state extended its influence into other sectors. In this connection two examples are particularly pertinent. The first regards the oil-producing and chemical sector. In 1953 the National Hydrocarbon Corporation (Ente Nazionale Idrocarburi) – ENI – was set up and was given a monopoly to search for methane gas and oil throughout the Po Valley and along most of the Adriatic continental shelf. At the same time it competed fiercely with the major foreign oil-producing countries in Third World countries to procure the necessary supplies. ENI was also engaged in the manufacture of chemicals and was to become one of the foremost producers in the sector.[50]

The other example concerns the electrical industry. Here, in contrast to the policy pursued during the period of autarky in the interests of the country's defence, the aim was not so much the growth of the nationalised sector as the possibility of using the price of the sector's products, that is the tariff, as a tool of economic policy. Underlying the nationalisation of the electrical industry was the idea of manipulating prices to encourage the development of certain sectors (agriculture, new or ailing industries), of certain developing areas (south Italy, for example), and of social groups that were especially needy.[51] Thus the National Electricity Board (Ente Nazionale per l'Energia Elettrica) – ENEL – came into being in 1962.

In the mid-1960s state enterprise was viewed as a tool of economic policy. South Italy was chosen as the area where IRI, ENI and ENEL were to set up new companies. Instead of pursuing the maximisation of profit, state enterprise was thus used to stimulate industrial growth in depressed areas. This policy led to the opening of the Alfa-Romeo (Alfa Sud) car-manufacturing plant at Pomigliano, which today belongs to Fiat, the opening of the iron and steel works at Taranto and several others.

Presented as a policy to foster the south's economic and social development, the creation of these enterprises financed and managed by the state repeated, in essence, the ideas and principles that had formed part of the nationalist economic school of thought at the height of its influence – that is, after the occupation of Abyssinia in 1936. Even though the new political class that emerged after the war mostly adhered to Marxist or Catholic ideology, which was quite different from nationalist thinking, it too was inclined to extol the role of the state in the country's economic development. This is borne out by the agrarian reform at the beginning of the 1950s, which led to the expropriation of 720,000 hectares of land, mostly in south Italy, and their division into small peasant holdings (a reform that from an economic and social point of view proved to be a complete failure[52]), and by the creation of state monopolies: that of ENI in the petrochemical sector, of ENEL in the electricity sector and the government monopoly over telecommunications. Measures to promote agricultural development moved in the same direction (mechanisation, land reclamation, irrigation, reafforestation and so forth), as did those to aid ailing industries and services (motorways and tourism, for example). Measures to support domestic manufactures were also carried out by way of tax concessions, government subsidisation of welfare contributions, credit facilities and transport facilities.) These measures have radically changed the distribution of labour in the different sectors resulting in a drastic reduction in the number of agricultural workers, which in some regions stands very close to the number of such workers in countries that have long been industrialised. The number of workers employed in industry and in the service sector has, on the other hand, increased considerably, according to a pattern that is common to all the most advanced western economies.

Lacking raw materials and endowed with inadequate sources of energy, Italy thus succeeded in creating an industrial system that is one of the largest among western economies, achieving primacy in certain manufactures which before the war scarcely existed. That all this came about due to a combination of international and domestic circumstances (Bretton Woods, the Marshall Plan and the European Union of Payments, for example), among which government intervention played an important part, is unquestionable. But it is equally true that the domestic and international situation has undergone profound change. Protracted government intervention – especially when this had gradually changed from being a tool of economic policy into a tool of social policy – has had its costs (the fragility of development and its discrepancies and the huge increase in the national debt), but it has become completely unacceptable and counterproductive in a world of free and global markets.

And yet Italy would have carried on its policy of government intervention in railways, banking, insurance and industry if the so-called Single Act had not been approved by the European Community in 1985 with the aim of creating a free European market, to free the movement of capital, to abolish restrictions over the establishment of foreign banks, and to privatise state-owned enterprises, especially those exercising monopolies, all objectives that should help to undermine the outdated areas of Italy's industrial system and remove old and deep-seated prejudices. However, although fifteen years have elapsed, Italy has not yet succeeded in completely satisfying the conditions agreed upon in the Single Act. It is true that several government-owned enterprises have been privatised, but privatisation has taken place without the whole property of companies being handed over to the free market. Unable to preserve 51 per cent of ownership, the government has taken pains to acquire a golden share to enable it to continue to exercise a kind of control over the companies it had previously owned. Moreover, there are still government-owned enterprises that are still a long way from being privatised, and there are some sectors which will never be privatised, at least in the short term, given the veto over their privatisation from political forces that, while defining themselves as Marxist, still harbour prejudices and fears that are strictly nationalistic.

It is true that these policies have aroused some strong criticism and opposition. They have been accused of slowing down the country's economic and industrial development and causing the huge growth of the national debt. This would lead on the one hand to a shrinkage in the capital market to the detriment of private enterprise and therefore ultimately to a lower rate of economic growth; on the other hand, the attempt to reduce the budget deficit would result in an increase in taxation, which by reducing demand would also lead to a fall in production.

But the general and very heavy increase in taxation has had another paradoxical outcome: it has fomented a new form of nationalism, much narrower in aspirations and scale but all the same deleterious. In areas where not big but small and medium-sized industry has established itself, the shrinking of the market, the high interest rates borne by such industry due to the pressure of the national debt on the capital market and, above all, the increase in taxation, have exacerbated parochialism to such a degree that proclamations are made about the existence of an oppressed nation of the Po (a nation that has never existed in history and that does not even have its own anthropological identity), and the revival of the Most Serene Republic of Venice, which was overthrown in 1797. In conclusion, the twentieth century began with movements aiming to exalt the Italian nation within its linguistic confines and on the basis of its cultural heritage and history; later, during Fascism, it witnessed not only the vindication of claims to annex Nice, Corsica and Malta but also vindication of the right to colonise Africa and other regions in the world. Now the century is closing with aspirations about a secession enclosed within narrow dialectical confines and the hypothetical and nostalgic rebirth of the old Lagoon Republic.

NOTES

1 From 82,719 tons in 1861 to 247,278 tons in 1900: see R. Romeo, *Breve storia della grande industria in Italia, 1861–1960* (Milan, 1988), p. 332.

2 From 33,531 tons in 1861 to 479,896 tons in 1900: *ibid.*, p. 332.

3 *Ibid.*, p. 337.

4 *Ibid.*, p. 346.

5 A. Gershenkron, *Il problema storico dell'arretratezza economica* (Turin, 1965), p. 75.

6 G. Prezzolini, 'Come fare l'espansionismo', *Il Regno* 30 (1904), 8.

7 *Il Regno* 14 (1904), 11–12.

8 See the articles 'Che cosa si deve fare nel Benadir', *Il Regno* 24 (1904), 13–14 and 'Ancora Benadir', *Il Regno* 25 (1904), 4.

9 G. Finazzo, *L'Italia nel Benadir. L'azione di Vincenzo Filonardi, 1884–1896* (Rome, 1966).

10 See *Il Regno* 9 (1904), 11.

11 *Il Regno* 5 (1904), 12–13.

12 *Ibid.*

13 M. Fanno, *L'espansione commerciale e coloniale degli Stati moderni* (Turin, 1906), pp. 435–6.

14 R. Michels, *L'imperialism italiano. Studio politico-demografico* (Milan, 1914), pp. 92–3.

15 Commissariato generale dell'emigrazione, *Annuario statistico della emigrazione italiana dal 1876 al 1925 con notizie sull'emigrazione negli anni 1869–1875* (Rome, 1926), pp. 6ff.

16 'Credete voi – si domandavano – che sarebbe la stessa cosa per il Mezzogiorno e per tutta l'Italia se quell'Africa fosse sotto dominio italiano invece che sotto dominio francese, credete voi che la Sicilia e il Mezzogiorno e l'Italia sarebbero nelle condizioni in cui sono.' See E. Corradini, *Scritti et Discorsi 1901–1914* (Turin, 1980), p. 170.

17 Fanno, *L'expansione commerciale*, p. 436.

18 Gershenkron, *Il problema storico*, p. 75.

19 L. De Rosa, *Storia del Banco di Roma* (Rome, 1982), vol. I, pp. 256ff.

20 L. De Rosa, *La rivoluzione industrial in Italia* (Rome and Bari, 1981), p. 45.

21 *Ibid.*

22 F. Gaeta, *Il nazionalism italiano* (Bari and Rome, 1981), pp. 110ff.

23 *Ibid.*, pp. 125–7.

24 *Ibid.*, pp. 126–8.

25 Corradini, *Scritti e Discoursi*, p. 177.

26 *Ibid.*, pp. 177–8.

27 Gaeta, *Il nazionalism italiano*, 135.

28 *Ibid.*, pp. 133 and 139–40.

29 A. Rocco, *La lotta nazionale della vigilia e durante la guerra (1913–1918)* (preface by B. Mussolini, Milan, 1938), p. 19.

30 A. Rocco, 'Economia liberale, Economia socialista ed Economia nazionale', *Rivista delle Società Commerciali*, 30 April 1914, pp. 296–7.

31 *Ibid.*, pp. 306–7.
32 A. Rocco, *Scritti e discorsi politici* (Milan, 1938), vol. II, pp. 693–9.
33 *L'idea nazionale*, 6 August 1914.
34 A. Caracciolo, 'La crescita e transformazione della grande industria durante la prima guerra mondiale' in G. Fuà (ed.), *Lo sviluppo economico in Italia* (Milan, 1969), vol. III, p. 233.
35 'A few great financiers and a few great industrialists', wrote an Italian economist at the end of the war, 'hold the power in the four major banks, and directly or through their representatives they also hold the power in the vast number of industrial, mercantile, and shipping, companies which form the customers of these banks and which are linked to them': R. Bachi, *L'economia in guerra* (Rome, 1918), p. 66.
36 Decree Law of 17 February 1916, no. 197.
37 De Rosa, *La rivoluzione industriale*, pp. 52–4.
38 Gaeta, *Il nationalisme italiano*, p. 195.
39 Cited in *ibid.*, p. 195.
40 *Il nazionalismo e i problemi del lavoro e della scuola* (Atti del secondo Convegno nazionalista di Roma, Rome, 1919), pp. 37–46.
41 *Ibid.*, pp. 97–109.
42 D. Veneruso, *L'Italia fascista* (Bologna, 1981), pp. 119–120.
43 *Ibid.*, p. 121.
44 R. Sarti, *Fascismo e grande industria* (Milan, 1977), p. 69.
45 De Rosa, *La rivoluzione industriale*, pp. 55–60.
46 F. Guarneri, *Battaglie economiche fra le due guerre* (Milan, 1953), vol. II, p. 295.
47 De Rosa, *La rivoluzione industriale*, pp. 60–75.
48 B. Barberi, *Consumi nel primo secolo dell'Unità d'Italia (1861–1960)* (Milan, 1971), p. 131.
49 Romeo, *Breve storia*, pp. 330–1.
50 L. De Rosa, *Lo sviluppo economico dell'Italia dal dopoguerra a oggi* (Rome and Bari, 1997), pp. 157ff.
51 *Ibid.*, pp. 152ff.
52 De Rosa, *Lo sviluppo economico*, pp. 73ff and 102ff.

CHAPTER TEN

National integration and economic change in Greece during the twentieth century

Margarita Dritsas

INTRODUCTION

Modern economic development in Greece was a process that unfolded parallel to political and territorial integration of the various regions that were liberated in the process of the breaking up of the Ottoman Empire at different points in time between 1821 and 1948.[1] Perhaps the most critical moment was when, in the wake of the First World War and during the final break-up of the Ottoman Empire, eastern Thrace and the region of Smyrna were placed under Greek control. The age-old irredentist dream of a 'Great Greece' extending over 'two continents and five seas'[2] and encompassing ancient lands where Hellenism survived and prospered despite repeated conquests from outside, became real. However, it proved a short-lived experience as Turkish nationalism, which had also grown since the end of the nineteenth century, was determined not only to overturn the corrupt and declining empire but also to cleanse it of all foreign economic domination (Greek, Armenian and so on). In 1922, the defeat of Greece by Turkey, after an ill-planned Greek campaign eastwards from Smyrna, resulted in territorial and unprecedented human loss for Greece. Eastern Thrace and the islands of Imvros and Tenedos were lost to Turkey and the Greek populations, which during previous centuries had prospered especially in the Aegean coastal areas of Asia Minor, were expelled or annihilated.[3] Henceforth, Greece's frontiers became fixed and attention was turned towards domestic economic development.

The two processes of nation-building and economic development did not have the same intensity and rhythm. Economic nationalism developed gradually and it implied, on the one hand, as in every case of late development, official action by the state and, on the other, spontaneous and/or concerted action by various social groups. This chapter attempts to establish, first, the determinants of the national effort and policy and, secondly, the consequences of national integration.[4]

THE BACKGROUND

National consolidation in the nineteenth and early twentieth centuries primarily implied a certain degree of homogeneity, which was dependent on the successful integration and/or assimilation of various diverse groups of people living in the areas that were eventually liberated. This was only gradually achieved through central state action and policies including economic measures. It can be argued with some confidence that Greece in the nineteenth century enjoyed a considerable degree of homogeneity since, until the end of that century, populations living in Greece but speaking different languages, such as Albanians, were fully assimilated into the Greek culture and political system and did not exhibit any separate national identity.[5] The annexation of the northern territories, however, at the beginning of the twentieth century proved to be more complicated. Amidst a fervour of nationalistic sentiment all over the Balkan peninsula, the territory of Greece doubled and different 'ethnic' groups previously belonging to the multiethnic Ottoman Empire – now undergoing rapid disintegration – had to choose whether to become Greek, Bulgarian or Serbian citizens. What previously was simply a geographical area belonging to a single political authority, was now divided among three states – Serbia, Bulgaria and Greece. Thus, Greek Macedonia included 'non-Hellenic' populations, prominent among which was the Jewish minority scattered all over the new provinces, though with a strong concentration in Thessaloniki, the second most important city of the empire until 1913. There, according to one estimate, they represented two thirds of the population,[6] most of them having settled in Macedonia in successive waves since the end of the fifteenth century after their expulsion from Spain. In addition, there were several Christian Orthodox Slav-speaking groups, which were loyal either to the Bulgarian Exarchate or to the Serbian Church and eventually became active in anti-Greek propaganda. There were also Albanians, Turks, other Muslim groups, some Koutso-Vlachs who maintained ancestral links with Romania, and Gypsies.[7] The 'Macedonian Question' as an expression of the 'National Question' became an issue after the 1870s and led to repeated bloody conflicts; it lay at the base of the two Balkan Wars whilst propaganda among the countries that claimed the territory of Macedonia as historically theirs inflamed public opinion for a long time. For Greece, it supposedly ended with the annexation of part of Macedonia and Epirus in 1913.[8]

After the Balkan Wars the question of minorities began to emerge,

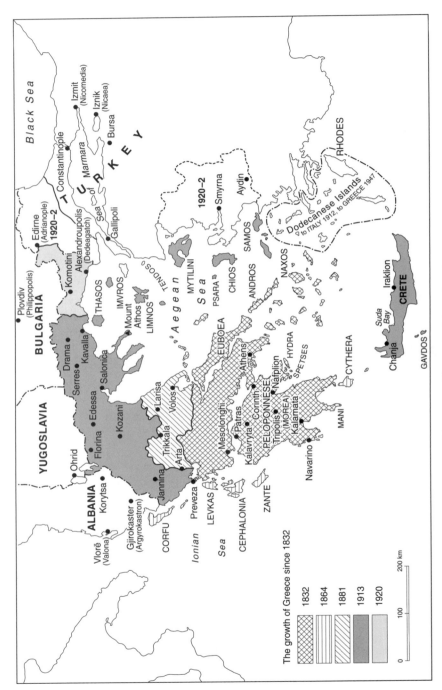

Figure 10.1. *The growth of Greece since 1832*

The growth of Greece since 1832

	1832
	1864
	1881
	1913
	1920

0   100   200 km

Black Sea

TURKEY

Izmit (Nicomedia)
Iznik (Nicaea)
Bursa
Marmara
Sea of Marmara
Constantinople
Gallipoli

Edirne (Adrianople) **1920–2**
Plovdiv (Philippopolis)
Komotini
Alexandroupolis (Dedeagatch)

BULGARIA

YUGOSLAVIA

Ohrid
Florina
Korytsa

ALBANIA

Gjirokaster (Argyrokastron)
Vlorë (Valona)

Drama
Serres
Kavalla
Edessa
Salonica
Kozani
THASOS
Mount Athos
IMVROS
LIMNOS

1920–2
Smyrna
Aydin

Dodecanese Islands
to ITALY 1912; to GREECE 1947

RHODES

SAMOS
NAXOS
ANDROS
CHIOS
PSARA
MYTILINI
TENDOS

A e g e a n   S e a

EUBOEA
Larisa
Volos
Trikkala
Arta
Jannina
Preveza
CORFU
LEVKAS
CEPHALONIA
ZANTE

Ionian Sea

Mesolonghi
Patras
Kalavryta
Corinth
Athens
Naftplion
HYDRA
SPETSES
PELOPONNESE (MOREA)
Tripolis
Kalamata
MANI
Navarino
CYTHERA

CRETE
Iraklion
Suda Bay
Chanja
GAVDOS

with successive Greek governments pursuing an integrationist policy for population groups of different ethnicity[9] living in the area. However, while it is useful to look at the various ethnicities and minorities living in Greece, this is not sufficient in itself to reach an understanding of the Greek situation: a further dimension needs to be taken into consideration. Refugees from those territories annexed by the other states in the area poured into Greece at different points in time, while a cultural integrationist policy was also directed towards the communities of the Greek diaspora. Until after the First World War, a number of Greek populations (Greek speaking, Christian Orthodox in faith and sharing similar national sentiments/consciousness with those Greeks living within the frontiers of the Greek nation state) lived outside Greece and were economically and socially as important (if not more so) as their helladic compatriots. They had been active for several centuries, founding prosperous communities both in European and Asiatic Turkey, as well as in several Balkan and central European states. They had also formed colonies, mainly of merchants, who had settled in various countries from America to India and Africa and who either returned to Greece in moments of crisis or maintained channels of emigration and communication for mainland or island Greeks throughout modern times. Their impact on the articulation of national policies and on the process of Greek economic development in the twentieth century was crucial.

If *ex post facto* national development is understood as a total phenomenon comprising state-building, cultural integration and economic growth, the emphasis in most analyses is usually placed on one of these aspects. As far as the economy is concerned, growth and progress is understood usually in terms of structural change as a result of industrialisation policies. However, if such an analytical framework is adequate for examining experiences of advanced countries, it is not always satisfactory for analysing late-developing countries.[10] In many cases agriculture and trade, not industry, were the sectors that developed at a faster pace and in fact inhibited the subsequent development of industry, while political modernisation also took precedence over the economy. In the early nineteenth century in late industrialisers such as Greece, ideas about what came to be termed 'development' took some time to find concrete expression and to be translated into policies. On the other hand, economic policies were not always viable and their implementation was rarely consistent. Such contradictions become intelligible if ideas and policies are examined against the background of political options and choices available. Furthermore, economic language in political statements was not used until relatively late; it is, therefore, difficult to infer economic preoccupations when dealing with older historical documents. Indeed, until the middle of the nineteenth century, turbulent political events in Greece not only detracted attention from the economy but determined the quality of information that we possess about it.[11]

For some time after independence, Greece generally remained an undeveloped – if not underdeveloped – country; agriculture was the main activity of helladic Greeks (whereas abroad, trade, shipping and banking were dominant). Land distribution and small family property as a way of compensation for services rendered during the war became a means of political, social and economic integration. Promotion of agriculture was given a high priority but little was actually done during the first two decades of independent life.[12] Small land tenure was accompanied by great shortage of local and of foreign capital, by high illiteracy rates, by an antiquated technology. As a result, agriculture remained stagnant, geared towards self-subsistence. Currant growing was the exception: gradually, due to a favourable trend in the European markets, it became the main export crop of the country. The possibility of increased profits from the cultivation of currants, some encouragement by the state for which exports were a vital source of revenue, and after 1841, the credit policy of the National Bank, eventually led to the establishment of a system of monoculture, which, however, made the Greek economy more vulnerable to foreign market fluctuations, contributed to serious crises and detracted investment away from industrial activity; nor did it solve the chronic deficit of the trade balance, which had also become a serious problem. The state became seriously preoccupied by the inefficiency of agriculture (that still absorbed over 60 per cent of the population) only after the Crimean War when Greek irredentist ambitions were violently frustrated. A government programme of moderate drainage works was undertaken and some care was shown for the construction of several small roads linking port areas.[13] As foreign trade was almost entirely seaborne, understandably its promotion depended on port improvement. Most importantly, the steps taken towards progress were *ad hoc* measures and did not form part of any coherent policy. For example, railway construction, which would have contributed to a much faster unification and homogenisation of the country, was postponed and was never adequately developed. Lack of sufficient capital resources, limited transfer of technology and the inadequacy of state policies were again among the main causes of retardation.

Ideas about development that did eventually emerge were rather vague and closely linked with the political ideology and aims of those early groups and statesmen that dominated events during the first phase of modern Greek history, closing with the end of the absolutist period (or the expulsion of King Otto in the 1860s). By the end of the first half of the century two contrasting views could be discerned. In one of them[14] nationalism became an instrument that would, on the one hand, unite the otherwise still divided Greeks, and that would, on the other, detract attention from any internal problems the country was facing. By extension, development was seen as dependent on the territorial expansion of Greece and on the cultural integration of those forces residing in still unredeemed areas (among which there were efficient entrepreneurs with talent and know-how who were active in international trade and banking). New lands, once liberated, would also theoretically be put to use, presumably as agricultural land. The emphasis was put not on industry but on agriculture and trade. An alternative view[15] favoured the creation of a strong unified country in the near east based on a centralised national government with a working constitution and with an efficient and honest bureaucracy, as free as possible of foreign influence.[16] By inference, it could be argued that the desire to establish a strong and efficient state would, on the one hand, induce development by allocating rationally both local and foreign capital resources – obtainable domestically through the major bank, and from foreign financiers through efficient diplomatic relations. On the other hand, the state would also prepare the development of human resources by establishing modern education and by encouraging the diffusion of innovations. In this project territorial expansion took second precedence and was made conditional on the prior domestic development of the productive forces. Both views were considered progressive, carrying the stamp of major European ideological trends and successful experiences of economic progress over the previous fifty years. In one of them, favoured by the statesman Ioannis Kolettes, nationalism engaged Greece in a constant struggle with Turkey and with its protectors, which ultimately truncated internal development, adulterated modernisation policies and detracted valuable economic resources.[17] Elements of these projects remained traceable in subsequent policies of development until well into the twentieth century.

Meanwhile, a more articulate developmental policy evolved in the 1870s and 1880s.[18] Whilst in 1871 foreign capital continued to be scarce[19] and the rate of investment was still low, land reform was finally proclaimed.[20] Further incentives for development included the suppression of brigandage and measures to end the isolation of the country. An early preoccupation with industry took the form of exploitation of local mineral resources. Mining was also seen as a means of allowing foreign investment to flow in and, therefore, concessions were granted to foreign companies.[21] The National Bank of Greece was beginning to emerge as the main instrument for the implementation of economic policy while the foreign debt had risen dangerously due, among other factors, to increased military expenditures for the support of Cretan refugees after the unsuccessful uprising on the island.

Developmental efforts became more systematic during the following decade, although, as will be shown, the outcome was uncertain, at least in the short and medium term. The successful settlement of the foreign debt question (1878) was followed by the annexation of Thessaly and part of Epeiros in 1881, and an ambitious reform programme was initiated by the successive Harilaos Trikoupis governments (1880–5, 1886–90, 1892–5). Developmental ideas were now strongly inspired by both political and economic liberalism, while the European aspects of Greek identity were emphasised and private initiative was encouraged.[22] The new policy was multifaceted with an interventionist role for the state. Priority was given to modernisation, which included not only the armed forces, the navy and the state administrative machine but also communications and transport (for example, railway construction, the Corinth Canal and the road network). Educational reform was also promoted, new taxation and a new system of tariffs were introduced. The main purpose of the latter was to secure additional revenue for the state, but agriculture was among the main beneficiaries since revenue was extracted from the urban bourgeois strata in favour of rural interests. It also proved beneficial for the protection of the nascent industries. Trikoupis sought to utilise whatever talent and ingenuity existed in the country and in the lands beyond the borders where Greeks prospered by appealing to progressive intellectuals, bureaucrats, professionals and entrepreneurs to take action. He contributed to the diffusion of innovations and technology by inviting foreign engineers and experts to advise on the reorganisation of the state administration and on ways to exploit national resources. Trikoupis' consistent policy of welcoming foreign investment, on the one hand, and the mid-1870s economic crisis that hit European markets, on the other, led to the attraction of foreign and of Greek (living outside Greece) investors. On the whole, reforms were not unsuccessful although overspending led to the eventual default on foreign payments in 1893 and a little later (1898) ushered in direct control of public finances by an International Finance Commission.[23]

Developmental policies, it could be argued, generally came rather late for the country and did not result in any important structural change. The crisis that had afflicted European economies as of 1873 forced investors to look for new markets and more profitable opportunities, which, however, led to speculative investment. Greek capitalists and financiers who operated in a wide area were also encountering problems: increasing competition by European capital and more effective methods of penetration in the Ottoman Empire forced Greek entrepreneurs to look for other outlets. Nationalism in other Balkan countries (Bulgaria, for example) had also started to constrain their activity, pushing them gradually out of those markets. Many among them chose to move to Greece where they assumed they could count on the support of the government and they would act as mediators between the latter and foreign investors with whom they were very familiar. Some also bought large plots of land from departing Ottomans in Thessaly and elsewhere, others invested in Greek bond loans, or they speculated on other titles and foreign exchange. What they did not do, however, was commit resources to productive activities.[24] This was a major weakness of the country, which the Trikoupis reform project did not alter. Despite its progressive character, it too was an expression of the older view and traditional conviction that agriculture and trade were the spine of the Greek economy that would guarantee the future and create prosperity for Greece. Reforms did not, in fact, prove incisive enough to change the traditional orientation of the dominant class nor did alternative views disappear. The economic logic of higher taxation that hit the lower strata harder and the heavier obligations that an inflated foreign debt entailed were neither accepted nor understood. Trikoupis was voted down in 1895, left Greece and died the following year in France. Meanwhile, public opinion had already been inflamed by developments in the north. Indeed, nationalism had become pervasive and irredentism cropped up as a central theme in the opposition's rhetoric. The situation had not been very different elsewhere. In addition to the grand national movements, for example Pan-Slavism and Pan-Germanism that gathered momentum, Italian and German unification was concluded and national mobilisation had led to the establishment of a Dual Monarchy in Austria-Hungary. But closer to Greece, the foundation of the Bulgarian Exarchate in 1878 and the occupation and subsequent annexation by Bulgaria in 1885 of Eastern Rumelia, an area where large Greek populations had for centuries prospered, created a major problem for Greece and caused conflict. Some of the Slavs in Macedonia opted for the Exarch while others remained under the protection of the Ecumenical Patriarch; others still acknowledged the National Serbian Church. Inflammatory propaganda was used by everybody and conflict was especially acute between Serbia and Bulgaria.[25] This was the beginning of an era during which national antagonisms in the Balkans became endemic. For Greece any further expansion in the future would no longer depend on the consent and/or support of the Great Powers, or on patience until the Ottoman Empire disintegrated completely.[26] Potential future confrontation with neighbouring countries would imply armed conflict, which necessitated extensive modernisation of the army, of the state and of the economy.[27] The disastrous engagement of the Greek and Turkish army in 1897 and the quick and dishonourable retreat of the former was the first intimation that disengagement from the conundrum would not be a simple affair. In fact it had severe repercussions domestically, which in 1909 culminated in a military *coup d'état* and soon afterwards in a new constitution and a new government headed by Eleutherios Venizelos.

TWENTIETH-CENTURY DEVELOPMENT

Early twentieth-century policies continued to be affected by circumstances that developed during the last years of the previous century, a period in which the last and more severe crisis of the Eastern Question occurred. Nationalism in the region reached its climax with the emergence of the Young Turk movement (1906–8), which marked the beginning of the end of the Greek presence in the eastern Aegean coast and beyond. The other major influence came from the postwar international economic situation. The year 1922 can be considered a turning point and as far as state interventionist policies are concerned, although they were initiated earlier, they were greatly strengthened after this date until the eve of the Second World War.

Two quotes by Eleutherios Venizelos, the Liberal leader whose personality and policies left a deep mark on the physiognomy of the country and the sentiment of the people, summarise in a rather succinct way the changes that had taken place, the framework of the policies followed and the mood of popular feeling and perception. Indeed, his words also unwittingly encapsulated the eventual fusion (if not reconciliation) of the two dominant views about nationalism. Venizelos' aim in 1909, 'to expand the stifling borders of our Nation', eighteen years later had changed into a 'dream to set the sound bases of an honest and well-run bourgeois state'.[28] In reality he tried to do both at the same time but the course of external and internal events determined the different emphasis at the beginning of each of his two terms of office.[29] His policies were largely successful but there was considerable failure, too, both because of the impact of international changes and that of domestic inertia.

The years 1900–17 were marked by the successful outcome of the Balkan Wars and the annexation of territories with 'multiethnic' characteristics, especially in the north. By 1917, Macedonia, Epeirus, Thrace, the islands of the eastern Aegean and Crete in the south had become parts of the national whole. It was gradually realised that cultural and social assimilation of the various populations in the new territories would be determined not only by effective cultural and social policies but would also be conditional on the degree of economic integration and homogenisation of the new provinces. The magnitude of the operation and at the same time the intricacies of securing peace necessitated much higher state intervention.[30]

Earlier national development policies had had a limited effect on the economy. Agriculture was still antiquated, the country exported much less than it imported, the degree of industrialisation was very low. Trade and banking continued to be the preferences of a rather weak – demographically, organisationally and economically – middle class. A large part of this class continued to reside abroad, its revenues being generated within foreign economies. Industry emerged towards the end of the century as a secondary activity, complementary to trade or as an alternative option during periods of crisis when trade was badly afflicted (for example, during the currant crisis in the mid-1880s and later in the 1890s). The absence of an important secondary sector also determined the weakness – in numerical and organisational terms – of a working class. In the countryside, a mass of small landholders were still engaged in subsistence farming. Periodic crises, low productivity and the very small size of holdings resulted in a constant outflow of human capital. People emigrated towards the Greek communities in the east, or towards the United States, or were pulled by the bigger towns where they filled the ranks of a burgeoning *petite bourgeoisie*. For most of them remittances and earnings from shipping which found their way back home to families that had stayed behind or filled the cash desks of banks as savings became the link with Greece. In addition to increasing consumption these remittances reduced the deficit in the balance of payments but only marginally improved the chances of development, to the extent that

they were invested in productive activities either privately or as credits
from the banks. What acted as a stronger bond, however, among these
disparate groups was the nationalist/irredentist *cause célèbre*. Until 1922,
ideas of economic expansionism and nationalism were still widespread
in the Greek offshore communities – notably in Asia Minor – while new
sympathisers appeared in mainland Greece itself. At the same time, a
sort of assimilationist nationalism started to develop, which transcended
both the ethnic and the 'class' dimension. Whereas during the previous
century nationalist slogans had mainly rallied peasant and *petit bourgeois*
forces, in the twentieth century, the indigenous helladic bourgeoisie,
which had by that time grown to some importance, began to appreciate
the economic implications of extending their businesses further east and
north. Extensive references appeared in the daily and economic press
about the advantages of a wider market, and in Macedonia itself economic action closely followed in the wake of political and military
events. Relations with the state became closer as businessmen donated
handsomely for the 'Hellenic cause', large land-holdings (*tsifliks*) belonging to departing Muslims were appropriated by wealthy Greeks (as was
done earlier in Thessaly). In fact, expropriation of rural land by Greeks
was seen by the Ministry of Foreign Affairs as a way to 'consolidate the
"Greek character" of Macedonia and Thrace'.[31] Greek populations
departing from Bulgaria in 1906 were assisted economically by the state
(and would benefit still more later from the general refugee settlement
policy undertaken by the Greek state and the League of Nations).
Between 1890 and 1910 chambers of commerce were founded in order
to assist the 'national' shipping, industry and trade sectors abroad.
Banks, especially the National Bank of Greece, which had traditionally
a very close relationship with the state, opened branches in the new areas
and in offshore centres of strong Greek presence not only because of the
lucrative business anticipated[32] but as part of a more general nationalist
policy.[33] Such activity was not devoid of hostile and violent incidences
as is indicated by the frequency with which businesses of Slav supporters of the Bulgarian Exarch were boycotted in Thessaloniki.[34]

Nationalism found expression, too, in the introduction of a new
institutional framework. Legislative modernisation of this period was
consistent with nationalist/expansionist feelings on the one hand, and
economic advancement on the other. A new system of tariffs was devised
in 1917 (although it was not actually put into effect until 1926): law
2190/1920 regulating the operation of joint-stock companies and law
2948/1922 for the promotion of industry both targeted the creation of
modern firms that would expand into Turkey and the Balkans.[35]

The defeat by Turkey in August 1922 frustrated such expectations and changed the orientation of the nationalist discourse. Large multidivisional companies failed to emerge, giving way to the more resilient small family enterprises, while monetary devaluation impeded further the in-flow and concentration of capital. While until 1921 emigration continued rising and divested Greece of potential manpower (thereby increasing labour shortages and contributing to the maintenance of relatively high wages), the possibility of a reversal of the trend was neutralised thanks both to the quota system introduced by the United States in 1921, and by the influx of 1.5 million refugees from Turkey. Labour scarcity now gave way to labour congestion and chronic unemployment. State interventionism was increased during the whole of the interwar period, in an attempt to attenuate the problems by means of labour policies and protectionist measures for industry and agriculture, but it failed because it lacked cohesion. Moreover, the defensive nationalist discourse was not sufficient to reconcile the conflicting interests of farmers, merchants, industrialists and workers and conceal the confusion of the aims of a policy based only on weak social forces, especially a weak middle class. The long Ottoman past (1453–1821), which itself preserved the byzantine tradition of a bureaucratic state, had not allowed the formation of a full-fledged bourgeoisie along the western pattern. Rather, it contributed to the formation of a less autonomous bureaucratic/merchant class. It was on this vestige that the modern Greek nation state was based and gradually cushioned the emergence of a weak national bourgeoisie (intra-border and extra-border) supported and protected by state interventionist and protectionist policies. Greek nationalism of the early twentieth century, therefore, continued to be part of the traditional liberationist ideology, only enriched now by a symbiotic relationship between the middle class and the state, but not leading to an effective emancipation of social forces.

The rise to power in 1910 of Venizelos and his Liberal Party was both a result of the support of this emerging force and the precondition for its full articulation and consolidation. Nationalism became the guiding principle of policy after the successful outcome of the Balkan Wars. In addition to Venizelos' diplomatic insight,[36] a wide programme of institutional reforms was undertaken with the dual purpose to modernise Old Greece and to homogenise the very diverse new provinces. The underlying assumption was that this would be easier if Greece maintained friendly relations with her traditional allies, the Entente powers, which in turn implied participation in the war effort. This brought Venizelos (and his supporters) into direct conflict with the more traditional forces (royalists) who favoured neutrality and, as a result, Greece was on the verge of civil war (*dichasmos*) for a number of years. It is in this period that the seeds of the subsequent civil strife were also sown. Among the immediate post-Balkan-war priorities the protection of border areas figured high and was perceived as concomitant with demographic, cultural and economic homogeneity. Incentives were given so that considerable numbers of people would move to the north from southern provinces. In Macedonia a cohesive local administrative network was organised, receiving direct instructions from the central government in Athens; ecclesiastical administration was introduced to achieve religious homogeneity; educational and linguistic integration of non-Greek speakers received immediate attention. Communications were also given a boost, carrying further the dynamism that was a result of the war as a number of roads, initially near Thessaloniki, were constructed for military purposes. In 1917, a new law provided for the construction of 3,205 kilometres of roads in the whole of Greece, of which 1,287 were in the new provinces. Railway construction, which had had its heyday during the Trikoupis era without ever leading to a complete or even adequate network, resumed after 1913. The most important Larissa– Thessaloniki line as of 1916 linked Greece directly with the continent. But it was also realised that successful integration of Macedonia and of the other provinces rested on the development of their local resources. With a shortage of population this was not an easy task. The emphasis was once again placed mainly on agriculture, which became the central instrument of economic policy. Improvement of the primary sector in Thessaly thirty years earlier had not borne the fruits expected. Methods of cultivation remained backward and agrarian reform ran into a stalemate. There remained substantial large holdings that had not been broken up. The situation in Macedonia, Epeiros and Thrace was not very different and full enforcement of the law promulgated in 1917 did not happen until after 1922 and the arrival of the refugees. Land reform was not fully enacted until 1923 and the pattern of small-holding – dominant until then in Old Greece – was now generalised. However, despite considerable innovation in the institutional framework, which included the foundation of co-operatives (since 1914), easier borrowing from the National Bank and the introduction of credit for smaller farmers, the break-up of large holdings (*tsifliks*) improved productivity levels only marginally whereas restructuring of agricultural production was still a desideratum. Land reform had over the years become a central political issue and was seen by the Venizelists primarily as a means of appeasement and control of an otherwise hostile and conservative (royalist) peasantry. Once again the rationale of policies was not purely economic, their implementation incomplete and the results remained mixed. It took over fifteen years for any changes to become obvious. Among those were a rise in the area of cultivable land,[37] and a certain restructuring towards industrial and export crops. Greek exports were now dominated by Macedonian tobacco, which had replaced currants, the main crop in Peloponnesos (Old Greece) since the nineteenth century. Cotton was also promoted, whereas the policy aiming to encourage cereal-growing was less successful.[38] The cultivation of cereal was seen by the governments of the period as the cornerstone of agricultural autarkic policy. The aim was to reduce the import of wheat – by far the major import item in the trade balance – to secure a measure of self-sufficiency and to limit the outflow of foreign exchange, and hence also reduce the deficit in the balance of payments. Cereal production, however, did not pick up until after 1927 when stronger interventionist action was taken, including measures to increase production and productivity and to improve concentration and distribution.[39]

The other aim of agricultural policy, that of converting farmers into a mass of consumers who would support import substitution industrialisation, also had only limited success. Agricultural machines were still imported in the late 1930s and fertilisers that were domestically produced were underused. Only light consumer goods production marked a steeper development, which, however, was also a mark of distortion. Given the low income of peasants, items produced were cheap, often of substandard quality. Moreover, small and inefficient production units competed for the same market with larger and more modern firms which, under the circumstances, had difficulties in surviving. Indeed, there was very little difference in industrial development between 1920 and 1930 and, if anything, industrial units were now smaller than before, whereas larger units remained unchanged. Industrialisation of the north depended on the existence of a communication network between Macedonia and the rest of Greece and only after the construction of the Thessaloniki–Monastir railway line did towns such as Verroia, Naoussa and Edessa start to modernise and industrialise. Local energy resources also remained untapped. To highlight this point it is sufficient to mention that in 1913, a mere three factories used electricity for lighting (because the Ottoman authorities prohibited the production of electricity).[40] Although the wealth of Macedonia belonged either to Greeks or to the large Jewish communities,[41] industrialisation was neither easy nor smooth. The growth of nationalism in the Balkan provinces and the

change in the role of large towns of Macedonia such as Thessaloniki
from metropolis to provincial towns of a small and weak nation, prevented their fast and successful integration. Already by the late 1920s the
trend of concentration of all industrial activity around Athens was
becoming obvious.[42]

A third facet of development policy was the promotion of large infrastructure works. Projects were designed immediately after the Balkan
Wars but did not actually materialise until the interwar years. They
absorbed large foreign capital resources, mainly foreign contractors
were involved and some of them became the object of serious controversy because of the extremely onerous terms of the loans involved.
Most of the projects aimed at improving agriculture although a few concerned utilities (the Athens water scheme and the electrification project).
Greek governments also considered large public works as a mechanism
of job creation. Among their most important consequences, however,
was the strengthening of technological dependence of Greece on
foreign countries, since most of the equipment and material was purchased abroad (often by virtue of stipulations included in the loan agreements) and Greek manpower was used only as unskilled labour. Despite
these serious shortcomings any assessment of this policy should take into
account the fact that those projects were indispensable and there was
little possibility that they would have been constructed without foreign
assistance. On the other hand, it should also be noted that the efficiency
of economic and developmental policies also depended not only on the
existence of well-worked-out plans but on the negotiating power and
ability of the borrowing governments and on the quality of bureaucratic
and advisory services provided. In the case of Greece, there was a serious
deficit on both these counts.

What is important to note is that the policies described above were
fully enacted when expansionism was no longer an option, when
emigration was seriously curtailed, both by the uprooting of the Greek
communities in the east and by quota constraints imposed by the United
States, and when pressure was exerted domestically on the economy, the
society and on the political system. Attention of decision-makers was
turned inwards as domestic resources had to be mobilised in order to
absorb the large refugee population that flowed in after the 1922 defeat
by Turkey. Whereas in 1919, the future of the country was still considered embedded in the expansion outward and the development of agriculture, shipping and trade,[43] in 1927 the situation was interpreted

differently: The National Bank of Greece, which was a central institution for policy enactment (including conducting negotiations with
foreign capital holders and investors – governments and private institutions – handling of properties belonging to departed Muslims, issuing of
national bond loans, co-operating with the League of Nations, planning
and applying economic and monetary policy until 1927), left no doubt
about the changes required. In his annual report of that year, the
Governor of the Bank emphasised that:

it was no longer possible for the Bank [and the Government] to argue whether
industry or agriculture or trade should be promoted. The sudden increase in
the urban population made imperative the development and support of large
and small industries, so that they may absorb the abundant labour manpower
of the towns. To ignore this would cause an immediate and acute social
problem.[44]

Already during the previous five years concerted efforts had been made
to that effect, especially by favouring the industrial class. In addition to
public commissions, subsidies, credit arrangements and tax concessions,
among the most direct and at the same time symbolic actions was the
appointment of a leading industrialist, Andreas Hadjikyriakos, as
Minister of National Economy in the first post-1922 government.

The influx of refugees in Greece in 1922 has been considered, with
reason, the biggest tragedy in modern Greek history; however, it may
also have been a blessing in disguise because it speeded up the enactment
of the development policies initiated after the Balkan Wars. Several
groups of refugees came into Greece between 1913 and 1925, as a result
of the rearrangement of frontiers in the Balkans, but the bulk of them
(57 per cent) arrived between 1922 and 1923, and 30 per cent between
1923 and 1925. As a result of these movements and of the abruptness of
the operation several imbalances were created, among the most important of which was the rural/urban distribution of newcomers. According to the settlement policy implemented, 46 per cent of refugees were
settled in towns and 54 per cent in the countryside as farmers. As regards
Macedonia and the north, for almost ten years there was no stability
since new settlers moved about every time one of the belligerent countries won a battle and later, after 1922, every time legislation regarding
refugee indemnities changed. Initially, the work of rehabilitation was
undertaken by the state, and an impressive body of legislation was introduced after 1913 for the regulation of the distribution of land belonging
to Muslims or about confiscating lands belonging to citizens of enemy

countries. The latter were later returned to previous occupants, causing serious confrontation and provoking outbursts of violence. Regulation was not always applied objectively and farms could hardly be put to use under such conditions of uncertainty.

In 1923, after the signing of the Treaty for the Compulsory Exchange of Populations between Greece and Turkey, Greek authorities appealed to the League of Nations for support. This led to the negotiation of a series of important foreign loans and to the establishment of the Refugee Settlement Commission (RSC) with extensive rights and possession of 500,000 hectares of land. The RSC had jurisdiction over refugee housing, health, employment, finance and other affairs. In addition to foreign resources, domestic loans were also raised amounting to 12 billion drs or 27.8 per cent of the public debt. Refugees were settled either as farmers or as urban settlers. Of the two kinds of settlement the one in agricultural activities was faster, more systematic and more effective due to the availability of land, to the fact that tools were relatively inexpensive, and that the duration of the need of settlers to be supported was limited, but mostly because it became part of an already articulated national agricultural policy. Agricultural settlement, moreover, had important political ramifications and was actively promoted by state, international and local authorities, primarily as a conservative response aiming to control the situation against the danger of potential social unrest.[45] Refugees were not likely to become proletarians nor would they remain idle, and even if their incomes were desperately low, they had a piece of land that they would sooner or later put to use. This would prevent them from forming a common front with workers and from being receptive to socialist ideas. In a similar spirit, refugees were never treated as a homogeneous group. They were dispersed all over Greece, although the bulk was moved to Macedonia, an area of 34,893 square kilometres whose population had grown between 1920 and 1928 by 31 per cent and which became a hothouse of authoritarian institutional reform.[46] Half of that population (around 450,000 people) were refugees and another 90,000 were settled in Thrace.[47] Their dispersion, on the one hand, halted any possibility of mass protest and rendered them more amenable to political influence while, on the other, it contributed to a faster homogenisation of the country.

Urban settlement was more complicated and largely ineffective, as housing without employment was not a sufficient condition for viability. Athens, Piraeus and Thessaloniki concentrated the greater volume of refugees, who were usually housed in temporary facilities in belt zones around the cities while rather primitive permanent housing was only gradually provided – sold – to them.[48] Overcrowding in the poorest refugee suburbs was common, unemployment high and living conditions generally appalling. Again there was no uniform policy as in other cases, houses were built by the more affluent refugees on their initiative and with their own resources. As there was no articulate industrial policy, nor any plan for their assimilation either according to their origins or according to skills or even to developmental requirements, urban refugees were left generally alone to fend for themselves. Much ingenuity was shown in devising strategies for survival on an individual, family or collective level and this determined their long-term prospects of success as well as the picture of the more general developmental process.[49] On the other hand, both farmer-refugees and urban settlers met with much hostility from indigenous resident groups to an extent that they were considered collectively as a minority on an equal footing with Muslims, Slavs or Jews. Despite integrationist policies, feelings of refugee separateness have never been completely eradicated from subsequent generations of descendants to this day. Similar situations arose also after the war with refugees arriving in Greece from countries such as Romania after the consolidation there of the communist regime, or later still with Greeks from Turkey (1955) or Egypt (late 1950s and early 1960s) who abandoned their countries after the establishment of staunch nationalistic regimes.

Among the darker sides of refugee activity and tactics was the brief re-emergence of the spectre of defensive nationalism in the 1920s and 1930s. It was expressed as anti-semitism and was directed mainly against the Jews of Thessaloniki and other towns in the north.[50] The two groups were competing within the same space and for similar economic resources, largely with a similar economic mentality but under very different ideological constellations. Thessaloniki, the prewar metropolis of the Balkans, had, after 1922, been relegated to the status of a provincial town, overcrowded and packed with refugees, many of them living below the poverty line, where Greeks from the south had also been encouraged to settle. The prewar dominant Jewish community was now officially a minority and the economic, social and political balance of the whole area had been upset for ever. Refugees were largely supporters of Venizelos but Jews, with the exception of a handful of elite personalities, were not: before Annexation, the latter supported first the Ottoman government and later the Young Turk radical nationalist republican movement, both of which were anathema for Greece. Over the years,

an important number of intellectual Jews who maintained close relations with the Jewish communities of western and central Europe
became involved in the socialist movement, of which Greek governments, including Venizelist ones, were rather suspicious. Refugees, on
the other hand, were encountering problems of subsistence arising from
the procrastination in finding a solution to the compensation problem
for properties left in Turkey; they were also victims of frequent unfair
discrimination – bordering on racism – by local or recently arrived from
the south populations. The ground was, therefore, fertile for extremist,
mainly fascist propaganda and the newly arrived inhabitants were
vulnerable to extreme activity emanating from various quarters.

To conclude by assessing the role of the refugees, it could be argued
that on the whole they seemed to have strengthened the traditional
aspects of the Greek economy and society. Although this might not have
been among the central aims of the settlement project, the dominance
of political considerations in designing national policy seems to have
tilted the scales in favour of tested methods and solutions. Substantive
foreign and domestic financial resources were used for the rehabilitation
of refugees, for monetary stabilisation and for balancing state budgets,[51]
but development policies as already mentioned were not always economically consistent or rational. The 'abundant refugee manpower' was
not systematically or primarily channelled to industry but mostly to
largely parasitic, handicraft production or tertiary activity, or to small-
holding agriculture. This was consistent with a social and political logic
dominant among the political and economic elite circles even within the
leading financial institutions of the country. Once again the Governor
of the National Bank was explicit:

the composition of the population of Greece includes many *petit-bourgeois* elements that have not yet been absorbed by large production. If these elements,
so precious for social balance, are not supported in their struggle to maintain
their position, we shall have committed a serious error. For that reason, the
Bank, without any reservation, has extended to the limit its credit despite the
difficulties involved in following the course of these loans.[52]

This logic was not in harmony with economic or organisational criteria.
It was especially found in public employment policies that contributed
to the functioning of the civil service as being something akin to an
agency of job creation.[53] In industry, policies were unclear as to their
aims and riddled with contradictions. Carpet industry is a case in point:
it was introduced as a completely new activity for which refugees had an
almost exclusive and excellent know-how. It failed completely because

of deficient organisation of production and distribution, inadequate and/or untimely state protection in securing co-ordination of production and distribution of products in external market outlets.[54] Carpet production was wrongly perceived mainly as a handicraft activity that could provide only supplementary income for farmers and craftsmen, often cheap female labour, or other small traders, not as an export sector based on big firms, skilled labour and modern organisation methods. As for encouraging industrial activity in general, there was no coherent plan, education was inadequate, capital if available was dear and anyway found its way more to agriculture and to the new provinces, at least until 1927. Nor did protectionism in the form of a new tariff system introduced in 1923 help industrial policy, as no particular branch of industry was targeted (cement production, fertilisers or heavy industry, for example); it functioned ultimately to the benefit of the state as a source of revenue (40 per cent of regular revenue came from this source) and much less to the benefit of Greek industry, which remained inefficient and without incentives to modernise. Moreover, protectionist policy was once again hampered by internal contradictions: for instance, sometimes taxing and other times granting exemptions to imported machinery, raw materials and intermediate goods; it was also designed strictly within the framework of import substitution industrialisation and ignored the possibility of certain sectors becoming export orientated, despite encouraging evidence to that effect. Other aspects of protectionism concerned the system of public procurement, tax relief, limited possibility of land expropriation and subsidies for transport and communications. Certain industries were declared 'saturated', and relocation of plants became impossible. The enactment of these measures was cumbersome, riddled with red tape and ultimately also open to abuse and corruptive practices. As for the 'saturation' or 'sufficiency' principle, a central concept in interwar development policy, it was probably the main cause for the delay in the modernisation and competitiveness of Greek industry. In fact, it satisfied short-term interests of certain entrepreneurs and at the same time expressed the deep belief by most politicians that industry was not a viable proposition for Greece. It was a self-fulfilling prophecy since by the mid-1930s, although the number of factories and workshops had doubled and production had increased, the structure of the secondary sector remained intact. As late as in 1932, the Minister of National Economy was still stating that Greece had a dual economic identity based on agriculture and trade.[55] The clearing agreements, he believed, were the best guarantee for placing Greek products abroad. It seemed as though the development policy had come full circle back to the old traditional ideas. A more definite push to industry that occurred during the last few years before the war (marked by the 1936–40 dictatorial government of Ioannis Metaxas) was not able to turn the tide. State intervention was strengthened especially in the area of labour legislation and social security but there was no change in the overall policy designed back in the 1920s and early 1930s. Although the decision to rearm could be seen as part of the new nationalist discourse that implied the exploitation of domestic energy resources, and placing mineral production and heavy industry high on the government priority list as a basis for technological development and military might, the poor performance suggests otherwise. In fact, under the influence of older German-inspired doctrines and the rise of socialist forces, economic liberalism quickly receded into the background and the dictatorial regime became anxious to enlarge its social base by emphasising political rather than only economic aims. Both projects of social security for the workers and more concessions for the middle class were, anyway, short-lived experiments, as was the life of the regime. The war interrupted any plans and the reshuffle of social forces and policies was postponed.

THE WAR YEARS AND THE POST-SECOND WORLD WAR PERIOD

The postwar years were marked by a radical break in ideas about development and policies. The new reality of United States hegemony and increased internationalisation of political decision-making soon brought Greece into the orbit of the American plan to stabilise national dependent economies. Because of the intensity of the ongoing civil war (1946–9) and the geo-strategic considerations in the escalating Cold War, Greece acquired a particular importance in the scheme as a pilot case. Industrialisation was central in the new scheme. It had already been at the core of debates since the last years before the war and during the occupation years, when the concept of a state industrial utility sector (especially a national energy network) gathered momentum both within bourgeois circles and within the resistance movement led by the National Liberation Front (EAM). The consensus on the need to develop heavy industry with state involvement continued after liberation, although important differences now arose between the left (CPG) and right-wing politicians, economists and intellectuals (PPG, DSPG).[56] Meanwhile, the productive capacity of the country had during the preceding war and occupation years been seriously reduced both in agriculture and industry, the transport system was utterly destroyed, public finances and banks were in chaos, and living conditions were particularly harsh due to starvation and disease. Over 500,000 people had perished between 1940 and 1944 as victims of war, of executions, of murders, of starvation and disease. Almost 2 million (over 25 per cent) of the population were, at the end of the war, dependent on relief organisations for their survival. Over 1 million were homeless, one third of the 9,000 villages and almost 23 per cent of buildings of any kind were either completely demolished or seriously damaged. Means of production were in a very bad state both in agriculture and in industry, while means of transport had almost disappeared, including the merchant fleet, which was largely destroyed.[57] The impact of war was equally important on the structure and on the moral fibre of Greek society. A part of the old bourgeoisie and almost the totality of the prosperous Jewish entrepreneurial community of Thessaloniki and other towns had either lost their property, went underground or perished in the harsh conditions of the triple occupation (German, Italian and Bulgarian) of the country between 1941 and 1945. Some joined the resistance movement, with organisations on the left and right, as did a mass of the *petit-bourgeois* and farmer population, while collaboration with the enemy was also considerable. Everywhere, but especially in Old Greece (south), old cleavages (republicans and royalists, socialists and liberals, and so on) were revived, and after liberation they contributed to the escalation of civil war which prolonged the generalised economic upheaval. Three attempts to stabilise the economy (in October 1944, summer 1945 and in 1946) having failed, hyperinflation, speculation and hoarding became rampant. In the absence of any social cohesion, but also because of the prewar tradition of state interventionism, recovery and reconstruction had to pass directly by the state, which eventually received and allocated considerable American 'AID' resources, exceeding 50 per cent of GDP. According to plans drawn up by international and national expert organisations,[58] industrialisation, which was to be the major vehicle of development, implied reinforcement of the state bureaucracy on the one hand and technical assistance from abroad on the other. However, in the specific conditions of Greece, neither was foreign technology accompanied by a corresponding business culture that would be grafted upon the new environment nor was the allocation of funds devoid of political considerations.[59] Consequently, resources were also used for non-economic purposes, including putting down the left-wing guerrilla fighters. Moreover, through a series of politically motivated state protectionist and subsidisation policy, it led to the consolidation of a 'nouveau-riche' entrepreneurial class.[60] This group consisted largely of elements that had become rich during the war through dubious practices (speculation, black market and contraband), including appropriation of foreign properties and collaboration with the occupation authorities.[61] In the new conditions, most of them showed a preference for short-term ventures, for trade or banking speculative transactions on foreign exchange that were supposed to fetch high and quick profits, as well as for government-endorsed bids of public works and construction projects. This turn of affairs, despite reactions from a number of elite economists, was not really opposed, since any opposition was offset by the prospects of economic growth that the promised recovery implied, by the desire to return to some kind of normalcy and by the ideological deadlock of anti-communism, which was accompanied by extended state repression against any dissident action or opinion. After the end of the civil war and the defeat of the left, the combination of American influence, the escalating Cold War and the short-term perspectives of the reinstated conservative political elite influenced both economic options and foreign issues. Weak governments, direct American intervention in national politics, confusion over policies and widespread corruption led to a sort of cynicism whereby acquiescence to government choices was rewarded. Rewards took the form of possibilities to collaborate with the state and to benefit from various kinds of concessions, which in turn allowed both the survival of new non-qualified entrepreneurs and a steady increase in the number of civil servants. Between 1941 and 1953 an impressive 40,000 new firms were founded, representing 50 per cent of the total number of industrial firms operating in 1953, while by 1951 the Greek economy had reached 1938 levels, and the industrial production index stood at 241 in relation to 1946 (100). Nevertheless, in the same year (1951), almost 95.5% of all industrial units – personal or family firms – employed fewer than ten people, suggesting that the structure of Greek industry had essentially remained unchanged compared with the prewar period. The number of civil servants also rose from 55,000 in 1940 to 132,000 in 1970, a rise of 140 per cent, against a 19 per cent population rise in the same period. From 1945 to 1952 half of the resources from Marshall Aid were channelled to military expenses for the civil war and 25 per cent was spent on imports of consumption goods, the remainder going to infrastructure investment and only a minimal amount finding its way to industry and production.[62] Modernisation without restructuring and high growth rates accompanied by the maintenance of a traditional economic structure was the result of policies that once more deviated from strictly rational economic considerations. Politically, the pendulum moved eventually further to the right, neutralising the voice of the moderate liberals and democrats who held power until 1951, while the uninterrupted economic growth had also made possible the survival of a multiparty institutional framework and the absence of overt authoritarian rule, until 1967. This was based on a materially prosperous new middle class, supported by the state, which was in turn supporting the strong anti-communist police state that managed to operate under a cloak of legitimate democratic parliamentary rule. Foreign relations during this period were also affected by the new circumstances, as territorial claims on northern Epeirus, Dodecannesos and southern Bulgaria were included in the manifesto of most bourgeois parties, which vehemently exploited the confusion about the Macedonian issue that characterised Greek communists faced with the aggressiveness of Balkan Communist parties. National territorial expansion was advocated on the basis of economic considerations such as, for instance, the need to tap energy resources in the north and offset the poverty of the Greek soil. These claims, however, were refuted by reports of international organisations on the postwar economic possibilities of Greece. After the cession of the Dodecanese by Italy to Greece in 1945, national issues definitely receded in the background. The intensity of the last two rounds of the civil war and the consequent violent repression and generalised fear, had virtually annihilated any possibility for alternative opinions to be expressed, leaving the way open for American influence and political intervention. The contradictions implied above were exacerbated with the military takeover in 1967.

Examining the imposition of the military dictatorship lies outside the scope of this chapter. Suffice it to say, however, that the contradictions outlined above were accentuated, the economy suffered severely from gross incompetence and corruption and the quality of political and cultural life was diminished. The seven-year authoritarian rule postponed yet again the resolution of the ideological and cultural cleavages created during the war and civil war, which finally became possible after the return to normalcy in 1974. On the economic front, important opportunities to benefit from the upward trend of the world economy until 1973 were lost, making recovery after 1974 more difficult. Close co-operation with American advisers and agencies, the memory of early postwar arrogant American political intervention and suspicion of involvement in the Turkish invasion of Cyprus coupled with a pro-Turkish stand as regards Graeco-Turkish negotiations provoked a wave of anti-American demonstrations after 1974. This was carried on into the 1980s and was exacerbated by the economic recession. Since the collapse of socialism in eastern Europe new realignments have occurred, but the massive in-flow of illegal immigrants from eastern European and Asian countries, especially from Albania, is creating tension marked by xenophobia, while there is also a general feeling that the question of the Muslim minority in the north needs to be reassessed, and both economic and cul-tural integration policies to become more dynamic.

CONCLUSION

The chapter has argued that policies of economic development and the evolution of the National Question in twentieth-century Greece cannot be separated from the general historical process of political, economic and cultural consolidation of the modern nation state that started in the early nineteenth century. Structural problems and ideas that contributed to their maintenance started early in the century; significant changes in social structure and economic policy were slow and difficult to achieve. Attention was drawn to the fact that, especially in late-developing coun-tries, the role of the state – and of a number of collaborating institutions – was important in devising and enacting economic policies – even in shaping social forces. In attempting to isolate the determinants of national policy and to assess the results of national integration, it was found that a non-economic logic prevailed in state policy-making that determined the degree of their efficiency. The activities of social agents themselves had an important part in shaping the outcome. The National Question has been inextricably linked with the development process and this relationship has often detracted and/or limited the ability to for-mulate rational policies. Nationalism emerged as a multifaceted process or concept, both regressive and progressive, with an expansionist and a defensive dimension, leading both to integrationist and assimilationist policies at different points in time. It shaped development ideas and poli-cies certainly until the Second World War but was not based primarily on industrialisation. Its importance as a mechanism of integration rather receded in the post-Second World War period when a significant change was observed as industrialisation became the central process under increased state intervention and American influence. Old contra-dictions, however, did not disappear, as many traditional features of the Greek economy and society prevailed until well into the 1980s.

NOTES

1 In 1829, the boundary of the mainland was laid down and the islands adjoining Peloponnesos, Euboea, the Cyclades and the Northern Sporades also became part of the Greek kingdom by the Protocol of 22 March and the Treaty of 21 July 1832 between the three Protecting Powers (England, France and Russia) and Turkey. In 1863 the Ionian Islands were ceded by Britain to Greece, while as a result of the Treaty of Berlin in 1878 the frontiers were changed and in 1881 Thessaly and the district of Arta were added to Greek territory. Finally, after the Balkan wars in 1912–13 and victory, Greece acquired Macedonia and Thrace, as well as the islands of the northern Aegean, and the frontiers with Bulgaria and Serbia were fixed. Turkey finally renounced its claims to the island of Crete in 1913. Crete had taken part in the war of independence and several uprisings occurred on the island. Two years after the last Cretan insurrection of 1896, Crete became autonomous, maintaining this status until 1906; subsequently, union with Greece was proclaimed (see map, figure 10.1).

2 An expression used by E. Venizelos after the conclusion of the Treaty of Sèvres.

3 The last phase of territorial expansion occurred in 1948 when the Dodecanese Islands – under Italian occupation – were finally ceded to Greece.

4 Whereas the literature on nationalism in general is extensive, there are relatively few works on economic nationalism. Moreover, they usually focus on recent third world development policies. A. Kahan's analysis is a welcome exception. See A. Kahan, 'Nineteenth-century European experience with policies of economic nationalism' in H. G. Johnson (ed.), *Economic Nationalism in Old and New States* (London, 1968), pp. 17–30.

5 Albanians in fact had fought in the war of independence as Greeks and became citizens of the new nation. The frequent occurrence of Italian proper names and the Catholic faith in the Cyclades Islands indicating descent from noble Genoese or Venetian families cannot be used as evidence of foreign influence, since these populations were, as a rule, of Greek extraction. See *Peace Handbooks*, Vol. III, Part I, 'Greece with the Cyclades and Northern Sporades', No. 18 (London, 1920), p. 14.

6 *Peace Handbooks*, Vol. IV, Part II, 'The Balkan States', No. 21 (London, 1920), pp. 14, 80 and 91.

7 For a detached and detailed contemporary presentation of the ethnic groups in Macedonia, A. A. Pallis, 'Racial migrations in the Balkans during the years 1912–1924', *The Geographical Journal* 66 (1925), 315–31.

8 The recent rekindling of the issue in the area lies beyond the scope of this chapter.

9 'Ethnicity' is a problematic term too, as different criteria of classification have been used over time. Within the Ottoman Empire, for instance, under the millet system, religion – and not language or national sentiment – was the determining factor. Once independent nations were created, or national

consciousness developed, criteria changed. In the case of Macedonia, there was an amazing confusion as the various groups adhered to national policies that reacted and responded to the manipulation of the Ottoman Empire, which harnessed local antagonisms to maintain her authority for a while longer.

10 As shown by G. Tortella, 'A latecomer: the modernisation of the Spanish economy 1800–1990' in M. Teich and R. Porter (eds.), *The Industrial Revolution in National Context, Europe and the USA* (Cambridge, 1996), pp. 184–200.

11 These events included the assassination of the first Governor of Greece, Ioannis Kapodistria, in 1829; civil war; the establishment of a kingdom under King Otto (1832) and the hegemony for a number of years of a Bavarian court; the granting of a constitution as late as 1843; the eventual expulsion of the king twenty years later and the hope of expansion often instigated by the ambitions and designs of foreign powers but also by a deep-rooted popular sentiment in Greece. Such events and concerns absorbed the minds of statesmen and the people in general and detracted attention from questions of economic organisation.

12 After independence all land was passed to the state. It was then gradually sold to the farmers. Because of the inadequate income of the population, and the inability of the state to draw a land registry (*cadastre*) and efficiently enact the relevant legislation, land distribution was delayed until a law was passed as late as 1871. Squatting became a widespread tactic by peasants. Among propositions for progress, colonisation was also suggested but the scheme failed as there has never been a concrete and homogeneous plan but rather vague ideas about the invitation of foreign immigrants.

13 In 1868 there were twenty-one roads of a total of 461 kilometres – three times that of the 1850s – but no major road was yet planned.

14 Ioannis Kolettes, an astute politician who had lived and studied in France, was among the main exponents of this policy. He favoured an expansionist foreign policy and integration of the Greek populations in several areas still under Ottoman rule. An ardent admirer of the principles of the French Revolution, he was the leader of the 'French' party, and acted often under the influence of the then French Prime Minister, François Guizot. Sensitive to the fact that his party was very heterogeneous, consisting of some of the most traditional sections of Greek society, Kolettes also used nationalism to maintain cohesion. His administration, however, became riddled with immobilism and corruption. For an extensive analysis of the early party system in Greece, see J. A. Petropoulos, *Politics and Statecraft in the Kingdom of Greece, 1833–1843* (Princeton, NJ, 1968), pp. 344–420.

15 Advocated mainly by another statesman, Alexandros Mavrokordatos, a westernised Phanariot, with strong sympathies and contacts among English philhellenic circles and leader of one of the early Greek parties, the 'English' party.

16 Since the inception of the Greek state, patronage – both foreign and local

– had become the basis of political integration and efforts to introduce an efficient bureaucracy had generally failed.

17 British control over the fate of Greece and its relations with Turkey, for instance, took rather extreme forms as in the first British blockade in 1850, the Franco-British occupation of Piraeus in 1854, at the time of the Crimean war when Greeks sympathised instead with Russia and saw an opportunity to claim Epeirus, Thessaly and Macedonia; and in 1886, during the Diliyannis mandate and Greek involvement in Macedonia, when a second British blockade was imposed.

18 This period coincided with a change in politics and the establishment of a constitutional monarchy under King George I. At the same time, the first important territorial annexation occurred when the Ionian Islands were united with Greece.

19 Greece was blacklisted in European stock markets after the inability of Greek governments to settle the question of the foreign debt, the service of which had stopped in the 1840s. In 1878 an agreement was finally concluded, the ban was lifted and a series of important loans were negotiated.

20 By the Koumoundouros government.

21 Any previous efforts to encourage industrial development had failed. See Christina Agriantoni, *Oi Aparches tes Ekviomechanises sten Hellada kata ton 19o aiona* [Beginnings of Greek industrialisation in the 19th century], (Athens, 1986).

22 Margarita Dritsas, 'He Hellada kai o Europaikos Oikonomikos Typos kata ten Trikoupiki periodo: Aparches tes politikes epikoinonias' [Greece and the European economic press during the Trikoupis period: The beginnings of a communication policy], *Ariadni* 8 (2000).

23 The construction of railways has been picked out by historians as an indication of ill-designed investment outlets that occurred during this period and led to the bankruptcy of the country. Although they could have induced industrialisation, they proved inadequate as they usually linked only coastal areas, and they diverted funds from investment in steamships, which had been for a long time the strongest sector of the economy. What has usually been underestimated in the analysis is the strategic importance of railways in mobilising army troops (see L. Papagiannakis, *Oi Hellinikoi Siderodromoi* [The Greek railways], (Athens, 1980) and G. Dertilis, *Koinonikos metaschematismos kai stratiotiki epemvasi 1880–1909* [Social transformation and military intervention 1880–1909], (Athens, 1985), p. 96.

24 For an example of the speculative and largely rapacious investment behaviour of Greeks from abroad during this period, see G. Dertilis, *To Zetema ton Trapezon* [The banking issue], (Athens, 1980).

25 Violent incidents in the north fuelled the opposition's scheme, advocated mainly by Theodoros Diliyannis, who called for immediate military action. He unrealistically aspired to preserve a hegemonic position for Greece in the east through various means, including the preparation of uprisings in foreign lands and/or the spreading of nationalist activity to counteract

propaganda by rival nations in the neighbourhood. Diliyannis succeeded Trikoupis as Prime Minister and the result of his policy was a brief war with Turkey in 1897 in which Greece was defeated. This adventure showed even more vividly the limits of expansive nationalism. With regard to the economy, although government rhetoric emphasised the need to strengthen domestic production and avoid foreign loans, government action was taken to strengthen exports rather than industry (e.g. establishment of chambers of commerce in Constantinople, Smyrna, and in Alexandria where trade was in the hands of Greeks): Ch. Hadjiossif, *He Gerea Selene, He Viomechania sten Hellenike Oikonomia 1830–1940* [The waning moon. Industry in the Greek economy 1830–1990], (Athens, 1993), p. 276.

26 These views and policies were articulated and used during all previous phases of the Eastern Question. A third view advocated collaboration with Turkey in order that Greeks inherit the empire. For an analysis of the issue of 'Megali Idea' (irredentism) in Greece, see Elli Skopetea, *To 'Protypon Vasileion' kai he Megale Idea* [The exemplary kingdom and the great idea], (Athens, 1988).

27 This statement does not imply agreement with the thesis that the requirements of military technology in nineteenth-century Europe forced the pace of industrialisation: Kahan 'Nineteenth-century European experience', p. 19.

28 Venizelos to Kanakaris-Roufos, cited in S. and K. Vovolinis, *Mega Hellenico Viographico Lexico* [Biographical Hellenic dictionary], (Athens, 1958), vol. I, p. 384.

29 Venizelos was Prime Minister for two successful full terms of government between 1910–15 and 1928–32.

30 One particularly sensitive area was that of foreign diplomacy. An example of problems created by a diplomatic oversight (or error) is furnished by the protocol signed between the Greek Foreign Minister and his Bulgarian counterpart in 1924, when, for the first time in the history of the two nations, the existence of a Bulgarian minority was officially recognised. It caused serious delays in the application of Greek policy in the region, it provoked protests from political circles and local groups who resented its implications and it inflamed public opinion. It was eventually revoked by the Greek parliament in 1925: A. Fergadi-Tounta, *Hellenovoulgarikes Meionotetes. To Protocolo Politis–Kalfov 1924–1925* [Greco-Bulgarian minorities, the Politis– Kalfov Protocol 1924–1925], (Thessaloniki, 1986). For its impact on one area, educational policy, see I. Michailides, 'Minority rights and education problems in Greek inter-war Macedonia: the case of the primer Abecedar', *Journal of Modern Greek Studies* 14(2) (1996), 329–43. The role of international organisations such as the League of Nations with its several Commissions (Section for Minorities, Mixed Commission, Refugee Settlement Commission, etc.) was also important. Some of the problems seem to be still around, as the re-emergence of the Macedonia question showed in recent years.

31 Historical Archives of the Greek Ministry of External Affairs (HAGMEA), B43, 17.IV. 1903–14.XI.1911, cited in Hadjiossif, *He Gerea Selene*, p. 279.

32 In 1912, it was estimated that Greek entrepreneurs operating in the Ottoman Empire, despite foreign competition, possessed 50 per cent of industrial capital and controlled over 40 per cent of internal trade. See Th. Veremis and K. Kostis, *He Ethiniki Trapeza sten Mikra Asia 1919–1922* [The National Bank of Greece in Asia Minor 1919–1922], (Athens, 1984). Among the most extreme propositions of this period was the wish to create an Economic League that would link the homeland with all national forces dispersed abroad. Not surprisingly, the German Zollverein and its importance for Pan-Germanism was used as an example worth imitating: K. Zografos, 'Peri tes Enischiseos tou Exo Hellenismou' [The support of offshore hellenism], *Hellenismos* (March 1900), 114–15.

33 Some historians have described this phenomenon as an 'extrovert economy', minimising the nationalist aspects: Hadjiossif, *He Gerea Selene*, p. 279; K. Kostis and V. Tsokopoulos, *Oi Trapezes s ten Hellada 1898–1928* [Banks in Greece 1898–1928], (Athens, 1987).

34 Just before and during the Balkan Wars, many business firms – insurance companies, etc. – were used as front organisations covering up for nationalist activities by Greeks. See Ch. Hadjiossif, '*Η Εξωστρέφια της Ελληνικής Οικονομίας στις αρχές του 20ού αιώνα και οι συνέπειες της στην εξωτερική πολικήη*' [Greek economic extroversion in the early 20th century] in *Ε.Λ.Ι.Α.* (ed.), *Η Ελλάδα των Βαλκανικών Πολέμων 1910–1914* [Greece during the Balkan Wars 1910–1914], (Athens, 1993), pp. 143–60.

35 M. Dritsas, *Viomechania kai Trapezes sten Hellada tou Mesopolemou* [Industry and banking in inter-war Greece], (Athens, 1990), pp. 99–110; Hadjiossif *He Gerea Selene*, pp. 96–7.

36 As soon as Venizelos came into power, in 1911, he formed a defensive alliance with Bulgaria against Turkey. The rise of the Young Turks and their racist policies against Christians and non-Turks had clearly shown to Balkan neighbours that they had to resolve their differences on their own. The treaty signed in 1912 pledged both parties to mutual aid, should either be attacked by Turkey, to secure the peaceful coexistence of the Greek and Bulgarian populations of Turkey and to co-operate in securing the rights of those nationalities. The content of the agreement was kept secret. In the subsequent war with Turkey, Greece was victorious in most battles. The crown prince anticipated the Bulgarians by entering Thessaloniki and the Turkish fleet was also defeated outside the Dardanelles. In the following year more victories followed in Epeiros (Treaty of London 1913) and after the outbreak of the second Balkan war in 1913, Bulgaria was completely defeated. Greece obtained eastern Macedonia and a large strip of the Thracian coast (Treaty of Bucarest in 1913).

37 In 1914 an area of only 2,823.4 square kilometres was cultivated. This had

risen to 4,418 in 1929 and to 6,697 in 1939: Ch. Evelpides, *He Georgia tes Hellados* [Greek agriculture], (Athens, 1944), p. 19.

38 K. Kostis, *Agrotike Oikonomia kai Georgike Trapeza* [Rural economy and agricultural bank], (Athens, 1987), pp. 39 and 58.

39 Measures included concentration of the produce, distribution and use of chemical fertilisers, advice to farmers, a price policy, introduction of import duties, regulation of relations with the flour industry, introduction of new credit arrangements, promotion of co-operatives and the creation in 1931 of a state Agricultural Bank.

40 Hadjiossif, *He Gerea Selena* p. 94.

41 Jewish entrepreneurs were particularly successful in the processing and trade of tobacco and cereal; they also concentrated almost exclusively in their hands trade transactions with the Ottoman Empire and the rest of the Balkan countries. Jewish presence was also prominent in textiles.

42 In 1913, wool factories, a traditional industry of the area, produced for the Turkish army but the industrialists were Greeks. After unification, they became part of the Greek industrial heritage but lost their main sale outlets and had to adjust to the new reality of regional concentration. Almost all of the Macedonian textile firms by 1938 had established affiliated companies in Athens, the size of the latter exceeding that of the Macedonian factories: Hadjiossif, *He Gerea Selena* p. 94.

43 Kostis, *Agrotike Oikonomia*, p. 248, cites a quote of E. Tsouderos, member of the Liberal party and later Governor of the Central Bank in 1919.

44 See Dritsas, *Viomechania kai Trapezes*.

45 In 1923, Venizelos underlined that Greece needed a particularly conservative agrarian policy. See S. Stefanou (ed.), *Keimena tou E. Venizelou* [Texts by E. Venizelos], (Athens, 1983), vol. III.

46 C. B. Eddy, chairman of the Refugee Settlement Commission, referred to the refugees as 'the salvation of Macedonia': *Greece and the Greek Refugees* (London, 1931), p. 139.

47 It is worth noting that during the height of the Macedonian campaign, before the arrival of the refugees, suggestions were made by government officials that farmers from Peloponnesos be moved to the north in order to offset the activity of Slavs. See K. Karavidas, *Ta Agrotika* [Agrarian affairs], (Athens, 1931, reprinted 1978).

48 In some areas house or flat provision was delayed until the 1960s.

49 Postwar industrial development studies have documented the contribution of first- or second-generation refugees to the building of modern Greek industry, but this was not a foregone conclusion before the war.

50 In 1927, a nationalist organisation was founded in which many refugees were members and which took an active part in anti-semitic demonstrations in 1931.

51 Between 1923 and 1930, foreign capital in the form of loans that flowed into Greece amounted to 907.8 million gold francs. Of it 48 per cent came from Britain, 31 per cent from the United States, 12 per cent from Belgium, 6 per

cent from Sweden and the rest from other countries. A small part of that was used by an Anglo-Hellenic trust for industry.

52 See Dritsas, *Viomechania kai Trapezes*, pp. 335–6.

53 Civil servant numbers had increased from 37,660 in 1915 to 72,610 in 1923–4.

54 Dritsas, *Viomechania kai Trapezes*, pp. 314–16.

55 *Ibid.*, p. 160.

56 The Communist Party (CPG) postulated the prerequisite of a radical change in the productive relations and the political institutions of the country as well as the mobilisation of domestic capital resources. The opposing right wing (Populist Party of Greece (PPG), Democratic Socialist Party of Greece (DSPG)) was united in advocating the attraction of foreign capital, the promotion of consumer industry first and heavy industry later, and the direct involvement of the state without touching, however, the socio-economic structure of the country. A growing anti-communism accompanied the fear of an eventual rise of the CPG via proletarialisation of the population. See Ch. Hadjiossif, 'Apopseis gyro apo te Viosimoteta tes Hellados kai to rolo tes Viomechanias' ('Opinions on the viability of Greece and the role of industry') in V. Kremmydas *et al.* (eds.), *Afieroma ston Niko Svorono* [Tribute to Nikos Svoronos], (Rethymno, 1986), vol. II, pp. 330–68 at pp. 354–6.

57 United Nations Relief and Rehabilitation Administration (UNRRA, 1946, 1947).

58 American hegemony in Greece became a reality with the Truman Doctrine, which was announced in April 1947, after the British Economic Mission in co-operation with the Greek government failed to bring about stabilisation.

59 See G. Stathakis, 'Finance and the industrial reconstruction: the case of the Marshall Plan in Greece' in A. Teichova, H. Lindgren and Margarita Dritsas (eds.), *L'Entreprise en Grèce et en Europe XIXè–XXè Siècles* (Athens, 1991), pp. 133–50. In 1952, in a critical appraisal of early postwar economic policy, Kyriakos Varvaressos, former Governor of the Bank of Greece and former Deputy Prime Minister, drew attention to the fact that an 'unprincipled economic oligarchy', prone to speculative activities had survived after the war, thanks to the lack of a taxation policy that would tap illegal war profits; that there was a need for a reorganised and strong interventionist state; that heavy industry was not *a priori* necessary but should follow economic development and the rise of living standards, that agricultural production and the construction industry – via the creation of small self-financed family firms – should be promoted because of their labour-intensive character and low capital requirements; and that dependence on foreign sources of capital, especially from the United States, should be reduced. Varvaressos' remarks met with general hostility from political and economic circles. See K. Varvaressos, *Report on the Greek Economic Problem* (Washington, DC, International Bank for Reconstruction and Development, 1952).

60 See K. Vergopoulos, 'The constitution of the New Bourgeois class 1944–1952' in J. O. Iatrides (ed.), *Greece in the 1940s and 1950s, A Nation in Crisis* (Athens, 1984), pp. 529–59.

61 A new sort of primitive accumulation of capital had occurred during the war years that had led to important investment as is indicated by the 5,000 new industrial enterprises which were founded between 1941 and 1948. See *ibid.* and K. Tsoukalas 'The ideological impact of the civil war' in Iatrides, *Greece in the 1940s and 1950s*, pp. 561–94. There is also a number of reports on the economic condition of Greece in the 1940s by the National Bank of Greece, compiled in view of the negotiations about reconstruction.

62 Stathakis, 'Finance and the industrial reconstruction', pp. 133–4.

CHAPTER ELEVEN

National identity and economic conditions in twentieth-century Austria

Herbert Matis

ECONOMIC DEVELOPMENT IN A MULTINATIONAL SETTING

Interest in questions of economic and political integration of regions with varying socio-economic levels and different ethnic and cultural backgrounds, understandable in the context of the establishment of the European Union, has drawn attention to the specific example of the former Habsburg Empire. From a retrospective view, the social reality has often been transformed into illusions. Historians asserted the existence of a wide, broadly cohesive common market, driven by market forces and based on comparative costs, a division of labour and a natural division of resources. But even before the outbreak of the First World War, one has to recognise a growing rivalry between different nationalities, nationally motivated boycotts and a growth of 'national industries'. The dominant nations of the time, the Germans and the Magyars, and to some extent the Polish aristocracy in Galicia, altogether represented only 43 per cent of the entire population. Nevertheless, they dominated in both the political and economic spheres. While Transleithania's feudal agrarian structure was dominated by Magyar magnates, in Cisleithania[1] the German middle class maintained strategic positions in cultural and social life, in politics and the economy. And it is an open question to what extent diverse reform projects, such as Austrian Prime Minister Ernest von Koerber's novel programme of economic development at the turn of the century, would have had a fair chance of overcoming national diversities and antagonisms[2] – diversities and antagonisms that arose not only from socio-economic causes but also from irrationally motivated mass-psychological phenomena. Although various attempts to balance domestic political and socio-economic inequalities failed, this can certainly not be attributed to discrimination against individual nationalities. This failure was more a result of an inability to realise a systematic and comprehensive policy for development. Added to this was the missed opportunity to transform the supranational state into a new form acceptable to all peoples. It would, however, be equally erroneous to make judgements about the special national, legal and political situation that obtained in the Habsburg Monarchy using the modern notion of a nation state as a yardstick. Similarly, it would be wrong simply to assess the monarchy's economic backwardness in the light of standards of present-day theories of economic growth. The question has to be asked whether the development strategies relevant for a present-day nation state could have been realised in the specific, historically determined structures of the supranational empire, with its intensifying domestic conflicts and nationality struggles. The main reason for the failure of the Habsburg Empire is simply that it functioned in its own time as a living anachronism. On the one hand, it was predominantly dynastic and, as such, a historical relic. On the other hand, as a supranational state, it was ahead of its time. The dilemma arising from these contradictory characteristics was that the empire's continued existence as a multiethnic, pluralistic society could not possibly be subordinated to a single, centralist and universally valid conception of a 'nation state' at a time of rising nationalism.[3]

While historians mostly emphasise political, legal and constitutional problems or cultural factors of national identity such as the 'language question', economic historians mainly deal with the impact of industrialisation as an integrative or disintegrative force. Due to the current fascination with integrated large-scale economies, one is tempted to overestimate unifying economic factors. In fact there really is a tendency – which anticipates later European attempts at integration – to select data that point in the direction of harmonious economic interaction. It was a fact that the pattern of industrialisation in the Habsburg Monarchy reflected that in Europe generally – a gradient from west to east and from north to south. This did initially reinforce existing socio-economic differences. The underdevelopment of whole regions necessarily relegated them to a quasi-colonial status. But in the long run, industrialisation had an equalising effect. Economic progress led to increasing productivity and steadily growing wealth, even in the backward provinces. Nevertheless, in the situation prevailing in the monarchy, steadily growing national sentiment was prepared to sacrifice all obvious advantages deriving from a common market comprising 52 million people for the sake of ideological and nationalistic motives. The relationships between the nationalities were not founded on economic partnership but on intensifying rivalry, so that centrifugal factors by far outweighed integrative ones.

The diverse nationalities all strove for more national independence and economic autarky. There was, however, one exception to this: the Habsburg hereditary lands of the Alpine and Danubian region, the area that comprises the heart of present-day Austria. This part of Austria-Hungary was, on the one hand, part of the German language and cultural area of central Europe; on the other hand, it constituted the core of the multinational empire. As such, it was very well situated to assume a central position, with Vienna as the economic centre. The peripheral regions found themselves economically in a position of asymmetric dependency. In the monarchy, the German-speaking population, not least due to their central role in the organisation of capital, occupied a hegemonial position. Vienna functioned as the empire's economic clearing house. Here were to be found the headquarters of the great industrial and services enterprises and, above all, the major banks, which exerted such a powerful influence on the whole economy. Compared with Vienna, the other major cities of Cisleithania, such as Prague and Brno, played a purely secondary role. Thus at the beginning of the twentieth century, many of the German-speaking Austrians found themselves in an ambivalent position. As members of a privileged nationality they benefited from the advantages offered by their position in the empire, albeit under the permanent threat of being eclipsed by the growing numbers and migration of the Slav population. On the other hand, like the empire's other 'nations', they also strove to achieve their own national identity. As a minority exercising growing political influence, Austrian Germans' wishful thinking did not centre around the idea of an 'Austrian nation' but on separatist Pan-Germanism. The latter has to be seen as a historical equivalent of other national movements (for instance, Pan-Slavism, Yugoslavism and Italian Irredenta), which were all directed against the empire's cohesion forces.

Thus, when in 1918 the Austro-Hungarian Monarchy collapsed, the fall of the empire was judged very differently by the various nationalities that had formerly been embodied in it. Some had to face losses of influence and territory, others gained their long-desired national sovereignty and political self-determination. In the economic sphere, the creation of successor states meant the disruption of a centuries-old inter-regional division of labour and the splitting-up of a large, fairly autarkic domestic market.[4]

In the 1920s most of the successor states pursued protectionist policies and aimed at economic autarky. Nationalism, even in its chauvinistic forms, was seen as a constitutional element of sovereignty. High tariff

barriers and neo-mercantilistic policies were seen as natural concomi-
tants to political independence. Historically evolved structural inter-
dependencies became obsolete with the fall of the monarchy, and the
successor states were confronted with a new economic situation. The
problem that most of the new nation states had was that they had to
build up functioning institutions in a new economic space. For Austria
the challenge was to adapt to the realities of what was now a small state,
which involved on the one hand scaling down surplus capacities, and on
the other carrying out an export drive. Austria was to become a country
dependent on international trade, much like Belgium, the Netherlands
or Switzerland.

THE FIRST AUSTRIAN REPUBLIC – A STATE WITHOUT A NATIONAL IDENTITY

One of the most striking features of Austria's history in the twentieth
century is the difference in economic strength between the post-1945
Second Republic and its predecessor, the First Republic (1918–38).
During the interwar period, Austrian per capita GNP decreased by an
annual average rate of 0.4 per cent. For the years 1929–37 alone, the rate
of decrease was 1.8 per cent. Industrial production in 1925 only reached
83 per cent of the output of 1913. In 1929 it came very close to the
prewar level (98 per cent), but then fell again until the incorporation of
Austria into the German Reich in March 1938. Unemployment was
already high during the 1920s (around 9.5 per cent of the labour force
between 1925 and 1929), but soared to a peak of 23.5 per cent after the
onset of the Great Depression. Thus, the First Austrian Republic displayed a picture of economic weariness and, consequently, political radicalism, marked by such events as the forced dissolution of parliament in
1933, the civil war in 1934 and, finally, the country's annexation by
Germany.

The First Austrian Republic was usually referred to as 'the state
nobody wanted'. This judgement also may require some critical
examination: Austria's potential for economic development after 1918
was certainly greater than most contemporary commentators and later
historians would have considered. The fact that the Alpine lands' close
ties with the east and south of the former Habsburg Empire were
severed after the latter's break up constituted an advantage for the new
Austrian Republic. National income per capita remained higher there
during the 1920s than in all other successor states, which indicates that

the country was able to reap some benefits of the political and economic break-up. The same conclusion can be drawn from a look at the sectoral division of national income and at labour force statistics.

Austria inherited 26 per cent of the territory and 23 per cent of the population of former Cisleithania (the Habsburg Empire's western portion). But calculations reveal that before the First World War almost one third of Cisleithania's GNP was generated by inhabitants of Vienna and the Alpine regions. The new republic possessed more than 30 per cent of all the factories of Cisleithania, and housed 30 per cent of Cisleithania's industrial manpower. Thus, it had a comparatively modern occupational structure: 41 per cent of the labour force were employed in agriculture, 35.6 per cent in industry and mining, and 23.4 per cent in services – a pattern similar to that existing in France, Switzerland or Germany at the time.[5] The Habsburg Monarchy (also Cisleithania), by contrast, had been characterised by a much greater relative weight of the primary sector.

New Austria also possessed large deposits of iron ore, magnesia and copper, huge exploitable forests and hydraulic energy. Her paper and leather industries, machine-building, metal-working, electrical and chemical industries were fairly developed. Available data on per capita national income can serve as evidence for Austria's relative economic strength. Not only was her GDP higher than that of Cisleithania, it also exceeded that of the former Bohemian crown lands in the early 1920s. How much Austria profited from disintegration comes out even more clearly when her statistical data are compared to those of the Habsburg Monarchy as a whole, and not only to figures relating to Cisleithania.[6] Concluding from this brief quantitative survey of Austria's resources after 1918, one can say that there was little justification in doubting the country's economic viability. Domestic industry was sufficiently strong; well-trained civil servants and highly qualified factory workers were available; there was a huge potential for hydroelectrical energy production; the Viennese banks administered a remarkable amount of foreign assets.

Some sides of the disintegration problem, however, defy attempts at quantitative analysis. Obviously, this is the case with functional disruption – that is, the separating of economically interdependent territories by means of new political borders. All the successor states of Austria-Hungary before 1918 belonged to a large economic unit with a complex division of labour between different geographical regions. Heavy industry provided an example for the kind of functional linkage bound to be destroyed by postwar politics. Within Cisleithania, huge deposits of iron ore in the Styrian Erzberg region were connected with coal-mining in the Czech Lands. Pig iron was produced mainly in the Alpine provinces, while cast-iron production concentrated in Bohemia and Moravia. A similar situation prevailed in the chemical and textile industries. Basic production in the chemical sector concentrated in the Bohemian north, final production in the Alpine lands. Most of Cisleithania's cotton-weaving mills were situated on Czech territory, but Austria possessed the bulk of textile printing and finishing industries.

The new borders drawn in central Europe (they added up to more than 1,300 kilometres in length) neither took into account the above-mentioned division of labour between regions nor that between different branches and sectors of the economy. Customs policies of the successor states directed towards achieving economic autarky further intensified the effects of functional disruption. The huge customs union of the Austro-Hungarian Empire, previously open to all domestic producers, broke up into a number of relatively small national markets protected by tariffs and other means of foreign trade regulation in order to secure autonomous development. With hindsight it can be said that strategies of international co-operation such as the concluding of customs treaties and trade agreements would have opened up more chances for economic prosperity in the 1920s.[7] But such strategies were prevented by a climate of widespread hostility and mistrust. If one tries to explain the difference in economic development between Austria's First and Second Republics, irrational factors such as national resentment, folkish pride and political hatred must certainly be taken into account. These weighed at least as heavily as the balance of economic resources and the attitudes of those who shaped commercial policy.

No doubt Austria's meagre economic performance in the interwar period failed to convince her own population that defending national sovereignty was worth the effort. Austrians during the 1920s and 1930s proved incapable of developing an emotional attachment to their small state. A vast majority did not object to German occupation in 1938, but warmly welcomed Hitler as the man who had defeated economic depression in Germany and would now achieve the same in his country of birth. There was, however, another reason for the Austrians' obvious lack of interest in national independence. Eric J. Hobsbawm has pointed out that the concept of 'nation' originating from the nineteenth century included the idea of territorial extension and space. Between the two world wars, many people refused to be loyal to the Republic of Austria precisely because this country was small. It had come into existence as a pitiful remnant after the dismantling of a powerful empire. The French Prime Minister, Clémenceau, had coined the derisory phrase of 'l'Autriche c'est ce qui reste'. How could such a creation claim to be more than a 'republic without republicans', a 'state without a nation', a 'state nobody wanted'?[8] Most Austrians considered it a product of political blackmail by the Allied Powers, sanctioned by the Treaty of Saint-Germain. Those Allied politicians who had been involved in the making of the peace treaty had been faithful to the principles of the western European nation state and determined to apply these principles while creating a new political order for central Europe. But in Austria the western concept of the nation state was rejected. Here, as in all other parts of the former Habsburg Empire, nation meant a community of culture and language, not people of common citizenship.[9] This is illustrated by the name the provisional Austrian state assembly gave to the republic born in November 1918: Republic of German Austria.

The new state was blamed for all the economic difficulties of the immediate postwar period, and was seen as being primarily responsible for the visible social decline of the urban middle class. Politicians of all parties shirked their obligation to educate the citizenry in a sense of making them understand the legitimacy and vocation of the Austrian Republic. Failing such efforts, very few people professed their faith in Austria's ability to survive economically. The country was held together mainly by coercion from outside, not by consent of the majority of its population. In the Alpine provinces, there was strong resentment against the idea of a centralised state, but also against the capital city, Vienna, seen as a hotbed of socialism. Those Austrians who refused to adapt to the conditions of life in a small state set their hopes on unification with Germany. In doing so they revived the old dream of the Paulskirche Assembly gathering at Frankfurt in 1848 to work out a constitution for one great German Reich stretching from the coast of the North Sea to the border of Hungary. Like the revolutionaries of 1848, the Austrian Pan-Germans of 1918–38 professed to be ethnic Germans. In the end they were so successful in propagating the notion of ethnic kinship between the Austrian and German populations that many foreign governments accepted the 1938 *Anschluss* as an inevitable act correcting the injustice of one nation compelled by its enemies to live in two separate political entities.

For many Austrians in the 1920s and 1930s the *Anschluss* also held out the promise of solving their country's economic problems. This is underlined by the fact that in years of acute economic distress, the idea of unification with Germany tended to gain support, while in those few interwar years witnessing modest growth, discussions about the *Anschluss* usually ebbed. Among the political and economic elites of interwar Austria there was far-reaching agreement that the Republic of Saint-Germain did not deserve loyalty. Two prominent figures of the Socialist party, Chancellor Karl Renner and Foreign Secretary Otto Bauer, pleaded for the *Anschluss* because they rejected the western concept of a nation state. But Ignaz Seipel, the undisputed leader of the Catholic conservatives, a man known for his careful approach to the German question, also once stated that 'the more we associate ourselves with the notions of folkish and cultural Germandom [*Volksdeutschtum* and *Kulturdeutschtum*], the easier it will be for us to accept the limitations of our state'.[10]

Just a handful of well-known personalities – among them industrialist Frederick Hertz, businessman Julius Meinl and the famous satirist Karl Kraus – welcomed the little Republic of Austria as an opportunity for a fresh start. 'In a republic', Kraus wrote, 'people are exactly as bad and foolish as under the rule of a monarch. But there exist no barriers to prevent them from altering this situation.'[11] Unfortunately, politicians in Austria did not seem eager to give republicanism a chance to unfold within the borders of their small state. Either they favoured association with Germany, or they were partisans of a return to the throne of the Habsburgs, in a Confederation of Danubian States to be set up under Austrian patronage. It was clear to them that, for the time being, they would have to conform to the political will of the Allied Powers, winners of the World War. But economic turmoil in Austria would, sooner or later, force the west to accept the inevitable and consent to a new political solution for the Danube basin. This assumption was shared in all of Austria's major political camps – that is, by the Christian Socialist Party, the moderately Marxist Social Democrats, and the Pan-Germans. Different reasons led all these parties to believe in political solutions that ran counter to Austria's independence. The Christian Socialists were inspired by the idea of a federation of Danubian states, holding the chance to bring the Habsburgs back as rulers of a Central European Empire sooner or later. Social Democrats hoped that union between Austria and the Weimar Republic would mean a powerful stimulus to social reform. After all, the joint workers' parties of Austria and Germany would have represented the strongest proletarian organisation in the capitalist world. Finally, the Pan-Germans acted as a lobby for a unified Germanic nation state, which they felt ought to have come into being already, in 1848.

There is plenty of evidence that the Austrian problem in the interwar period was caused mainly by the local political leadership's inability or unwillingness to compromise. But also the situation was complicated by conflicts of interest between the major European powers concerning the Danubian region. Austrian domestic policies were shaped after 1920 by changing coalitions of more or less radical anti-Marxist forces, but also by those groups abroad who felt they could use the Republic as a card in the central European power game played by Germany, Italy, France and – to a lesser extent – Great Britain. Cohesive forces within Austria proper were so weak that group particularism in most cases defeated common national interest. The consequences of this are clearly discernible if one looks at the four subsequent stages of economic policy-making in Austria during the interwar years:

1. After the armistice of 1918, Austrian politics were characterised by a stalemate between left and right, neither side being strong enough to force its will on the other. From 1918 to 1922 there was a coalition government of Social Democrats and Christian Socialists, who were unable to agree upon drastic measures of economic reconstruction, as such measures would inevitably hurt the voters of either the workers' or the bourgeois parties. No decisive steps were taken to reorganise industrial production and banking, while budget deficits soared and the currency was allowed to depreciate in order to give exporters an advantage over foreign competition and keep unemployment under control. The Socialists could not prevent the dismantling of nationalised industry in the name of free enterprise, and they failed to carry through rigorous taxation of property, as originally intended. On the other hand, the right had to accept far-reaching measures of social legislation, tenants' protection and the linking of workers' wages to the price index.

2. The victory of the Christian Socialists in the elections of 1920 set the stage for a gradual return to classical *laissez-faire* attitudes of the nineteenth century. A League of Nations reconstruction loan was granted to Austria in 1922 under conditions that her government would follow a rigorous policy of tight money and reduced public spending. Chancellor Ignaz Seipel, with foreign help, succeeded in stabilising the Austrian crown and linking it to gold and the dollar, an achievement that earned him widespread recognition at home, and even more in western financial circles. But currency stabilisation also put an end to the inflationary boom and brought with it a painful crisis of readjustment. Austrian workers and civil servants were hit hard by

deflation but were told that continuing foreign assistance depended on precisely such measures of austerity. Unemployment started to rise again, and soon reached the figure of 200,000.

3. During the second half of the 1920s there were signs of economic improvement in Austria, but chances for a fundamental reorganisation of the industrial and financial sectors were missed. Critical commentators point to the fact that the large Viennese banks after 1925 returned to their prewar strategy of 'informal imperialism' in eastern central Europe, tightening their hold on industries in the region by fuelling them with capital taken up in Britain, France and the United States. Consequently, the banks were accused of ignoring the financial requirements of business in new Austria, and of contributing to the country's low rate of investment and high unemployment. This was not the complete truth, though. Investing in Austria involved a high political risk, due to the fact that both the right and the left had their armed militias and there was latent danger of a civil war. In the light of this it seems at least understandable that Vienna's banks refused to withdraw from their traditional financial strongholds in the former Habsburg lands and to place the liquidation proceeds at the disposal of Austrian industry.

Also, there was no significant change in the geographic pattern of Austria's foreign trade. Commercial activities during the 1920s continued to concentrate on the area once united under the Habsburg crown. Only after the outbreak of the Great Depression were Austria's close ties with the Danubian world loosened, and her trade balance became dependent on exchanges with the two fascist powers, Germany and Italy.

4. The crisis years after 1930 were a traumatic experience for most Austrians, especially for those out of work. While unemployment rose to a record level of more than 25 per cent, political antagonisms remained as sharp as ever. In May 1931 Austria's largest bank, the Credit-Anstalt, collapsed. Panic spread over all of eastern central Europe, where the Credit-Anstalt had played a formidable role as a creditor to industry and partner of local financial institutions. The two major parties in the Austrian parliament, Christian Socialists and Social Democrats, although they united in a hurried (and ill-advised) effort to rescue the Credit-Anstalt, did not form a coalition government that could have tackled the country's economic problems seriously. Instead, they threw themselves into a bitter fight over the question of whether Austria should accept or decline foreign loans in

exchange for political concessions to the west. The so-called Lausanne loan contract was finally signed after Chancellor Dollfuss had formed a right-wing coalition of Catholics and fascists (Heimatschutz) in May 1932. Eleven months later, Dollfuss closed down the *Nationalrat* in Vienna and established an authoritarian regime that exposed the socialist workers' movement to various measures of oppression, until open civil war broke out in February 1934. On 25 July, the Chancellor lost his life in the course of an attempted *putsch* staged by followers of Adolf Hitler. Austria continued to be a clerical dictatorship after this date, but her political leaders were mistrusted both by the working class and the traditionally pro-German provincial intelligentsia. In its foreign policy, the government in Vienna relied upon Mussolini's support against Nazi aggression from across the German border. Economically, Austria followed a line of formal adherence to the gold exchange standard and rigorous deflation, occasionally breaking the rules of orthodoxy by subsidising agriculture and financing a small number of public works. But such half-hearted steps failed to impress a population tempted to compare the obviously ailing Austrian economy with its booming German counterpart. One may see it as a paradox of history that the government in Vienna, which fought National Socialism on the political stage, simultaneously played into Hitler's hands by its inflexible economic policies.[12]

The rise to power of National Socialism in Germany in 1933 affected Austrian political life in different ways. Pan-Germanic circles felt encouraged by Hitler's 'national revolution' and opted for the *Anschluss* with more conviction than ever before. At the same time, both Social Democrats and Christian Socialists felt obliged to modify their standpoints concerning the national question. Unification with Germany now became an anathema for them. Instead, Catholic conservative thinkers began to depict little Austria as a 'civilised' German state set against Nazi Germany, the symbol of perverted Germandom. For Dollfuss and his successor, Schuschnigg, Austrian national sovereignty became a necessary prerequisite to defend what they thought to be 'true' German culture, as opposed to the neo-paganism of Hitler's followers.[13] Not incidentally, the early 1930s also witnessed the emergence of a new concept of 'Austrianity', somewhat vague but clearly inspired by reminiscences of the Habsburg Empire's cultural pluralism. The poet Anton Wildgans spoke of *der österreichische Mensch* called to fulfil a cosmopolitan mission, and the dramatist Hugo von Hofmannsthal noted that the idea of Austrianity was tantamount to universalism.[14]

For Social Democrats in Austria, the defeat of the once so proud German workers' party at the hands of the Nazis made it impossible to continue demanding an *Anschluss*. But seeing the hostility they met with from part of Austria's governing right-wing coalition, Socialists found it equally impossible to adopt the Catholics' strategy of appealing to a new mystical sentiment of Austrian patriotism. The myth of Austria the 'genuine' Germanic state, morally and culturally superior to its northern neighbour, was designed to render the population immune to the myth of the Third Reich. Obviously this strategy failed, not least because the men in power in Austria never stopped to think of themselves as belonging to a united German nation. In his last speech on Austrian radio before Hitler's invasion of his country, Chancellor Schuschnigg spoke of a 'German mission of Austria', and bade his countrymen farewell 'with a German salute'.[15]

In the First Austrian Republic one could find a National Bank, a Provisional National Assembly, a National Council (the name for the lower house of parliament), a National Library and so on, but very few people were willing to accept the existence of a nation to which these institutional names alluded. Only the marginal Communist Party of Austria in accordance with Stalin's writings on the national question defended the concept of Austrian nationhood during the 1930s. Some Catholic conservative writers and publicists, such as Ernst Karl Winter, Hans Karl Zessner-Spitzenberg and Richard Schmitz, who later won much praise for their intellectual contributions to shaping Austrian national consciousness, also spoke of an Austrian nation. However, their interest focused on Habsburg restoration rather than on anything else, and their works reached only a minority among the politically educated Viennese bourgeoisie.[16]

THE AWAKENING OF AUSTRIAN NATIONALISM UNDER NAZI OCCUPATION

Austrians began to support the idea of their forming a distinct nation only after some years of life under Nazi rule. Their rejection of mentalities and everyday practices common among Germans from the Reich made them more conscious of their own culture and paved the way for the emergence of Austrian patriotism after 1945. Austrian national identity gained shape in opposition against the exaggerated Prussian-style militarism of the Nazi regime. Also, the German Nazis made the mistake of banning the terms 'Austria' and 'Austrian' from public use.

They insisted upon such verbal monstrosities as 'Ostmark' or 'Alpen-und Donaureichsgaue', thus creating a nostalgic attachment of the population to what should have been obliterated. Finally, the concept of nation propagated by National Socialism meant nothing but a community of people of the same 'race'. It ran counter to all western individualistic theories, which was in tune with Austrian traditions of thought, but nevertheless was unacceptable to those Austrians who had believed in cultural values as constituting the core of Austro-German national unity (*Kulturnation*).

As Austrians learnt to dislike German rule in general, and the increasingly offensive behaviour of some high-ranking Nazi administrators in particular, their vision of the Austrian Republic of 1918–38 changed. Looking back, it seemed to have been an advantage living in a small sovereign state, and the once-convincing arguments of economic non-viability lost their persuasive power. After regaining independence in 1945, Austrians did not voice these any more. The common experience of those who had suffered in German concentration camps (politicians of both the left and the right in Austria had been imprisoned during the war) helped to create a new climate of pragmatism and loyalty to the Second Austrian Republic. For some Austrians the courageous attempts at resistance against the Nazis played a major role as a symbol of new national identity.[17] But even the majority of those Austrians who in 1938 had welcomed the *Anschluss* turned away from their earlier enthusiasm for the Nazis as the war went on. In 1945 they considered themselves to be loyal Austrian citizens. Depicting Austria as the first victim of National Socialism, these people completed the process of repressing embarrassing memories of the past, including their own involvement in the crimes of the Hitler regime – in this respect, the Waldheim case of 1986 was a timely reminder that one has consciously to confront one's own past.

When the Republic of Austria was reconstituted after the Second World War, it defined itself purely as 'Austria'. The new political leadership in 1945 could make use of the mental reorientation described above, which took place during the war. Added to this was the pressure of the ten-year Allied occupation, accompanied by the danger of a dismemberment of Austria into western and eastern zones. The common experience of rebuilding the country also helped to strengthen the sense of national belonging. Simultaneously, regional loyalties declined in the face of an emergent unified demos. The fact that the country was run by a 'grand coalition' and a system of 'social partnership' contributed both to the political stability of Austria and to the emergence of a renewed national identity. The year 1955 marked a high point in this process. Austrian independence was legitimated by the State Treaty. On the other hand, one must view critically certain efforts made at this time (frequently the fanatical results of the newly converted) to create a separate Austrian national language. The word 'German' was so rigorously avoided that even the subject 'German' was no longer taught in the schools, but instead the term 'language of instruction' was used. Such attempts at differentiation, accompanied by the promotion of local dialects, sprang from the desire to distance oneself from everything that was German, and, by implication, the crimes of the Nazis. The assumption that a common standard language must have an integrative function had proved to be a fiction in any case. The writer Karl Kraus' witticism still holds good – that there is nothing that divides the Austrians from the Germans so much as their common language.

In contrast to the interwar period, the Second Republic's economic performance after 1945 was stunning, despite a number of obvious handicaps: extensive war damage, ten years of costly presence of Allied troops, and the existence of the Iron Curtain between east and west since 1948, placing Austria in an uncomfortable position on the outermost fringe of the non-communist world. But already in 1951 Austrian real GDP exceeded the prewar level by one third. In the course of the 1950s Austria's economy grew faster than those of all other OEEC countries, namely by an average 7.7 per cent per annum. Between 1952 and 1960 nominal GNP doubled. In real terms its increase amounted to 80 per cent. Although the pace of growth slowed down after this first stage of economic reconstruction, expansion continued at a faster speed than in the rest of Europe. Over the period of 1955–82 Austrian per capita GDP grew at an average rate of 3.3 per cent annually, compared with an average of 2.3 per cent among the OECD countries. It is certainly not exaggerated to say that Austria had already developed into one of the most dynamic modern economies before its accession to the European Union in 1995 (see figure 11.1).[18] In a 1997 ranking of EC countries, Austria held the third position after Luxembourg and Denmark with a GDP per capita of 22,445 ecu, followed by Germany and Sweden.[19] Comparing the economic performance of twenty OECD members (excluding the smaller countries) in the period from 1900 to 1997, Austria's economic position also demonstrates the country's steady improvement after the Second World War (see table 11.1).[20]

Partly, this astounding achievement can be explained by the strong

Figure 11.1. *Gross domestic product, 1920–1995 (1913 = 100)*

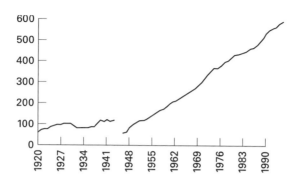

drive for economic integration in western Europe, for which Marshall Aid and the need to face the emerging communism in eastern Europe were responsible. After 1947, Austria was quickly drawn into the process of western European economic integration, subsequently joining the OEEC (later named OECD), EFTA, EEC, EC and EU, or in terms of currency the EPU and ECU. Nothing comparable had existed before 1945: on the contrary, in the interwar period European states were used to viewing each other as opponents in a zero-sum struggle for resources and markets. Only in rare cases were plans for international co-operation put forward; but they usually met with staunch political resistance and, in the end, were doomed to failure.

In addition to the more favourable conditions of western economic co-operation after 1945, many historians have underlined the importance of domestic factors contributing to Austria's economic success after the Second World War. It is a moot question, though, to what extent these factors were able to justify a statement like that of the late Pope Paul VI, who once called modern Austria an 'island of the blessed'. Also, there obviously exists a certain inter-relation between economic and psychological factors: since 1945, an Austrian national consciousness arose at grass-roots level through an ongoing process of increased solidarity. This was helped on by a new orientation among educators and teachers, espousing new values. This affirmative conviction was also supported by an outstanding economic success story and, vice versa, growing national identity also contributed to economic self-confidence, competitiveness and performance, associated with the trademark 'Made

Table 11.1. *Economic performance of OECD countries, 1900–97: Real GDP per capita (Purchasing power parity 1990) (OECD = 100)*

	1900	1938	1950	1960	1970	1980	1990	1997
USA	155	152	196	167	148	141	138	138
Norway	61	90	95	92	88	107	109	122
Switzerland	139	168	162	166	155	138	132	119
Japan	43	65	33	51	86	95	110	112
Denmark	102	117	113	106	105	101	102	110
Austria	95	78	67	87	90	102	104	109
Belgium	121	103	98	92	96	104	103	108
Canada	101	92	126	112	107	116	113	106
Germany	99	104	66	94	94	98	99	106
Netherlands	111	100	102	104	103	101	99	101
France	98	93	94	100	106	110	107	100
Australia	148	120	125	111	104	101	99	100
Sweden	67	107	118	113	114	107	105	96
Italy	70	75	66	80	90	98	101	95
United Kingdom	148	126	120	113	97	93	98	95
Ireland	–	65	62	56	55	61	71	94
Finland	58	79	74	81	85	93	100	94
New Zealand	190	128	142	123	101	90	83	84
Spain	65	54	46	52	66	68	73	75
Portugal	44	36	36	37	47	53	58	67
OECD countries	100	100	100	100	100	100	100	100
EU 15	96	93	80	89	91	94	96	96

in Austria'. For example, the gigantic Alpine electro-hydraulic power plant of Kaprun, besides its economic importance, was seen as a national symbol, strongly associated with Austria's economic reconstitution and recovery after 1945. The joint efforts of European countries in connection with the distribution of the Marshall Plan Aid not only helped Austria to participate in western integration but also to develop a new national identity within this transnational context.[21]

For the first time in history, a clear majority of the population owned up to an Austrian national identity in connection with the State Treaty and the declaration of permanent neutrality in 1955. From this time on, the question of the small republic's non-viability was not up for discussion. The new political and economic reality had thrusted aside backward-orientated dreams of a revival of the former Habsburg Empire as well as pan-Germanism. Since 1956 the loyalty to an Austrian nation was also underlined by opinion polls: recent quantitative research has shown that it is, above all, among the young generation that Austria was accepted as a separate nation with its own identity. The acceptance of a distinct national identity among Austrians between 1964 and 1995 grew from 47 to 85 per cent, while the percentage of people denying the existence of the Austrian nation declined from 15 to 4 per cent.[22] The idea of Austrianity was rejected mainly by elderly people, while younger and urban people accepted it. Thus, from the 1960s on, Austrian self-confidence has grown to such an extent that one can now, without reservation, speak of a specific Austrian national identity.[23]

CONCLUSION

In summary, on the basis of a survey of Austria's resources after 1918, there was no practical reason to doubt the new republic's economic viability. Nevertheless, the majority of Austrians could not manage to free themselves from the economic, social and political fetters of their times. After twenty years of half-hearted and unsuccessful struggle, Austria was swallowed up by Nazi Germany. The true problem of Austria lay in adapting herself to the new situation of now being only a small country after the Habsburg Monarchy's dissolution. In the interwar period, Austria never experienced the evolution of a distinct national identity. This was obviously an obstacle for the country's economic performance between 1918 and 1938. From the very beginning influential personalities of all political directions searched for an alternative ('Anschluss' or 'Danube Confederation') to the 'state nobody wanted'. Only a very small minority welcomed republican Austria as an opportunity for a fresh start. The situation changed as a result of German occupation, and after 1945 Austrians developed a common feeling of being a distinct 'Austrian nation'. A steadily strengthening national identity – empirically confirmed by many opinion polls – supported the economic upswing of the 'Wirtschaftswunder' after the Second World War and, vice versa, the booming economy strengthened Austrian national identity.

NOTES

1 The river Leitha marked the borderline between Austria and Hungary. 'Transleithania' was used as a synonym for the Lands of the Holy Crown of Saint Stephen, 'Cisleithania' was often substituted for the official term 'Kingdoms and lands represented in the Reichsrat'.

2 Alexander Gerschenkron, *An Economic Spurt that Failed. Four Lectures on Austrian*

History (Princeton, NJ, 1977), challenges the widespread belief among scholars that the disruptive forces of nationalism decisively influenced the Habsburg Empire's economy.

3 Herbert Matis, 'Austria: industrialization in a multinational setting' in Mikuláš Teich and Roy Porter (eds.), *The Industrial Revolution in National Context. Europe and the USA* (Cambridge, 1996), pp. 226–46 at pp. 244ff.

4 Cf. Alice Teichova and Herbert Matis (eds.), *Österreich und die Tschechoslowakei 1918–1938. Die wirtschaftliche Neuordnung in Zentraleuropa in der Zwischenkriegszeit* (Vienna, Cologne and Weimar, 1996).

5 Gerschenkron, *Economic Spurt*, p. 271.

6 Cf. Herbert Matis, 'Disintegration and multi-national enterprises' in Alice Teichova and Philip L. Cottrell (eds.), *International Business and Central Europe 1918–1939* (New York and Leicester, 1983), pp. 73–96 at p. 76.

7 Peter Berger, 'The Austrian economy, 1918–1938' in John Komlos (ed.), *Economic Development in the Habsburg Monarchy and in the Successor States*, (New York, 1990), pp. 270–84 at p. 272.

8 Norbert Leser, 'Im Kontrast zum Staat, den keiner wollte', in *Die Republik. Beiträge zur österreichischen Politik* (Vienna, 1975), vol. XI, pp. 26ff.

9 This makes understandable the disappointment when the victorious powers failed to apply their own principle of national self-determination in the cases of the South Tyroleans, South Carinthians, South Styrians and the Bohemian Germans.

10 Ignaz Seipel, *Nation und Staat* (Vienna and Leipzig, 1916), p. 6.

11 Berger, 'The Austrian economy', pp. 272.

12 *Ibid.*

13 Ernst Bruckmüller, 'The national identity of the Austrians' in Roy Porter and Mikuláš Teich (eds.), *The National Question in Europe in Historical Context* (Cambridge, 1993), pp. 196–227 at p. 220.

14 Anton Wildgans, *Rede über Österreich* (Vienna, 1947), p. 21; Albert F. Reiterer, 'Vom Scheitern eines politischen Entwurfs. Der "österreichische Mensch" – ein konservatives Nationalprojekt der Zwischenkriegszeit', *Österreich in Geschichte und Literatur* 30 (1986), pp. 19–36.

15 Grete Klingenstein, *Die Anleihe von Lausanne* (Vienna and Graz, 1965), pp. 96ff.

16 Cf. Gerhard Jagschitz, 'Die Jagd nach dem Gamsbart oder Österreichs Suche nach seiner Identität' in Robert Hettlage *et al.* (eds.), *Kollektive Identität in Krisen. Ethnizität in Region, Nation, Europa* (Opladen, 1997), pp. 175–8.

17 Bruckmüller, 'National identity', p. 199.

18 Cf. Felix Butschek, *Die österreichische Wirtschaft im 20. Jahrhundert* (Stuttgart, 1985); Felix Butschek, *Statistische Reihen zur österreichischen Wirtschaftsgeschichte. Die österreichische Wirtschaft seit der industriellen Revolution* (Vienna, 1977).

19 Eurostat 1997.

20 Anton Kausel, *Ein halbes Jahrhundert des Erfolges. Der ökonomische Aufstieg Österreichs im OECD-Raum seit 1950* (Vienna, 1998), table 1, p. 15.

21 Cf. William T. Bluhm, *Building an Austrian Nation. The Political Integration of a Western State* (New Haven and London, 1973).

22 Max Haller and Stefan Gruber, 'Die Österreicher und ihre Nation – Patrioten oder Chauvinisten? Gesellschaftliche Formen, Bedingungen und Funktionen nationaler Identität', in Max Haller (ed.), *Identität und Nationalstolz der Österreicher* (Vienna, Cologne and Weimar, 1996), pp. 431–500.
23 Bruckmüller, 'National identity', p. 221.

CHAPTER TWELVE

Economic, social and political aspects of multinational interwar Czechoslovakia

Jaroslav Pátek

THE BIRTH OF INDEPENDENT CZECHOSLOVAKIA: ITS STATE AND NATIONALITIES

The idea behind the founding of an independent Czechoslovakia was Thomas Garrigue Masaryk's (1850–1937) liberal-democratic conception of a (putative) Czechoslovak nation consisting of a Czech and a Slovak branch that was to uphold European humanist and democratic traditions. Thus, he believed, Czechoslovakia's existence as a fully fledged nation state would be guaranteed. Intellectually, Masaryk's political programme derived from the philosophy of human existence and history, developed by František Palacký (1798–1876). Masaryk saw the principal tasks and problems of human existence in terms of a concept of humanity rooted in the religious humanism of the Czech Reformation and founded on democracy. These ideals were presented as values implicit in the Czech national historical tradition that had begun with the medieval Hussite revolution and been reborn with the national revival of the nineteenth century. When Masaryk, in 1915, took the final step of linking the humanist tradition of the Czech Reformation to the idea and historical precedent of independent Czech statehood, he promoted the idea of an independent Czechoslovak state of which he became the first president. Among historians, Masaryk's interpretation of Czech history had its supporters (such as Kamil Krofta) and its opponents (such as Josef Pekař).[1]

Brought into being on 28 October 1918, the new state was multinational. A kind of new, miniature Austria-Hungary was created on the ruins of the multinational Habsburg Monarchy.[2] The borders of the new Czechoslovakia established by the peace treaties of Versailles, St Germain and Trianon were the results of a combination of three principles: national self-determination, historical development and economic self-sufficiency. Also, strategic considerations played a role markedly displayed in the Paris peacemakers' decision that Ruthenia, a

Table 12.1. *Territorial division of the Czech and Slovak branches of the Czechoslovak nation, 1921*[5]

Land	Czech branch	Slovak branch
Bohemia	4,376,159	6,657
Moravia–Silesia	2,338,974	8,973
Slovakia	71,733	1,941,942
Subcarpathian Ruthenia	9,477	10,298
Czechoslovakia overall	6,796,343	1,967,870

part of Hungary, became, as Subcarpathian Ruthenia, the easternmost constituent of Czechoslovakia, along with the Czech Lands (Bohemia, Moravia–Silesia) and Slovakia.

Independent Czechoslovakia contained, in addition to Czechoslovaks (made up of Czechs and Slovaks), Germans, Magyars, Russians and Little Russians (Ukrainians), Jews, Poles, and other ethnicities, who found themselves in a minority position. According to the census of 1921, Czechoslovaks formed 65.5 per cent of the population of the new state. Other national groups were represented in the following proportions: Germans 23.4 per cent, Magyars 5.6 per cent, Russians and Little Russians 3.5 per cent, Jews 1.4 per cent, Poles 0.6 per cent and others, including foreign nationals 0.2 per cent.[3]

The statistics show that Czechs and Slovaks, numerically the largest group, had settled largely in the interior of the new state.[4] Based on the 1921 census the division between the Czech and Slovak branches of the Czechoslovak nation was as shown in table 12.1.

Of national minorities, numerically the strongest were the native Germans. In 1921 they represented 23.4 per cent and in 1930 22.3 per cent of the population of the Czechoslovak state.[6] Germans were to be found in all the territorial components of the state, with the highest proportion in Bohemia (32.4 per cent), rather less in Moravia–Silesia (22.8 per cent) and fewer in Slovakia (4.5 per cent) and Subcarpathian Ruthenia (1.9 per cent).[7] The native German population lived mainly in the border areas of the Czech Lands, and their pattern of settlement was often very complex and intricate. In some areas the Germans made up the majority of the population. In Bohemia this was the case in ninety-one judicial districts, and in Moravia–Silesia in thirty-one districts. It was, however, common to find very mixed districts, where Czechs and Germans lived side by side. There was some German-speaking presence even in apparently wholly Czech-language localities of the interior. In

Bohemia Germans made up at least 20 per cent of the population in nine districts, in Moravia–Silesia in eleven, and in Slovakia in five districts. There were Germans living in the large cities: Prague (30,429), Plzeň (8,251), České Budějovice (11,642), Brno (55,816) and Bratislava (31,159). In addition to native Germans there were approximately 100,000 Austrian and Reich German nationals living in Czechoslovakia.[8] There were also Jews living in all territorial components of Czechoslovakia. Their numbers increased as one travelled east. While in the 1930 census the number of people identifying themselves as Jews was 12,735 in Bohemia, this increased to 17,267 in Moravia–Silesia, to 65,385 in Slovakia and in Subcarpathian Ruthenia to 91,255. The Jews did not live in compact, coherent settlements and did not have a unified mother tongue, using the language of other nationalities.[9] The Magyar population inhabited a narrow belt along the southern frontier of Slovakia and Subcarpathian Ruthenia. The census of 1930 showed a relative decline in the Magyar population as compared to other nationalities, but this was the result of the fact that in previous censuses a number of Slovak and Jewish inhabitants had opted for Magyar nationality. Poles, three times less numerous than Jews in Czechoslovakia, lived concentrated in one district of Těšín where they formed a majority and in two other districts as a minority.[10]

THE ECONOMIC CHARACTER OF INDEPENDENT CZECHOSLOVAKIA

At the time of its birth as a state, Czechoslovakia's economy was agricultural-industrial (39.6:33.8 per cent). It was not until 1930 that employment in industry overtook employment in agriculture and forestry, in a ratio of 34.9 to 34.7 per cent.[11] Even before the First World War the Czech Lands had become industrial in character. The new state had joined together two geographical areas of the Republic at different stages of development: the industrial west (Czech Lands) and the agrarian east (Slovakia and Subcarpathian Ruthenia).

Estimates suggest that the production of a ten-hectare agricultural enterprise in Slovakia equalled that of a four-hectare agricultural enterprise of the same production type in the Czech Lands. In some parts of Slovakia and in Subcarpathian Ruthenia the barter system survived, together with remnants of medieval practices. Production for the market had spread only in the more fertile areas of southern Slovakia. It was not until 1920 that obligations to give a proportion of produce to the Church were abolished, together with the duty to perform unpaid labour on a major estate in return for lease of land.[12]

While Slovakia and Subcarpathian Ruthenia were backward, 60 to 70 per cent of the industry of the former Habsburg Monarchy was concentrated in the Czech Lands, which could also boast of intensive agricultural production linked to a well-developed food-processing industry and a relatively advanced system of agricultural co-operatives. There were four main industrial regions, centred on Prague, Plzeň, Brno and Ostrava, with fully developed mining, mechanical engineering, electrotechnical, chemical and other industries. The most important of these regions was that of Prague, where there existed dozens of technically sophisticated industrial enterprises, well supplied with capital capable of extensive investments. The favourable location of this region at the biggest rail junction and crossroads facilitated domestic and foreign trade. Apart from brewing, the Plzeň industrial region was characterised mainly by the Škoda joint-stock company (formerly the Škoda Works) in Plzeň. Thanks to excellent capital and technical equipment this company was able to manufacture a broad range of metal, mechanical engineering and electrotechnical products. The Brno industrial region could also rely on substantial sources of capital and nodal points of communication. It was also an important centre of mechanical engineering and the textile industry. The Ostrava industrial region was orientated towards heavy industry, mining and smelting. The favourable factor here was the presence of cokeable black coal allowing mechanical engineering and the heavy chemicals industry to develop. In addition to these four major regions, there were other localities where industries developed such as Ústí nad Labem, Kolín and Pardubice (chemicals), Mladá Boleslav (automobiles) and Zlín (Baťa shoes). Essentially, only southern Bohemia and the Czech–Moravian Uplands remained primarily agrarian in character.

Looking specifically at the German-speaking and ethnically mixed areas, west Bohemia, which was dominated by mining, pottery and construction industries, occupied an important position. So too did the north Bohemian brown-coal basin with its heavy industry and chemicals production. Light industry had developed in other areas of north Bohemia, for example textiles and glass in the Liberec/Jablonec area, and textiles in north-east Bohemia extending into north Moravia.[13] In the Czech Lands 44 per cent of the native German population was employed in industry and 27.3 per cent in agriculture. The Czech Lands indisputably formed a relatively strongly integrated economic whole, in which the more industrial German-speaking areas were conveniently complemented by the more agriculturally orientated Czech-speaking areas.[14]

By contrast, the development of industry in Slovakia and Subcarpathian Ruthenia had been lagging behind that of the Czech Lands. The eastern territories did not have access to sufficient financial resources, either from the state or private investors, for more intensive industrialisation. Any major upswing in production was inhibited by relatively meagre sources of raw materials and lack of a skilled workforce. It was not until the 1930s that Slovakia experienced some substantial industrial growth with the development of the arms industry (Dubnica nad Váhom), the leather and shoe industry (Bat'a works) and some branches of heavy chemicals. The mining of brown coal in the Handlová and Nováky areas in southern Slovakia had a certain importance, and large quantities of pyrites were mined in central Slovakia. More important was the extraction of magnesite ores in the eastern part of the mountainous region Slovak Rudohorie. Nickel and zinc mining were generally of negligible significance and the traditional mining of precious metals between Kremnica and Banská Štiavnica had ceased almost completely. Salt-mining in the vicinity of Prešov and in Subcarpathian Ruthenia, however, was important, and covered most of the needs of Czechoslovakia as a whole. As far as the smelting industry was concerned, the most important centre was the River Hron basin complex of the state ironworks in Podbrezová, with the blast-furnace works in Tisovec and a few ancillary works. The Pohornadská and Rimamuránská companies respectively owned the Krompachy ironworks and the Union sheet-metal factories in Zvolen. The Coburg Mining and Metallurgic Works had their main establishment in Trnava. Many of these enterprises were taken over as early as the 1920s by the Mining and Metallurgic Company in Třinec and the Vítkovice Mining and Foundry Works in Ostrava.[15] The output of the metal-working industry represented 23.2 per cent of total industrial production in Slovakia, and the food industry had a 33.4 per cent share. Of the other branches the next most significant was the textile industry with 12 per cent, followed by chemicals at 7.4 per cent, timber processing at 7.7 per cent and the paper and leather industries.[16] In most cases there was little concentration of industry and enterprises were scattered and fragmentary. The population of Subcarpathian Ruthenia was almost exclusively agricultural. Statistics show 81.78 per cent of the population in Subcarpathian Ruthenia to have been employed in agriculture, forestry and fishing, with only 6.36 per cent in industry and 2.08 per cent in transport. Among the native Germans, only 0.55 per cent were active in agriculture, with 21.11 per cent in industry and 3.16 per cent in transport, and among Magyars the figures were 61.51 per cent in agriculture, 17.85 per cent in industry, and 3.67 per cent in transport. The Jewish population in Subcarpathian Ruthenia was mainly engaged in trade and banking – 33.7 per cent – with 24.31 per cent in industry and 21.48 per cent in agriculture. In Slovakia, the Slovaks were predominantly an agricultural people: 57.61 per cent of Slovaks worked in agriculture, 18.8 per cent in industry and 5.69 per cent in transport. The Russians and Little Russians showed an even greater majority in agriculture – 89.63 per cent – with only 3.32 per cent in industry, and of the Magyars 65.35 per cent were in agriculture, with 16.92 per cent in industry. In contrast, the Germans in Slovakia worked predominantly in industry (34.34 per cent) with significantly fewer (29.22 per cent) in agriculture. A substantial percentage of native Germans were also employed in trade and banking, with 53.04 per cent in trade and banking, 20.24 per cent in industry and only 7.06 per cent in agriculture.

In the Czech Lands the census of 1930 shows most Poles employed in industry; this was undoubtedly because of their proximity to Ostrava. 56.36 per cent of Poles worked in industry, and of these almost a third were employed in the coal-mines of the Ostrava-Karviná mining district. In the Czech Lands 48.16 per cent of native Germans were active in industry and only 20.7 per cent in agriculture. The proportion of Czechoslovaks (Czechs and Slovaks) in industry was 38.81 per cent in Bohemia and 40.57 per cent in Moravia. The proportion of Czechoslovaks (Czechs and Slovaks) in agriculture was 26.04 per cent in Bohemia and 29.67 per cent in Moravia–Silesia. The Jewish population in the Czech Lands was to be found working mainly in trade and banking (46 per cent) in the free professions (29.48 per cent) and in industry (19.34 per cent). The situation was similar in Moravia, with 48.45 per cent of Jews working in trade and banking, 21.26 per cent in industry and 22.84 per cent in the free professions. As one travelled east the number of Jews increased, and so too did the proportion of poor Jews. Overall, Jews were important as doctors, lawyers, scientists and writers. Those involved in industrial enterprise usually identified themselves as Czech by nationality. In many Jewish families, however, German (Magyar in Slovakia) continued to be the language of communication.[17]

In the Czech Lands the German population lived mainly in the border areas rimmed by mountain ranges from Jeseníky through

Krkonoše, Krušné Hory, Český Les to the Šumava. These were areas covered in thick forest and the soil was poor. Only in a few places was it possible to cultivate cereals or root-crops. The most productive agricultural areas in Bohemia were around Litoměřice and Lovosice, where fruit and vegetables could be produced as well as grain, and, in the Žatec and Podbořany areas, hops and sugarbeet. In southern Moravia the market-gardening area around Znojmo, and the Mikulov wine area, were also outstanding for their agricultural production. In Silesia and the adjacent north Moravian districts, building materials could be quarried; in north-east Bohemia there was the minor coal basin near Trutnov, and in the Liberec area the raw materials for glass production. The most important mineral resources consisted of the brown coal of the north Bohemian basin, mainly around Most and Sokolov. In addition, in west Bohemia there were important mineral springs and substantial deposits of kaolin. The Šumava area offered practically no mineral wealth but only timber and building materials. Overall, however, the industrial importance of the north and west Bohemian border areas was striking. The Šumava area and western Silesia, with their logging, paper industry, stone-quarries and cottage industries, were less economically significant. Any industry to be found in the towns consisted mainly of workshops and small businesses.[18]

On average, industry in the border areas was of considerable importance. In one of his reports in 1934 the German Ambassador to Prague, Walter Koch, estimated that the contribution of native Germans to the Czechoslovak economy was two to three times greater than their relative numbers would have suggested. Although this estimate was exaggerated, it remains clear that the Germans were important in industry.[19] According to the 1921 census, the participation of Czechoslovaks and native Germans in different branches of industry was as shown in table 12.2.[20]

The results of the census of 1930 show that differences between levels of industrial employment in Czech areas with a Czech-speaking and German-speaking population were gradually levelling out.

On average, industry in the border areas had a more significant position than in the interior. The consequences were manifest in the social structure of the German population, which was predominantly employed in industry, trade and transport, while in agriculture its share was less in comparison to other ethnic groups (25 per cent). In 1921 the German population represented 33.5 per cent of those employed in industry, of whom 32 per cent were in trade, banking and transport, 27.4

Table 12.2. *Industrial employment of the Czechoslovak and German population in 1921*

Sector	Czechoslovaks (numbers per 1,000 actively employed)	Germans (numbers per 1,000 actively employed)
Mining and smelting	29.8	34.4
Metal industry	54.4	59.9
Quarrying	15.8	25.9
Glass industry	7.9	23.5
Chemicals	6.2	10.6
Timber industry	32.1	40.7
Textiles	39.2	113.8
Paper industry	5.0	10.6
Construction	55.7	59.4

per cent in state public service and 32 per cent in other occupations. Identification of the percentage of German population in individual branches of industry is likewise important. Among economically active members of the population, the Germans enjoyed relative preponderance over Czechs and Slovaks in mining, smelting, metal-working, stone and earth industry, glass-making, chemicals, lumbering, the paper industry, textiles and construction. In the social field it was also manifest in the very distinct predominance of wage-earning workers over independent entrepreneurs.

THE SOCIAL AND ECONOMIC CHARACTERISTICS AND NATIONAL RELATIONS OF INTERWAR CZECHOSLOVAKIA

In Czechoslovakia between the wars, the economically active population represented not quite half of the total population (6,537,384). The 1930 census statistics broke down this active population into three categories: independents (owners/employers); officials and white-collar employees; and workers, hired labourers and apprentices. The results of this categorisation showed that there was a rough equilibrium between the social categories of independents and workers.

The most numerous social group was that of workers (2,599,089), which, when hired labourers and apprentices were added, reached 3,281,238. Most were working in industry (1,953,880) with only 749,887 in agriculture and still fewer in the other sectors. In the social group of independents the 1930 census showed a total of 2,290,958, among them

Table 12.3. *Occupational distribution in Czechoslovakia, 1930*

Sector	Per 1,000 persons actively employed		
	Independents	Officials	Workers, servants, hired labourers
Agriculture, forestry, fisheries	530.2	7.7	462.1
Industry and trades	124.9	47.3	827.8
Commerce, banking and transport	279.7	476.1	544.2
Civil service, professions and military	58.1	405.4	536.5
Domestic and personal services	102.3	1.5	896.2
Other professions and professions not specified	890.8	–	109.2

886,997 in agriculture and 823,711 in other fields. Persons living off rents and social security, wards of institutes and students were also included in this group. In industry the number of independents was only 312,400, and in trade, banking and transport it was 225,148. This shows the relative concentration of industrial and commercial enterprise, transport and finance, as compared with agricultural enterprise.

The category of officials and white-collar employees was numerically strongest in trade, banking and transport, in which 390,777 people were working. The next largest number worked in public service, the free professions and the military (301,142), followed by industry (235,364) and agriculture with only 35,980. These figures show the level of tertiarisation of the Czechoslovak economy.[21]

Among the rest of the population the numerically largest group was that of people without gainful occupation (children, housewives, pensioners and so on), which represented 6,917,097 persons. This was followed by auxiliary family members (1,071,598) and servants (203,457). The largest percentage of this non-employed population was affiliated to industry and agriculture. Table 12.3 shows the status of the active working population in 1930.[22]

The tertiary sphere was expanding in the interwar period with the development of modernisation and the rationalisation of the Czechoslovak economy. The relatively high level of industrialisation in the Czech Lands and the growth of services linked to it meant that the proportion of independents in the Czech Lands was less than in Slovakia or Subcarpathian Ruthenia.

The different economic and social character of the western and eastern parts of the Republic caused difficulties in the economic and political integration of the state. Although Slovakia had previously been one of the most industrialised areas of the former eastern half of Austria-Hungary (Transleithania), and had slightly exceeded the Hungarian average in volume of industrial production, only 17.6 per cent of its population was employed in industry, with 59 per cent occupied in agriculture.[23] Immediately after the establishment of the independent state, Czech capital attempted to gain control of Slovak sources of raw materials and to take over the Slovak market for its own industrial products. The major role in economic penetration of Slovakia and Subcarpathian Ruthenia was played by Czech banks (Legiobanka and Agrární banka).[24] The postwar period saw the collapse of a series of enterprises in heavy industry in Slovakia, especially in smelting and mechanical engineering, but there was also growth in the importance of light industry, particularly in timber processing, food and textiles. In this period Slovakia became the market for between 13 and 17 per cent of the industrial products of the Czech Lands. In return, it supplied principally agricultural products and raw materials (iron ore, wood, leather and, in small quantities, magnesites), but also included were such industrial products as cables, and electrotechnical and rubber manufactures. The Slovak timber and food industries and the mining of iron ores[25] enjoyed significant development in the prosperous years of the 1920s. With the world economic crisis, however, the fall in industrial production in Slovakia was greater than the decline in the Czech Lands. The worst affected was the timber industry, which had been orientated towards exports. In the poorest areas of Slovakia, such as Horehronie, Kysúca and Orava, this led to mass unemployment. The extraction of copper ores ceased and the mining of iron ores declined steeply. The demise of the relatively backward smelting industry continued. Several enterprises were closed down and a substantial part of smelting production from Podbrezová was relocated to Vítkovice. In the textile industry, cotton and linen production was severely curtailed. The cotton works in Ružomberok-Rybárpole cut production down to 40 per cent. In the glass industry only three of the original twelve glassworks remained in operation. There was also a steep fall in production in the food industry, especially the production of sugar and beer. In Subcarpathian Ruthenia the crisis took its toll mainly in logging, wood-processing and salt-mining. The agricultural crisis also had a very severe impact on Slovakia and Subcarpathian Ruthenia. The paucity of arable soil and its unequal arable distribution exacerbated the effects. In Subcarpathian Ruthenia a fifth of the land belonged to the French-owned Latorica company, which let it out in small parcels for high rents. The eastern territories suffered from chronic agricultural overpopulation, the migration of the population for seasonal work and emigration.[26]

The situation in the Czech Lands was very different in that the relations between Czechs and native Germans reflected the position of both as industrially developed groups. Until roughly the middle of the nineteenth century it was possible, if with certain qualifications, to speak of a unitary Bohemian society that included both the Czech- and German-speaking population. A certain number of people could speak both languages and from the economic and civic point of view made up a homogeneous whole. Nationalist movements within both ethnic groups gradually deepened the division of this society into its Czech and German components, which came frequently into conflict. Roughly from the end of the 1860s the Czech ethnicity was gaining in strength, above all, because of the migration of the Czech population from the countryside to the towns.[27] Developments in the later nineteenth century challenged the thesis propounded by the publicist Franz Schuselka in his work *Ist Oesterreich deutsch?* arguing that the more advanced urbanisation of the German-speaking population justified its primacy.[28]

By the end of the nineteenth century, the Czech Lands were already an industrial-agricultural society comparable to the Scandinavian countries, and not too far behind countries such as France and Germany. The industrialisation of the Czech Lands led to the growth of the Czech industrial working class, and also strengthened the Czech bourgeoisie, competing with its German-speaking counterpart. The results of the First World War opened up the way to profound changes. Following the establishment of the new state, the political and economic position of the Czech bourgeoisie was fortified through currency reform, nostrification and land reform. After immediate postwar economic difficulties had been overcome with the help of foreign loans, modernisation proceeded on all sides.[29]

Leaving on one side the immediate postwar attempt to create German-Austrian provinces out of the border regions of Bohemia and Moravia, the relationship between the native German and Czech ethnic groups stabilised. Co-operation developed in the economic fields and also in politics – from 1926 the German Agrarian, Christian Social and Social Democratic parties participated in coalition governments.[30] Indigenous German capital also had a share in Czech banks. At the beginning of the 1920s, the Deutscher Hauptverband der Industrie, as the representative body of German industrialists in Czechoslovakia, was set up. It established co-operation with the Central Union of Czechoslovak Industrialists by joining it for a certain period. Native German business in Czechoslovakia was represented principally by the Hauptverband der deutschen Kaufmannschaft in Teplice-Šanov and the Verband deutscher Kaufleute, likewise in Teplice-Šanov. The main organisations of small tradesmen included the Hauptverband des deutschen Gewerbes in Prague, the Reichsverband deutscher Gewebevereine im tschechoslowakischen Staate in Brno, and the Deutscher gewerblicher Landeskreditverband in Ústí nad Labem.[31] A significant element in the economic life of Czechoslovakia was Reich-German and Austrian capital. In 1923, for example, twenty-seven Reich-German and thirty-four Austrian joint-stock companies were active on Czechoslovak territory.[32] As indicated, much of the textile and glass-making industries and also of the timber, paper and porcelain industries, as well as a part of the chemical industry, were in native German hands. The restricted market of a small country such as Czechoslovakia could scarcely absorb the production of indigenous light industry with its large capacity. Thus the *bijouterie* industry was manufacturing 90 per cent for export, while in porcelain the figure was 85 per cent, in glass 82 per cent, in glove production 80 per cent, in haberdashery 80 per cent and in textiles 40 per cent. By contrast, the proportion of ironworks production destined for export was only 35 per cent, for chemicals 21 per cent, for cement 20 per cent and for black coal 7 per cent.[33]

The radicalisation of the native German population, which eventually led to its embracing Hitler's National Socialism, occurred in the course of the world economic crisis, which had a particularly severe impact on the border areas and their light industry. This crisis was accompanied by a fall in tourism that had a damaging impact on spas (Karlovy Vary, Marianské Lázně and Františkovy Lázně). Unemployment in the border districts was usually higher than in the country's interior. At the end of 1935, districts with more than 80 per cent German-speaking population had an unemployment rate of 19.2 per cent of economically active persons, and the figure for districts with 50 to 80 per cent German-speaking population was 17.46 per cent. Meanwhile, the unemployment rate was 9.16 per cent of economically active persons in districts with less than 20 per cent German-speaking population. The overall national unemployment rate was 12.16 per cent of economically active persons. The worst affected districts were Kraslice, Nejdek, Krnov and Rýmařov.[34] It should, however, be acknowledged that the Czechoslovak coalition government failed to solve the social problems in time.

It was an historical tragedy that at a time when democrats in Germany saw in Czechoslovakia a refuge from Nazism, many native Germans in Czechoslovakia were expressing a contrary sympathy for it.[35]

NOTES

1 T. G. Masaryk, *Česká otázka* [The Czech question], (Prague, 1990); T. G. Masaryk, *Palackého idea národa československého* [Palacký's idea of the Czechoslovak nation], (Prague, 1992); J. Pekař, *Masarykova česká filosofie* [Masaryk's Czech philosophy], (Prague, 1927); M. Kučera, *Pekař proti Masarykovi* [Pekař against Masaryk], (Prague, 1995); J. Pátek, 'Die tschechoslowakische Aussen-und Europapolitik in der Zeit zwischen den beiden Weltkriegen' in F. Boldt, R. Hilf and W. Reiter (eds.), *München 1938* (Essen, 1990).

2 P. Feldl, *Das verspielte Reich. Die letzten Tage Oesterreich-Ungarns* (Vienna and Hamburg, 1968), pp. 72–3; L. Fialová, P. Horská *et al.*, *Dějiny obyvatelstva českých zemí* [History of the population of the Czech Lands], (Prague, 1996), p. 264.

3 A. Boháč, *Národnostní mapa republiky Československé* [Nationality map of the Czechoslovak Republic], (Prague, 1926).

4 *Československá statistika* [Czechoslovak statistics], (1934), vol. VI/7, *Sčítání lidu v republice Československé* [Census of the population of the Czechoslovak Republic 1930], Part I, p. 46.

5 *Ibid.*, p. 46.

6 *Československá statistika* (1924), vol. 9, cited also by Z. Deyl, 'Demografický vývoj a profesní národnostní a sociální složení obyvatelstva' ['Demographic development and national and social composition of the population'] in V. Lacina and J. Pátek (eds.), *Dějiny hospodářství českých zemí od počátku industrializace do současnosti* [Economic history of the Czech Lands from the beginning of industrialisation to the present], (Prague, 1995), p. 38.

7 *Československá statistika* (1934), vol. VI/7, pp. 46–7.

8 A. Oberschall, 'Die Nationalitätenfrage in der Tschechoslowakei' in *Československá statistika* (1934), vol. 9, Section VI, pp. 41–2.

9 *Československá statistika* (1934), vol. VI/7, pp. 46–7.

10 *Ibid.*

11 J. Pátek, 'Vývoj zemědělství a lesnictví' [Development of agriculture and forestry] in Lacina and Pátek, *Dějiny hospodářství českých zemí*, pp. 43–70 at p. 43; see also *Zprávy SÚS (Státní Úřad Statistický)* [Reports of the State Statistical Office], 104 (1933), Section D, No. 17.

12 Pátek, 'Vývoj zemědělství a lesnictví'.

13 J. Novotný and J. Šouša, 'Vývoj průmyslové výroby' ['Development of

industrial production'], in Lacina and Pátek, *Dějiny hospodářství českých zemí*, pp. 71–96 at pp. 71–3.

14 *Statistická příručka republiky Československé* [Statistical Handbook of the Czechoslovak Republic], vol. VI (1932), p. 17.

15 Novotný and Šouša, 'Vývoj průmyslové výroby', pp. 73–6.

16 V. Král, M. Kropilák and J. Křížek *Přehled československých dějin* [Outline of Czechoslovak history], (Prague, 1960), p. 846. (See also R. Holec, 'Economic aspects of Slovak national development in the twentieth century' in this volume.)

17 *Zprávy SÚS* (Prague, 1933 and 1934), vols. XIV and XV, Section D, No. 26, 2, 13. For the Jewish population see A. M. Rabinowicz, *The Jews of Czechoslovakia* (New York, 1968).

18 J. César and B. Černý, *Politika německých buržoazních stran v Československu v letech 1918–1938. Exkurze o hospodářských a společenských poměrech německé menšiny v Československé republice* [Politics of German bourgeois parties in Czechoslovakia in the years 1918–1938. Notes on economic and social conditions of the German minority in the Czechoslovak Republic], (Prague, 1962), p. 437. (See also C. Boyer, 'Nationality and competition: Czechs and Germans in the economy of the First Czechoslovak Republic (1918–1938)' in this volume.)

19 J. W. Brügel, *Tschechen und Deutsche* (Munich, 1967), p. 146.

20 *Československá statistika* (Prague, 1935), vol. 116, Section VI, No. 10, p. 17.

21 *Zprávy SÚS*, (1933), vol. XIV, Section D, No. 17.

22 *Ibid.*

23 Král, Kropilák and Křížek, *Přehled československých dějin*, Part 3, p. 52.

24 *Ibid.*, p. 50.

25 *Ibid.*, pp. 153–6.

26 *Ibid.*, pp. 316–19.

27 L. Fialová, P. Horská *et al.*, *Dějiny obyvatelstva českých zemí* [History of the population of the Czech Lands], (Prague, 1996), p. 268.

28 F. Schuselka, *Ist Oesterreich deutsch?* (Leipzig, 1843); see also A. Klíma, *Češi a Němci v revoluci 1848 až 1849* [Czechs and Germans in the Revolution of 1848 to 1849], (Prague, 1988), pp. 11–18.

29 Fialová, Horská *et al.*, *Dějiny obyvatelstva českých zemí*, pp. 274–82.

30 César and Černý, *Politika německých buržoazních stran*, p. 460.

31 *Ibid.*, p. 462.

32 *Statistická příručka republiky Československé* (Prague, 1925), vol. II, p. 596.

33 A. Dobrý, *Hospodářská krize československého průmyslu ve vztahu k Mnichovu* [The economic crisis of Czechoslovak industry in relation to Munich], (Prague, 1959), pp. 23–4.

34 M. Weirich, *Staré a nové Československo* [The old and the new Czechoslovakia], (Prague, 1938), pp. 162–3.

35 A. Teichova, *An Economic Background to Munich International Business and Czechoslovakia 1918–1938* (Cambridge, 1974); A. Teichova, *The Czechoslovak Economy 1918–1980* (London and New York, 1988).

CHAPTER THIRTEEN

Nationality and competition: Czechs and Germans in the economy of the First Czechoslovak Republic (1918–1938)

Christoph Boyer

THE BASIC SITUATION

The nationality issue

The nationality issue was an element of cardinal importance in the political, economic and social life of the First Czechoslovak Republic. The background of this issue was the presence of a strong native German population ('Volksgruppe') in a state that defined its identity not as multinational but as the state of the Czechoslovaks. To some extent, the Germans were conceived of as a menace to this identity and as a threat to the newly gained national independence. These statements are very general; they only characterise mainstream or average attitudes.

The *Volkstumskampf* ('ethnic struggle'), as it was called by contemporaries, characterised the First Republic from its foundation in the autumn of 1918 until its end following the Treaty of Munich.[1] However, talking about conflict alone would draw a strongly distorted picture. Reality was characterised by a complex mixture of antagonism and co-operation. The result was a modus vivendi – sometimes arduous but viable on the whole. The element of conflict was predominant in the first years after the First World War. It faded into the background in the second half of the 1920s when the 'activist' German parties – that is, those that professed to be loyal to the state – co-operated with the Czech parties and participated in government. Antagonism tended to arise again in the 1930s, when the peaceful coexistence of Czechs and Germans in the Republic was overshadowed by the rise of National Socialism in Germany. The Sudetendeutsche Partei (SdP – Sudeten German party), basically a puppet of the Nazi party,[2] was undoubtedly perceived as a threat to the unity and security of the state, and therefore the Germans within the country were suspected of being the 'fifth column' of the Reich.

The nationality issue and the economy

The nationality issue was also troublesome in the economic sphere. The goal of an independent economy – a precondition and a complement of political autonomy – was a constant factor in the history of the First Republic. Because the Czechs feared that German economic hegemony would be the first step towards political supremacy, they were afraid of being subjugated by the economic power of the Reich – a circumstance that had various consequences for bilateral economic relations that cannot be dealt with here. For similar reasons, the Czechs considered the strong German economic position within the country to be dangerous. In the eyes of the Czechs, the German influence had two aspects. The first critical point was the impact of capital from the German Reich in Czechoslovakia, especially in technologically advanced key industries such as chemical production, electrical engineering and mechanical engineering. A second problem was the native Germans; roughly speaking, their resources were concentrated in the 'old' light and consumer goods industries – textiles, glass and porcelain, for example.

At this point, some remarks have to be made about basic concepts. For several reasons it would be almost impossible to quantify the size and borders of the 'ethnic economies' of the Czechs and the Germans.[3] In the first place, it is not clear if the basis for the classification of an enterprise as 'Czech' or 'German' should be the nationality of its owner, the shareholders, the management or the workers. The nationality of these persons or groups was by no means necessarily identical. The language used by the internal administration of an enterprise could be a criterion, but it is not complex enough. Secondly, talking about the nationality of the owners already presupposes that national identity can be clearly defined. In fact, nationality is nothing natural or organic but is a historical phenomenon based on a large variety of criteria such as language, national feelings or loyalty towards certain historical traditions.[4] This implies that for people to ascribe a nationality to themselves, or for nationality to be defined by means of a bureaucratic procedure such as the population census in the First Republic, national identity could yield quite different and varying results. Moreover, it was even possible to change one's national identity. The diffuse character of the concept is illustrated by the case of the Jews in Czechoslovakia, a group that played a prominent part among the entrepreneurs of the country: the Jews opted to be 'Czech' or 'German' or 'Jewish'. Also to be taken into account are the 'cosmopolitans', who showed a very weak adherence to a nationality or confessed no national loyalties at all – a type of person usually found in circles of business leaders with international interests and a supranational outlook. Apart from these conceptual problems there are practical difficulties with statistics: companies from the German Reich, which were not very welcome in the Republic, often preferred mimicry, which means that the basis for the quantification of German economic resources, at least, is fragile.[5]

To sum up: only a rough concept of a 'Czech' or 'German' economy can be used.[6] Nevertheless these entities are indispensable – utterly diffuse and blurred though the borderlines may be. They were rooted in the minds of the people of the time and they were at least distinct enough to form the precondition for conflict between the ethnic businesses. This struggle between Czechs and Germans about 'nationaler Besitzstand' ('national property') was embedded in the whole situation of *Volkstumskampf*, in which both parties considered a strong economic position to be an important prerequisite for a good standing. German contemporary agitation denounced aggressive 'Czechisation' ('Tschechisierung'), a policy that constituted in the Czech perspective the legitimate attempt to form a Czechoslovak national economy, not least with the intent to reverse the Habsburg policy of 'Germanisation' ('Germanisierung').

The Czech policy of economic nationalisation was directed against all forms and variants of German economic influence – against enterprises from the German Reich as well as against the economy of the Germans of Bohemia and Moravia. The different structure and importance of these two economic bodies were mostly ignored. The economic assets of the native Germans significantly exceeded their share of the population, but they were less imposing than they looked in statistics because German industries were relatively backward and their productivity was low. Nevertheless, in the political perspective Germans of Czechoslovakia never completely got rid of the image of being unreliable; in this respect they were a menace equal to the impact of capital from the Reich. Economic nationalism, aimed at extending Czech capital as well as personal influence in the economy, found expression in a bundle of measures initiated and supported by the majority of Czech political parties, by the cabinets and the administration, by political and economic organisations, industrial enterprises and the Czech banks. A not unimportant factor was the Národní rada, the 'national council' – the central organisation of Czechoslovak regional nationally oriented bodies. The essence of its programme was the completion of the nation state in every respect.

Already at this point, however, an important restriction has to be imposed. What holds true for the nationality issue as a whole is especially important in the economic field: factors limiting conflict intensity were stronger in this field than elsewhere. The goal of balanced interests was especially prominent in the domain of material interests. In other areas of the *Volkstumskampf*, for example in the field of language and school politics, nationalism was much more infectious and could become virulent with considerably less risk of material loss. This chapter presents three case studies demonstrating that Czech–German relationships in the economic area were intermingled with an especially strong element of co-operation. The studies do not deal primarily with the quarrel over the control of national capital. Rather, they concentrate on the conflicts between the two ethnic groups about personal or organisational influence. They focus on the networks that led, organised and represented the two ethnic economies: configurations of persons of the same nationality, sometimes loosely organised groups, sometimes formal organisations. These networks operate on the basis of material power, but their influence is also correlated with their intellectual, technical and administrative capacities, their political standing, their tactical skill, their knowledge, energy and motivations as well as the conflicts, the political alliances and contexts in which they act – in this case, the political system of the Czechoslovak state.

FIELDS OF CONFLICT AND CO-OPERATION

The organisations of industry

After the Czechoslovak state was established, two organisations of industrialists along national lines, one Czech and one German, were founded: the ÚSČP (Ústřední svaz československých průmyslníků – Central Association of Czechoslovak Industrialists) and the DHI (Deutscher Hauptverband der Industrie in der Tschechoslowakei – German Central Association of Industry in Czechoslovakia). In both cases the motivating force had obviously been the foundation of the state; the political rearrangement made the adaptation of the industrial organisation to the new frontiers necessary. Because the 'industry of the Germans' was concentrated in the border regions of the western part of the country, whereas 'Czech industry' was mostly to be found in the heartlands of Bohemia, the organisations had different regional centres of gravity. But they both possessed a fully developed structure inclusive of almost all industrial branches.[7]

Within the rather flexible frame of Czechoslovak association law these two private organisations had the liberty to form coalitions on the basis of a rational calculation of respective interests. Such agreements were not completely independent from the political sphere, but they were concluded at a relative distance from the political arena. The history of the relationship between the two organisations shows a clear tendency: in the beginning – in the years immediately after the First World War – relations were rather inimical. In the following stage there was sporadic harmonisation, a convergence of respective interests from time to time. In the next phase, co-operation was organised under the aegis of a common covering organisation. In the final stage, the Hauptverband joined the Czech organisation *in corpore* – a symbiosis that remained stable almost until the end of the Republic. The details of this development can be described as follows.

The identity of the Ústřední svaz was ambivalent: it had been founded before the end of the First World War as an organisation for the protection of national 'Czech industry' against the disadvantages it suffered in the Austro-Hungarian war economy.[8] After the Republic was established, the Ústřední svaz declared itself to be the official representation of Czechoslovak industry as a whole, a claim that was acknowledged by the first cabinets of the Republic, which consisted only of Czech ministers.[9] But at the same time the Ústřední svaz regarded itself as a national Czech body. The leading personnel were rooted in the Czech emancipation movement; at least in the first years after its foundation the Ústřední svaz showed a certain inclination towards the National Democratic Party, which had strong nationalistic tendencies.[10]

Under these circumstances it was somewhat natural for the Hauptverband to justify its segregation by the fear of annexation, with alleged negative consequences for the 'German industry' of Bohemia. The preservation of 'national property' became the primary reason for its existence. It was not by chance that the foundation of the Hauptverband took place at a time when tensions between the two nationalities were especially grave: the rallying of 'German industry' under the national flag was a counterpart to the project of a united front of the German parties against Czechisation,[11] which, to a certain extent, was real; but on the other hand, a certain element of paranoia could be

found in this context, too. The first years after the war were characterised by a serious economic crisis, and the 'German industry' of Bohemia
was inclined to place the blame for all problems on the official economic
policy of the new state, thereby blurring the difference between those
problems that stemmed from real anti-German resentment and those
produced by objective circumstances such as the crisis of foreign trade
caused by the new frontiers of the successor states of the Habsburg
Monarchy or by particular deficits of the administration.[12] The background of this paranoia was psychological trauma, stemming from the
fact that the Germans of Bohemia, who had perceived themselves as the
elite in the Habsburg Empire, found themselves in the position of a
minority in a state they did not consider to be theirs. In the same way,
'German industry' found itself degraded to the economy of a national
minority.

It is not surprising that on the German side there was a tendency to
'withdraw into a citadel'. But very soon in the leading circles of the
Hauptverband this tendency was superseded by the insight that the
policy of preserving German 'national property' could be successful
only if 'German industry' co-operated with the Czechoslovak administration, trying to influence the government and the parliament. Very
soon the Hauptverband demanded political participation and rights
equal to those of the Ústřední svaz; it started to use the German bourgeois parties as a parliamentary lever. Thus the Hauptverband at least
implicitly came to accept the existence of the Republic. It became part
of the 'activist' element – that is, the political forces that proclaimed
loyalty to the state and were in principle ready for a constructive political relationship with the Czechs.

Very soon it also became evident that the queries of the
Hauptverband in the central fields of economic policy were in most
cases identical to those of the Ústřední svaz.[13] This leads to the conclusion that to a great extent 'bad economic policy' really was 'bad policy'
from the point of view of industrialists and it had little to do with a
national bias on the Czech side. For example, the main social conflicts
were between the classes and not between nationalities. There were
conflicts over questions of economic order, tax policy, public finance and
trade or currency policy, but between different branches and only very
rarely between the 'Czech economy' on the one hand and the 'German'
on the other. Soon it became obvious that the differences between the
aims of the two bodies were only a matter of nuance. But the schism
considerably weakened the power of the industrial lobby; moreover, the

existence of two organisations was uneconomical. Until the end of 1921, there were parallel programmes and claims. Under the pressure of a new economic crisis that started around the beginning of 1922, co-operation was for the first time institutionalised in the form of a central committee of the two bodies. The motive for bridging the gap was the economy, at a time when political tensions between Czechs and Germans were about to rise to a new height.

In 1928 the co-operation was fully institutionalised, when the Hauptverband *in corpore* joined the Ústřední svaz.[14] This time, the alliance was not born out of a crisis; on the contrary, it was forged in a rather pleasant economic climate. The motive for the union was the rel-atively weak impact of the industrial lobby *vis-à-vis* an economic policy that, again from the point of view of the industrial organisations, was insufficiently oriented towards industrial interests. Economic policy, for example in the cardinal question of customs tariffs, was mainly directed by a coalition of the Agrarian Party and the representation of workers' interests. Politics essentially consisted in a trade-off between these two groups, whereas industry was relatively distant from the centre of power.[15] The amalgamation of the two bodies was also favoured by certain background conditions, such as a general softening of the ethnic conflict in a period when German activist political parties joined the cabinet.[16] Moreover the activist course of German industrial interests was supported by a newly founded activist party, the DAWG (Deutsche Arbeits- und Wirtschaftsgemeinschaft – German Association for Work and Economy).[17] At the same time, bilateral political relations with the Reich improved.[18]

The first years after the Hauptverband joined the Ústřední svaz were characterised by this congruence of political activism and economic co-operation.[19] The situation changed almost completely with the rise of Sudeten German National Socialism in the 1930s: the SHF (Sudetendeutsche Heimatfront – Sudeten German Patriotic Front), later renamed SdP (Sudetendeutsche Partei – Sudeten German Party) devel-oped a new, intransigent position on the nationality issue. The pro-gramme of this party contained at least implicitly, later also explicitly, the postulate that the Hauptverband should give up co-operation with the Ústřední svaz within the political framework of the Czechoslovak state. Instead, the Hauptverband was now urged to incorporate itself in the *Sudetendeutsche Volksgemeinschaft* (the Sudeten German people's com-munity), which was conceived of as a part of the all-encompassing *Deutsche Volksgemeinschaft* (German people's community), with the SdP or even the Nazi party as political leaders. The economic counterpart of this *Sudetendeutsche Volksgemeinschaft* was to be an autonomous 'Sudeten German economy', separated from the 'Czech economy' and orientated towards the Reich. Another implication of this concept was that German industrialists in Bohemia should give up the moderately liberal and democratic principles they shared with their Czech partners and adopt the National Socialist totalitarian political credo and the authoritarian model of an economic order.[20] But even in this situation the Hauptverband was relatively reluctant to give in, to acknowledge the supremacy of the party and cut the narrow links tying it to the Ústředni svaz.[21] The reasons for this were the material interests of German industrialists in Bohemia: severing the ties to the part of the economy that was considered 'Czech' seemed almost impossible, because it would have required a complete restructuring.

To sum up: the co-operation of the two industrial organisations was based on calculation of economic interests that were basically identical and that superseded nationalistic sentiments. This basic harmony was to a considerable extent immune to political disturbances. At times, politics even constituted an outright counterpart to economics.

The Chambers of Trade and Commerce

The conflict and co-operation in the Chambers of Trade and Commerce were different from those in the industrial organisations. For a systematic explanation of these differences we have to look at the characteristic features of the respective bodies. The Chambers were rooted in the continental Chamber law – in the case of the Czechoslovak Chambers this was basically the corpus of the Austro-Hungarian Chamber law. According to this tradition, Chambers were not private associations but corporations of public law; membership of firms, regardless of their nationality, was compulsory. The relationship of the Chambers with the state was relatively close: Chamber statutes were fixed by the authorities or at least they had to be approved by the Ministry of Trade and Commerce; the rights of this ministry to intervene in the internal life of the Chamber were quite far reaching.[22]

With this background and compared with the industrial organisations, the problem of national representation and the possibilities of co-operation and conflict between Czechs and Germans took a different shape: within a clear-cut frame of organisation, ways had to be found that secured both parties fair representation within the Chambers. The mandates in the leading bodies of the Chambers, the *Verwaltungs-kommissionen* ('administrative commissions'), were distributed proportionally between Czech and German interests. German and Czech commission members were organised in respective 'parliamentary groups'. The mandates were originally to be distributed according to the results of Chamber elections, but this procedure was drawn out over at least the next twenty years; in fact the Ministry of Trade and Commerce appointed the members of the commissions, thus fixing the national quota.[23]

At this point it is important to stress that the distribution of the mandates by the ministry was not simply dictated by government authorities. The ministry had to rely on information from below. The process was highly political because the Chambers, as corporations of public law, interpreted their role as the representation of the economy as a whole – the parliament of the economy – which meant that very different claims had to be taken into account: those of industry, trade, commerce and finance. There was a conflict between big business and small business; there were ethnic or even nationalistic sentiments and, of course, there were the demands of political parties representing economic interests. In Chamber politics, the consequence of this highly complex system of manifold and often diverging claims was a very complicated, often arduous and lengthy process of bargaining in the phase preceding the appointment of the Chamber members. This trade-off normally did not take place in public; it usually meant scheming in the back room. The appointment principle also created sinecures that were at the disposal of party politicians.[24]

Immediately after the foundation of the Republic the composition of the administrative commissions was adapted to the new situation, which meant that the Czech quota was raised. This first shift was meant to be compensation for an undeniable under-representation of the Czech element before 1918. In 1926/7 and again in 1936 the membership of the administrative commissions was extended. Whereas in 1926/7 the Germans got a share of the additional mandates that on the whole allowed them to preserve the status quo, they significantly lost ground in 1936. There are several reasons for this. In the first place, the number of political parties – most of them Czech – that claimed to be represented in the Chambers had risen in the 1930s compared to the 1920s. On the whole, Czech political parties representing economic interests were much keener on extending their influence in the Chambers, whereas on the German side similar party influence was not to be found. The second reason that the majority of the additional mandates fell on the side of the Czechs in 1936 was the strong impulse to strengthen the small-business element, which played an important role in the economy of the First Republic. Because the Czech position in the handicraft and the small-trade sector was stronger than the German position, favouring small business meant strengthening the Czech element.

To conclude: in the long run, the importance of the German element in the administrative commissions declined significantly. But the reason for this loss of weight was not ethnic aggression on the Czech side. There was no long-term plan to extend the Czech position in the Chambers at the cost of the Germans by taking away mandates from the Germans and giving them to the Czechs. Now and then such projects were devised by isolated chauvinists; but they remained largely irrelevant. The explanation has to be sought in the almost automatic working of the appointment mechanism described above. Given the nature of party politics, this mechanism produced as a side effect a bias in favour of the Czech element, but the system as such was a result of the given political structures. It was not a result of Czech acrimony. This can be proved by the fact that there was ample protest against this swamp of intrigue not only on the German side but on the Czech side, too.

Everyday life in the Chambers, which consisted of a wide range of activities supporting trade and commerce irrespective of its nationality, was relatively harmonious and mostly free of nationalistic resentment. In some isolated cases there were quarrels about the language to be used in the Chamber, in some other cases certain other symbolic issues were disputed.[25] But on the whole these cases were an exception.

The industrial elites

Another very important dimension of the fight for influence and control over the economy of the First Republic was the over-representation of German personnel in the leading positions of Czechoslovak industry. This problem of 'národnostní poměry' – that is, the 'national conditions' in the economy – was basically a heritage from the Habsburg Monarchy. Because of their administrative, technical and economic know-how, these technicians, engineers, leading managers and directors were of immense strategic importance in the economy of the Republic. Some members of this business elite were natives of Bohemia or Moravia and Czechoslovak citizens. Many of them were Austrian citizens; but there were also a great number of immigrants from the Reich – the state to which Czechoslovakia most feared being subjugated. Here, again, in the eyes of the Czechs all Germans regardless of their citizenship tended to be perceived as potentially dangerous. The menace was all the greater because a concentration of Germans was to be found not only in the higher echelons of enterprises classified as German; the situation in Czech firms was not much different. An especially delicate matter were the Germans in those enterprises on which the defence of the country was based: mining, metallurgy, chemicals, mechanical engineering and electrical engineering. In Czechoslovak military circles, which were closely interconnected with the Národní rada, this aspect of national security played an especially important role.[26]

Nationalistic currents in public opinion, the Národní rada, the lobbies of Czech qualified employees and professionals and, of course, the pressure of the military all urged a replacement of the Germans already employed in Czechoslovakia; at the same time they supported measures aimed at reducing any further influx of Germans into leading positions in the future. The issue of *národnostní poměry* became virulent for the first time after 1918 in the context of the so-called 'nostrification' – the policy by which the Prague government tried to urge enterprises producing on the territory of the Republic to move headquarters from the old capital, Vienna, to Czechoslovakia. The intention of this measure was to gain sovereignty in the field of economic policy. It went hand in hand with attempts at extending the influence of Czech capital, and this was to be the means by which the *národnostní poměry* at the top of the enterprises were to be changed.[27] A few years later, in 1923 and again in 1928, Czechoslovakia tried to introduce certain legal and practical restrictions on the occupation of foreigners, primarily Germans; but in both cases an escalation was prevented by way of negotiations with the Reich. The conflict became sharper in the 1930s: this time it was provoked by the Nazi regime, which quite brutally removed most Czechoslovak workers employed in Germany. This policy, which was part of the Nazi anti-crisis policy trying to raise employment, was answered in Prague by retaliation measures against German employees in Czechoslovakia. Things came to a head in 1936 when the parliament in Prague passed the Law for the Defence of the State. This law, which was the Czech response to the National Socialist threat, enabled the military to intervene in the economy in order to guarantee the security of the country and to prepare it for an eventual war. It also significantly extended the rights of the administration to intervene in all matters of *národnostní poměry*.[28]

In summary, Czech policy aiming at improving *národnostní poměry* showed significant results, especially in the 1930s – results that the German side bitterly regarded as consequences of 'Czechisation'. Certainly this process aggravated the tensions between the ethnic groups. But on the other hand it would be exaggerated to interpret this as total 'ethnic cleansing'. In many cases it was impossible to remove Germans in leading positions because there were no Czech substitutes. In other cases, a Hegelian 'cunning of reason' was operating: the rising influence of Czech capital in German enterprises, originally intended as a prerequisite for changing the *národnostní poměry*, stimulated the interest of Czech capital owners in the smooth functioning of these enterprises and reduced their interest in nationalistic experiments. Industry was, in general, very sceptical about measures threatening the existence of managers and experts. Finally, the risk of complications with the Reich and Austria was an argument against rigorous restrictions; Czechoslovak citizens employed in the neighbouring countries were in danger of being taken hostage.

SUMMARY

It is a myth that Czech–German relations in the First Republic consisted of nothing but bitter conflict caused by Czech malevolence and intransigence. Although there was sometimes aggressive conflict over the extension of 'national property' and a rather short-sighted chauvinism on both sides of the ethnic frontier, there was also co-operation and compromise.

First, maybe the mainstream of Czech politics in the First Republic was permeated by a basic anti-German inclination; this disposition was, however, not translated into a comprehensive and consistent policy programme. In other words, German nationalistic agitation was wrong in assuming the existence of a Czech master-plan intending to ruin the Germans. Nationalistic sentiments had their ups and downs. Very often they were instrumentalised by power politics; nationalistic topics were, for example, very popular in election campaigns. Not all pronouncements by chauvinists should be taken as gospel truth.

Secondly, not all Czech measures that looked nationalistic at first sight were motivated by resentment: discrimination against Germans was in many cases due to objective economic or political constraints, structural weaknesses of the political system, especially the characteristic mechanisms of party politics or the dilettantism of an administration that in many cases was characterised by the slackness in the tradition of the

Habsburg bureaucracy. Typically enough in many cases, for example in matters of economic policy, there were German complaints, but there were parallel concerns on the Czech side as well.

Thirdly in Czechoslovakia, there were several safeguards against a solution to the nationality issue by force. For example, the German activist parties took part in the political process. Even if it is controversial how far their influence reached, it is plausible to assume that they had a certain bargaining power. Also, Czechoslovakia was a constitutional state with a properly working legal and judicial apparatus, which in most cases prevented arbitrary interventions of the authorities into the sphere of private business. This meant that there existed a curb against arbitrary anti-German measures. The German position in the Chambers, for example, could not be erased, and the legal status of citizens of the Reich could not be changed arbitrarily.

A fourth point to note is that Czechoslovakia was bound by international juridical norms, in the first instance the treaties for the protection of the minorities. Although there were many queries about Czechoslovak infringements of these treaties, they acted as a minimal curb to arbitrary measures.

Finally, especially in the economy there was relatively far-reaching goodwill regarding living together profitably – 'profitably' in the strict sense of the word, because this attitude was mainly the expression of economic pragmatism. Damaging those enterprises that, in the eyes of contemporaries, were considered as a part of the 'German economy of Czechoslovakia' would in many, if not most, cases also have meant damaging the sector of the economy that was considered to be 'Czech' – whereas co-operation across ethnic frontiers produced synergetic effects. This taming of nationalistic feelings may not always have been a matter of the heart, but goodwill motivated by profit is perhaps apt to generate a more stable modus vivendi than noble, but volatile, emotions.

NOTES

1 For the political background, see Rudolf Jaworski, *Vorposten oder Minderheit* (Stuttgart, 1977) and Ferdinand Seibt, *Deutschland und die Tschechen. Geschichte einer Nachbarschaft in der Mitte Europas* (Munich and Zurich, 1995), pp. 227–334.

2 See Christoph Boyer and Jaroslav Kučera, 'Die Sudetendeutsche Heimatfront/Sudetendeutsche Partei und der Nationalsozialismus' in Horst Möller, Andreas Wirsching and Walter Ziegler (eds.), *Nationalsozialismus in der Region. Beiträge zur regionalen und lokalen Forschung und zum internationalen Vergleich* (Munich, 1996), pp. 273–85, and Christoph Boyer and Jaroslav Kučera, 'Die

Sudetendeutsche Heimatfront/Sudetendeutsche Partei 1933–1938: Zur Bestimmung ihres politisch-ideologischen Standortes', *Bohemia* 38(2) (1997), 358–68.

3 Although such trials do exist. The most prominent are to be found in Jiří Hejda, 'Komu patří československý průmsyl' ['To whom does Czechoslovak industry belong?'], *Přítomnost* 4 (1927), 709–11, 724–6, 742–4, 759–61, 787–9, 805–7, 822–4 and *Přítomnost* 5 (1928), 20–4, 38ff., 54–6, 70–2, 86ff., 104ff., 117ff.

4 See, for example, Ernest Gellner, *Nationalismus und Moderne* (Berlin, 1991).

5 Whereas the position of western capital can be much better quantified: see Alice Teichova, *An Economic Background to Munich* (Cambridge, 1974).

6 'German economy', 'German industry', 'Czech economy' and 'Czech industry' are in inverted commas from now on, to indicate the problematic character of the concepts.

7 For the DHI, see *Mitteilungen des Deutschen Hauptverbandes der Industrie* 1 (1920), 9 and 123, and 2 (1921), 116 and 189.

8 *Observer* 15 (1933), pp. 247–50.

9 Státní ústřední archiv (Central National Archive, SÚA), Ústřední svaz československých průmyslníků (Central Association of Czechoslovak Industrialists, ÚSČP), Box 24, 0/50/1, letter of the ÚSČP, reporting the founding of the organisation, 19 June 1918.

10 SÚA, ÚSČP, Box 10, speech by President Malinský in the General Assembly of the ÚSČP, 10 May 1919.

11 Politisches Archiv des Auswärtigen Amtes, Bonn ('PA'), R 9103, German embassy in Vienna to Auswärtiges Amt ('AA'), 24 October 1919.

12 As a typical statement, see Rudolf Teltscher, 'Wirtschaftliche Diktatur. Ein Jahr tschechoslowakischer Wirtschaft', *Die Wirtschaft* 2 (1921), 472–4.

13 For a representative list of those queries, see Karl Janovsky, *Drei Jahre tschechoslowakischer Wirtschaftspolitik* (Prague, 1922).

14 Report on the committee meeting of the DHI on 18 September 1928, *Mitteilungen des Deutschen Hauptverbandes der Industrie* 9 (1928), 833ff. See *Prager Tagblatt*, 19 September 1928.

15 *Observer* 6 (1924), p. 285.

16 PA, R 73 778, Memo Röpke, March 1927 (no exact date).

17 PA, R 73 833, letter from German Embassy in Prague to the German Foreign Ministry, 7 August 1928. See *Die Wirtschaft* 10 (1928), 990.

18 PA, R 73 778, Memo Röpke, March 1927 (no exact date).

19 See, for example, the report on the general assembly of the DHI on 5 April 1930, *Mitteilungen des Deutschen Hauptverbandes der Industrie* 11 (1930), 269. Speech by Mr Preiss, president of the ÚSČP, 22 May 1929. See *Observer* 11 (1929), 229–31.

20 See, for example, the report on the Conference of Teplitz-Schönau, 20 February 1938, *Hospodářský archiv* 17 (1938), 134.

21 This was obvious, for example, in the general assembly of the DHI on 2 April 1938: *Mitteilungen des Deutschen Hauptverbandes der Industrie* 19 (1938), 136.

22 Franz Geissler, 'Die Entstehung und der Entwicklungsgang der Handels-kammern in Österreich' in Hans Mayer (ed.), *Hundert Jahre österreichischer Wirtschaftsentwicklung 1848–1948* (Vienna, 1949), pp. 21–126 and Herbert Matis, *Österreichs Wirtschaft 1848–1913. Konjunkturelle Dynamik und gesellschaft-licher Wandel im Zeitalter Franz Josephs I* (Berlin, 1972), pp. 48ff.

23 This was widely criticised. See Hellmuth Freytag, *Die Organisation der wirtschaftlichen und berufständischen Selbstverwaltung in der Tschechoslowakei* (Leipzig, 1934), p. 25.

24 This process is analysed in detail in Christoph Boyer, *Nationale Kontrahenten oder Partner? Studien zu den Beziehungen zwischen Tschechen und Deutschen in der Wirtschaft der Ersten Tschechoslowakischen Republik* (Munich, 1999).

25 Speech of Matys Pokorný, Vice-President of the Chamber Pilsen, in the general assembly of the administrative commission of the Chamber on 14 July 1919, *Věstník obchodní živnóstenské komory v Plzni* 1 (1919), 141.

26 SÚA, Ministerstvo průmyslu, obchodu a živnosti (Ministry of Industry, Trade and Handicraft, MPOŽ), dod. (addenda), Box 7, P-4045/1, Czechoslovak Ministry of National Defence to Czechoslovak Foreign Ministry, 5 January 1933.

27 Vlastislav Lacina, *Formováni československé ekonomiky* [The formation of the Czechoslovak economy], (Prague, 1990), pp. 91ff.

28 A good impression can be won from the parliamentary debate on the law. See *Prager Tagblatt*, 29 and 30 April 1936.

CHAPTER FOURTEEN

Economic aspects of Slovak national development in the twentieth century

Roman Holec

In the twentieth century the central European region experienced frequent political and systemic changes. Due to the complex and sensitive nature of Slovakia's national and political development, questions were asked about the meaning of Slovak history, which have polarised the entire society. Slovakia's economic development faithfully conformed to all stages of political changes, which outwardly appeared as economic nationalism. During the greater part of the twentieth century Slovaks remained on the defensive regarding their legal status and their position in the state.

Under the conditions of the Austro-Hungarian Monarchy Slovaks had to resist strong Magyar national – political as well as economic – pressures. Liberal legislation and the decisive role of the state in the economy, characteristic of Hungary, were accompanied by efforts to control and restrict non-Magyar business activities. This became evident in strong tendencies towards centralisation affecting banking, as well as co-operatives with the intention to prevent the use of accumulated capital in the furtherance of political goals hostile to the interests of the state.[1]

In such conditions a significant defensive role was played by active Czech–Slovak co-operation. While publications have dealt with the political aspects, less attention has been paid to economic co-operation between the two nations, which supported the Slovaks' endeavour to achieve national emancipation and assisted in furthering their own economic activities. As Slovak economic nationalism was strengthened during this process, it gradually created conflicts and contradictions in the economic field. Nevertheless, Czech–Slovak economic co-operation positively influenced several areas of Slovak development. An important part, for instance, was played by the education of economic personnel at schools in Bohemia and Moravia, the so-called Apprenticeship Scheme of the Českoslovanská jednota (Czechoslav Union), whose co-ordinating organisational activities consisted of expanding trade relations between individuals and firms, purchasing property and land in Slovakia, organising extensive educational courses in business management, assisting in the development of the Slovak co-operative movement and initiating numerous other activities. An exceptionally positive effect of Czech–Slovak co-operation of lasting significance was the work of numerous Czech experts and engineers in Slovak business enterprises and financial institutions.

Slovakia was, before 1918, an integral part of the Hungarian market and transport system. In their efforts to challenge economic discrimination, Slovaks adopted the Czech slogan of economic nationalism, 'svoj k svojmu' (ours to us), and tried to strengthen capital links with Czechs. Since the end of the nineteenth century Czech capital had begun to expand into Slovakia where it met with greater acceptance than in other areas of Austria-Hungary, such as Galicia, Dalmatia or Croatia. The existence of a strong consciousness of Czech–Slovak mutuality and the lively interchange in practically all spheres of life created one of the most viable forms of the movements of national emancipation. Within this framework, however, Czech capital and its financial institutions found themselves unintentionally in conflict with the ideals of brotherly assistance and the reality of business practice. In other words, Czech business got involved in the political struggles in Slovakia where the economic nationalism of the ruling (Magyar) and the ruled (Slovak) nation faced each other in irreconcilable antagonism.

In August 1911, speaking in the Moravian spa town of Luhačovice, the banker Július Markovič made an unusually critical statement about the activity of Czech capital in Slovakia. Whilst he attached great importance to Czech assistance, he rejected Czech–Slovak unity and mutuality merely on a materialistic basis and also emphasised ideological and ethnical topics. From the beginning Czech assistance focused on providing credit, thus aiding Slovak financial institutions to achieve greater independence. Large credits did not, however, correspond to the Slovak banks' own financial strength and evoked various 'megalomaniac' moods that resulted in excessive investment activities. Good intentions changed into the sword of Damocles as liquidity of the majority of Slovak banks was threatened because they were unable to cover the servicing and repayment of loans. Markovič ascertained that, while credits of 6 million crowns had been taken up by Slovak banks in Hungary, 14 million crowns of credits came from Cisleithania, mainly from Bohemia and Moravia, even though interest was 0.5 per cent higher than from

Magyar or German institutions in Hungary (7.25:6.75 per cent). At the same time a gradual change could be observed in the behaviour of Czech capital, which, also under the threat of discrimination from the Hungarian state, entered increasingly into business relations with Magyar or Jewish capital. According to Markovič, the spirit of altruism faded and 'exclusively the bankers' spirit of self-interest and exploitation' gained preponderance – that is, the spirit and direction, though entirely correct from the banker's point of view, was not suitable to further brotherly links on the basis of racial and ethnographic mutuality.[2]

A prewar survey undertaken by the periodical *Prúdy* concerning Czech–Slovak mutuality identified two basic problems in the economic area.[3] In the first place, Slovaks sharply criticised business practices of Czech financial institutions towards their Slovak partners. This has to be seen not only against the background of the less developed asking for an altruistic approach from the richer partner but rather as reproaches concerning the connections of Czech with Magyar capital, or the higher interest rates and rediscount practices that discriminated frequently against Slovaks. In spite of great expectations by Slovaks very little assistance was given to them by Budapest-based Czech institutions. Efforts by Milan Hodža, Igor Hrušovský and other Slovak prominents failed to found a Czech–Slovak bank in which Slovaks would wield greater influence and which would take up a central position in Slovak finances. In due course the repercussions of capital investments of Czech banks in Slovak joint-stock companies evoked disenchantment and indignation.

Differences in approaches as well as divergent views and tactical considerations were tangibly revealed at several occasions: for example, at a confidential meeting of Českoslovanská jednota in Prague in March 1907, at several negotiations in Luhačovice, and in particular at the secret consultation of Rudolf Pilát, one of the initiators of Czech– Slovak cooperation at the Živnostenská banka (Trade Bank), with representatives of Slovak political and business life in Ružomberok (a small industrial town in central Slovakia) in June 1909, devoted to the project of the Dunajská banka (Danube Bank) in Budapest. Not always entirely justified reproaches, raining down on Pilát's head during the discussions in Ružomberok, were mainly directed against persons belonging to the circle of the banker and politician Alois Rašín in the Živnostenská banka who, in their struggle against German economic superiority, saw a suitable counterpoise in close Czech–Magyar financial and economic collaboration. Real fears of the expected dominance of Czech capital in Slovakia existed in the wake of a possible Czech–German understanding, which would doubtless be followed by a federalist reconstruction of the Dual Monarchy. 'Economic control of Slovakia and subsequent cultural dominance is only a matter of time; as soon as only an approximate key to a Czech–German compromise will be found Czech power will be released and quite naturally transferred to us!'[4] This fear literally emanated from the commercial-entrepreneurial activities of Czech banks, which, on the Slovak side, were accompanied by correspondingly greater disappointment because all steps of Czech capital in Slovakia were undertaken under the flag of Czech–Slovak unity or Slav mutuality. Contrary to these claims it was critically asserted that 'people belonging to Czech financial circles . . . are often not aware of the national mission of Czech capital in Slovakia'.[5]

The second problem arising from the *Prúdy* survey was connected with various aspects of the well-known slogan of Czech economic nationalism, 'svoj k svojmu'. Here, more pronounced than anywhere else, political aspects came to the fore, particularly because it openly contravened the programme of Magyar policy to achieve greater customs and economic independence from Austria – that is, from Cisleithania, to which the territory of the Czech Lands belonged.

From the above characterisation it is obvious that, in spite of the many positive aspects of Czech–Slovak economic co-operation before the First World War, not a few disproportions existed emanating chiefly from the unequal position of the partners. The very problems that had troubled mutual capital relations before 1918 began to rise to the surface, became politically relevant and determined all aspects of Czech–Slovak relationships after the establishment of the new Czechoslovak state.

In the last year of the war the unequal economic strength of both partners became fully manifest during the discussions about the economic nature and the economic priorities of the future state. While in the Czech press and in the pronouncements of representatives of Czech political parties the inevitability of socialisation, land reforms and other questions were discussed, generally without specific plans, Slovakia had not yet got that far. Even deliberations about the nature of a future common state and about the position of Slovaks in it were absent. This was formulated only in the so-called Martin Declaration of 30 October 1918, which was an official act of the Slovak National Committee confirming the decision to establish a common state of Czechs and Slovaks.

Doubtlessly, Czech society had made substantial progress towards national emancipation and had developed a high degree of political consciousness. Evidence of this can be found in the preparation and drafting of the political and economic programme of the future state in the summer of 1918, the authors of which belonged to a group of experts headed by the director of the Živnostenská banka, Jaroslav Preiss, and the director of the Městská spořitelna pražská (Municipal Savings Bank of Prague), Vilém Pospíšil.[6] It is symptomatic that the programme was created without Slovak participation. Indeed, no consideration was given to the specific features, the different composition and levels of development of the economies of the Czech Lands and of Slovakia. Only in two marginal cases was Slovakia mentioned in the programme. Even during the first postwar years no adequate attention was paid to the economic reality and complexity of Slovakia.

In spite of their evident unpreparedness, it cannot be maintained that Slovaks were unaware of the danger emanating from an economically substantially stronger partner. A young Slovak economist, formerly a clerk of the Živnostenská banka, Tomáš Tvarožek, drew attention to these problems in an internally circulated memorandum that he independently drafted in summer 1918, essentially concurrently with the above-mentioned Czech proposal of the economic programme.[7] Tvarožek analysed the financial situation in Slovakia and tried to impress that timely preparations should be made for the event of new economic conditions by using the positive and eliminating the negative features of the operations of Czech capital. His deliberations reflect the uneasiness emanating from previous experiences with Czech capital. The ideas contained in the memorandum were approved by Milan Hodža and other economists. However, Slovak possibilities were restricted and conditional upon the character of Slovakia's inclusion in the Czechoslovak Republic.

The establishment of the Czechoslovak Republic in 1918 afforded Slovaks unthought-of possibilities of self-realisation in political, cultural, economic and other areas. However, in none of these was general satisfaction achieved. On the contrary, tensions arose, mutual communication faltered and mutual misunderstanding grew. After 1918 somewhat less than one fifth of the industrial capacity of Hungary remained in Slovakia, which amounted to somewhat over 8 per cent of the total industrial potential of the new state. As part of the Czechoslovak Republic, Slovakia faced entirely new tasks in the framework of building new economic relationships. At the same time, it was

economically weakened as a consequence of the war and, particularly,
due to military events and plundering of 1918 and 1919, military dictatorship, the fleeting establishment of various east-Slovakian republics,
sabotage, the negative effects of the removal of entire industrial facilities, factories and raw-material stores as well as machinery. What could
not be removed (railway lines, for example) was destroyed by retreating
Magyar or, later, bolshevik troops. In addition, the process of currency
separation from Hungary in 1919 proved to be much more complicated
and damaging than that of the Czech Lands from Austria. All this must
necessarily be considered when describing the catastrophic economic
situation of Slovakia at the time it entered the new state.

In the postwar period a whole range of objective factors stymied the
integration of the two diverse economies, not least because Slovakia was
assigned the role of an agrarian appendage. Proponents of the concept
of industrialisation had to challenge views that industry in Slovakia was
of a greenhouse nature and that its development was artificial rather
than natural. Naturalness was seen in the light of Czech and Slovak
equality but this view of equality objectively disadvantaged the weaker
– that is, the Slovak – economy. In fact, the liberal, in principle egalitar-
ian, economic policy proclaimed initially by the state – that is, the programme of non-intervention into market forces by rejecting giving
preference to one part of the Czechoslovak Republic over another –
paradoxically caused damage to Slovakia. Namely, no consideration was
given to Slovakia's substantially lower economic performance, neither
were specific conditions taken into account, for example the fact that, as
a result of Hungarian legislation that was still in force, a higher tax
burden existed in Slovakia until 1927 (speculators used this for evading
substantial tax payments), or the fact that tariffs on private and state railways differed, which disadvantaged Slovakia where transport costs were
much higher. Industrial development was held back by the absence
of coal mining and mechanical engineering production. Similarly, the
unified system of quotas of distilling, introduced in 1919, damaged
Slovakia where conditions of production were entirely different and
where the economic importance of distilling was greater than in the
Czech Lands. Equally, quotas for lower taxes on spirits, decreed in 1920,
discriminated against Slovakia.

Uniting Slovakia with the industrially more advanced Czech Lands is
often appraised from the point of view of the captains of Czech industry, who regarded the eastern region as compensation for the lost
markets of the Austro-Hungarian Monarchy. However, the limited

possibilities of consumption in Slovakia and Subcarpathian Russia could not, by any stretch of the imagination, replace the whole Dual Monarchy but, on the contrary, the Czech economy represented a potential consumer of Slovak raw materials and semi-finished goods (for several interwar years Slovakia's trade with the Czech Lands showed an active balance). Slovaks felt discriminated against because of disproportions in orders placed by the Czechoslovak state: the share of Slovakia in state orders has been estimated as 5 per cent, whereas the share of Slovakia's taxes in total tax revenue of the Czechoslovak state varied between 15 and 18 per cent. Although parliament granted enterprises in Slovakia a so-called 5-per-cent advantage according to which a Slovak firm could receive state orders even though its estimated costs would be up to 5 per cent higher than those of a firm in the Czech Lands, the reality in this case was also different – namely, Czech firms evaded this regulation by transferring the seat of their enterprise to Slovakia.

In the very first years of the Czechoslovak Republic's existence Czech financial circles launched a relatively large expansion of capital investment in Slovakia with the aim of dislodging the strong Budapest banks and to establish themselves in the key enterprises and industrial branches on Slovak territory. Logically, and in a market economy as is to be expected, interest centred on lucrative enterprises with good growth prospects: paper mills, iron works, textile factories, breweries, malthouses, spas, mineral wealth and so on. The foundations of this expansion of Czech capital were already being laid during the last year of the war, in co-operation with the strongest Slovak banks and also owing to the prewar connections of Czech banks in Slovakia and lively capital and commercial dealings. However, this process did not have entirely positive repercussions. Thus, using the excuse of the unitary state quota system on distilling, the modern distillery in Leopoldov – mainly in the hands of Slovak capital – was forbidden to distil from sugar beet. Spirit had to be distilled from molasses but all seven Slovak sugar refineries were already under contract for these with distilleries across the Morava river in the Czech Lands.[8] Similar economic or, rather, extra-economic pressure was applied to other efficient Slovak enterprises by competing Czech business groups. Enterprises within the sphere of interest of Czech capital managed to overcome the postwar recession more easily and were in a position to register economic growth by the second half of the 1920s. At the same time, the acute shortage of credit, investments and transfer capital in Slovakia led to steep rises in interest rates.

When the postwar recession deepened, calls for state intervention in the economy became louder in Slovakia. As the state's economic policy was based on the principle of non-intervention into the market mechanism, public support was afforded only to those enterprises that had been taken over from the Hungarian state and which thereafter developed relatively successfully. As a result of the postwar crisis of 1921–3, the interest of Czech financial and business circles in Slovakia faded away and many industrial enterprises stagnated, went bankrupt and into liquidation. This produced highly restive repercussions as works closed down and thousands lost their jobs. Social deprivation engendered political tensions and the culprit was sought in Prague. It was in this connection that the myth of the 'dismantling of industry' arose, which was kept alive by the press and misconstrued for political purposes. It became much more difficult to 'dismantle' the myth than to invent and perpetuate it. The so-called dismantling of Slovak industry resulted from the reality of competition during which enterprises failed because of their less efficient equipment and high production and transport costs.[9]

While the state rejected intervention into private business,[10] it attempted to pacify social tensions by a long-term rescue action for Slovak banks to help them cope with the huge deficits the First World War had left them. Among others the Ružomberok Ľudová banka (People's Bank) of the parish priest Andrej Hlinka (leader of the Catholic autonomist People's Party) was rescued as its fall would have morally discredited this leader, who was becoming an uncomfortable politician for Prague. Irritation was caused in Slovakia by the state's dilatory attitude to solving urgent economic problems concerning transport, taxation and conditions of production, or to alleviate the damaging effects of the currency reform on Slovakia's exports. On the financial market the concentration of banks in Czechoslovakia led in many cases to the fusion of Slovak with Czech commercial and savings banks which, in the process, replaced former Slovak branches. In the political sphere resentment was caused by the insufficient representation of Slovaks in the state's central economic institutions (the Czechoslovak National Bank) where Slovak presence was largely symbolic or even non-existent.

Slovakia's economic problems in the interwar period were doubtlessly caused by unfavourable objective conditions. Although misused as a weapon in the political struggle these economic realities could not speedily be changed. Political aspects were of secondary significance whilst their existence and impact cannot be overlooked. Many negative aspects in Slovakia's economic life even became targets of Magyar propaganda, which suddenly not only discovered Slovak ethnicity but also warned

with touching solicitude against 'Czech colonialism'. Real and fabri-
cated economic problems were made the most of by individual Slovak
politicians, which weakened the young republic from the very first years
of its existence.

Slovaks may have accepted the new Czechoslovak statehood but did
not necessarily identify with it; its reality very slowly penetrated their
consciousness. Conditioned as the process was, both regionally and
socially, its acceleration depended largely on the improvement of the
economy: the Czechoslovak framework would meet with growing
approval should economic well-being increase. Thus political and economic aspects were closely intertwined. Slovaks wanted a substantially
greater share in political power, which in November 1921 had already led
to demands regarding customs jurisdiction and a dualistic regime of the
Czechoslovak economy. These demands were repeatedly voiced in the
Slovak, the central organ of the Slovak People's Party led by Hlinka, as
for instance:

autonomy of Slovakia is economically based, for the economy is Slovakia's vital
issue. Economic vassalage brings about political subjection and stagnation of
economic life . . . Slovak industry, in its present state, is not strong enough to
maintain its markets in its competitive struggle with Czech business . . . the only
solution is: economic dualism. The introduction of duties on industrial goods is
an indispensable condition of its reconstruction . . . i.e. a sliding scale of duties
which would decrease the competitiveness of Czech industrial products and
would equalise production costs . . . The passivity of the government in economic affairs in Slovakia directly forces working people to become supporters
of autonomy . . .[11]

Also, the Protestant Slovak National Party (Slovenská národná strana)
demanded autonomy (excepting protective tariffs between the western
and eastern halves of the state). Its influence in interwar Czechoslovakia
fell far below its prewar position. Experiences with the process of
integration also led people close to Prague to recognise the pitfalls, as is
evident from the opinion of the agrarian politician and economist Ján
Cablk (1930):

It was our fault that frivolously, superficially and consciencelessly we overlooked
the problem of how to integrate economic conditions of Slovakia into the new
state successfully. As a consequence, the weaker filled the world with its complaints, the stronger made use of all its options of skill and strengths.[12]

While discussions continued among Slovak economists about conceptual questions regarding the agrarian or industrial character of
Slovakia, distressing social consequences of the economic crisis of the

early 1930s further extended the contagion of national conflicts and, above all, separatism in the ranks of the opposition in Slovakia. In this atmosphere Hlinka's Slovak People's Party – after a short spell in government (1927–9) – rejected the budget at the beginning of 1930 and, in May, again presented a bill to parliament demanding autonomy for Slovakia. In 1931 this was followed by a proposal for state support of Slovak industry. Before the elections of 1932 the Slovak People's Party mounted a signature campaign against 'the economic damage caused to Slovakia' from which a memorandum was presented to Prime Minister František Udržal by a delegation led by Andrej Hlinka in February 1932. Among its seven points were demands for tax relief, cheap credit, depoliticising the agrarian credit co-operatives (dominated by the Agrarian Party) and state orders for Slovakia.[13]

Also, after the experiences of the world economic crisis other political currents in Slovakia turned their attention to the economic dimension of the Slovak question. For example, ideas of the new Slovak generation within the governing Agrarian Party gave rise to the movement of 'regionalism'. While autonomy was not demanded, such visions pointed in that direction.

In the mid-1930s, when the existence of the Czechoslovak Republic came under threat, the centre of the government's industrial-strategic plans shifted to Slovakia where a number of armament and engineering works were founded and work on taming the rapids of the River Váh for electric power was begun. There was talk about the reindustrialisation of Slovakia. However, the failure to solve the national-political question undermined the stability of the state and weakened its internal and external security. But also the autonomy of Slovakia (proclaimed on 6 October 1938), during the short period of Czecho-Slovakia, the so-called Second Republic, was unable to solve the country's economic problems. The question 'who is paying for whom' dogged all economically motivated conflicts between Prague and Bratislava.

The Second Republic ceased to exist when Slovakia, with the support of Germany, seceded and declared its state independence on 14 March 1939 and the German army occupied Bohemia and Moravia on 15 March 1939. The disintegration of the Second Czechoslovak Republic created dissimilar economic conditions in the German-instituted Protectorate of Bohemia and Moravia and in the Slovak state. Whilst the former became part of the German Third Reich and was brutally plundered, the latter, due to its formally independent status, was more slowly sucked into the system of the German war economy. Following the establishment of Slovakia as a vassal state of Germany, Czech–Slovak relations were not furthered by the purges of Czech civil servants and employees in all walks of Slovakia's life, including the economy. All Czechs were forced to leave the territory of Slovakia without regard for the significance of the positions they held, or for the length of their services to the country, or for interventions on their behalf at the highest places.

A particular feature was the demand of Slovak entrepreneurs for the so-called nationalisation of capital, that is the transfer of Czech property into the hands of Slovak nationals. In general, Slovakia benefited from the relatively high degree of militarisation of its industry, which, in fact, was inherited from the last years of the Czechoslovak Republic. For instance, at the height of the boom 15,000 people were employed at the armament works in Dubnica. The demise of Czech competition coupled with the favourable conditions of booming war production engendered economic growth. If the economic gains from 'aryanisation' are added, the result is a picture of a German satellite enjoying social security and a sound living standard within a Europe suffering from war. This greenhouse dynamism of a war boom makes up the background to the myth of the 'economic miracle' and prosperity of the Slovak state, which did not last long, as the horrors of war also reached its territory. As popular dissatisfaction with German domination of the Slovak state grew, the Slovak resistance movement developed and reached its culmination in the Slovak National Uprising in August 1944. Its aim was the renewal of the Czecho-Slovak state in which Slovaks would have complete equality with Czechs.

The restoration of the Czechoslovak Republic brought about the recognition of the Slovaks as an independent nation and the declaration of equality with the Czech nation, anchored in the Košice Programme of the Czechoslovak government of 5 April 1945. It was based on the experiences of Munich and on the recognition of Slovak resistance during the Second World War. Slovak national organs were constituted, which, however, had no counterpart on the Czech side. On the one hand, this asymmetric model expressed the reality of Slovak emancipation and, on the other hand, Czech society, in the absence of feelings of national discrimination, identified itself with the whole of Czechoslovakia.

From the point of view of the interplay of political (national) and economic forces the new situation created a number of controversial issues. In view of the more satisfying economic conditions as well as the better

situation in the supply of provisions in the Slovak state in comparison
with the Protectorate of Bohemia and Moravia, the Slovak population
regarded the postwar state and the introduction of food rationing as a
deterioration of their standard of living. A further serious irritation was
felt by the unification of the currency at an exchange rate between the
Slovak and the Protectorate crown thought to be unfavourable to
Slovakia.

The resolution of the Slovak National Council of 2 March 1945
confirmed the economic, customs and currency independence of
Slovakia for a transitional period. At that time the Commissioner of
Finance, Tomáš Tvarožek, openly stated that 'from the point of view
of Slovak finances one of the most acute and important problems is the
decision about the exchange value of the Slovak crown . . . and its equalisation with the Czech Protectorate crown'.[14] Unification of the currency was complicated for several reasons: different movements of prices
and wages in Slovakia and in the Czech Lands, different inflationary
developments, differences in purchasing power and in levels of indebtedness to Germany and, last but not least, a different situation because
the front line had passed through Slovakia. The Ministry of Finance
and the Czechoslovak National Bank formulated a secret document on
the *Principles of Currency Reform and Financial Policy*, dated 23 August 1945,
which states that:

it is extremely important not to create the impression that one part of the state
gained more than the other during unification of the currency, especially . . .
dangerous would be a situation in which the Slovak part of the republic would,
one way or another, be damaged. Therefore, equalisation should be performed
in such a way that Slovakia would not be made to carry a burden which to a
greater part was created in the Czech Lands rather than in Slovakia.[15]

In spite of these words on the economic, social and political approach
to the currency reform, a course was chosen that was to pacify the Czech
campaign claiming that Czechs 'were worse off by having to pay for
Slovakia' rather than trying not to hurt Slovak feelings of injustice. In
the end, the currency reform was introduced by decree of the President
of the Czechoslovak Republic on 19 October 1945, which received, especially in circles of experts, an adverse reception in Slovakia. The
exchange rate of the Slovak to the Protectorate crown was fixed at 1:1,
which did not correspond to its real value and did lifelong damage to the
holders of Slovak currency. Disadvantaged Slovakia was to be compensated by the introduction of a programme of industrialisation[16] to which
all political parties in Slovakia agreed, however much their opinions

differed about the role of the state and the private sector. At the same time, agreement was reached about the rejection of liberalism and the inevitability of state intervention in the economy.

The idea that economic solutions would also resolve political and national imbalances characterised the postwar opinions of President Edvard Beneš who, when receiving representatives of the Czechoslovak Society on 22 March 1946, pronounced: 'It is important to realise . . . that the difference in economic levels in Slovakia and in the Czech Lands is the substance of all difficulties between Czechs and Slovaks.'[17]

With regards to the main aims of the re-established Czechoslovak state's economic policy, the laws on nationalisation of October 1945 and the confiscation of property of enemies and collaborators had a bigger impact on the industrially more developed Czech Lands than in Slovakia. In the course of the land reform, especially during its second stage, which began in 1947, regional specificities and traditions in Slovakia were largely disregarded. However, in comparison with the development after 1918 it was generally accepted that changes in the economy and in the social structure of Slovakia had to take place. During the industrialisation programme of the first postwar years industrial enterprises of the Czech border regions were transferred to Slovakia (337 enterprises capable of employing 24,000 workers). At the end of 1948, these had absorbed 13 per cent of the total employed in Slovakia's industry. On the Czech side this programme was not accepted without reservations. While the Czech National Social Party did not agree with the weakening of Czech industrial capacity, it advocated the increase in the flow of workers from Slovakia to Bohemia and Moravia. On the Slovak side the Slovak Democratic Party demanded the transfer of production capacities to Slovakia where the required workforce was available. It is obvious that in this political argument economic efficiency played only a subordinate role.[18]

After the Communists came to power in February 1948, the policy of the centralistic-authoritarian regime with regards to the Slovak questions concentrated solely on eliminating Slovakia's economic backwardness. The main, indeed key, design of achieving economic, social and civil equalisation of Slovakia with the Czech Lands consisted of the so-called socialist industrialisation – that is, the programme of industrialisation in Slovakia significantly affected the process of national emancipation of Slovak development. The then Czech as well as Slovak Communist leadership reduced the Slovak question exclusively to its economic dimension. It acted under the illusion that industrialisation of

Slovakia would bring about Czech–Slovak consensus and understanding at the same time as the asymmetric constitutional model could be maintained. In reality industrialisation had the opposite effect – it contributed to the growth of dissatisfaction with the rigid centralism of Prague and the weak competence of Slovak authorities. All the more so, as the decision-making power of Slovak authorities was being lowered year by year in rough proportion to the rise of Slovakia's economic potential. During the 1950s, disparate opinions about the course of industrialisation and critical voices addressed to Prague within the framework of the Communist Party were judged to be indications of Slovak nationalism and 'economic separatism'. Industrialisation was considered to be the lawlike transition period from capitalism to socialism – later to be replaced by the slogan 'the more industrialisation, the more socialism' – and, based on the same axiomatic approach, preference was given to the buildings of heavy industry. Paradoxically, the positive emphasis on the need to raise the economic level of Slovakia to that of the Czech Lands was accompanied by the virtual liquidation of the executive and limitation of the legislative within Slovak political organs. In reality the Slovak question was reduced merely to industrialisation, that is to an economic equalisation. Therefore, a policy that could be defined as vulgar economism was unable to succeed.[19]

In spite of the problems discussed above, industrialisation provided the economic basis for the solution of the national question. Slovakia changed from an agrarian to an industrial-agrarian country. Industrial employment exceeded agrarian employment by the mid-1960s and Slovakia's share of the national income steadily increased.

The Action Programme of the Communist Party of Czechoslovakia of April 1968 formulated the main aims of economic and social policy of the state. The part concerning the economy contained a new system of steering and control. From the point of view of Czech–Slovak relations the Action Programme contained two contradictory formulations, which triggered a polemical discussion between Czech and Slovak economists. On the one hand a unified Czechoslovak economy was talked about; on the other hand the economy of the state was seen as the integration of two national economies. While the Action Programme demanded the broadening of competences of Slovak national organs, no mention was made about setting up similar specific Czech national bodies. In the economic sphere the task of Slovak organs was to work out and sanction a national economic plan, including a budget for Slovakia. The process of economic equalisation of Slovakia with the

Czech Lands was to be completed by 1980. In practice, this would have meant speeding up the course of industrialisation, the intensification of agricultural production, the expansion of tourism and the support of economically backward regions.

During the reform days of 1968, the government of the Czechoslovak Socialist Republic presented its programme, together with a critical analysis of former policies, to the National Assembly on 24 April 1968. In the critique of the state of the economy the following areas were mentioned: overemphasis on heavy industry; pursuit of autarkic policies; overextended demand on materials and energy, investments and imports; restrictions on consumption; lack of integration into the international division of labour; underestimation of technical progress and an unconsidered approach to economic reform.[20]

The invasion of troops of the Warsaw Pact countries terminated any efforts at reform. The Constitution of the Czechoslovak Federation of 27 October 1968 remained an empty frame without a picture with regards to relations between the two nations, particularly because of the suppression of civil rights and the restriction of civic freedom, gaps in legislation and the problematic division of powers between the national and federal organs. In economic affairs the federal government, in charge of the central planning authority, was substantially strengthened to the detriment of the national governments, and the declared integrity of the state often generated conflicts with Slovakia. Although differences in the level of the economies still persisted, on the basis of overall indices the process of economic, social and cultural equalisation between Slovakia and the Czech Lands was officially declared completed in the mid-1980s.

After the fall of communism in 1989, the economic experiences of the past four decades became part of the general Czech–Slovak discussions and polemics. They were conducted in the strained political atmosphere that accompanied the conversion of the armament industry begun in 1991 and which, in the course of two years, reduced the production of military equipment by 90 per cent. The share of the output of the Slovak armament industry amounted to 64 per cent of total armament production of the federative state of Czechs and Slovaks. Thus the socio-economic effects of the conversion reached catastrophic dimensions in Slovakia.

The industrialisation of Slovakia arose from the principle of developing a unified Czechoslovak economy – that is, instead of duplication there should have been mutual complementarity of the Czech Lands and Slovakia. After the division of the federative state in 1992/3 into two separate republics (the Czech Republic and Slovakia) many problems emerged – more so on the Slovak than on the Czech side, which nobody had envisaged and had never contemplated.

Again the question arose 'who has paid for whom?', indeed 'who has robbed whom?' In this atmosphere negotiations took place about the new regulation of relations between the two republics, which, after the elections of 1992, against the will of the majority of the population in both republics, led to the division of the state. Historical reality shows that, on the one hand, Slovakia's share in total state investments was higher than its share in the generation of the total common national income while, on the other hand, the complementarity of mutual economic relations strengthened both partners.

The common state fell apart at a time when all, including economic, differences in both republics were less than at any time during the common existence of the state. Thus the break up of the unified economic system of the former Czechoslovakia damaged both economies but, with regards to its structure, more serious damage was inflicted upon Slovakia. Negotiations about the division of the common wealth led to insurmountable differences between the two new states. As for Slovakia, the economic and geopolitical aspects of the Slovak national-political development were pushed into the background as preference was given to selfish interests of the political elite hiding behind the cover of the process of national emancipation.

NOTES

1 Activities in the field of industrial entrepreneurship were confronted with non-economic, distinctly political measures. See R. Holec, 'Zápas o martinskú celulózku ako najväčší projekt česko-slovenskej hospodárskej spolupráce pred I. svetovou vojnou [Struggle for the pulp mill of Martin as the largest project of Czech–Slovak economic collaboration before the First World War], *Historické štúdie* 35 (1994), 48–72; R. Holec, 'Medzi slovanskou vzájomnosťou a podnikateľskou aktivitou. Pražská banka Slávia v Uhorsku v druhej polovici 19. storočia' [Between Slavic mutuality and business activity. The Prague bank Slávia in Hungary in the second half of the nineteenth century], *Hospodářské dějiny – Economic History* 21 (1995), 145–72.

2 J. Markovič, 'Vývin slovenského peňažníctva zo stanoviska česko-slovenskej jednoty' [Development of Slovak finance in the light of Czech–Slovak unity], *Slovenský peňažník* 4(3), 20 March 1912.

3 'Anketa o československej vzájemnosti' [Investigation concerning Czech–Slovak mutuality], *Prúdy* 5(9–10), July–August 1914 (May 1919), 456–565.

4 P. Blaho to F. Houdek, 7 May 1911, Slovenský národný archív (SNA) Bratislava, fond F. Houdek, box 2, inv. 10.

5 'Československá vzájomnosť a peňažníctvo' [Czechoslovak mutuality and finance], *Slovenský denník* 2 (88), 11 May 1911.

6 V. Lacina, *Formování československé ekonomiky 1918–1923* [The forming of the Czechoslovak economy], (Prague, 1990), pp. 59–64.

7 Tomáš Tvarožek, probably to Anton Štefánek, 15 November 1917. Archív literatúry a umenia Matice slovenskej Martin, sign. 42 Z 38; Články a rozpomienky [Articles and reminiscences]. SNA, fond J. Cablk, box 10, inv. 798.

8 SNA, fond M. Dula, box 10, IV s/1, inv. 211.

9 See L. Hallon, *Industrializácia Slovenska 1918–1938. Rozvoj alebo úpadok?* [The industrialisation of Slovakia. Growth or decline?], (Bratislava, 1995).

10 See V. Lacina and L. Slezák, *Státní hospodářská politika v ekonomickém vývoji první ČSR* [Policy of the state in the economic development of the First Czechoslovak Republic], (Prague, 1994).

11 'Autonómia' (Autonomy), *Slovák*, 7(173–4), 4–5 August 1925.

12 Spolky (Associations), SNA, fond J. Cablk, box 10, inv. 796.

13 D. Jančík, 'S Prahou či proti Praze: ľudácka politika na rozcestí' [With Prague or against Prague: People's Party policy at the crossroad] in J. Dejmek and J. Hanzal (eds.), *České země a Československo v Evropě XIX. a XX. století* [The Czech Lands and Czechoslovakia in nineteenth- and twentieth-century Europe], (Prague, 1997), pp. 249–76 at pp. 261–2.

14 Report of the Commission for Finance about the financial situation, 2 March 1945, SNA, fond V. Šrobár, box 12, inv. 76.

15 *Zásady měnové reformy a finanční politika* [Principles of the currency reform and financial policy] formulated by the Ministry of Finance and Czechoslovak National Bank: SNA, fond V. Šrobár, box 12, inv. 76.

16 See Š. Horváth and J. Valach, *Peňažníctvo na Slovensku 1945–1950* [Finance in Slovakia 1945–1950], (Bratislava, 1984), pp. 43–103.

17 Report on the reception of the Czechoslovak Society by President Beneš on 22 March 1946. SNA, fond V. Šrobár, box 12, inv. 81.

18 M. Barnovský, 'Problematika industrializácie Slovenska v rokoch 1945–1950' [Problems of industrialisation of Slovakia during the years 1945–1950], *Historický časopis* 16 (1968), 169–91; M. Barnovský, 'Premiesťovanie priemyslu z českého pohraničia na Slovensko v rokoch 1945–1948' [The transfer of industry from the Czech border areas to Slovakia during the years 1945–1948], *Hospodářské dějiny – Economic History* 6 (1980), 101–45; A. Bálek, 'Specifické rysy a vzájemné vztahy české a slovenské ekonomiky v letech 1945–1948' [Specific features and mutual relations of the Czech and Slovak economy during 1945–1948] in *Hospodářský a sociální vývoj Československa (1945–1992)* [Economic and social development of Czechoslovakia (1945–1948)] in *Acta Oeconomica Pragensia* 3 (1996), 15–35; M. Londák, 'K problematike industrializácie Slovenska v období príprav plánov na 2. päťročnicu' [Problems of industrialisation of Slovakia during

the preparations of the second five-year plan], *Historický časopis*, 46 (1998), 64–78.

19 M. Barnovský, 'Determinanty a problémy industrializácie Slovenska' [Determinants and problems of industrialisation of Slovakia], *Česko-slovenská historická ročenka*, 3 (1998), 149–59; M. Barnovský, 'Ekonomická politika KSČ a hospodářský rozvoj Slovenska v prvej polovici šesťdesiatych rokov' [Economic policy of the Communist Party of Czechoslovakia and the economic development of Slovakia in the first half of the 1960s] in A. Gabal (ed.), *Rozvíjanie socializmu na Slovensku v prvej polovici šesťdesiatych rokov* [The development of socialism in Slovakia in the first half of the 1960s], (Bratislava, 1979), pp. 13–69 at p. 36.

20 V. Průcha, 'Hospodářská politika a vývoj československého hospodářství v období od roku 1960 do 21. srpna 1968' [Economic policy and the development of the Czechoslovak economy from 1960 to 21 August 1968] in *Hospodářský a sociální vývoj Československa (1945–1992)* [Economic and social development of Czechoslovakia (1945–1992)] in *Acta Oeconomica Pragensia* 3 (1996), 107–49 at pp. 124–5.

CHAPTER FIFTEEN

Economic change and national minorities: Hungary in the twentieth century

Ágnes Pogány

In a recent article, Heinrich August Winkler pointed out a general characteristic of research on nationalism: 'Until recently the history of nationalism . . . has mainly been treated as the history of its thinkers, with the focus on ideas and not on interests. The research methods have been those of the intellectual historian and not of the social historian. They tend to be phenomenalist rather than analytical.'[1] This statement could be complemented by another, namely that the aspects of economic history have also hardly been taken into account when studying not only the questions of nationalism but the problems of ethnic minorities and national identity. Although these are complex phenomena and it would be an oversimplification to explain them in purely economic terms, they are strongly intertwined with economic matters.

In the case of Hungary, the connection between economic transformation and national assimilation has been evaluated in very different ways. On the one hand some authors state that modernisation leads to the assimilation of ethnic minorities: 'it is undeniable that a natural assimilation was taking place, especially in the fast developing towns and industrial centres. The natural assimilation went on understandably as a result of modernization and industrialization. Therefore this affected those nations with a more modern social structure, whereas those with a more archaic structure resisted more effectively.'[2] In the opinion of others, however, economic development results in the awakening of the national feelings by the creation of a national middle class: 'As a consequence of capitalist modernization and of unfettered development of bourgeois conditions of labour and life the national efforts of non-Hungarian nations also gathered momentum in the second half of the 19th century.'[3] The main focus of this chapter is how economic factors influenced national minorities in twentieth-century Hungary.

ECONOMIC TRANSFORMATION AND ETHNIC MINORITIES

Hungary has been a multiethnic society since the Middle Ages. Slavic people lived in the Carpathian basin as early as the ninth century. Saxon immigrants were drawn by the regional development of the mining industry in Upper Hungary and Transylvania from the twelfth century onwards. In the sixteenth century Serbs came from the Balkans seeking refuge from the Ottoman conquest. During the Turkish occupation of Hungary, population numbers declined dramatically. In the seventeenth and eighteenth century, after the expulsion of the Turks, peasants from other parts of the Habsburg Monarchy (mainly Swabians, Franconians and Slovaks) settled the abandoned regions to cultivate the depopulated land. They were even granted certain privileges in order to make the hard task of moving to an uninhabited territory more attractive.[4] In the nineteenth century ethnic Hungarians made up less than 50 per cent of the population. Romanians, Slovaks, Germans, Serbs, Croats and Ruthenes were the most important ethnic groups living on the territory of Hungary.

In the Austro-Hungarian Monarchy the national question was strongly intertwined with the disparities in regional development. Before 1890 modern economic growth took place mainly in the western and central parts of Hungary, which were populated mostly by Magyars. There were only some regions with a mixed population that were able to take part in the rapid industrialisation process; the grain-producing southern plain (Bácska, Bánát), the mining districts of central Upper Hungary (Gömör/Gemerská župa, Zólyom/Zvolen, Szepes/Spišská župa)[5] and certain parts of Transylvania. In that period the regional economic disparities widened. Increasing regional differences in per capita income manifested themselves also in the uneven economic development of the various national groups. Ethnic minorities that lived on the northern, eastern and southern perimeters of the country remained in their traditional ways of life and showed a poor standard of living. Relative overpopulation and poverty led to mass-emigration movements towards the rapidly developing parts of Hungary and towards overseas countries.[6] Although the unevenness of growth was not induced by a definite discrimination policy on the part of the Hungarian government, it contained elements of social tension. While in territories with dynamic growth, Hungarian-speakers made up two thirds of the population, the proportion of Slovaks, Romanians and the Ruthenes living in the stagnating parts of the country exceeded 75 per cent.[7] Industrialisation in the central and western parts of the country, especially in Budapest, induced strong personal and generational mobility among the ethnic minorities and strengthened the process of assimilation.

In the years after 1890, modern economic growth also reached those territories where the majority of the population consisted of national minorities. Areas where economic and social conditions were backward began to be transformed. Economic and income inequalities were reduced, although they did not disappear. Before the outbreak of the First World War the level of economic development of the border regions was well above those of the country's eastern and Balkan neighbours. Economic integration in the Austro-Hungarian Monarchy contributed towards overcoming the unevenness of economic development. The growth rates of the less-developed eastern and southern parts of Hungary were well above those of the industrialised parts of Austria, Bohemia or Moravia.[8] In spite of these processes, the occupational structure and the rate of literacy of the different ethnic minorities showed significant differences in 1910. Germans had a more modern structure, the proportion of those employed in industry and services was much higher than in the case of the other ethnic groups, including the Magyars. Ruthenes, Romanians and Serbs had a more traditional structure. Among these latter nationalities, the proportion of those engaged in agriculture remained above 70 per cent. In the case of the Ruthene and Slovak populations, the share of white-collar workers could be considered astonishingly low (see table 15.1).

Between 1890 and 1914 the network of railways and roads spread into territories inhabited by ethnic minorities. The number of factories and credit institutes tripled or quadrupled. Significant industrialisation took place in West Transdanubia, where Germans and Croats lived in great number, and in regions inhabited by Slovaks (Kisalföld, the north and central part of Upper Hungary). In these regions, traditional heavy industry was complemented by textile, leather, chemical, glass and paper industries. New industrial plants emerged in Petrozsény (Petroseni) and Vajdahunyad (Hunedoara), where coal-mining and heavy industrial firms were founded. Food processing and engineering enterprises were established in southern Hungary as well.[9] At the turn of the twentieth century, 21 per cent of the Hungarian industrial plants employing more than twenty workers were to be found in the northern parts of the country inhabited by Slovaks. The proportion of factories employing 50 to 1,000 workers was 26.1 per cent in the same territory. Only 16 per cent of the Magyar population lived there.[10]

Table 15.1. *The occupational structure and the rate of literacy of various*
Hungarian nations in 1910

Nations	Occupational structure (%)			Rate of literacy (%)	
	Agriculture	Industry and commerce	Professionals and civil service	Men above 6 years	Women above 6 years
Slovaks	70.8	20.1	1.0	75.6	64.4
Serbs	76.8	14.7	2.5	57.8	38.1
Croats	69.7	21.5	1.2	64.2	48.4
Romanians	86.3	7.9	1.4	41.4	24.7
Ruthenes	89.2	4.8	0.5	32.5	23.6
Germans	49.7	37.2	2.7	86.0	78.7
Hungarians	55.0	30.6	4.8	82.8	75.5

Source: Lásló Katus, 'A nemzetiségi kérdés és Horvátország története a 20. század
elején' [National question and the history of Croatia at the beginning of the twentieth
century] in P. Hanák (ed.), *Magyarország története, 1890–1918* [The history of Hungary,
1890–1918], (Budapest, 1978), vol. VII, p. 1010.

The Industry Development Laws of 1881, 1890, 1899 and 1907
granted state subsidies, tax exemption or railway freight rate allowances
to newly founded industrial plants. Comparing the regional distribution
of per capita industrial development subsidies, the majority of the state
subsidies were paid to the industrial companies in west Hungary, Upper
Hungary and the district around Brassó (Brasov). Although these territories were inhabited mostly by Germans, Slovaks and Romanians, the
new enterprises were founded mainly by Austrian, Hungarian or foreign
capital. Many Czech entrepreneurs established firms in Upper Hungary
in order to get state subsidies or tax exemption.[11]
    Entrepreneurs of the ethnic minorities only had access to smaller
amounts of capital and founded mainly smaller or medium-sized firms.
Strong competition hindered the substantial increase of their industrial
undertakings.[12] According to Imre Polányi, in 1905 there were only seven
industrial plants employing more than twenty workers under Slovak
ownership.[13] At the same time, local money markets offered some
chance for success. Banks, saving banks, credit co-operatives and economic associations were founded. From the 1880s the number of credit
institutes founded by the nationalities began to increase. In 1890, 62
Slovak, Saxon, Serb and Romanian banks existed; they numbered 285
in 1912.[14] Their share capital grew ten times during this period.

Although most of these banks were only smaller institutes, some of them grew rather significant, for example the Romanian Albina at Nagyszeben (Sibiu), Victoria at Arad (Oradea), or the Slovak Tatra Bank in Turócszentmárton (Martin) and the Credit Bank in Rózsahegy (Ružomberok). The main activity of these banks consisted of granting mortgages and loans to smallholders and artisans. They also collected and transferred the money sent by emigrants living in the United States to their relatives.[15] Well-to-do Slovak, Serb and Romanian peasants founded consumer and seller co-operatives, too. National political motives appeared also, since the 'ethnic banks' wanted to attract customers by slogans about national aims and interests. It was hoped that marketing along ethnic lines would provide a shield against the strong competition of local branches of the big Budapest and Vienna banks. Although Slovak banks offered cheaper loans, these hopes were not wholly realised.[16]

The emergence and strengthening of the above-mentioned new economic institutions brought about a change in the political activities of the national minorities. A new generation of politicians appeared, which turned away from the passivity of the previous generation. The new leaders of the various national movements were often bank managers of the credit institutes mentioned above. The Slovak, Romanian, Saxon and Serb banks supported the cultural and political activities of their respective nationalities.[17] Business connections were promoted across frontiers between ethnically related nations. Czech entrepreneurs, in particular, showed keen interest in investing in territories with Slavic, mainly Slovak, populations. Under the slogan of 'Neo-Slavism' new firms and credit institutes were promoted by them.[18] The Živnostenská banka was one of the most active in investing in Upper Hungary. It acquired a majority of the shares of the Rózsahegy (Ružomberok) Credit Bank, one of the biggest Slovak banks, and together with the Sporobank held shares of another significant Slovak credit institute, the Tatra Bank. Other smaller Slovak banks also belonged to the clients of the Czech banks (money institutes in Nagyszombat (Trnava), Szered, Zohor, Szakolca (Skalica), Miava (Myjava) and others). In the first years following the turn of the century, Prague banks and entrepreneurs founded industrial firms in Upper Hungary as well (the wood paper mill at Rózsahegy (Ružomberok), the cellulose works at Zsolna (Žilina) and the Kovács & Stodola leather factory at Liptószentmiklós (Liptovský Mikuláš).[19] Magyar business groups protested vehemently against the spread of Czech ventures, criticising the 'Pan-Slavic agitation' of the Slovak banks.[20]

Table 15.2. *The population of Hungary according to mother tongue, 1910–1990*

Year	Total	Hung	Slovak	Roman.	Croat	Serb	Slovene	German	Gypsy	Others
1910	18,264,533	9,944,627	1,946,357	2,948,186	282,653	461,516	77,398	1,903,357	108,825	591,614[b]
1910[a]	7,612,499	6,730,299	165,317	28,491	62,018	26,248	6,915	553,179	–	40,032
1920	7,980,143	7,147,053	141,882	23,760	59,786	17,131	6,087	551,211	6,989	26,244
1930	8,685,109	8,000,335	104,786	16,221	47,332	7,031	5,464	477,153	7,841	18,946
1941	9,316,074	8,655,798	75,877	14,142	37,885	5,442	4,816	475,491	18,640	27,983
1949	9,204,799	9,076,041	25,988	14,785	20,423	5,158	4,473	22,455	21,387	14,161
1960	9,961,044	9,786,038	30,690	15,787	33,014[c]	4,583	–	50,765	25,633	14,534
1970	10,322,099	10,166,237	21,176	12,624	21,885	7,989	4,205	35,594	34,597	17,462
1980	10,709,463	10,579,898	16,054	10,141	20,484	3,426	3,142	31,231	27,915	17,122
1990	10,374,823	10,222,529	12,745	8,730	17,577	2,953	2,627	37,511	48,072	22,079

Notes:
[a] Trianon territory of Hungary.
[b] Gypsies and others.
[c] Croats and Slovenes.

Source: Árpád Mészáros and János Fóti, 'Nemzetiségek, etnikai csoportok a 20. századi Magyarországon' [Nationalities and ethnic groups in twentieth-century Hungary], *Regio* 3(1995), pp. 3–34; István Fehér *Az utolsó percben, Magyarország nemzetiségei 1945–1990* [In the last minute, nationalities in Hungary 1940–1990], (Budapest, 1993), pp. 57–60.

NATIONAL ASSIMILATION IN TWENTIETH-CENTURY HUNGARY

The size of the ethnic minorities in Hungary shrank significantly during the twentieth century. While at the beginning of the twentieth century, non-Magyar nationalities made up 11.6 per cent of the population of the Trianon territory, in 1990 it was only 1.5 per cent (see table 15.2). The causes of this dramatic decrease were defined and evaluated in various ways. Authors in the neighbouring countries have usually blamed the Magyarisation policy enforced by Hungarian governments during the whole of the twentieth century. In trying to draw an objective picture, however, several demographic, economic and social factors have also to be considered when examining the process of assimilation.

The great transformation beginning at the end of the eighteenth century has brought about the formation of political nations and national markets. This process forced groups of people that lived in a world not yet tinged by national self-awareness, to make choices about their new national identity. States, the evolving legal and administrative structures and public education pressed for a common language and culture. This was to promote political unification and the unification of national markets. The choice of national identity became a central political issue from the late nineteenth century on in Hungary. Hungarian governments forced linguistic Magyarisation in order to achieve a stable majority of ethnic Magyars within the Dual Monarchy and also within the boundaries of Hungary. The creation of a national language out of the numerous dialects, and the creation of a national history (or myth) were considered as essential preconditions for the emergence of national feelings among other nations of central and eastern Europe as well.[21] Hungarian governments wanted to increase assimilation by spreading the Hungarian language among ethnic minorities. After 1880 Hungarian censuses were taken on the basis of mother tongue and not of nationality.[22] In this respect education became one of the central issues in enforcing assimilation. Magyarisation was a main aim of Hungarian educational policy. Teaching of Hungarian became compulsory in secondary schools from 1888 and in elementary schools from 1907 onwards.[23] The number of schools teaching in the mother tongue of ethnic minorities was drastically reduced after the turn of the century. This kind of educational policy remained characteristic in the interwar years and after the Second World War until the late 1960s.[24] The number of Slovak schools declined considerably, because the Slovak minority did not have its own national Church that could have maintained schools instructing in the mother tongue, as did Romanians, Serbs or Saxons. Although the Magyarisation policy was carried out very rigorously, it did not prove 'successful' in reality. It did not succeed in increasing national assimilation. At the turn of the century only a small proportion (7 per cent) of the Slovak population spoke Hungarian. The majority of Slovaks speaking Hungarian lived in settlements with a mixed population. Most of them were workers in bigger industrial plants or had middle-class occupations (professionals, civil servants, merchants or craftsmen) and lived in urban centres. According to the census of 1910 the situation had not changed very much by then. Obligatory instruction of the Hungarian language was hardly practical in the closed communities where pupils did not understand a word of Hungarian.[25] The absence of Slovak secondary schools can be regarded as being more harmful because it hindered the formation of a self-conscious Slovak middle class. The assimilation of the Slovak professional classes should not be overestimated, however. Most of them retained their bilingualism and their links to the original Slovak culture, which was clearly shown by their rapid re-Slovakisation in the years following the First World War.[26]

The process of national assimilation was the most spectacular in the case of the rapidly developing cities. By the end of the nineteenth century, German-speaking towns became almost completely Hungarian-speaking.[27] At the end of the eighteenth century, 75 per cent of the 50,000 inhabitants of Pest-Buda had been German-speaking. In 1910 86 per cent of the population of the capital, with nearly a million inhabitants, had Hungarian as their mother tongue and the other ethnic groups also understood Hungarian.

The size of the national minorities was further reduced by the assimilation and demographic processes in the interwar years. However, the most significant decrease was a result of the traumatic events following the Second World War. The deportation of the German population according to the Potsdam decisions and the Slovak–Magyar population exchange reduced the number of German and Slovak minorities in Hungary. These measures had a long-lasting effect as well, because they led to the disintegration of the remaining German and Slovak communities. This made it easier for the relatively small number of Germans and Slovaks who remained to be absorbed by the Hungarian majority.[28] In the opinion of László Szarka, however, the data of 1949 (table 15.2) seem to be unrealistic. In the postwar atmosphere of fear and atrocities many Germans and Slovaks did not dare declare themselves to be ethnically German or Slovakian. In his estimation the real number of the

Germans may have been 250,000, and that of the Slovaks 40,000 in 1949 (see table 15.3).[29]

Beside the political interventions such as deportations and population exchanges, the process of assimilation was aggravated by other demographic factors. In the years after the Second World War the incidence of intermarriage increased. The proportion of homogeneous marriages was lowest among Romanians, Slovaks and Serbs (44 to 49 per cent) in 1990. Among Germans it was 50 to 55 per cent in the same year.[30] According to recent investigations, the chance of transmitting the mother tongue of the minority parent is much lower in mixed marriages than in ethnically homogeneous ones.[31] Only about 40 to 50 per cent of the children of mixed marriages involving Slovaks adopted the Slovakian language, while 80 per cent of German and Slovene children took over their family's language. According to statistical investigations, the fertility of married women was significantly below average in the German population, while it was above average among Slovaks, Croats and Romanians in 1990.[32]

The economic transformation brought about permanent interactions with the majority society and required adaptation to the changed circumstances. These included increased internal mobility and radical changes in the country's settlement structure. Forced urbanisation resulted in a changing ethnic structure as well. According to the analysis of Holger Fischer, the assimilation and socio-economic transformation of the German minority in Hungary were strongly influenced by the forms and size of settlements. In the years between 1920 and 1980, Germans had a greater chance of retaining their ethnic culture in the settlements where the ethnic German population exceeded 80 per cent than in the multiethnic or minority German townships.[33] After 1920, there was no Hungarian town where either Germans or Slovaks would have been in a majority and there were only a few villages where a single nationality formed the majority.[34] In the interwar years internal migration from German settlements (5.3 per cent) exceeded the national average (0.9 per cent), which can be attributed to the preference of the German population for urbanisation and mobility. This kind of mobility coincided with a partial loss of the national culture and identity in the cities. From 1920 to 1930 the proportion of Germans making up the population of Hungarian towns declined from 21.4 per cent to 17 per cent.[35]

Ethnic communities could respond to the changes in various ways. Recent research has found several possibilities open for these communities, ranging from assimilation to ethno-cultural revival. The reactions

Table 15.3. *The population of Hungary according to nationality, 1941–1990*

Year	Total	Hungarian	Slovak	Romanian	Croat	Serb	Slovene	German	Gypsy	Other
1941	9,316,074	8,918,686	16,677	7,565	4,177	3,629	2,058	302,198	27,033	33,869
1949	9,204,799	9,104,640	7,808	8,500	4,106	4,190	666	2,617	37,598	34,674
1960	9,961,044	9,837,275	14,340	12,326	14,710*	3,888	–	8,640	56,121	13,744
1980	10,709,463	10,638,974	9,101	8,874	13,805	2,805	1,731	11,310	6,404	16,369
1990	10,374,823	10,161,712	10,459	10,740	13,570	2,905	1,930	30,824	123,042	19,640

* Together with the Slovenes
Source: Mészáros and Fóti, 'Nemzetiségek', p. 22.

of the ethnic minorities to economic interaction with the majority society could be very different, depending on the geographical position, social structure and commercial relations of the given communities. In the case of the Slovak communities in Trianon Hungary, it can be seen that different types of settlement had different kinds of ethno-cultural models. Some of these could guarantee optimal economic and cultural development, while others led to an early loss of ethnic characteristics.[36]

Contrary to the generally accepted belief, Slovaks in Hungary had a differentiated social structure. As early as in the eighteenth century, glass works and iron foundries employed Slovak workers. In the last century the male population of many Slovak villages worked as coal miners. In the 1920s the number of Slovak coal miners increased further when new coal mines were opened in the Slovak villages around Tatabánya. In the interwar years and in the period following the Second World War many Slovak industrial workers commuted from the villages and suburbs around the capital to Budapest.

The most successful adaptation to economic change can be observed in the case of some market towns of south-east Hungary. As early as the second half of the nineteenth century, Slovak communities with complex societies comprising well-to-do peasants, a significant middle class, professionals, craftsmen, civil servants and many agrarian labourers lived in these towns. Due to the prospering of agricultural and commercial activities, these market towns (Tótkomlós, for example) had their own autonomous local governments and cultural institutions, essential for their ethno-cultural development. Communities such as these could successfully maintain their Slovak national identity and participate in modern economic life until the Slovak–Magyar population exchange in 1946.

Other types of settlement could not preserve their national culture. In the case of Kiskőrös, a rapid assimilation took place as early as the end of the eighteenth century. The social structure was more simple in this case. This market town was inhabited mainly by poor, landless agrarian labourers who had to seek work in the neighbouring Magyar settlements. Due to the one-sided labour and commercial relations with the majority society, the Slovak inhabitants of Kiskőrös had to learn the Hungarian language and customs, which led to an early loss of their original Slovak culture. The same can be observed in the case of the industrial settlements around the newly established factories.

A third type of Slovak settlement was the small closed villages that could be found in the mountain areas. Here the traditional way of life

Table 15.4. *The occupational structure of the Hungarian population by nationality in 1990 (%)*

	Total active population	Slovaks	Romanians	Croats	Serbs	Slovenes	Germans	Gypsies
Industry and construction	38.1	32.5	37.6	32.7	29.0	46.7	37.9	44.2
Agriculture and forestry	15.3	22.3	20.9	25.6	20.9	21.1	18.0	21.3
Material services	22.0	17.9	18.0	19.6	21.3	15.3	18.7	18.7
Non material services	24.6	27.3	23.5	22.1	28.8	16.9	25.4	15.8
Total	100.0	100.0	100.0	100.0	100.0	100.0	100.0	100.0

Source: Mészáros and Fóti, 'Nemzetiségek', p. 31.

and the peasant culture helped preserve the original culture mostly untouched until the 1960s. Because of the low incidence of interaction with the majority society and the slow rate of economic development, the evolution of a strong national identity is not clearly evident in this type of community. In the absence of a middle class, local government and differentiated cultural institutions of their own, these communities could not organise themselves as complex societies and could not participate in modern economic growth.[37]

CONCLUSION

Modernisation brought about the emergence of the nation state, the centralisation of power by governments and the curtailment of the power of the local self-governing bodies. At the end of the nineteenth century, modern economic growth narrowed the development gaps within the various regions of Austria-Hungary. Economic integration led to the emergence of a nationwide market. These institutions, together with the speeding up of communications, strengthened the challenge of assimilation. A complex web of demographic and social changes, urbanisation processes and migration furthered the loss of ethnic culture. After the Second World War political decisions (the deportations of the Germans and the Slovak–Magyar population exchange) led to the significant diminution of the ethnic minorities (see tables 15.3 and 15.4).

On the other hand, the minority communities could respond in different ways. The modern economy (the establishment of local economic and cultural institutions – banks, co-operatives, newspapers and so on) offered possibilities to defend or even to revive national identity. Ethnic communities with a flourishing economy and a complex social structure seem to have been the most successful in preserving or renewing their national culture. In the communities that were one-sidedly dependent on interactions with the majority society, assimilation took place very rapidly.

NOTES

1 Heinrich August Winkler, 'Nationalism and nation state in Germany' in Mikuláš Teich and Roy Porter (eds.), *The National Question in Europe in Historical Context* (Cambridge, 1993), pp. 181–95 at p. 181.
2 Emil Niederhauser, 'The national question in Hungary' in Teich and Porter, *The National Question*', pp. 248–69 at p. 261.

3 Ferenc Glatz (ed.), *Hungarians and their Neighbors in Modern Times 1867–1950* (Boulder, CO, 1995), p. XVI.

4 *Ibid.*, p. XIV.

5 Hungarian and Slovak versions of the various countries.

6 László Katus, 'A nemzetiségi kérdés és Horvátország története a 20. század elején' [National question and the history of Croatia at the beginning of the twentieth century] in P. Hanák (ed.), *Magyarország története, 1890–1918* [The history of Hungary, 1890–1918], (Budapest, 1978), vol. VII, pp. 1003–65 at p. 1003.

7 *Ibid.*, p. 1004.

8 David F. Good, *The Economic Rise of the Habsburg Empire, 1750–1914* (Berkeley and London, 1984), p. 157.

9 Katus, 'A nemzetiségi kérdés', p. 1004.

10 Imre Polányi, *A szlovák társadalom és polgári nemzeti mozgalom a századfordulón 1895–1905* [Slovak society and the national movement at the turn of the century 1895–1905], (Budapest, 1987), pp. 23–7.

11 György Kövér, *Iparosodás agrárországban Magyarország gazdaságtörténete 1848–1914* [Industrialisation in an agrarian land: economic history of Hungary 1848–1914], (Budapest, 1982), pp. 34–5.

12 Polányi, *A szlovák társadalom*, p. 28.

13 *Ibid.*, p. 33.

14 Zoltán Szász, 'Banking and nationality in Hungary, 1867–1914' in A. Teichova, T. Gourvish and Á. Pogány (eds.), *Universal Banking in the Twentieth Century* (Aldershot, 1994), pp. 32–44 at p. 34.

15 Katus, 'A nemzetiségi kérdés', p. 1005.

16 Polányi, *A szlovák társadalom*, pp. 29–31.

17 István Tóth, 'Szlovák hitelegyletek a századfordulón' [Slovakian credit societies at the turn of the century], *Aetas* 4, 62–70 at pp. 62–5; Szász, 'Banking and nationality', pp. 33–5; G. Gábor Kemény, *Iratok a nemzetiségi kérdés történetéhez Magyarországon a dualizmus korában* [Papers relating the history of the nationalities in Hungary during the Dualism], *vol. III, 1900–1903* (Budapest, 1964), pp. 416, 424–7 and 584.

18 Zdeněk Jindra, 'Vizsgálódások a csehországi német-cseh gazdasági kapcsolatok tárgyában a 19. és 20. század fordulóján' [Thoughts on German–Czech economic relations at the turn of the twentieth century] in Éva Ring and Dorottya Lipták (eds.), *Tradíciók és modernitás, Közép- és kelet-európai perspektívák* [Traditions and modernity, central and eastern European perspectives] (Budapest, 1996), pp. 109–22 at p. 112; László Szarka, *A szlovákok története* [The history of the Slovaks], (Budapest, 1993), p. 114.

19 Polányi, *A szlovák társadalom*, pp. 32–3.

20 *Ibid.*, p. 34.

21 Niederhauser, 'The national question', p. 250.

22 Zoltán Dávid, 'The Hungarians and their neighbors, 1851–2000' in Stephen Borsody (ed.), *The Hungarians – A Divided Nation* (New Haven, 1988), pp. 333–45 at p. 334. (The census asked about nationality from 1941 on.)

23 Niederhauser, 'The national question', p. 260.
24 Lóránt Tilkovszky, *Nemzetiségi politika Magyarországon a 20. században* [Government's policy concerning nationalities in Hungary in the twentieth century], (Debrecen, 1997), pp. 44–6; László Szarka, 'Asszimiláció a 20. századi Magyarországon (Adatok és adalékok a hazai német és szlovák kisebbség elmagyarosodásának történentéhez)' [Assimilation in twentieth-century Hungary] in P. Hanák and M. Nagy (eds.), *Híd a századok felett, Tanulmányok Katus László 70. születésnapjára* [Bridge over the centuries, in honour of László Katus], (Pécs, 1997), pp. 397–409 at p. 401.
25 Polányi, *A szlovák társadalom*, pp. 46–7.
26 Szarka, *A szlovákok története*, p. 132.
27 Dávid, 'The Hungarians and their neighbors', pp. 334–5.
28 Szarka, 'Asszimiláció a 20. századi Magyarországon, pp. 397–8.
29 *Ibid.*, p. 400.
30 Arpad Mészáros and János Fóti, 'Nemzetiségek, etnikai csoportok a 20. századi Magyarországon' [Nationalities and ethnic groups in twentieth-century Hungary], *Regio* 3 (1995), pp. 3–34 at p. 7.
31 *Ibid.*; Erika Garami and János Szántó, 'A magyarországi szlovákok identitása' [Identity of the Slovaks in Hungary], *Regio* 2 (1995), pp. 113–35 at pp. 128–9.
32 Mészáros and Fóti, 'Nemzetiségek', pp. 7–8.
33 Holger Fischer, 'A magyarországi németek 20. századi társadalmi-gazdasági átalakulásának térbeli aspektusai' [Spatial aspects of the socio-economic transformation of German Hungarians in the twentieth century], *Regio* 2 (1992), 147–66 at pp. 151–3.
34 Szarka, 'Asszimiláció a 20. századi Magyarországon', p. 402.
35 Fischer, 'A magyarországi németek', p. 151.
36 Anna Gyivicsán, 'Nemzetiség-gazdaság-kultúra' [Ethnic minorities, economy and culture] in Ring and Lipták, *Tradíciók és modernitás*, pp. 122–35.
37 *Ibid.*

CHAPTER SIXTEEN

Economic background to national conflicts in Yugoslavia

Neven Borak

INTRODUCTION

Yugoslavia (1918–91) was a conglomerate of several different ethnic groups (table 16.1), two alphabets, three major religions, five languages, it was known for large socio-economic disparities and inequalities and a unique state system. It has threaded the way from a unitary state (1918–41), often accused of being just a hegemony of one nation over the others, to the state of eight federal units (1945–91). After the break-up of Yugoslavia in the 1990s, four of them, namely Slovenia, Croatia, Bosnia-Herzegovina and Macedonia, became internationally recognised independent states, whilst the remaining four (Serbia, Vojvodina, Kosovo and Montenegro) are at the time of writing united under one state, which has, quite unjustifiably, retained the name Yugoslavia. Figure 16.1 reveals one of the most important characteristics of the former Yugoslavia: the further south-east one goes from the north-western part of the country, the smaller is the national homogeneity of the former federal units; in Slovenia 90.5 per cent of the population were Slovenians, in Croatia 75 per cent of the population were Croats, in Serbia 66.4 per cent of the population were Serbs (including Vojvodina and Kosovo), in Macedonia 67 per cent of the population were Macedonians and in Montenegro 68.5 per cent of the population were Montenegrins. Muslims were the most numerous nation in Bosnia-Herzegovina, accounting for 39.5 per cent of the total population. Serbs represented the second most numerous segment of population – 32 per cent – and Croats were the third, representing 18.4 per cent of total population. According to the OECD[1] estimate, Yugoslavia was at the level of Turkey in terms of per capita gross domestic product at purchasing power parity in 1985. Kosovo, the less-developed part of Yugoslavia, was at the level of Pakistan. The most developed part, Slovenia, was compared with Spain and New Zealand. Vojvodina and Croatia approached Greece and Portugal. Bosnia-

Table 16.1. *National structure of Yugoslavia and its federal units in 1981 (%)*

	Serbs	Croats	Muslims	Slovenians	Albanians	Macedonians	Montenegrins	Other	Total
Slovenia	2.2	3.0	0.7	90.5	0.1	0.2	0.2	3.2	100.0
Croatia	11.6	75.1	0.5	0.5	0.1	0.1	0.2	11.8	100.0
Serbia (total)	66.4	1.6	2.3	0.1	14.0	0.5	1.6	13.5	100.0
Serbia Proper	85.4	0.6	2.7	0.1	1.3	0.5	1.4	8.1	100.0
Kosovo	13.3	0.6	3.7	0.0	77.5	0.1	0.2	3.2	100.0
Vojvodina	54.5	5.4	0.2	0.1	0.2	0.9	2.1	36.3	100.0
Montenegro	3.3	1.2	13.4	0.1	6.5	0.2	68.5	6.8	100.0
Bosnia–Herzegovina	32.0	18.4	39.5	0.1	0.1	0.1	0.3	9.5	100.0
Macedonia	2.4	0.2	2.1	0.1	19.7	67.0	0.3	8.4	100.0
Yugoslavia	36.3	19.7	8.9	7.8	7.7	6.0	2.6	10.9	100.0

Source: Calculated from *Statistical Yearbook of Yugoslavia 1991* (Belgrade, 1991).

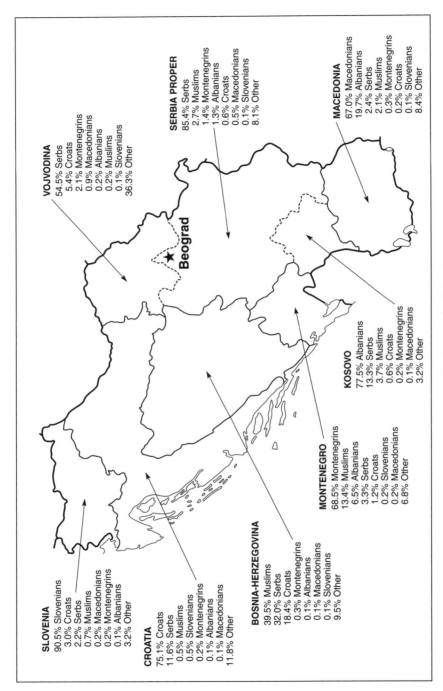

SLOVENIA
90.5% Slovenians
3.0% Croats
2.2% Serbs
0.7% Muslims
0.2% Macedonians
0.2% Montenegrins
0.1% Albanians
3.2% Other

CROATIA
75.1% Croats
11.6% Serbs
0.5% Muslims
0.5% Slovenians
0.2% Montenegrins
0.1% Albanians
0.1% Macedonians
0.1% Slovenians
11.8% Other

BOSNIA-HERZEGOVINA
39.5% Muslims
32.0% Serbs
18.4% Croats
0.3% Montenegrins
0.1% Albanians
0.1% Macedonians
0.1% Slovenians
9.5% Other

VOJVODINA
54.5% Serbs
5.4% Croats
2.1% Montenegrins
0.9% Macedonians
0.2% Albanians
0.2% Muslims
0.1% Slovenians
36.3% Other

SERBIA PROPER
85.4% Serbs
2.7% Muslims
1.4% Montenegrins
1.3% Albanians
0.6% Croats
0.5% Macedonians
0.1% Slovenians
8.1% Other

MACEDONIA
67.0% Macedonians
19.7% Albanians
2.4% Serbs
2.1% Muslims
0.3% Montenegrins
0.2% Croats
0.1% Slovenians
8.4% Other

MONTENEGRO
68.5% Montenegrins
13.4% Muslims
6.5% Albanians
3.3% Serbs
1.2% Croats
0.2% Slovenians
0.2% Macedonians
6.8% Other

KOSOVO
77.5% Albanians
13.3% Serbs
3.7% Muslims
0.6% Croats
0.2% Montenegrins
0.1% Macedonians
3.2% Other

Beograd ★

Figure 16.1. *Yugoslavia's nationalities 1981*

Herzegovina and Macedonia were compared with Thailand and Mexico, and Serbia with Turkey.

A unique state organisation can be added to this diversity, governed in fact at three government levels: the level of federation, republics and autonomous provinces, and communities (the latter cannot be directly compared to local governments, as they had a much greater portfolio of authorities and tasks). Bearing all this in mind, it is not difficult to understand why the country – in times of breaking up – was often compared with the tiger's skin: the further one went along its axis, the more diversified it was.

This chapter focuses on the economic background of national conflicts in Yugoslavia.[2] It offers an insight into Yugoslav economic practice and its interference with political and constitutional processes. It is therefore proper to begin by giving an example of a joint project in which historians of all Yugoslav nations took part. The result of this joint project was two parts of an unfinished publication with the title *A History of the Nations of Yugoslavia*.[3] It seems fortunate that the title of the last chapter (which is, by the way, chapter 13) of the second book is 'Reaching the conditions for the rise of national movements and the struggle for liberation'. The third and fourth parts of the publication, which were to include the nineteenth and twentieth centuries, were never written. Therefore, Yugoslavia had no general or political history that would be acceptable to all the nations and neither had it a comprehensive economic history. There are, however, some parts and fragments of the economic history of former federal units that were more or less systematically studied, and are patiently waiting to be integrated and properly interpreted. In addition, nationalism and national conflicts are not considered to belong to the mainstream of economic research, since this science is thought to be too rational and too equilibrium-oriented to study these irrational phenomena, often considered disturbances. It has not been until recently that some experiments were made to apply some parts of public-choice theory, fiscal federalism and local government finance to generalise the experiences of the disintegration of countries and emergence of new countries on the territory of the former communist Europe and to deliberate about economic and political aspects of break-ups and disintegrations.[4]

These findings, however, do not prevent us from making the following assertions:

- Yugoslavia did not emerge for economic reasons;
- Yugoslav nations built their new country on large contradictions and diversities;

- the main conflicts in the Kingdom of Yugoslavia (1918–41) were political. They moved from centralism and unitarism on the one hand to federalism and national equality on the other. Economic reasons served only as excuses for conflicts;
- the main conflicts in Communist Yugoslavia (1945–91), which ensured that federalism prevailed over centralist tendencies, were economic and all ethnic groups and federal units took part in the conflicts;
- the normative economic area failed to become a long-term functioning area either in the first or the second Yugoslavia;
- nationalism was the last and the most decisive weapon in the fight for domination in Yugoslavia. This fight entailed either the capture of the federal state or its abolition.

HERITAGE

When they became united under one state in 1918, the Yugoslav nations were all mature nations. They were aware of their identity and had their cultural and historical traditions.[5] They did not know each other well. Moreover, they all had different economic bases. They all brought along their own heritage in the form of national programmes expressing aspirations and tendencies of their cultural and political elites. Some of them even brought along their former states or, at least, memory of it. The image of the main protagonists of the Yugoslav drama – Serbs, Croats and Slovenians (whose names were also a part of the name of the new kingdom till 1929) – is as follows:

1. The national and foreign-policy programme of Serbia – the so-called Garašanin's Plan (*Načrtanije*) of 1844 – was restricted to southern Slavic nations, in particular to the Serbian nation under Turks and the provinces they considered Serbian, namely Serbia, Montenegro, Bosnia–Herzegovina, historical Old Serbia and northern Albania, the latter to provide access to the sea. On the basis of historical law founded on the tradition of Serbian medieval statehood, Serbia was to expand to embrace these provinces gradually and through diplomacy, and not to unite them on the basis of their self-determination.[6]

2. Slovenians had their roots in the programme United Slovenia (*Zedinjena Slovenija*), which was slightly younger than the Serbian plan and called for the unification of all Slovenians. The programme was based on ethnic and natural law (not historical) and required the

amalgamation of all Slovenian territories into one autonomous unit, regardless of the existing historical borders. The Yugoslav idea emerged at the turn of the twentieth century when the German–Slovenian conservative alliance broke up.

3. Regarding the Croats, the Illyrian movement ideology, which had been formed gradually until 1835, expressed two levels of integration movements – Croatian and South–Slav.[7] The latter movement gave way to Croatian integration and co-operation between Croats and Serbs in their attempts to set up joint institutions required to protect the political position of the so-called 'triple kingdom' against Hungarian national expansionism.[8] In part, these aspirations were fulfilled by the Croatian–Hungarian treaty of 1868, which granted the Croats recognition as a political nation, in principle territorially integral, and with certain administrative independence. The Croatian aspirations did not go beyond the borders of a triple structure of the monarchy, whose duty was to ensure the amalgamation of all Croatian territories, including the so-called *Vojna krajina* (Borderland or Military Croatia), and thereby realisation of historical Croatia, and after that also the unification of South–Slav nations into a monarchy.

The development of events in the period from the emergence of the programmes to the formation of a new state included rises and falls, approaching to and withdrawing from the Yugoslav idea, and constant shifting from minimalist to maximalist tendencies. It can nevertheless be established that in essence the national programmes and their derivatives did not refer to a Yugoslavia such as that which was actually formed in 1918. Serbs expected it to be a country uniting all Serbs. Slovenians expected it to be a South-Slav state in which they would be united with historical Croatia. The Croats expected it to be a state founded on their own historical law. Considering it from this point of view, Yugoslavia was in a way a residual option for all three nations. It just happened. The nations found themselves there because of geopolitical and international changes. Yugoslavism is a complex concept that had more than just a single meaning. In general, it meant togetherness of ideas about closer co-operation and integration among southern Slavic nations. At the time of the First World War no fewer than four variations of Yugoslavism could thus be found.[9]

As early as 1914 the Serbian National Assembly, in the famous Niš Declaration, linked the fight for the integration of all Serbs living in Serbia and in the Austro-Hungarian Monarchy with the idea of integration of Serbs, Croats and Slovenes. The Niš Declaration became the programme of realisation of the Serbian state idea in the war that Serbia was fighting. In this programme, Serbia saw itself in the role of Piedmont in uniting Serbs, Croats and Slovenes into a unitary southern Slavic state.

The second version of Yugoslavism could be founded at the Yugoslav Committee, which was founded in exile by Croatian, Serbian and Slovenian politicians from the Austro-Hungarian Monarchy. It aimed at founding the Yugoslav state, but it did not have a united view as to what it should look like. The Committee was caught between the options of Serbian unitarian Yugoslavism and Croatian Middle European federalism. Unification of views of the Yugoslav Committee with the views of the Serbian government – and to the former's advantage – came about in the famous Corfu Declaration (1917).

The third version of Yugoslavism is represented by the May Declaration of Yugoslav Club 33 members of Slovenian, Croatian and Serbian origin in the Vienna parliament, which called for unification of southern Slavs in the Austro-Hungarian Monarchy in the Autonomous Southern Slavic entity. This was the basis of the massive Declaration movement, particularly in Slovenia, where Yugoslavism became a part of the national programme.

The idea of the Yugoslav Club later, as it became clear that the monarchy would break apart, led to the creation of the National Council of Slovenes, Croats and Serbs, the fourth version of Yugoslavism, which led to the creation of the state of Slovenes, Croats and Serbs, a southern Slavic state that lasted only one month, which was outside the boundaries of monarchy and without Serbia, Montenegro and Vojvodina. This short-lived state formation, which had neither precisely determined borders nor an army, did substitute the Yugoslav Committee in the negotiations with Serbia on their integration into a common state, but was not able to impose on Serbia its view on the shape and structure of the new state. So the new kingdom was created mostly in line with Serbian views and was based on national unitarism of Serbs, Croats and Slovenes. The amalgamation of Slovenian, Croatian and Serbian national territories into a new state became their main task, as well as the search for balance between the centralist and federalist tendencies. The national programmes, at least the memory of them, became the benchmark according to which the nations or their political elite assessed their positions and relevance in a new state. The assessments of economic situations of selected nations and administrative formations in which they lived had an important role in times of a common state. The question of its constitutional arrangement had an important role in the political life of the Kingdom of Yugoslavia. Differing views on the organisation of the state to a large extent determined characteristics of the political parties, their functioning and their programme directions; parties and nations disagreed primarily over the question of whether the organisation of the state should be unitarian or federal.

The Second World War brought a new test for Yugoslavia. German attacks on Yugoslavia also had as an objective its destruction as a state. After the military defeat of Yugoslavia the four occupational forces split the country, annexed its individual parts, created quisling states and also divided its individual parts according to military responsibility. All this was meant to strengthen the conviction that the state no longer existed and that thereby the incorrect decision made by the Versailles peace treaty was eliminated. On Yugoslav ground the civil war erupted, particularly among Serbs, Croats and Muslims, and the resistance against the occupying forces developed in the same time. The only real power, which united all nations in the fight against the occupying forces, was the Communist Party of Yugoslavia (CPY). The slogan of 'Common state of equal voluntarily united nations' was manifested throughout numerous documents of the CPY and the liberation movement under its leadership. The Declaration of the First Session of AVNOJ (Anti-Fascist Liberation Movement of Yugoslavia) in 1942 already contained a distinct structure of the future state community (Serbia, Montenegro, Croatia, Slovenia, Bosnia–Herzegovina, Macedonia), although the term federation had not yet been mentioned. For the communists and the national liberation movement the main issue was not Yugoslavia yes or no, but what kind of Yugoslavia. The answer to this came soon, in the Second Session of AVNOJ in 1943, when the decision on federal organisation of the future Yugoslav state was taken.

BACKGROUND TO THE FEDERAL STATE

When joining Yugoslavia, Slovenians and Croats expected that national hegemonies that they knew in the previous system's monarchy would disappear, but were in fact encountered with a new hegemony. The era of the Kingdom of Yugoslavia was marked by political struggle for autonomy and movements towards the centre. Croats wanted political autonomy. By setting up Ban's Country Croatia, they came close to it; this caused a strong reaction by Serbs and Slovenians. All three nations felt exploited and they all thought that the other two nations had gained more. In Slovenia, beliefs that Croats improved their situation in Yugoslavia and that Slovenia lagged behind were not rare. Serbs were also stirred. The Croatian economist Rudolf Bičanić triggered a number of discussions with his booklet *Economic Basis of the Croatian Question.*[10] In Slovenia, a booklet with similar substance was written by Andrej Gosar,[11] and in Serbia by a group of authors.[12]

Founding of the Ban's Country Croatia pushed Yugoslavia towards federalisation in 1939, which was brutally interrupted by the Second World War. In the years 1939–40, there was a general and lively interest in the organisation and operation of federal states.[13] Under the 1929 Constitution, the Kingdom of Serbs, Croats and Slovenes was renamed as the Kingdom of Yugoslavia and restructured: thirty-three provinces were abandoned and nine regional units called 'banovine' – ban's countries (some authors translated this as 'banate') – were established with river valleys as focal points for the new regions. They were named after the rivers. The internal borders of new regions were not historical, with the exception of Drava and Zeta Ban's Countries, which corresponded to Slovenia and Montenegro respectively. In 1939 Serbian and Croatian politicians agreed to restructure the state. The main result of this Serb–Croat agreement was the establishment of Ban's Country Croatia, which contained almost 30 per cent of the kingdom's population and territory, its own parliament and a ban (governor) appointed by the monarchy, with autonomous budgetary and internal affairs and Belgrade-controlled foreign affairs, foreign trade, defence, transportation and communication. Moreover, there were realistic expectations that other Ban's Countries would be formed following the Croatian model. In fact all the draft provisions for the renaming of the Dravska Ban's Country into the Slovenian Ban's Country were prepared but their implementation was delayed due to a rapid deterioration of international relations and the threat of approaching war. The third Ban's Country was expected to be Serbian ('Serbian Territories').

It is quite easy to agree with many researchers dealing with the Yugoslav reality who claim that regional economic disparities matched the classic north–south division. J. K. Galbraith found in his report on an imaginary trip to eastern Europe, which was to have taken place in 1880 and again 100 years later and which also included some parts of the later Yugoslavia, that regional disparities in the country were no less significant 100 years later. According to Galbraith, communism improved the social and economic situation in absolute terms but failed to narrow a relative lag of these countries behind their western and northern neighbours. 'Eastern Europe . . . shows the practical unwisdom of stressing the economic system as a cause of or an antidote for poverty.'[14] He also claims that it is more crucial for a researcher dealing with the Yugoslav reality to have knowledge about who lived where before the foundation of Yugoslavia than the fact that it belonged to communism. New development theories call this 'path-dependence'.

The OECD report, cited above, on the regional development of Yugoslavia, which was completed after the break-up of the state, shows no surprise about the above fact. According to this report the two main obstacles to internal convergence have been a qualitative and quantitative lack of capital formation in the less-developed regions and the system of self-management and its effects upon the mobility of capital and labour.[15]

Economic researchers often deal with the question whether poor countries or poor regions within the countries grow at faster rates than developed countries or regions and in this way catch up with them and narrow the disparities. Although some economic theories forecast convergence, the existing empirical evidence raises doubts about that. The Yugoslav experience fails to confirm the hypothesis on convergence. On the contrary, there has not been any researcher in the past that would not report about the persistence of relative and absolute disparities, or even their widening. It is my intention to summarise their findings using a modern analytical approach that has become quite popular when analysing convergence between countries and regions within them. I shall confine myself to the period of 1952 to 1990 using the data on the most synthetic development indicator – social product per capita at constant prices of 1972. In the Yugoslav statistics, these data, which were based on the concept of material production, were available in aggregate terms for the whole country as well as for each separate federal unit.

Two concepts of convergence prevail in the economic growth and development theory.[16] The first concept is β-convergence. It presumes that convergence exists under the condition that a poorer country or a region within the country rises faster than the wealthier one in terms of per capita product or income. The second concept is σ-convergence. It measures dispersion of the selected indicator in the observed units in each selected year. This concept presumes that convergence exists if the dispersion decreases over time. However, there is a relation between the two concepts: the first convergence (the poorer grow faster than the wealthier) generates the second convergence (decreasing of dispersion

Table 16.2. *Cross-units regressions*

	β-convergence	Sectoral composition	R²
All units			
Year to year	−0.0004	0.971	0.629
	(−0.100)	(21.0)	
5-year averages	−0.004	1.035	0.711
	(−2.61)	(24.82)	
Seven units (without Kosovo)			
Year to year	0.0023	0.947	0.65
	(0.586)	(19.95)	
5-year averages	0.00108	0.958	0.763
	(0.601)	(21.48)	
Four units (Bosnia–Herzegovina, Montenegro, Macedonia and Serbia Proper)			
Year to year	0.001	0.908	0.589
	(0.141)	(12.88)	
5-year averages	0.003	0.893	0.573
	(0.353)	(11.492)	

between the poor and the wealthy). This relation does not exclude a temporary increase in the second – that is, σ-convergence as a consequence of some economic disturbances increasing the disparities. The econometric estimations of β-convergence (with t-values under the coefficients) are presented in table 16.2. Pooled time-series cross-sections were estimated with non-linear least squares.[17] The estimations were made for the eight federal units together, for the seven units excluding Kosovo and for four units (Bosnia–Herzegovina, Montenegro, Macedonia and Serbia proper). Unconditional convergence (dependence of growth rate on the initial level of social product per capita) is assessed, as is conditional convergence, which includes an additional explanatory variable. The additional variable measures the sectoral composition of social product in each federal unit. It captures the effects of changing sectoral weights within a federal unit and would equal the growth rate of per capita social product in unit i between two time periods if each of the unit's sectors grew at the Yugoslav average rate for that sector. This variable captures the effect of sectoral composition of federal units' economies on convergence. As shall be shown later, this

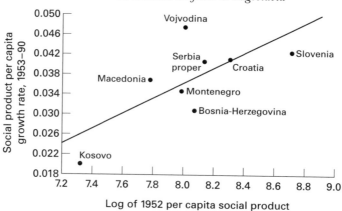

Figure 16.2. *Divergences of per capita social product across Yugoslav federal units, 1953–1990*

variable had more than marginal significance. The calculations were based on the basic data and their five-year averages.

The results are additionally explained by figure 16.2, which shows the dependence of the average growth rate of per capita social product in the period 1953–90 on the initial level of per capita social product in 1952. If β-convergence existed the line in the graph would have a different direction: it would be a downward line from north-west towards south-east. The estimated convergence for developed countries (the United States and European countries) had a value around 2. This value means that in thirty-five years the initial disparities would be cut by half. On the contrary, in Yugoslavia an extreme divergence can be seen, as the orientation of the line indicates that the disparities widened.

The σ-convergence is a different measure than the β-convergence, although they are closely related. This measure is in fact a standard deviation of the logarithm of per capita social product in one year. The movements of σ are presented in figure 16.3. There are three curves in the graph, the first indicating the movement σ for the eight Yugoslav federal units, the second indicating its movement for seven units without Kosovo and the third its movement for seven units without Slovenia. This graph also shows a strong divergence rather than convergence in the observed period. The graph also reveals some periods in which disparities decreased for a short period of time, which, however, was not enough to reverse the trend of constantly increasing disparities.

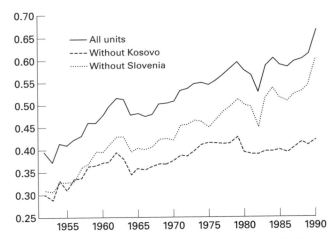

Figure 16.3. *σ-divergences of social product per capita across Yugoslav federal units*

The results in table 16.2 show only the results that contain the estimations of conditional convergence (conditional on the sectoral composi-
tions of units' social products). The estimated β coefficients are very low,
and here and there statistically insignificant. The estimation for all eight
units shows a divergence. As for dependence on the initial per capita
social product they show that the poor remain poor. Although the exclusion of Kosovo changes the sign of the estimated β coefficient, it is
entirely statistically insignificant. Therefore, the conclusion for all eight
units remains unchanged: the poor remain poor. The estimation of the
β coefficient for four federal units is somewhat surprising, revealing
that between them there is no convergence as for the initial size of per
capita social product. The importance of sectoral composition is quite
different. Apparently, it was the sectoral composition that was the key
promoting or restraining factor of convergence in growth rates. It is also
the basis for all the discussions about investment, the leading sectors and
the leading regions, which are presented in the following section of this
chapter.

A Slovenian economist, Pavle Sicherl, shed some light on the time
dimension of disparities. He calculated that the time distance (the
number of years needed for the less developed to catch up with the more
developed) increased. The increase was different for different economic
and social indicators. In 1971 the time distance between developed and
underdeveloped regions in Yugoslavia was 11.5 years in terms of per

capita social product, 5 years in terms of productivity, 15 years in terms of employment, 40 years in terms of demographic factors.[18] He also made comparisons for Slovenia and Yugoslavia in terms of per capita social product in the period 1955–85.[19] He found that disparities in growth rates are considerably wider when comparing selected units in selected time periods than when disparities between Slovenia and Yugoslavia are compared. His results also highlight the periods when disparities narrowed, visible in figure 16.3. Although the relative disparities narrow – which is largely related to the periods of stagnation – the time distance increases. The developments were as follows: a decline in economic growth goes hand in hand with narrowing of relative disparities and increasing of the time distance of disparities. As regards per capita social product, the time distance was constantly increasing and Yugoslavia's lag behind Slovenia was wider every year: the lag of 7.3 years in 1960 rose to 17.5 years in 1985. Sicherl also noticed a general tendency that the lags were less significant for social indicators than they were for economic indicators.

There is another fact that draws the attention of economists. The disparities between Yugoslavia and its federal units on the one hand and other countries on the other have also widened.[20] Sicherl found that Slovenia increased its lag – in terms of time distance – behind western countries and the European Union but at the same time increased its advantage over other parts of Yugoslavia, which needed increasingly more time to catch up with Slovenia.[21] Sicherl made two main conclusions. One is that the economic background for mounting tensions in Yugoslavia was not only the stagnation and falling behind in economic indicators in absolute terms, but also the increasing disparities between the regions. This frustration is the same as is felt by Slovenia today, whose stagnation makes the prospects of catching up with Europe and developed countries even more distant. The second conclusion is that the increasing disparities should be attributed to the inefficiency of all, and not to exploitation among the regions.[22]

With this insight into divergence movements it will be easier to understand the importance of the discussion about development orientation and development model of the country, which will be discussed next.

FROM NATIONAL PROGRAMMES TO DEVELOPMENT MODELS

In the Kingdom of Yugoslavia, the redistribution mechanisms were limited to the taxation system. Therefore a unification of a tax system became a sufficient cause for disputes among nations. The more developed parts of the country felt that they were exploited as their tax burden was higher due to more efficient tax collecting than was the case in other parts of the country. On the other hand, these more developed areas benefited from the protection of an internal market assured by the customs system. The actual economic conflicts in fact began in times of communist Yugoslavia. With the formation of republics and the transfer of a number of state functions, including economic functions, to the republics as well as with the decentralisation of the state, the conflicts moved to the economic area and politics become subordinated. The politicians had to provide an acceptable development programme that would embrace the country in all its diversity. It never succeeded in providing one. This phenomenon and the developments that followed were not overlooked by researchers. In the preface to his book, Joseph Bombelles wrote: 'The pattern and volume of investment seem to be very important elements for an understanding of changes and conflicts in Yugoslavia.'[23] This thought shall be used as a starting point for the overview of various development concepts advocated by economists and politicians. Sabrina P. Ramet bases his book about Yugoslavia on the theory of equilibrium between sovereign states.[24] A Serbian economist, Kosta Mihailović, one of the most prominent participants in the discussion about regional development and the position of the Serbian nation in Yugoslavia and coauthor of the famous *Memorandum of SANU* (Serbian Academy of Science and Arts) issued by the Serbian Academy of Science and Arts, also talked about this phenomenon.[25] Moreover, he added to it the role of individual leaders of nations.[26]

The story about investment has been in fact the so-called *file rouge* of the majority of professional and political polemics about centralisation and decentralisation, division of powers between the federation, republics and autonomous provinces, and the role of the market and a planned economy. These polemics were actually debates about the economic basis of a society and the establishment of social organisation. Politics, on the other hand, was only a means of fulfilling certain development aspirations.

Since any detailed presentation of the polemics goes beyond the scope of this chapter, it shall be restricted only to those parts that fall within the subject of discussion or present different views of the development models. In this way the link with the initially listed national programmes and the disparities between the federal units shall be preserved. This is even more justified given the fact that the abolition of Yugoslavia itself did not abolish different development views, which were inherited by the newly emerged countries. The break-up of Yugoslavia did not diminish these conflicts: it only changed their form. They used to be inter-republic or inter-regional but could easily become inter-state conflicts.

The most important development views that were exchanged in communist Yugoslavia are, basically, the views advocating that a leading region should be established which would provide a momentum for the development of other regions. These are not all development views. Different views can also be found within nations or federal units. The development concepts written down in the federal units' or Yugoslavia's plans have been more or less avoided in this chapter; they mostly manifested the substance of the concepts that follow.

a) *The Donava development concept or the concept of the development of a central region.* This concept has been attributed to the aforementioned Serbian economist Kosta Mihailović.[27] According to this concept, in order to ensure stable and rapid development Yugoslavia should develop in the first place the production of electricity, basic chemicals, basic iron and steel, basic non-ferrous metals, machinery and equipment, agriculture and food industry. The most favourable conditions for these economic sectors were in medium and less-developed regions of Yugoslavia – the water resources in Serbia (the Drina and Donava rivers) and Bosnia, coal mines in Kosovo, Bosnia and Serbia, and gas and oil resources in Croatia, Vojvodina and Slovenia. Bosnia, Macedonia and Serbia were rich in iron ore, so the main steelworks were set up there. Bauxite as a resource for aluminium production was found in Montenegro, Dalmatia and Herzegovina. Copper and lead, used in the production of non-ferrous metals, were abundant in Serbia and Kosovo. The best conditions for agriculture were in Vojvodina, Slavonija, northern Serbia and Bosnia and, hence, the food-production industry should be developed there. Given all this, the priority area for industrialisation would incorporate the Sava, Tisa, Tamiš and Morava river basins, all flowing into the Donava river, and the Vardar river basin. Investment in navigable rivers would make these rivers a skeleton of the transport infrastructure. This concept is close to the concept of a leading nation, in this case the Serbian nation, which was the most heavily populated nation in Yugoslavia.

b) *The Adriatic development concept.* This is a joint project by a group of Croatian economists. Instead of orientation towards the north-east implied by the Donava concept, the Adriatic development concept turned to the west and implied closer co-operation with the whole world.[28] The Adriatic concept incorporated the development of a transport network throughout the whole territory of Croatia, which has the interesting shape of an open pair of compasses that also embraces a part of Bosnia–Herzegovina. This network was the last and most important stage of the integration of Croatian economy. The ends of the compasses could not be linked without main road connections, which would, however, lie on the territory of the neighbouring federal unit of Bosnia–Herzegovina. At the same time, orientation towards the Adriatic would imply the shift of the Yugoslav development priorities to the Adriatic belt, thus becoming a leading region.

c) *K-concept or a decentralised Slovenian concept.* The letter K coincides with the first letter of the surnames of the main Slovenian politicians in the period of both Yugoslavias (Korošec, Kardelj, Kidrič, Kavčič and Kučan), who had the most decisive influence in the formation of the Slovenian idea about Yugoslavia. The notion of the *Slovenian model*[29] was used by Susan Woodward, and the notion of *Kavčič's liberalism* by a Slovenian historian, Božo Repe.[30] This model can be in general described as a Kardelj–Kidrič development model of socialism, based on the macroeconomic proportions in distribution, emphasising the role of productivity, market, demand, technological innovation, exports, manufacturing – all the components leading to so-called market socialism. Quite justifiably, Rudolf Bičanić added that according to this concept the role of the leading region belongs to the most developed region, which by promoting rapid development accumulates investment resources for development of other regions, which in turn follow the development of the industrially most developed part of the country.[31] The investment resources should be ensured by banks and enterprises and not by external or political force.

This overview, like the findings about divergence in the previous section, lead to the conclusion that Yugoslavia as such never really prospered as one single economic area able autonomously to reproduce without strong and constant political intervention.

DENOUEMENT

As already mentioned in the introduction, the state system of communist Yugoslavia functioned at three levels: the level of federation, republics, and autonomous provinces and communities. The same three-level system also applied to the economic content of the constitutional law. Prior to the constitutional amendments of 1963 the entire economic system was built around the federation. The 1963 Constitution still observed hierarchical relations among the three levels of the state and provided corresponding ground rules. It obliged the federation to ensure unity of economic structure and the system of social product distribution, leaving relatively little space for direction by the republics themselves as regards economic structure. The adoption of the Constitution opened a new front of changes, which reflected a tendency to strengthen the economic role of the republics and provinces and lessen the role of the federal centre. According to the belief prevailing at the time, the solution to the national problem was closely connected with republic/province-level sovereignty, which was supposed to grant republics the right to decide on issues other than under the federal authority. Power and authority that the federal units gained at the expense of the federal centre, however, did not reduce disparities in the national structure of the population nor address the issue of national inequality within federal units. And no matter how harsh the subsequent critiques of the events may have been, none of them ever expressed any doubts in the belief that equality of nations is achieved through autonomy of federal units.

Many research reports on the economic system of Yugoslavia were written in the 1960s, all of them addressing the issue of the economic aspect of the federation and the economic role of federal units. They all spoke in favour of the belief that the economic role of the republics was the most important element of their autonomy and that this autonomy was based on equality and independence of nations as the fundamental principle of Yugoslavia. It is understandable that recognition of the economic role of the republics instantly raised questions as to what position national economies (economies of federal units) could assume in a multinational state and, for that matter, in the single economic system of Yugoslavia. Furthermore, national equality and the economic role of the republics were recognised as being closely connected with two issues: the question of economic system and the question of economic policy. All the studies regarded co-operation of all republics as the best solution to be applied in designing economic regulation on the federal level, in preparing medium-term and long-term plans and in adopting current or short-term economic policies. Along with their economic role, the very existence of the republics was generally believed to encourage and confront different interests, particularly economic and development ones. Yet in reality the studies only confirmed what politics was already using as the basis for the new constitution. The authoritarian regime in power made it unlikely for the established economists to come up with views different from the ones described above. Nevertheless, two more views on the Yugoslav federation are examined below, as they provide a better illustration of the situation. Both standpoints were considered marginal at the time since they express negative attitude towards the Yugoslav federation, a sentiment that was, in a varyingly articulate form, present in all periods of the federation's existence. A booklet from 1968, for example, states that:

> it is clear that, economically speaking, to the Slovenian people Yugoslavia is a constant loss of funds and an obstacle to a normal economic development . . . It does not allow us to independently manage resources to obtain the standard of living the Slovenian economy makes possible, the standard of living we could have if our development was not held back, the development the nation deserves for working hard and could have already reached if a large part of its resources had not been alienated from it against its will. The present situation is not so much a result of the faults of the leading officials in the present regime but primarily of the fact that we are in Yugoslavia. As it is, Yugoslav economic integration is not very highly valued by Slovenians and is even considered a great economic loss.[32]

Šime Đodan, a Croat, showed more courage. In the time of 'Croatian spring' he published an article in which he presented an evaluation of the economic position of Croatia in Yugoslavia and concluded that Croatia was lagging behind other republics. In addition, he proposed some changes that were considered incomprehensible at the time: the break-up of all federal finance and foreign trade institutions, the formation of separate financial systems of federal units, the formation of central banks across federal units and co-ordination of anticyclical economic policy and protection measures with appropriate (but not defined) central organs of the Socialist Federal Republic of Yugoslavia (SFRY). According to his view, the framework of the Yugoslav economic system should be broad enough to ensure the realisation of the positive aspects of the economic model of each republic.[33]

Views considered marginal at the time of publication found their place in the official statements of state and political elites, which arose soon after the multiparty elections only twenty years later.

The economic contents of the federation as provided for in the 1974 Constitution also need addressing.[34] The Constitution guaranteed equality of nations in the federation as regards making decisions about mutual interests, which among other things include common economic and social development, based on principles of agreement, solidarity and mutuality, equal co-operation of federal units in the federation bodies and direct co-operation and agreements between federal units. With these provisions the Constitution aimed to ensure national and social equality of nations and abolish domination of the central state or of a particular nation. As a result, the federation's role was to enforce the foundations of the single Yugoslav market, which consisted of free movement of production factors, a single currency with a single monetary and foreign exchange regulation, and common monetary, foreign exchange and credit policies and a single customs system with a common customs policy. The Constitution foresaw a system of compensations for the entities, including the federal units, which would be affected by the common economic policy, the formation of a Yugoslav social plan through agreements of federal units on the economic policy of mutual importance and a federal credit fund to accelerate development of less-developed federal units. Federal units became responsible for their own social and economic development and also accepted their share of responsibility for the development of Yugoslavia as a whole. Constitutional functions of the federation and its republics, consistent fiscal decentralisation and a common policy package prepared by the Federal Assembly and confirmed in talks with federal units removed the obstacles to formation and implementation of a number of different federal units' policy mixes and styles. According to the assumption that the socio-economic environment is the primary determinant of public policy and due to the huge differences between federal units, the new Constitution order gave the ultimate incentive to interplay of different and in many circumstances opposite and conflicting interests and attitudes.

Today people still believe that the inappropriate social and economic regulation was the main cause for the crisis. This view, however, needs to be modified. There were also external economic and political factors, two of which are of key importance. The first factor was the disintegration of the USSR and the collapse of communism. It appears that the existence of Yugoslavia was no longer necessary. The second reason is the mechanism of solving the foreign debt crisis. Foreign creditors managed to impose on Yugoslavia the concept of total internal solidarity in repaying debts, which required the adaptation of internal economic order to assure the net out-flow of resources abroad. Finding a solution to this problem became the primary task of economic policy and economic system restructuring. It gave an additional impetus to dis-integration of the single market and single economic space of the state and increased the conflicts over the distribution of resources through federal government. The expectations that the reform programmes and their positive results would automatically remove all the accumulated conflicts among federal units seemed to be on shaky ground.

In the beginning of the 1980s the outbreak of the foreign debt crisis set Yugoslavia off on the road where the existing tensions and conflicting interests between federal units again strengthened the conflicts between the developed and the less developed. This conflict was followed by a dispute about the centralisation or decentralisation of the state, which was stirred up by central Serbia.[35] Serbia determinedly embarked on the path of restructuring the Serbian Constitution and abolishing the auton-omy of the provinces of Kosovo and Vojvodina, and later endeavoured to reform the federation and remove all its confederal components. In these efforts Serbia was guided by a report that stated that central Serbia was lagging behind in economic development and by dissatisfaction with the constitutional position it had within the Yugoslav federation, where it was, in practice, structurally equal to the two autonomous regions.

The above-mentioned outbreak of the debt crisis was just the most obvious among the deep-rooted causes of economic failure. It indicated ultimate failure of the investment cycle of the 1970s, which was financed with recycled oil dollars and triggered by estimates that on the world level there was to be another long-term increase in the prices of primary products. These circumstances gave a fresh impetus to those advocating a development policy of autarky, based on domestic natural resources and the strategy of import substitution. Internal credit transfer, required by a turnaround in foreign financial flow, which unsuccessful investments made even harder, was designed to cover the losses banks and compa-nies made and to collect funds to repay foreign debts. The transfer of resources applied several mechanisms: solidarity cycles (three levels of solidarity were established: between enterprises, banks and federal units) to repay foreign debts, budget and off-budget financing of the federa-tion, and expansive money creation. From the point of view of macro-economics, these fundamental mechanisms of redistribution functioned within two adjustments in the balance of payments: the international balance of payments and the (less obvious) inter-regional balance. Both adjustments are known in theory but the problem of adjustment in the inter-regional balance of payments was not acknowledged by Yugoslav economists, although they had lively debates on the problems of less-developed regions, 'extra income', investments and the operation of the single Yugoslav market. An interesting feature of the discussion was that it introduced issues known from the debates on the worldwide problems of developed and less-developed regions, but said very little about the characteristics of the formation of the European internal market, emerging on the other side of the western Yugoslav border.

With rising economic and political crisis the country entered into constitutional crisis, too. The legal system of federal units was closely connected with the legal system of Yugoslavia. Under the Yugoslav Constitution a single socio-economic order and the same foundations of the Yugoslav market were to apply to the entire area of the state. Key economic issues were regulated by federal legislation, which included the current economic policy measures. The situation called for the preparation of appropriate constitutional groundwork. Two republics were at the forefront of these changes. Preparations for the changes in Slovenian constitutional laws were undertaken simultaneously with the preparations for constitutional changes of the Yugoslav Constitution. But changes in the constitutional position of the Republic of Serbia, which subordinated the provinces of Vojvodina and Kosovo and retained their votes in decision-making processes at a federal level, introduced a request for the constitutional and legal position of Slovenia in Yugoslavia to be changed as well. After both republics, first Serbia and then Slovenia, had undertaken constitutional change, Yugoslavia became an asymmetric federation. In Slovenia the amendments to the 1974 Constitution of the Republic of Slovenia and constitutional acts for their implementation created the necessary conditions. These formed the constitutional framework for either the gradual abolition of federal legislative and regulations or their integration into the legal system of the Republic of Slovenia. The procedure may well be understood as an answer to the amendments to the Yugoslav Constitution, which aimed at promoting further centralisation of the federation. In his assessment of the amendments Ciril Ribičić stated: 'With these constitutional rights Slovenia has taken a right to decide for itself, up to a point, which decisions made by the federation bodies concern it and which do not, and which it will apply and which not. It is a right to nullification, which opens for Slovenia the door to an asymmetric and confederal position in Yugoslavia.'[36]

In the autumn of 1990 Croatia and Slovenia published a joint document that contained a proposal of confederation accord.[37] The two republics proposed that the Yugoslav federation be transformed into a confederal state, formed by sovereign states with an aim to implement their common goals. The first condition for the model to be adopted was the basic economic interest – a guaranteed common market – and the second, participation in European integration processes. In the proposed confederation accord special emphasis was placed on economic issues. The model confederation would have a common market, protected with a customs union and some form of monetary union. In the fields of transport, communications, energy production and agriculture the states would harmonise their policies or create a common policy. A constituent part of the agreement would be anti-monopoly provisions and regulations governing competition, dumping prevention, and public invitations for tenders and subsidies. But the economic content of this proposed accord was not the crucial question. The transformation of federal units into independent states announced the change of status of previously equal nations: they were offered the option only to exchange national equality for status of minorities or even foreigners. This was especially unacceptable for the Serbian nation: the only preferred option for them was to retain full sovereignty in Serbia, to be a constituent nation in Bosnia–Herzegovina and a minority in Croatia. Thus the essence of the Yugoslav problem – the question of the Serbian nation and its relation with the Croats – was revealed again.

Response to the Slovenian–Croat confederation accord arrived in the form of a proposed Yugoslav constitutional order based on federal foundations, which was prepared by Serbia and Montenegro.[38] The document regarded republics as independent states that assert a part of their sovereign rights in the Federal Republic of Yugoslavia. Yugoslavia was defined as a single economic territory where all forms of property are protected and business initiatives encouraged. Its single market was to consist of the free flow of goods, services, labour force and capital; it was to have a single monetary, foreign exchange, customs and banking system and a common monetary and foreign exchange policy, a single fiscal system and a common fiscal policy, a common policy regulating foreign affairs and common development and economic policy and the strategy of scientific and technological development of the state. Economic functions of the federation would be: regulation of ownership rights; regulation of corporate law and the fiscal and banking system; regulation and provision of the monetary system, foreign trade and foreign exchange system, and the system of protection measures; protection of competition, commodity reserves and large technological systems; formation of a common economic policy and a policy to encourage development of less-developed areas; and regulation of areas important to the entire state such as transport and communications, water management and the environment. The key part of the proposal, which was radically changing relations within the federation and could therefore not count on the support of Slovenia and Croatia, was the introduction of majority decision-making in the Federal Assembly, which would be elected on the principle of one-man-one-vote. This would remove from the constitution the issue of key importance and great delicacy in the Yugoslav federalism – consensual voting of republics and regions.

Yugoslavia entered the final phase of its existence with two diametrically opposed proposals, and without any willingness to harmonise its views.

CONCLUSION

The break-up of the Austro-Hungarian Monarchy after the First World War and the formation of the Yugoslav state meant that the united southern Slavic nations were faced with a change in the economic area. What these nations brought into the new state has been developing in different circumstances and in different settings. Unification of the new state was also a unification of its different inherited economic institutions and of the economic and social order. The processes of unification were painful. They included the question of property rights (sequestration, nationalisation or nostrification, and agrarian reform), currency reform, liberalisation of exports, return to the gold standard, custom and taxes laws, company law, resolution of internal (agricultural) debt crisis and introduction of a social security system, the beginnings of labour-market policies and the subordination to German economic pressures in the late 1930s. Before the Second World War economic development was based predominantly on liberalist market principles, although the 1930s saw a decisive shift to state interventionism in the economy. The impact of these changes was unequal across the country. During the Second World War the country was brutally dismembered and its resources were used to support the German war effort. The tribute that the country paid was among the heaviest in occupied Europe.

With changed social relations and a new philosophy after 1945, the situation altered in several respects. Initial recovery from the war was successful. But economic incentives were denied at the very core of the state and society. The role of the state became omnipotent: a planned economic system and ownership of means of production were concentrated in the state party apparatus, which made all decisions and coordinated everything. When resulting obstacles were recognised by the architects of communist Yugoslavia, a series of broad reforms were launched trying to find a proper governance system, which would reconcile the need for decentralised decision-making in the economy with a one-party political system and growing statehood of federal units. Constitutional transfer of power from the federal state to federal units was seen as a proper solution for Yugoslav microcosms. But it was soon understood that these changes were not enough. A bridge was looked for to ensure cohesion. It was anticipated that this bridge was to be constructed by the last great transformation of Yugoslav socialism: the introduction of free associated labour and of the system of delegation as a basis of political system, which was the last attempt of the founders of communist Yugoslavia to build a society without granting market forces and a multiparty system any significant role. Ironically, the concept of associated labour and the constitutional responsibilities of federal units for their own development and for the development of Yugoslavia as a whole was very well understood by foreign creditors, who imposed total federal responsibility for foreign debts of Yugoslavia after the outbreak of the foreign debt crisis. This federal responsibility and total socialisation of foreign debts was a greater blow to economic incentive even than the socialist system itself. In such circumstances the country was defeated. What happened later was only the search for a mechanism of allocation of the burdens imposed by the defeat.

The growing gap and the timescale of catching up among the federal units was a central problem of Yugoslav economic development. Inability to solve these growing economic disparities led to the never-ending restructuring of the country's constitutional order, its political and economic system. Being at the same time a peripheral European country with a mixture of south-, central- and east-European development characteristics the country was in constant search for the proper development model that would satisfy the requirements and aspirations of its different nations and their political elite. It seems that this search was influenced by geopolitical changes after the demise of socialism. It seems that the country was born in blood and it died in blood due to a combination of internal (southern Slav) and external circumstances. The proper role and weight of each of them is yet to be evaluated.

NOTES

1 *Regional Disparities and Developments in the Republics of Yugoslavia*, (Paris, March 1992, unpublished).
2 Similar attempts were made by Slovenian economist Franjo Štiblar in 'The rise and fall of Yugoslavia: an economic history view' in Alice Teichova (ed.), *Central Europe in the Twentieth Century: An Economic History Perspective* (Aldershot; 1997), pp. 61–82 and Serbian economist Milica Uvalić in 'The disintegration of Yugoslavia: its costs and benefits', *Communist Economies & Economic Transformation* 5 (1993), 273–93.
3 *Zgodovina narodov Jugoslavije, Prva in druga knjiga* [A history of Yugoslav nations, Books 1 and 2], (Ljubljana, 1953 and 1959).
4 Patrick Bolton, Gerard Roland and Enrico Spolaore, 'Economic theories of the break-up and integration of nations', *European Economic Review* 49 (1996), 697–705.
5 In Charles Jelavich, *South Slav Nationalism Textbook and Yugoslav Union before 1914* (Columbus, OH, 1990) one can find a detailed discussion about the role of educational process in the development and preservation of national identity.
6 *Enciklopedija Jugoslavije*, 2. izdaja, četrta knjiga [Encyclopedia of Yugoslavia, 2nd edn, vol. IV], (Zagreb, 1989 – Slovenian edition), p. 312. The second edition of *Enciklopedija Jugoslavije* [Encyclopedia of Yugoslavia] remained an unfinished project.
7 The main idea of Illyrianism – to create a common culture for all South–Slavs on the basis of a unique literary language – was rejected by those nations. From 1848 the terms Yugoslav and Croatian replaced Illyrian to designate the national movement. The role of Slav nationalism and Yugoslavism in the 1860s in Croatia is explained in Mirjana Gross, 'The union of Dalmatia with northern Croatia: a crucial question of the Croatian national integration in the nineteenth century' in Mikuláš Teich and Roy Porter (eds.), *The National Question in Europe in Historical Context* (Cambridge, 1993), pp. 270–92.
8 *Enciklopedija Jugoslavije*, šesta knjiga [Encyclopedia of Yugoslavia, vol. VI], (Zagreb, – Croat or Serbian edition, in Latinic transcription), p. 133.
9 Janko Pleterski, *Narodi, revolucija, Jugoslavija* [Nations, revolution, Yugoslavia], (Ljubljana, 1986); Branko Petranović, *Istorija Jugoslavije 1918–1978* [A history of Yugoslavia, 1918–1978], (Beograd, 1980).
10 Rudolf Bičanić, *Ekonomska podloga hrvatskog pitanja* [Economic basis of the Croatian question] (Zagreb, 1938).
11 Andrej Gosar, *Banovina Slovenija. Politična, finančna in gospodarska vprašanja* [Ban's Country of Slovenia. Political, financial and economic issues], (Ljubljana, 1940).
12 *Istina o Ekonomskoj podlozi hrvatskog pitanja – Odgovor g. dr. Bičaniću* [The truth about the economic basis of the Croatian question – Answers to Dr Bičanić], (Beograd, 1940). The authors were Gojko Grđić, Vladimir Đorđević, Jovan Lovčević, Milan J. Žujović, Bogdan Prica and Slobodan M. Drašković.

13 Aleksander Bilimovič, 'Privredno uređenje Jugoslavije: sporazum od 26. avgusta 1939 god' [Economic system of Yugoslavia: the agreement from August 26, 1939], *Narodno blagostanje* 24 (1940), 531–4; Jovan Đorđević, *Osnovna pitanja federalnih država* [The basic issues of federal states], (Beograd, 1940); Ljubomir S. Dukanac, *Privredno uređenje federalnih država* [Economic system of federal states], (Beograd, 1940).

14 J. K. Galbraith, *The Nature of Mass Poverty* (Harmondsworth, 1980), pp. 17–18.

15 OECD, *Regional Disparities*, p. 25.

16 R. Barro and X. Sala-I-Martin, *Economic Growth* (New York, 1995), pp. 25–32.

17 The formulae for convergence calculation are available in *ibid.*, pp. 383–7.

18 Pavle Sicherl, 'Time-distance as a dynamic measure of disparities in social and economic development', *Kyklos* 26 (1973), 559–75.

19 Pavle Sicherl, 'Novi vidiki merjenja razlik v razvitosti: Primerjava Slovenije in Jugoslavije' [New issues in measuring the differences in development: comparison between Slovenia and Yugoslavia], *Zbornik znanstvenih razprav* 49 (1989), 181–201.

20 Aleksander Bajt, 'Trideset godina privrednog rasta' [Thirty years of economic growth], *Ekonomist* 38 (1980), 1–18; Pavle Sicherl, *Slovenija zdaj. Primerjava indikatorjev razvitosti* [Slovenia now: comparison of development indicators], (Ljubljana, 1990); Ljubomir Madžar, *Suton socijalističkih privreda* [Decline of socialist economies], (Beograd, 1990).

21 Sicherl, *Slovenija zdaj*, pp. 130–1.

22 *Ibid.*, p. 131.

23 Joseph T. Bombelles, *Economic Development of Communist Yugoslavia* (Stanford, 1968), p. vi.

24 Sabrina P. Ramet, *Nationalism and Federalism in Yugoslavia, 1962–1991* (Bloomington, IN, 1992).

25 *Memorandum SANU* [Memorandum of the Serbian Academy of Sciences and Arts], (Duga, June 1989), special issue.

26 Kosta Mihailović, *Regionalna stvarnost Jugoslavije* [A regional reality of Yugoslavia], (Beograd, 1990), pp. 77–96.

27 Kosta Mihailović, 'Regionalni aspekti privrednog razvoja' [Regional aspects of economic development], *Ekonomist* 11 (1958), 1–41.

28 R. Bičanić, 'O jadranskoj koncepciji ekonomskog razvoja Jugoslavije' [On the Adriatic development concept of Yugoslavia], *Pomorstvo* 9–10 (1964), 286–7. Before the break-up of Yugoslavia, this concept was mentioned in the study by Josip Deželjin and Dragomir Sundać (eds.), *Pomorska orientacija Jugoslavije* [A maritime orientation of Yugoslavia], (Rijeka, 1988).

29 Susan L. Woodward, *Socialist Unemployment. The Political Economy of Yugoslavia 1945–1990* (Princeton, NJ, 1995).

30 Božo Repe, *Liberalizem* [Liberalism], (Ljubljana, 1992). Although Repe did not invent this notion, he was the one who most thoroughly dealt with its substance.

31 Rudolf Bičanić, *Economic Policy in Socialist Yugoslavia* (Cambridge, 1973), p. 201. See also Repe, *Liberalizem*, pp. 40–6.

32 *Slovenija 1968 kam?* [Slovenia 1968, where are you going?], (Trieste, 1968; reprinted Ljubljana, 1990), pp. 10–11; quoted after the 1990 issue.

33 Šime Đodan, 'Evolucija gospodarskog sustava SFRJ i ekonomski položaj Hrvatske' [Evolution of the economic system of SFRY and economic position of Croatia], *Hrvatski književni zbornik* 2 (1971), 3–102.

34 *Ustava Socialistične federativne republike Jugoslavije* [Constitution of Socialist Federative Republic of Yugoslavia], (Ljubljana, 1974).

35 Ivan Stambolić, *Rasprave o Srbiji* [Discussions on Serbia], (Zagreb, 1988). The author was a former president of Serbia and became the first victim of Milošević's march to Yugoslavia. The book begins with a chapter 'Serbia lagging behind' and finishes with the chapter 'Explanation of a proposal for the change of the Socialist Republic Serbia Constitution'.

36 Ciril Ribičić, *Ustavnopravni vidik osamosvajanja Slovenije* [A constitutional aspect of the Slovenian road towards independence], (Ljubljana, 1992), p. 23.

37 *Model konfederacije v Jugoslaviji* [A confederate model for Yugoslavia], (Zagreb and Ljubljana, Presidency of the Republic of Croatia and the Republic of Slovenia, joint expert working group, 4 October 1990).

38 *Koncept ustavne ureditve Jugoslavije na federativnih temeljih* [A concept of a constitutional system for Yugoslavia on a federal basis], (Beograd, 16 October 1990).

CHAPTER 17

Economic differentiation and the national question in Poland in the twentieth century

Jerzy Tomaszewski

The share of national minorities in Poland in 1931 can be estimated at about 36 per cent of the total population. The basic data are shown in table 17.1.[1] The characteristic feature of these minorities were significant differences in their social structure and economic situation connected with the regional differences between the provinces of the Polish Republic. Regional differentiation and specific social and economic features of national minorities and the dominating Polish nation were caused by the historical development of the country. In some cases these differences were rooted in medieval times (for example, the different structure of land ownership) and deepened during the nineteenth century, when the territory of the former Polish Commonwealth was divided between the three neighbouring powers – Austria, Prussia and Russia – and incorporated into the three economic and political units of greatly differing size, economic structure and policy.

At the beginning of the twentieth century the three parts of the future Polish Republic included in these three political and economic units varied significantly. The lands included at the end of the eighteenth century and after 1815 in the Prussian Kingdom developed a strong and relatively modern agriculture with small industrial enterprises and services related to the needs of the agricultural population. The future Poznań and Pomorze provinces were agricultural lands delivering their products to the industrial regions of the German Empire. The Prussian administration supported the German minority in these provinces, organised and financed the influx of German farmers, businessmen and officials from the western part of the monarchy and tried to impose the German language and culture upon the local Polish and Jewish population. Polish landlords, farmers and small businessmen developed a net of Polish co-operatives and institutions, which helped to defend their interests against the state administration and their German neighbours. The financial centre of the Polish co-operatives and small business was the

Table 17.1. *The ethnic structure of the population in Poland, 1931*

Nationality	Thousands	Per cents
Total	32,107	100
Poles	20,650	64
Ukrainians	5,245	16
Jews	3,133	10
Belorussians	1,966	6
Germans	784	2
Lithuanians	200	1
Russians	140	1
Others	89	0

Note:
The numbers include soldiers in barracks.
Sources: J. Tomaszewski, *Ojczyzna nie tylko Polaków* [A fatherland not only of Poles], (Warsaw, 1985), p. 50 and E. Makowski, *Litwini w Polsce 1920–1939* [Lithuanians in Poland 1920–1939], (Warsaw, 1986), pp. 26–8.

Bank Związku Spółek Zarobkowych (Bank of the Union of Co-operatives).

Many Jews (most often poor people who were expendable from the point of view of the German administration) emigrated – either voluntarily or involuntarily – to the Russian part of the Polish lands, while their more affluent co-religionists were assimilated (not without legal and economic pressure exerted by the German administration) into the German culture and language. They were not numerous in these lands and many of them settled later in the central or western regions of Germany.

The German administration introduced a similar policy in Upper Silesia, mainly inhabited by the Polish-speaking population but with a significant number of German workers and peasants who had settled there since the thirteenth century. This region was one of the most important industrial centres of Germany. The mines and most of the other enterprises remained in the hands of wealthy German aristocratic families, although with growing influence of the businessmen from other social classes. Some of the owners were descendants of or akin to old Slavic local royal families.

Silesia had a complicated history. In the past it had belonged to the

Polish Kingdom, later to the Czech Kingdom and was incorporated –
together with other parts of the Crown Lands of St Venceslav – into the
Habsburg Monarchy; but in the eighteenth century a greater part of it
was conquered by Prussia. Only a small part of Silesia (Teschen Silesia,
Śląsk Cieszyński or Těšinské Slezsko) remained in the Habsburg
Monarchy and after 1918 was divided between Poland and Czechoslovakia.

The southern provinces of the old Polish Commonwealth, included
in the Habsburg Monarchy, consisted of relatively poor agricultural land
with large estates and small peasant farms. The more developed western
regions were inhabited by Polish peasants; in the almost exclusively agricultural eastern part (a notable exception here was the oil industry) the
majority of peasants were Ukrainians with, however, a significant
number of Polish peasants. The towns and cities had a numerous Jewish
minority; however, in several small towns the Jews constituted a majority of the local population as a kind of industrial and commercial class.

A significant part of the territories of the former Polish Commonwealth became the so-called Congress Poland created after the Vienna
Congress in 1815 and subordinated to the Russian emperor, who
assumed the title of the King of Poland. Congress Poland was deprived
of all remnants of autonomy after the uprisings of 1831 and 1863 and
incorporated into the Russian Empire. It was an important industrial
region of Russia; however, a majority of the population was engaged in
agriculture, which was backward in comparison with western Europe
(including the Polish lands incorporated in Germany) but relatively well
developed compared with Russia. The population was mainly Polish
with a significant Jewish minority engaged in trade and industry (mainly
small businessmen, peddlars, artisans and workers) and a tiny group of
Russian government officials, teachers, policemen and other professionals.

The lands east of Congress Poland (so-called 'lost lands' incorporated
into Russia in the second half of the eighteenth century) were economically least developed. These areas were mainly inhabited by
Belorussian, Lithuanian and Ukrainian peasants; however, in some
regions, notably the country around Vilna (Vilnius or Wilno) and south
from this city, Polish villagers prevailed. The towns were mostly inhabited by Jews with a significant minority of Poles, Russians and other
national groups. Vilna was the most important city of this region. It was
the centre of flourishing Polish, Jewish and Belorussian culture and the

historical capital city of Lithuania. The most backward province was Polesie, with strong remnants of a pre-capitalist economy – in some remote places a barter economy still.

These regional differences were accompanied by the no less important specific social features of individual ethnic groups. The nobility (a political nation) of the old Polish Commonwealth before the partitions was, as a rule, Polish. It is true that this nobility had incorporated different ethnic groups in the past, notably Ruthenians and Lithuanians, in some regions Armenians and Tartars, and sometimes Jews who were baptised. Almost all of them were influenced by the dominating Polish culture and at the end of the eighteenth century these ethnic differences lost their importance in most cases, remaining only as a cherished tradition of a famous past of particular families. Several of them were proud of their ancestors, who had been princes and dukes of the Great Duchy of Lithuania.

There lived, however, in many rural settlements the descendants of the small gentry (*szlachta zagrodowa*), more or less similar to English yeomen, who had small farms and lived side by side with peasants. They spoke vernacular (local peasant) dialects, attended the village churches, worked on their plots and remembered only that their ancestors were knighted by the Polish kings. The gentry maintained social distance from the peasants; the economic situation of both groups was, however, similar.

The policy of the three powers in the nineteenth century caused significant changes. A number of estates in the German part of Poland were bought by German landowners and farmers, often with the help of authorities and not without pressure on former Polish owners. The Russian authorities confiscated several Polish estates (especially in the 'lost lands') and offered them to loyal Russian landowners. In the second half of the nineteenth century in all parts of these territories several estates were divided among small farmers or sold to people not belonging to the nobility; among them were Jewish businessmen, especially in the south-eastern provinces belonging to Austria.

These changes did not influence the general conviction of Belorussian, Lithuanian and Ukrainian peasants that the Poles were 'lords' and the Polish language was the 'language of lords', whereas their languages were the 'languages of peasants'. The language was a symbol of social status. Small gentry used single Polish words and addressed socially equal persons with the Polish word *pan* (Sir) or *pani* (Lady). The peasants were addressed – and used among themselves – a simple *wy* (you), which is the same in the Polish, Belorussian, Ukrainian and Russian languages.

It is useful to note that this difference (*pan* or *wy*) when addressing the people from different social classes was known before 1939 in other provinces of Poland, too (I remember this well from my boyhood); it was, however, not burdened with ethnic prejudice (with the notable exception of poor Jews). In contemporary Poland the word *pan* lost its old meaning and is used when addressing people independent of their social status (with the possible exception of very old ladies from aristocratic families).

A similar situation existed in the south-eastern territories, under Habsburg rule. The Polish writer Stanisław Vincenz, a descendant of a landlord's family, related how the people spoke in his native country of Lwów (Lviv).[2] His uncle, when meeting a local Jewish peddlar, spoke the vernacular, that is the local Hucul dialect of the Ukrainian language. The Polish language was used when speaking with the people belonging to the Jewish (Hassid) patriciate and the Greek-Catholic Ruthenian (Ukrainian) priests. These people were considered members of the upper social strata. These priests used the Polish language even among their families.

National differences in the eastern parts of Poland more or less reflected the social differences. In Upper Silesia similar national differences were connected with the social difference between the German aristocracy, businessmen and administration and the Polish peasants and workers. It is necessary to add, however, that in Upper Silesia a significant proportion of workers, in some places the peasants as well, were German. The Poles (in general, the people speaking Polish and insufficiently fluent in the German language) belonged as a rule (with only scarce exceptions) to the lower social strata. The assimilation (or, at least, acculturation) was a price paid for social advance. The complicated history of this region, the nationalist policy of the German government, and social and ethnic relations influenced a sharp Polish–German antagonism in extreme cases. There existed, however, significant groups of native population, Germans and Poles as well, who maintain normal contact between themselves and the people who declared themselves to be Silesians rather than Poles or Germans, speaking the local Polish dialect.

The Jewish population was traditionally engaged in commerce and small industry (mainly as artisans). This was changing slowly and – after they had achieved legal emancipation – the Jews entered other professions, often connected with academic education (such as lawyers and doctors). The Jews, however, were often seen as middlemen between village and town. This stereotype did not change – at least in most cases – after 1918 in independent Poland and was quite popular, notably among peasants.

The Polish Republic after 1918 (see figure 17.1) included territories that had earlier belonged to the three powers and constituted parts of different economic and political units. During twenty years of independence significant economic changes occurred; the period of independence, however, was short and the basic regional social and economic differences could not be removed in such a brief time.[3]

The characteristic feature of the ethnic structure was the territorial concentration of the so-called Slavic minorities in the agricultural provinces, with the exception of the agrarian Lublin province, which had a relatively small Ukrainian minority in its eastern region (see table 17.2).[4] Peasants of the eastern provinces, formerly part of Russia, were mainly Belorussians or Ukrainians; a relatively small number of Lithuanian peasants lived in the north. There were, however, villages or even regions with a Polish peasant population, most significant in the Wilno province. The Bialystok province was on the border between Polish and Belorussian ethnic territory.[5] In Bialystok – the main city of this region – there were, however, workers (Jews, Belorussians and Poles) engaged mainly in the textile industry.

The same eastern provinces were known as having a strong tradition of pre-capitalist social relations. The traditional social differences between small gentry (*szlachta zagrodowa*) and peasants were maintained in spite of the constitutional equality of civil rights for all the citizens, contrary to the real economic situation of villagers. An author well acquainted with the Polesie province wrote of these people:

'Gentry' constitutes here a separate social class. The membership of it is independent of wealth or education. A nobleman can be poor or illiterate. The basic question is only the descent. 'The Polish nobleman' – this definition stands often for the nationality and for all the affiliation . . . The religion is without importance. The majority is Orthodox. There are, however, villages totally Roman Catholic.[6]

People belonging to the small gentry considered themselves, as a rule, to be a higher and better category of people, 'the Polish noblemen', most often being poor farmers similar to the majority of peasants and speaking the same 'local' language – that is, dialects of the Belorussian or Ukrainian languages. Polish authorities tried to strengthen the Polish

KEY

–·–·– International boundary
– – – – Provincial boundary
――― Railway
――― River

◉ Towns of over 100,000 inhabitants
◎ Towns from 50,000 to 100,000 inhabitants
○ Towns of under 50,000 inhabitants

PROVINCES:
1 - Warszawa, 2 - Łódź, 3 - Kielce, 4 - Lublin,
5 - Białystok, 6 - Wilno, 7 - Nowogródek,
8 - Polesie, 9 - Wołyń, 10 Poznań,
11 - Pomorze, 12 - Śląsk, 13 - Kraków,
14 - Lwów, 15 - Stanisławów, 16 - Tarnopol

Source: *Mały Rocznik Statystyczny 1931*
[Concise statistical yearbook 1931]

Figure 17.1. *The Polish Republic, 1931*

Table 17.2. *The agricultural population and the main minorities by province in Poland, 1931*

Province	Population (thousands)	Agricultural (%)	Germans (%)	Belorussians and Ukrainians (%)	Jews (%)
Poland	31,916	60.6	2.44	22.15	9.76
Warsaw city	1,172	0.4	0.17	0.17	30.12
Warsaw	2,529	60.8	2.92	0.08	8.66
Łódź	2,632	48.6	5.89	0.04	14.40
Kielce	2,936	56.8	0.27	0.03	10.80
Lublin	2,465	71.0	0.65	5.03	12.74
Białystok	1,644	69.9	0.43	16.61	11.98
Wilno	1,276	72.3	0.08	32.21	8.70
Nowogródek	1,057	82.4	0.00	58.37	7.85
Polesie	1,132	80.6	0.09	77.12	10.07
Wołyń	2,086	79.4	2.25	69.42	9.97
Poznań	2,107	47.1	9.16	0.05	0.33
Pomorze	1,080	51.5	9.72	0.00	0.28
Śląsk	1,295	12.2	9.16	0.00	1.47
Kraków	2,298	59.5	0.39	2.57	7.57
Lwów	3,127	68.6	0.38	41.73	10.94
Stanisławów	1,480	74.7	1.15	72.91	9.46
Tarnopol	1,600	79.6	0.19	54.50	8.38

Note:
The numbers do not include soldiers in barracks.
Sources: Mały Rocznik Statystyczny 1937 [Concise statistical yearbook], pp. 30, 31 and 32, and Z. Landau and J. Tomaszewski, *Robotnicy przemysłowi w Polsce 1918–1939. Materialne warunki bytu* [Industrial workers in Poland 1918–1939. Economic conditions of life], (Warsaw, 1971), pp. 94 and 130–3

tradition and influence the gentry (for example, an association of the small gentry was organised), introducing additional frictions into the life of the local population.

An important question was connected with the existence of large estates. The majority of landowners, especially the wealthiest, were Poles (tables 17.3 and 17.4) belonging to old aristocratic families. These families maintained often specific habits rooted in the feudal past that stressed their superiority over the simple people from the villages. There are a number of quite intriguing examples of these traditions.[7] This linked the ethnic differences to economic and social conflicts. Poles in the eastern provinces were often identified with the 'lords' and the peasants, rooted deeply in the tradition of feudal conflicts, considered that the lands of their estates should belong to the local villagers. This was a

Table 17.3. *Nationality of owners of estates above 50 hectares by province in Poland, 1921*

	Nationality of owners (%)						
Province	Poles	Germans	Ukrainians	Belorussians	Russians	Jews	Others
Poland	82.0	10.3	1.3	2.5	1.9	1.6	0.5
Warsaw city	83.3	–	–	–	–	16.7	–
Warsaw	97.8	0.6	–	–	0.4	1.1	0.1
Łódź	97.2	0.5	–	–	0.4	1.7	0.2
Kielce	95.9	0.2	–	–	0.2	3.7	–
Lublin	97.1	0.1	–	–	1.0	1.8	–
Białystok	93.3	0.1	–	2.4	3.0	0.9	–
Wilno	86.0	0.2	0.2	8.2	3.0	0.9	1.5
Nowogródek	87.4	0.2	–	8.2	2.8	0.8	0.6
Polesie	65.4	–	4.6	17.8	9.3	2.0	1.1
Wołyń	61.5	1.3	17.6	0.3	15.1	0.1	4.1
Poznań	58.6	40.9	–	–	–	0.1	0.1
Pomorze	67.6	32.2	–	–	–	0.1	0.1
Śląsk	42.3	55.6	–	–	–	–	2.1
Kraków	94.9	1.0	0.5	–	–	2.6	1.0
Lwów	87.2	2.3	1.6	–	–	8.5	0.4
Stanisławów	84.8	0.9	6.0	–	–	5.7	2.6
Tarnopol	90.7	0.5	3.1	–	–	5.5	0.2

Source: W. Roszkowski, *Landowners in Poland 1918–1939* (Boulder, CO, 1991), p. 27.

fundamental reason for the radical character of the Belorus national movement, which often showed sympathy for the Soviet Union. It is true that the collectivisation in the USSR changed these attitudes significantly, but social radicalism did not vanish and even the Christian-Democratic Belorus movement was accused by the Polish archbishop, Romuald Jałbrzykowski, of the 'sin of Bolshevism'.[8] The followers of this movement demanded radical land reform, namely the expropriation of big estates.

The Polish authorities tried to strengthen Polish influence and supported Polish people settled among the local population.[9] Therefore, large estates were often divided (in connection with the land reform) between Polish peasants coming from the provinces that suffered from significant agrarian overpopulation. This policy fostered ethnic conflicts as the newcomers were considered to be thieves of land that should be divided according to human justice and the Lord's laws and given to the local (mainly Belorussian or Ukrainian) peasants.

Table 17.4. *Nationality of owners of estates above 50 hectares by size in Poland,* 1921

Nationality of owners	Groups of estates in hectares and % of owners				
	Total	50–100	100–500	500–1,000	over 1,000
All owners	100.0	100.0	100.0	100.0	100.0
Polish	82.0	77.1	84.7	84.6	81.8
German	10.0	15.3	7.1	8.9	7.9
Ukrainian	1.3	1.2	1.4	1.2	1.6
Belorussian	2.5	3.5	2.4	1.2	1.6
Jewish	1.6	1.3	2.0	1.0	1.5
Russian	1.9	0.9	1.7	2.7	4.8
Czech	0.2	0.3	0.2	0.1	0.3
Other	0.5	0.4	0.5	0.3	0.8

Source: Roszkowski, *Landowners in Poland*, p. 28.

The town people were mainly Polish (administrators, teachers and so on) and Jewish (shopkeepers and artisans), with minority groups of others, for example Belorussian or Ukrainian workers. Workers from these last two nations constituted, as a rule, a majority among the workers hired by the owners of affluent peasant farms and – less often – by owners of estates.[10]

These provinces were economically least developed and the poverty of peasants added another reason for animosity towards the Polish administration and Polish 'lords' to the traditional social and ethnic conflicts. The Polish administration was seen not only as the foreign power defending the landlords but as a kind of colonial system. Although there were significant changes for the better in the relatively short time of less than two decades of Polish administration (the net of state-owned schools teaching mainly in the Polish language was developed and the productivity of land was growing), the eastern provinces remained far below the level of the other parts of the Polish Republic in almost all spheres of life (see table 17.5). The poverty of non-Polish peasants contrasted with the relative affluence of the Polish administration, the more so with the luxury of Polish landowners, which was an important source of social conflict. Many people (not only peasants) cherished illusions that national independence (or the Soviet system) would be a sufficient remedy for all economic, social and political pains.

A similar – at least to some extent – situation existed in the former

Table 17.5. *Selected indices of living standard by province in Poland, 1931*

Province	Illiterate persons aged 10+ (%)	Apartments with 1 room (%)	People in 1-room apartments (% of total population)	Average number of people in each 1-room apartment	Hourly wages of industrial workers (% of the average level in August 1937)
Poland	23.1	46.9	43.4	3.9	100
Warsaw city	10.1	42.5	36.9	4.0	134
Warsaw	22.4	46.7	42.3	4.0	109
Łódź	21.4	52.8	47.3	3.8	106
Kielce	26.2	58.5	55.7	4.1	89
Lublin	24.2	53.8	50.9	4.2	78
Białystok	23.5	37.9	34.4	3.8	73
Wilno	29.1	60.0	57.8	4.2	75
Nowogródek	34.9	63.7	61.3	4.1	46
Polesie	48.5	60.6	58.6	4.0	63
Wołyń	47.8	48.7	47.0	3.5	67
Poznań	2.8	17.9	13.2	3.3	85
Pomorze	4.3	18.4	14.2	3.4	87
Śląsk	1.4	19.2	12.9	2.8	112
Kraków	13.7	37.1	32.2	3.6	99
Lwów	23.1	49.6	47.6	3.7	88
Stanisławów	36.6	61.6	58.7	3.7	55
Tarnopol	29.8	60.5	58.1	3.9	64

Sources: Statystyka Polski, seria C, No. 62, pp. 2, 3, 6 and 47. Landau and Tomaszewski, *Robotnicy przemysłowi w Polsce*, p. 594.

eastern Austrian provinces, with an important exception: the Polish village population was more numerous in the Tarnopol province, and the western part of the Lwów province was mainly Polish (the ethnic border was not sharp and the population speaking Ukrainian dialects even lived in several villages in the southern part of Kraków province). The number of Ukrainians engaged in non-agricultural professions was relatively (in comparison with the Belorussian population) significant and this was connected with the existence of numerous private Ukrainian schools, co-operatives and associations. An analogy can be drawn between the Ukrainian movement in the former Austrian provinces of Poland and the Polish movement before 1918 in the Poznań and Pomorze provinces. One of the most important points of contention was the land. Ukrainian peasants and their political organisations demanded land reform in favour of the local villagers. The Polish administration tried to strengthen the Polish population and the land reform was often introduced in favour of the polish peasants, discriminating against Ukrainians. Also, Ukrainian associations, co-operatives and schools were discriminated against. The Polish government refused to create an Ukrainian university in Lwów and the Ukrainians managed to organise underground academic studies.

There were often serious reasons for this policy as the Ukrainian institutions were misused by an illegal terrorist organisation that killed Polish officials and Ukrainians who tried to find a kind of compromise (at least on a temporary basis) with the Polish authorities, burned Polish estates and robbed banks. The often brutal methods used by the authorities helped to maintain order but aroused numerous protests and added fuel to the developing enmity of Ukrainians towards the whole Polish population. The radical left believed that the only solution was unification with the Soviet Ukraine; their popularity diminished, however, when the news about collectivisation and famine in the USSR reached Poland. The radical right-wing groups co-operated with Germany and deceived themselves that the Third Reich would help to establish an independent Ukrainian state. The moderates (far from both extremes) tried to achieve a modus vivendi with Poland, in the justified conviction that neither the Soviet Union nor Germany could or would solve the Ukrainian question.

The Jews were mainly concentrated in towns of the former Russian and Austrian provinces (table 17.6). They were engaged in trade, especially in local commerce.[11] Jews in the eastern and south-eastern provinces were in fact a kind of commercial class dominating the retail trade with a somewhat smaller share in the wholesale trade. A Jew was in many villages a synonym for a peddlar, shopkeeper, innkeeper or purchaser of agricultural products, that is a representative of a market economy with all its attendant troubles for the average peasant. The economic conflicts between the town and village, between the small farmer and small tradesman, were personified in these poor people who often had to suffer for all the sins of the capitalist economy. The popular opinion of peasants (and even shared to some extent by many politicians) was a kind of homespun physiocratic doctrine. They considered agriculture to be the only (or at least the most important) source of national wealth, with the other social strata living at the expense of farmers. This added an ideological sanctification to the everyday quarrels in local markets. No wonder that the radical social movements in

Table 17.6. *The town population and Jews by province in Poland, 1931*

Province	Population (thousands)	Population of towns (thousands)	Jews as % of town population
Poland	31,916	8,731	27.3
Warsaw city	1,172	1,172	30.1
Warsaw	2,529	583	29.7
Łódź	2,632	1,104	31.2
Kielce	2,936	750	30.2
Lublin	2,465	434	43.7
Białystok	1,644	396	38.4
Wilno	1,276	261	29.2
Nowogródek	1,057	103	42.6
Polesie	1,132	149	49.2
Wołyń	2,086	253	49.1
Poznań	2,107	838	0.8
Pomorze	1,080	348	0.9
Śląsk	1,295	418	3.9
Kraków	2,298	580	24.8
Lwów	3,127	776	33.2
Stanisławów	1,480	295	34.8
Tarnopol	1,600	272	34.7

Note:
The numbers do not include soldiers in barracks.
Source: Mały Rocznik Statystyczny 1937, pp. 23 and 24.

some regions of Poland were frequently accompanied by anti-Jewish riots. This was especially so in the southern provinces in the years 1918–19.[12]

Significant changes were going on, however, in the south-eastern provinces (where Ukrainian co-operatives developed) and in the central and southern provinces (where Polish co-operatives developed). The co-operative movement was proclaiming its own ideology and political programme, akin to some extent to non-Marxist socialism, but on the local level there existed more important current and practical questions. The co-operative shops and other enterprises were rivals of the local shopkeepers and sometimes, independent of the will of left-wing activists, co-operative propaganda drifted towards anti-Jewish declarations as the local private tradesmen were often Jews. The economic conflicts between the commercial class and the village population were therefore connected with ethnic differences and religious conflicts. Many Christian priests (who had a strong influence on the minds of peasants)

Table 17.7. *The German population by province in Poland, 1931*

Provinces	% of Germans of the total population	Germans (thousands)	% of Germans occupied as workers
Poland	2.4	780	20
Warsaw city	0.2	2	–
Warsaw	2.9	74	21
Łódź	5.9	155	40
Wołyń	2.3	47	0
Poznań	9.2	193	22
Pomorze	9.7	105	23
Śląsk	10.0	130	12
Stanisławów	1.1	17	0
Other	0.0	57	0

Sources: Tomaszewski, *Ojczyzna nie tylko Polaków*, p. 50; Landau and Tomaszewski, *Robotnicy przemysłowi w Polsce*, pp. 94 and 130–3.

believed in ritual murder, and such accusations were printed in popular Catholic journals distributed among the half-literate population.[13] Economic conflicts, religious superstitions and anti-semitic propaganda were often a dangerous mixture and ended in tragedies.

The radical peasant leaders during the first two decades of the twentieth century were often proclaiming war against the 'Jewish swindlers and usurers'. It was only in the 1930s that the influential Polish peasant politicians began to understand that the anti-Jewish slogans were only helping the anti-democratic trends in the country.

The central, southern and western provinces of the Polish Republic had a dominant Polish majority. The Germans in the western provinces (which had earlier belonged to Germany) were a minority[14] (after 1919 a significant number of Germans and Jews who accepted the German language and culture emigrated), but they retained a privileged economic position and remembered their political domination before the First World War (see table 17.7). They were often owners of estates (see tables 17.3 and 17.4) and relatively large farms, businessmen and professionals. The agriculturally most developed provinces – Pomorze and Poznań – had a relatively small percentage of Germans but their share in ownership of big estates was much more significant. German farmers and landlords developed a strong net of co-operatives, which received financial help from Germany.[15] This state of affairs was inherited from

German policy prior to 1918 and was one of the important sources of resentment of the Polish population against Germans. On the other hand, the German population was afraid of the policy of the Polish authorities, notably of the land reform, which meant that the big estates were divided mainly among Polish peasant buyers of land. A somewhat different situation was to be found in Silesia, where among the German-speaking population were not only businessmen, landowners and private officials but workers in mines and industrial enterprises as well. The German Social Democrats had a relatively large number of supporters among them.

Another region with a significant German minority was the Łódź province, where the German-speaking population consisted of industrial workers (mainly in the textile industry), clerks and businessmen. The Germans in this region had never been a ruling nation and local Polish–German relations were not the same as in the western provinces. It is true that after 1933 the influence of a radical German nationalism grew even in this region. Many Germans, however, remained loyal to the Polish Republic, and not only Social Democrats did not welcome the *Wehrmacht* in September 1939. Some of them were murdered by the Nazi authorities. The Nazi policy during the Second World War inevitably changed Polish–German relations in Łódź for the worse.

The economic strength of the German upper classes and the memory of German anti-Polish policy and discrimination were the reasons behind the conviction, popular among the Polish population, notably in the western provinces, that the Polish administration should regain the economic losses of Poles suffered before 1918. The realisation of this belief was limited because of international treaties and the Polish law. It was, however, an additional reason for the alienation of the German minority in the Polish Republic and also for political conflicts.[16]

Economic and social differentiation in Poland was to a large extent connected with ethnic differences. This helped to maintain several traditional stereotypes, which sometimes survived to the present day. The Belorussian and Ukrainian population was often considered by the Poles as a kind of primitive folk without national tradition or culture. The Belorussians and Ukrainians considered the Poles to be their oppressors from the economic, social and political points of view. The Jews were seen by all three peoples, especially villagers, as the economic exploiters who lived at the expense of the native population. Often religious bias was added.

The growing surplus of the village population who could not find work and sources of income, and similar trends in small trade together with enormous unemployment in industry and administration, influenced rivalries between different social and professional strata as well as within them, often in the shape of ethnic conflicts. The policy of the government, which aimed to promote narrowly interpreted interests of the Polish nation at the expense of national minorities, poured oil on the flames. The Jews had almost no chances to change their profession from the poor independent shopkeeper or artisan to a worker or clerk in industry or administration. On the other hand, they suffered growing pressure from Christian rivals coming from the villages to towns or from the western provinces to the eastern ones. The co-operative movement became an additional threat. In spite of the poverty prevalent among the Jews (the rich stratum was relatively narrow and without significant political influence), there was a general conviction that the Jews were the most influential and affluent group in the country and had enormous backing from abroad. This conviction was even shared by several Polish politicians who were apparently quite reasonable in other areas. Belorussian, Lithuanian and Ukrainian peasants were under the pressure of administration and suffered discrimination in connection with the land reform and in some other matters. The Polish population continued an economic war against their more affluent German neighbours, trying to regain the losses suffered before 1918.

It was not the aim of this chapter to discuss the economic or social policy of the Polish government in its ethnic (national) aspects. Two decades were too short a period to achieve any stable solution to the conflicts that were inherited from past centuries and intensified during the Great Depression, at least not without an instigation from abroad. It is necessary to stress that any solution required – at least from the purely economic point of view – the solution of the agrarian question (that is, the significant diminishing or disappearance of the agrarian over-population) and the creation of new jobs for the people in towns. This would have required vast investments of private capital, which was absent in Poland and which failed to come from abroad. The efforts of the Polish government, lacking time and sufficient financial resources, were inadequate to meet the need.

Most historians, Polish and foreign as well, stress the political aspects of the national question in Poland between the two world wars. There were, no doubt, significant political reasons for the national conflicts. The analysis of the socio-economic situation of the national minorities and the differences between the main regions of the Polish Republic indicates, however, a more complex situation. There were fundamental social conflicts at the bottom of the national question, connected with the past development of individual provinces. It would be impossible to find any solution – even a temporary one – without fundamental changes in the economic and social structure of Poland, rapid economic growth and diminishing differences between backward and developed regions. Without this, social, economic and regional differences constituted a great danger for the Polish Republic and all her citizens. It is, of course, always possible to try out different policies, even in the worst situations, in an attempt to find solutions for existing problems.

The inter-war Polish Republic was by no means the only east European country that contained a mixture of economic, social and ethnic conflicts connected with regional differences. The interconnection of these differences and conflicts was suffered in Czechoslovakia, Romania and Yugoslavia and, to a lesser extent, was known in other countries as well. This situation made the political and ideological conflicts, known in all democratic countries, more complicated and difficult to solve. The difficulties were often even more entangled and impossible to solve because of external intervention, notably from Germany after 1933.

The Second World War strengthened these controversies and clashes of interests as the national strivings of particular nations appeared in conflict. The resettlement of populations and the expulsion of great numbers of people after 1945 decided by the three Allied powers and by individual governments appeared to be the way to solve at least the most dangerous ethnic conflicts. Another solution was the federal reconstruction of the state, as undertaken in Yugoslavia and Czechoslovakia. All these endeavours introduced by the authoritarian political systems failed and could not solve the existing problems. The Communist parties that were at the head of the governments superficially fought ethnic enmity and chauvinism and promoted internationalism. At the same time they exploited the nationalist feelings and ethnic biases in internal feuds of the ruling groups. Often the tragic results of this policy and the heritage of the still-remembered past can be seen in contemporary Europe.

NOTES

1 Official data about the population according to mother tongue were not always in accordance with the reality. This was particularly true in the provinces of Lwów, Stanisławów and Tarnopol. See Edward Szturm de

Sztrem, 'Prawdziwa statystyka' [The true statistics], *Kwartalnik Historyczny* 3 (1973), 664–7. The estimation is from Jerzy Tomaszewski, *Rzeczpospolita wielu narodów* [The republic of many nations], (Warsaw, 1985), pp. 25–37.

2 Stanisław Vinzenz, *Po stronie dialogu* [On the side of dialogue], 2 vols. (Warsaw, 1983), vol. I, p. 193.

3 For a general outline, see Zbigniew Landau and Jerzy Tomaszewski, *The Polish Economy in the Twentieth Century* (London and Sydney, 1985).

4 The basic studies on the Slavic minorities are Krystyna Gomółka, 'Białorusini w II Rzeczypospolitej' [Belorussians in the Second Republic], *Zeszyty Naukowe Politechniki Gdańskiej*, No 495, *Ekonomia* 31 (1992); Ryszard Torzecki, *Kwestia ukraińska w Polsce w latach 1923–1929* [The Ukrainian question in Poland 1923–1929], (Kraków, 1989). On the Lithuanians, Edward Makowski, *Litwini w Polsce 1920–1939* [Lithuanians in Poland, 1920–1939], (Warsaw, 1986).

5 For more detailed analysis of the Belorussian population in Poland, see Jerzy Tomaszewski, 'Białorusini w społecznej strukturze Polski (1921–1939)' [Belorussians in the social structure of Poland (1921–1939)] in Marek Nadolski (ed.), *Między polityką a historią. Księga pamiątkowa na sześćdziesięciolecie profesora Zygmunta Hemmerlinga* [Between politics and history. The memorial book for the sixtieth birthday of Professor Zygmunt Hemmerling], (Warsaw, 1995), pp. 39–49.

6 Roman Horoszkiewicz, 'W poleskich zaściankach szlacheckich' [In the villages of small gentry in Polesie], *Ziemia* 6–7 (1935), p. 127.

7 See Jerzy Tomaszewski, *Z dziejów Polesia 1921–1939. Zarys stosunków społeczno-ekonomicznych* [From the history of Polesie. An outline of the socio-economic relations], (Warsaw, 1963), pp. 136–40.

8 See Jerzy Tomaszewski, 'Białoruska Chrześcijańska Demokracja. Uwagi o kryteriach ocen' [The Belorus Christian democracy. Comments on the criteria of appraisal] in Jerzy Tomaszewski, Elżbieta Smułkowa and Henryk Majecki (eds.), *Studia polsko-litewsko-białoruskie* [Polish–Lithuanian–Belorussian studies], (Warsaw, 1988), pp. 166–9.

9 A basic study on Polish policy is Andrzej Chojnowski, *Koncepcje polityki narodowościowej rządów polskich w latach 1921–1939* [The ideas of the nationality policy of the Polish cabinets, 1921–1939] (Wroclaw, 1979).

10 For more about workers, see Jerzy Tomaszewski, 'Robotnicy Białorusini w latach 1918–1939 w Polsce' [The Belorussian workers in Poland 1919–1939], *Acta Baltico-Slavica* 5 (1967), 93–116; Jerzy Tomaszewski, 'The national structure of the working class in the south-eastern part of Poland 1921–1939', *Acta Poloniae Historica* 11 (1968), 89–111.

11 On the Jews, see Józef Adelson, Teresa Prekerowa, Jerzy Tomaszewski and Piotr Wróbel, *Najnowsze dzieje Żydów w Polsce w zarysie (do 1950 roku)* [An outline of the contemporary history of Jews in Poland (to 1950)], (Warsaw, 1993).

12 See Jerzy Tomaszewski, 'Spring 1919 in Rzeszów: Pogrom or Revolution?' in János Buza, Tamás Csató, Sandor Gyimesi (eds.), *A gazdaságtörténet,*

kihívásai. Tanulmányok Berend T. Iván 65. születésnapjára. [Challenges of economic history. Essays in honour of Iván T. Berend] (Budapest, 1996), pp. 183–91.

13 See Anna Landau-Czajka, 'The image of the Jews in Polish religious periodicals in the Second Polish Republic', *Polin. Studies in Polish Jewry* 8 (1994), 148, 155–64.

14 About the Germans, see Przemysław Hauser, *Mniejszość na Pomorzu w okresie międzywojennym* [The German minority in Pomorze between the two world wars], (Poznań, 1998); Dariusz Matelski, *Mniejszość niemiecka w Wielkopolsce w latach 1919–1939* [German minority in Wielkopolska province 1919–1939], (Poznań, 1997).

15 There is a detailed analysis in Tadeusz Kowalak, *Spółdzielczość niemiecka na Pomorzu 1920–1938* [The German co-operatives in Pomorze 1920–1938], (Warsaw, 1965).

16 See Dariusz Matelski, 'Polityka repolonizacji Wielkopolski w latach II Rzeczypospolitej' [The policy of repolonisation in Wielkopolska in the times of the Second Republic], *Studia Historica Slavo-Germanica* 20 (1995), 47–82.

CHAPTER 18

Economy and ethnicity in the hands of the state: economic change and the national question in twentieth-century Estonia

Anu Mai Köll

Inside the multiethnic states of Imperial Russia and the Soviet Union, the Baltic peoples have been nationalist forces of importance. The Baltic area (see figure 18.1) is on the verge between 'europeanness' and 'otherness', as it has been termed in the discussion on Russian nationalism. In this context, Estonians in the late nineteenth century chose to commit themselves to European culture, partly obliged by Baltic German overlords, partly choosing between them and the Russian central power. German romantic nationalism and its organic view of the state have been recurring in Estonian thought, not only in the nineteenth century, but also in the interwar years. In this, Estonians adhered to the central European rather than to a Scandinavian pattern. This, however, also influenced their way of managing the economy.

Here, economic aspects of nationalism in Estonia will be discussed in the period between the so-called national awakening in the late nineteenth century up to the demise of the Soviet Union in 1991. In this period, Estonia has been subject to four different economic regimes; as part of tsarist Russia, as an independent capitalist nation state, as a socialist republic within the Soviet Union, and again as an independent state with a capitalist and liberal economic policy. Three different aspects of the problem will be addressed here. One is the ethnic division of labour and its consequences. The second aspect is the economic and ethnic policy of the successive governments. Thirdly, attention will be paid to the preservation of the Estonian language and culture as the main concern for nationalist forces. Foreign domination, immigration and very low rates of demographic growth have been perceived as the main threats to survival of the Estonians as a nation.

ESTONIAN NATIONALISM AND INDUSTRIALISATION 1890–1917

In 1897, there were almost a million inhabitants in the area that later became Estonia: 90 per cent were Estonians, 4 per cent Russians and

Figure 18.1. *The Baltic nations*

almost 4 per cent Germans.[1] In tsarist Russia, the provinces were called Estland, Livland and Kurland. Estonians inhabited Estland and northern Livland; Latvians inhabited southern Livland and Kurland. These two peoples speak very different languages. They were ruled by diets, dominated by Baltic German landlords, the *Ritterschaft*, together with Russian governors, and had recently undergone a process of russification. In this way, the Baltic peoples were squeezed between Russians and Germans in an even more literal sense than elsewhere in central and eastern Europe. Power had shifted somewhat from the *Ritterschaft* to Russian administrators, but some also fell, at the local level, on to native Estonians.[2]

The Estonians were mostly peasants, living in the countryside. Since the 1860s it had been possible to buy land from the large estates in pieces of over 20 hectares on average. Thus among the peasant population a small group of yeomen farmers had been formed. Most of the peasants, however, were landless, working on the estates as tenant crofters or labourers. There was also a small, educated countryside elite of schoolteachers, agronomists, parish clerks and so on, who were the mainstay of the national movement that dated back to the 1860s.[3] Before this point, Estonians had not defined themselves as a nationality, but as country folk.[4]

The national movement was inspired by German romantic nationalism, in particular by Johann Gottfried Herder, who actually lived in Riga in Livland during his formative years.[5] The definition of nation was based on language, not race or religion. The language is Finno-Ugric, closely related to Finnish. It is, however, very different from German, Russian, Latvian and Lithuanian. It was emerging as a common national and literary language in the latter part of the nineteenth century, whereas German had earlier been the language of intellectual communication.[6] It is written with a Latin alphabet.

The dominant religion was Protestant Lutheranism. Baltic Germans, the Baltic bishops taking part in the Reformation process from its early days, administered the Church.[7] Russian Orthodox religion was, however, gaining some ground; there were substantial movements of conversion in the 1840s and 1880s among the peasant population.[8] This had, of course, wider cultural implications for the converts, some 10 to 20 per cent of the Estonian peasantry. Religion was thus an area of contest between the two ruling ethnicities.

The Lutheran Church was closely related to the Baltic German minority and the local government of the provinces. The German landlords elected the clergy. Estonians made up most of the congregations, had posts up to parish clerks and were occasionally even appointed as pastors. The Church had an important role in education as well, with literacy being more advanced in the Protestant provinces of Russia than in the Orthodox ones. In the second half of the nineteenth century almost 90 per cent of the population over ten years old could at least read, if not write.[9]

The national movement had a close relationship to economic improvement with the introduction of a yeomanry and educational possibilities for native Estonians. In the late nineteenth century, the russification process opened up some opportunities for Estonians to become civil servants as well. There was, however, no ruling class, and no bourgeoisie among Estonians, their social structure thus being 'incomplete' in the sense of Miroslav Hroch.[10]

The Baltic Germans were, in spite of being only 3.5 per cent of the population, the dominating group. Economically and politically most important were the landlords who also governed the area as *Ritterschaft*, with almost exclusive control of the local diets. Besides the landlords, or the nobility, Baltic Germans lived mostly in the cities. Town dwellers were a diverse group, from intellectuals and professionals, craftsmen and shopkeepers, to paupers.

It is not easy to define the relationship between the Baltic Germans and Germans in the German lands. It is obvious that the economic management of the Baltic estates was inspired by examples in eastern Prussia. When land was sold off to peasants, their land was also consolidated. The productivity of German estates was high compared to the Russian average. As the example of Johann Gottfried Herder shows, there was a certain amount of exchange with other parts of Germany, but this was probably due to the nobility being more international, or at least inter-European, in the early nineteenth century. When, however, Germany was united, the independence of Baltic Germans seemed more menacing to the central power in Russia. The jurisdiction, police force and education were transferred to the Russian governors and there were (very limited) elections for local townships.[11]

In the countryside, class and nationality coincided. Landlords were mostly German, peasants were almost exclusively Estonian. The Baltic Germans made no distinction between class and nationality in their attitudes towards Estonians. The Estonians perceived the social gap as absolute and contradictory. In 1905 and 1917, as well as in 1919, the Baltic German estates were the principal targets for expropriation, insurrection and even arson. In an attempt at class analysis, made in a handbook produced during Soviet rule, 60 per cent of the population before the revolution belonged to the peasantry. Almost half of these, or 25 per cent of the total population, were landless. Industrial workers and their families were 31 per cent, *petite bourgeoisie* 12 per cent and the bourgeoisie 2 per cent, consisting of non-Estonians.[12]

With russification in the 1880s the Russian central power became locally tangible. The economic significance of Russians was principally due to their role as representatives for the state. Besides this, there was a Russian minority in most realms of society, as landlords, merchants, workers and peasants, mostly in the eastern border areas. However, Russian culture and identity were not widely spread except in the border areas. When, for instance, Russian was introduced as the language of education, the situation in the schools became chaotic because the Estonian teachers mainly knew their own language and German. However, as Toivo Raun has shown, this did not contribute to literacy rates going down in the area.[13] The Cyrillic alphabet and the Orthodox religion contributed to the cultural differences.

Unlike the Germans, the Russians thus did not constitute a class or social group. As for the tsar, the Estonians wrote the same kind of very subordinate petitions to him as did other subjects, implying that injustices would be rectified if he took notice of them. This must be regarded as stereotypical behaviour. In the Estonian nationalist movement, discussions of their position towards German and Russian rule were frequent. A pro-German and a pro-Russian orientation developed, and it seems that the pro-Russians were in the majority by the turn of the century.[14]

Industrialisation in Estonia was very rapid in the last decades of the nineteenth century. It came about largely as a result of state intervention, the forced industrialisation initiated by Finance Minister Count Sergei Yulievich Witte. In the Estonian realm, moreover, industrialisation was induced by military needs. Thus, the state was responsible both for investments and for demand. Large-scale textile factories in Narva district produced the goods for army orders. Metallurgic industry in the Tallinn area consisted of shipyards for the reconstruction of the imperial navy, and of workshops for railway material as the trans-Siberian railway was constructed. Besides these state-oriented factories, others developed as well – factories for food products, a furniture factory, and production of paper pulp and paper. This, however, does not change the general dominance of state-generated industrialisation.[15]

Did industrialisation have any national bias? If so, it was not very visible. Initiative was with the Russian modernisers, who made the process work at the central level. One of its basic features was its openness towards foreign investment. Certainly, the process was related to high tariffs and a protected domestic market, and to imperial armament, and was thus a highly nationalist project. But in this period of rapid growth, people from different ethnic groups were invited to participate.

It is probable that the Baltic provinces had higher rates of investments by German capital than other parts of Russia because of cultural contacts with the Baltic Germans. On the other hand, French investment, frequent in the St Petersburg area, was more scarce here. Baltic Germans on the whole did not combine agriculture with industrial activity: they remained agrarian producers, craftsmen and traders. Russians were among investors, but also among workers. Estonians did not participate to any substantial extent as entrepreneurs and industrialists, but they were drawn into the factories as workers and clerks. Urbanisation was rapid, and soon Estonians outnumbered other ethnic groups in the cities. Simultaneously, there was an influx of workers of Russian origin into the area.

By 1914, the Baltic provinces were among the most industrialised parts of Russia. The localisation of industries in this part of the empire was due to harbour facilities in the Baltic Sea and to the vicinity of St Petersburg. There were few local raw materials for the industries, except in the case of paper-making. Cotton, coal, iron and steel were transported by boat or railway. High literacy rates and levels of education contributed to attracting investment, as did the contacts with Germany. But allocation was mainly made according to administrative decisions, not according to calculations of profitability.

The position as one of the economically most developed provinces in the Russian Empire had an impact on the consciousness of Estonians and their attitude towards the rest of the empire. As political crises arose in Russia, the nationalist movement took on attitudes more European than Russian, alleging its closeness to German culture, its Protestant religion and its kinship to the more independent people of the Finnish archduchy. Industrialisation was not exactly an Estonian achievement, but it contributed to the formation of the national consciousness.[16] But it must also be acknowledged that the Estonian population was not united behind the nationalist movement. The leadership of the nationalist movement, as in most places, consisted of the *petite bourgeoisie*, mostly educated countryside officials.[17] The consciousness of workers and landless peasants took other expressions as both the revolution of 1905 and the revolution of 1917 took place in the Baltic provinces. The revolutions were by no means supported by the Russian minority alone, and were carried out with violence.[18]

INDEPENDENCE AND ECONOMIC NATIONALISM 1917–1940

The situation in the area totally changed with the First World War. Bolsheviks took power in the Baltic provinces, and the nationalist movement decided to declare independence and fight the Red Army. Earlier, independence had not been the official goal for the national movement, more realistically discussing forms of local autonomy.[19] Now, the Baltic provinces of Estland, Livland and Kurland were, following the February Revolution, divided into one Estonian-speaking and one Latvian-speaking province, later, with some territorial additions, these became Estonia and Latvia.

Independence was achieved in a chaotic situation. The role of Estonian nationalism in this process was, of course, crucial, but on the other hand the neighbouring Latvia and Lithuania, and also a number of small states in the area, achieved independence at this point. If nationalism was one factor, a larger political game of security in the area was probably also necessary to make the 1920 peace agreement in Tartu possible.

In the new Republic of Estonia, inhabitants were more homogeneous from an ethnic or national point of view than in the same area before the war (see table 18.1). The number of Germans in the Estonian area had fallen by more than half, from 3.5 to 1.7 per cent, by 1922. The population with Russian origins in Estonia had increased with industrialisation, and even if part of the industrial workers went back to the Soviet Union in the years of fighting, the Russian minority became the largest in Estonia.[20] Estonians made up, after independence, 88 per cent of the population in the new republic. A law of cultural autonomy regulated the legal situation of minorities, where minorities had rights to their own language, their own schools and cultural institutions. From 1925 they also had the right to state-supported governing councils to deal with their cultural affairs.[21]

The war arrested rapid economic growth in the area. When Estonians proceeded to take hold of the economy in their territory, there were two factors they did not control. Non-Estonians owned enterprises in Estonia. Practically no Estonians owned the large-scale factories in the territory, although there were a number of lesser enterprises in their

Table 18.1. *Ethnic composition of Estonia in the twentieth century, 1897–1989*

Year	Total population (1,000s)	Estonians (%)	Russians (%)	Germans (%)	Ukrainians (%)	Belorussians (%)
1897[22]	958	90.6	3.9	3.5	–	–
1922[23]	1,107	87.7	8.2	1.7	–	–
1934	1,126	88.2	8.2	1.5	–	–
1945[24]	800 ± 25	94 ± 2	–	–	–	–
1950	845	76 ± 2	–	–	–	–
1970[25]	1,356	68.2	24.6		2.1	1.4
1989[26]	1,583	61.5	30.3		3.1	1.8

hands. Secondly, as explained above, large parts of the local industry were not only tightly linked to the Russian market, it was directly dependent on Russian state orders.

Economic policy at first aimed at finding new markets for existing industries, particularly in western Europe. This did not succeed very well. While the Baltic industries had been advanced, and the Baltic provinces highly economically developed inside the Russian Empire, they still had a development gap in relation to their neighbours to the west. This gap has been discussed elsewhere, particularly in relation to Finland.[27] Finland, although part of the empire, had not been part of the protected domestic market, and so had already had to meet western competition in the nineteenth century.

The crisis was deepest for the metallurgic industry in the area. Paper and pulp production went through a successful restructuring and even showed some growth in relation to prewar production.[28] The textile industry did not resume activity at the same level as before, but survived through export of semi-processed products such as cotton yarn. Its second line of development was to diversify production for the needs of the small domestic market.[29] Shipyards and railway carriages, however, did not find any new outlets, and these enterprises went into a prolonged crisis.

This crisis was also an ownership crisis. Economically dominant groups among the Baltic Germans had probably fled to Germany as the war front crossed the Baltic provinces and, after the war, they faced an entirely new situation. Far from all of them decided to stay on under Estonian or Latvian rule. Alternatives were presumably less forthcoming for Baltic Germans with small economic means, such as craftsmen or shopkeepers. Russian industrialists faced other difficulties, and apparently did not choose Estonia as a new field for activity. English and French capital had been limited in the earlier period.

Estonians had, however, had smaller enterprises in the past, and a great number of new small enterprises were started in the period of independence. Their need for labour was small in comparison with the failing large-scale works from the prewar period. Unemployment was high throughout the 1920s. A small number of workers, both Russians and Estonians, had, on ideological grounds, been joining the Red Army and withdrew with it. This diminished the unemployment numbers somewhat.[30]

In agriculture, revolutionary change took place. A large-scale land reform expropriated the land of all large estates into a state land reserve. This amounted to an expropriation of the Baltic German landlords. The land was subsequently shared among Estonians, those who had participated in the nationalist army having first priority, previous tenants and landless labourers coming next. The land was still sparsely populated, due to low birth rates since the 1880s. The land reform was consciously designed to construct viable farms, with an average around 15 hectares, which, in comparison to contemporary land reforms in eastern Europe, was quite sizeable.[31]

Production on the farms was diversified in the early nineteenth century, and this movement became accentuated with the land reforms. Grain and spirits had been the dominating export articles previously. In the years before war and revolution, some specialisation towards providing the St Petersburg market with fresh livestock products took place. After the land reform this transition continued, in spite of the loss of the Petersburg market. Dairy production and meat production found outlets in Britain and Germany, and the producers chose a co-operative form for processing and marketing, after Nordic, particularly Danish, models.[32] The management of agriculture in the new republic thus passed from Germans to Estonians without losses in productivity and with fairly good success. Butter, bacon and eggs soon became the most important exports of the republic. The extensive rate of organisation among the peasantry and moderate economic success also contributed to the political stability of these turbulent times.

Of course, the land reform did not solve all the problems. The transition to dairy production was only undertaken by approximately half of the farms and, in addition, landlessness remained a problem, although the landless had become a minority in the countryside. But on the whole, giving the land to the tillers gave the agrarian sector and, above all, the individual farm families a standard of living that improved with exports in the 1920s.

The Great Depression hit the agrarian countries harder than the industrialised ones. However, in Estonia it was in the towns, with their prevailing high unemployment rates, that the situation became desperate. There, as in most other central and eastern European countries, a movement with fascist leanings called the League of Veterans (from the struggle for independence) quickly earned support among the young and the unemployed, but also among students.[33] In the countryside they had less support, but the risk was obvious that they might take power in elections.

A preventive *coup d'état* took place before elections in 1934. The interpretation of this event is debated and admittedly complicated. It seems as if racism was not one of the most frequent tenets of the League of Veterans, but they were extremely nationalistic, had an organic view of the state and, above all, fought against ideologies of class struggle and individualism. This was done with the violent methods common to the paramilitary movements of these years. The problem for historians seems to be that the authoritarian government, preventing their takeover, went in precisely the same ideological directions, except for the violent methods. Nationalism was the main ideological component, directed against socialism but also against liberalism, called the 'politics of self-interest', egotism and group egotism. The self-interest ought to be replaced by 'higher interests', which were common to the whole society and for which the state was the representative. Politics favoured groups who wielded state power with violent methods – the army and the police. In the rather well-known typology of Juan Linz, the Estonian authoritarian government would probably be organic conservatism with an invented tradition.[34]

The economic corollary to this kind of thinking was a high degree of state intervention in the economy. Capitalism and profits belonged to the realm of self-interest, although private property was considered natural. In particular, competition was seen as the economic counterpart to party politics, creating splits in society and destroying unity. The higher, common interests were represented by the state.[35] The state became an investor and an entrepreneur on quite a large scale. This was naturally partly due to the lack of other willing investors, foreign because of the crisis, domestic that were few to begin with. Now, necessity was made a virtue. Moreover, the Ministry of Finance, as the central state authority in these matters, was given powers to decide which investments should be allowed in the private sector. It was even given powers to close down existing plants in cases of 'destructive competition'. Finally, the state held monopoly powers in foreign trade and had the right to intervene in the price system.[36] The policy, which was carried through in 1934, was thus very thoroughly state interventionist, and also promoted a nationalistic economy.

The question is whether this rupture with market economics was more radical in Estonia than in other parts of central and eastern Europe. It seems to be the case that the role of the Ministry of Finance was more prominent than in most places. The models explicitly used in the contemporary sources in Estonia were Italy and, more cautiously, Germany; however, the industrialisation policy of Minister Witte was quite close to the Estonian economy after 1934 as well.

The main aim of economic nationalism in this case was probably that the economy should serve the nation, not private interests. But the policy also clearly favoured, as the slogan had it, 'Estonian-speaking Estonian citizens'. The nostrification policy had three different levels. The management of any enterprise should include a majority of Estonians. A number of persons having the essential qualifications of being Estonian-speaking Estonian citizens were added to the boards of directors in private enterprises, without changing the actual ownership structure. Foreign specialists and skilled workers were allowed to have work permits on condition that they had Estonian apprentices who would be able to replace them eventually. According to official statements, only a few foreign specialists were left in the late 1930s. Casual checks do not quite support these statements – for instance, there were foreign specialists in the shale oil industry. Finally, among unskilled workers, Estonians were simply supposed to replace foreigners. Such cases exist, although there is no full picture as yet.

So, as far as I understand, there was no racism in the sense that a particular group was officially denounced as scapegoat for the Depression, but there was a formal nostrification policy, where nationality, interpreted as citizenship and skills of language, were made a condition for economic activity.

Unemployment in Estonia was eradicated in a few years, by both orthodox and unorthodox means, such as demands on enterprises, and particularly state enterprises, to take on workers regardless of need. With the armament boom coming up in the late 1930s, there was a scarcity of manpower. There is some documentation on the importation of labour in the files of the Ministry of Finance.[37] It is evident that work permits were given to seasonal workers in agriculture, but that the restrictions on foreign labour in industry were more severe. To extract shale oil, an important export product with the German marine as a main customer, permits were given only grudgingly to specialists, while applications from less strategic industries were rejected.[38]

In sum, during the period of independence 1919–40, the political as well as a large share of economic power was transferred to Estonians, an ideological dogma having wide support in the country. As market-oriented peasants with co-operative forms of organisation they were quite successful, considering the circumstances. However, the lack of entrepreneurs and of a bourgeoisie was more difficult to overcome in this period, full of economic hardship. Almost all large enterprises had been owned by foreign capital, and many of these failed in the 1920s, so a virtual deindustrialisation took place. Following depression and the *coup d'état*, the state took on the responsibility and was a substitute not only for private financing but also for private management of industry. It is probable that the disadvantages frequently following from protectionism and state enterprises – inefficiency and nepotism – were also present here, but the time up to the outbreak of the Second World War was too short to make any firm conclusions. Finally, the nostrification policies were resolute, economic resources and employment being reserved for Estonian citizens speaking Estonian.

Why did the market economy collapse? In this case, collapse coincided with the demise of parliamentary democracy and was part of a larger European pattern. The backdrop was doubtless difficulties in competing on foreign markets with the most advanced western producers, and the high rate of unemployment resulting from this failure of competition. In my analysis of the Estonian case, however, nationalism, as the ideological opposite to socialism but also to liberalism, has a leading role. It was used as a state ideology to avoid social conflict in the years of economic hardship. When the state had been proclaimed as the true expression of common national interest, the interventionist economic policy was being formed accordingly. No democratic checks were foreseen for the Ministry of Finance, according to the belief expressing a higher interest than individuals and social groups.

INDUSTRIALISATION AND IMMIGRATION IN THE SOVIET PERIOD
1940–1985

Identity does not reside in essential and readily identifiable cultural traits but in relations, and the question of where and how borders towards 'the Other' should be drawn therefore become crucial.[39]

It seems the Estonians were ambiguous in defining the Baltic German nobility as 'the Other' in the nineteenth century. However, with the Russian occupation in the Second World War, the identification of Russians as 'the Other' seems to have been generalised in Estonia.

Soviet rule in Estonia is divided into two periods: the first the occupation in 1940, in conditions of war, soon broken off by German occupation; the second from 1944 to 1991, to which attention is given in this chapter.[40] With a rapid influx of Russians into the Baltic area in the 1940s, continuing into the 1970s, there was national resentment against a new ruling ethnicity, with ideological, but without clear class, connotations.

In the discourse of these years, two expressions convey important aspects of the national problem and its connections with politics and economics. One is the concept of Yestonians (in the vernacular, *jeest-lased*). The Yestonians were ethnic Estonians who had been living in Russia during the period of independence. They were often communists, some of them had withdrawn with the Red Army in 1918, and others had been living in Russia since tsarist times. The nickname is due to the heavy Russian accent with which they spoke Estonian. The concept conveys the importance of language in the definition of nationality in Estonia. Blood was not the criterion, but command, and degree of command, of the language. In this connection it must be remembered that the language is specific and different from Germanic and Slavic languages. Speakers of Estonian number only about 1 million, and in the area there exist a number of languages and national cultures that are on the verge of extinction or extinct, such as the Livs, the Vots and the Ingrians.[41] Extinction is thus the backdrop of Estonian, and probably Baltic, nationalism.

In nationalist historiography written in exile, the Yestonians are typically influenced by the time they had spent in Russia, and their russified names, which were eventually changed to Estonian versions.[42] Clearly, this is not only a question of their language, but also of their being communist and appointed to the leadership after communist takeover. Their personal history bears witness of closeness to Russia, where nationalists want to draw a distinct borderline, and to ideological affinities that are considered non-Estonian. Of course, Estonian bolshevism has existed but, typically, the problem is seen as a dichotomy between communism on the one hand, nationalism on the other.

The second concept is 'bourgeois nationalism', used by Soviet authorities. Whenever there was a purge of the Estonian Communist Party or detentions of *kulaks* or dissidents, they were accused, not of being class enemies or traitors, but of bourgeois nationalism.

Both the concept of Yestonians and of bourgeois nationalism thus indicate that nationalism, in spite of Stalin's stance on the national question, was regarded as the ideological opposite of socialism from both sides, not as a different category that would be compatible with several ideologies. This double function is close to the use of nationalism in the interwar years.

The first years of Soviet rule were characterised by rapid, heavy industrialisation of Estonia of the crash-style typical of Stalinist times. There was a five-year plan for 1946–50, which directed investments to the republic, and the investment per inhabitant was several times higher than investment per inhabitant in the Russian SSR.[43] Strategic investments were made in power plants using local oil shale, producing energy for the north-western area, including Leningrad.[44] Shipyards and machine works, some of them with traditions from the tsarist period, were put to use. Raw materials were imported from distant parts of the Union, and markets were also there. Trade with the west was almost non-existent.[45] Industrial production increased tenfold before 1970, according to available but dubious Soviet statistics. In the same period, the more reliable figure, showing the number of industrial workers, more than doubled (see table 18.2).[46]

This growth was achieved partly through the immigration of workers from other Union republics. Peak influx was in 1945–7, with an estimated 180,000 non-Estonians arriving in Estonia. In this age of late Stalinism, labour mobility had the character of forced labour. After this period, immigration slackened somewhat, but the percentage of ethnic Estonians (including Yestonians) continued to fall from 88 per cent in 1939 to 72 per cent in 1953.[47] In Soviet historiography, the immigrants are presented as specialists and skilled workers, coming to the aid of the new republic when there was a lack of labour power after the war.[48] The level of education of non-Estonians was, in fact, higher than that of the Estonians.[49]

In the so-called thaw period after the death of Stalin, immigration

Table 18.2. *Occupational structure of Estonia in the twentieth century, 1916–94*[50]

Year	Total workforce	Agriculture (%)	Industry (%)	Construction (%)	Trade (%)	Transport (%)	Services, other (%)
1916	[950]	62	21	–	–	–	–
1922	[1,107]	59	15	1	4	3	18
1934	471	45	18	3	6	4	24
1950	290	11	36	6	8	13	26
1970	613	11	37	8	9	10	25
1989	733	20	30	8	7	8	27
1994	649	12	26	7	13	9	32

continued, but on a more voluntary basis. Higher living standards compared to Russia and available housing were pull factors. There was also a certain reflux of Estonians who had been deported to Siberia.[51]

The immigrants from other parts of the Union, mostly Russians, were concentrated in certain branches, certain factories and in certain parts of the land. They dominated industrial work in general, and heavy industry in particular. In industries within the military-industrial complex Estonians were almost entirely absent. This also applies to strategic sectors such as high-sea fishing or the police force.[52]

85 per cent of the non-Estonians lived in towns. They were geographically concentrated in Tallinn and to a district in north-eastern Estonia. In the capital, Tallinn, where most of engineering and metallurgic industry grew up, 47 per cent of the population was Estonian in the 1980s. The share of Estonians in the north-eastern towns of Narva was 4 per cent, in the oil-shale districts Sillamäe, 3 per cent, and Kohtla-Järve 21 per cent.[53] Sectorally and territorially, therefore, segregation was upheld in spite of the large numbers of immigrants.

Language, as the crucial aspect of Estonian nationalism, was part of the segregating forces. Only 13 per cent of the non-Estonians in the republic spoke Estonian. Only a third of Estonians actually admitted having a good command of Russian, in spite of Russian being the first foreign language in the school system, according to a study published during *glasnost* in Estonia.[54]

Only 15 per cent of the non-Estonians resided in the countryside, but the dramatic collectivisation process was still one aspect of the national question. Soviet rule began by a land-to-the-tiller reform, abolishing all holdings over 30 hectares, which was reasonably popular. From 1947 on,

pressures towards collectivisation were made, but the *kolkhozes* made slow
progress. From the highest central authorities in the Soviet Union,
orders were given to direct a blow against the local *kulaks* to speed up the
process. The Estonian Communist Party (ECP) prepared detention lists,
but argued that the need for labour in the local oil-shale mines was such
that there was no need for deportations to Siberia. They were severely
reproached, and eventually, with the help of commissars from other
Union republics, effectuated a large-scale deportation in March 1949.
The estimations of the numbers deported range from 20,000 to 80,000
people, making this probably the most brutal collectivisation process of
the postwar era.[55] In the following two months, the number of collectiv-
ised farms rose from 10 per cent to 70 per cent.[56] Agricultural production declined dramatically.[57]

The deportations were important enough to tilt the population
balance in themselves. The epilogue was that the ECP leadership was
taken to account at the Central Committee meeting of the Communist
Party of the Soviet Union (CPSU) in February 1950, and charged with
bourgeois nationalism. All the Estonians in leading positions were
replaced by Yestonians. The purge reached beyond the party leadership
to, for example, intellectuals, all close to the ECP, and comprised some
3,000 persons. Thus, Estonian communism was practically uprooted.[58]

During the Stalin era, economic decision-making was strongly
centralised. With the thaw period in the latter part of the 1950s, the grip
slackened somewhat. In particular, the *sovnarchozy* reform in 1957 meant
a quite far-reaching decentralisation of economic decisions. Each
republic became a unit of economic administration, and the local *sov-
narchoz* decided something over 80 per cent of the industrial production
in the Estonian Republic, while the rest were responsible to the union
level. The reform, happily received on the local level, created chaos,
however, in the large-scale division of labour, and production tended to
fall due to want of strategic inputs, produced in a distant region.[59] A
mere five years later a wave of recentralisation started throughout the
Soviet Union. In this phase, strategic areas such as power production,
construction and fisheries were subordinated to suprarepublic, regional
sovnarchozy. And in 1965, after the fall of Khrushchev, the *sovnarchozy* were
abolished inside the Soviet Union.[60]

They were replaced with a system of three different levels. Strategic
sectors, such as military industries, but also civil production with military use, for instance electronics, were submitted to all-Union ministries
with central planning. In 1988, there were 171 such enterprises in

Estonia, making up 29 per cent of total industrial production.[61] The engineering and metallurgic industries, and energy and infrastructure, belonged to this level. A predominantly Russian workforce manned these industries. One reason for this was that recruitment was also made at the central level, in Leningrad and Moscow.[62]

The planning committees in the different republics were to prepare projects for other industries, and submit these projects to an all-Union committee. Thus there was participation from both, but the final decisions were taken on the Central Committee on this Union–republic level. The majority of industries in Estonia, including wood processing and textiles, belonged to this middle group. These industries had a higher percentage of Estonian workers.[63] Finally, consumer industries, such as food processing were managed at the republic level. This part of the industry was estimated at 25 per cent in 1965 and only 10 per cent in 1985, but increased in the last years of Soviet rule under Gorbachev.[64] The Baltic republics were used as a laboratory for economic experiments of self-management.[65]

In this way, Soviet Estonia was segregated in both economic and geographical terms, with the all-Union industries conceived as Russian enclaves inside the country. When independence was discussed in 1990–1, before the fall of Gorbachev, the all-Union industries were at the centre of the discussion; they could not be considered as national assets, Soviet negotiators maintained.[66]

From 1949 onwards, there seems to have been a strong element of distrust from the central power towards the ethnic Estonians. The preference for 'Yestonians' as power brokers conveys both a need for national legitimacy and a need for an integrative force, which are contradictory. The tendency not to accept Estonians in the strategic factories and the police force, and the recurring accusations, invariably of bourgeois nationalism, which did not stop with the death of Stalin, express the same attitude.

Politically, of course, the Communist Party was dominant. There was actually an investigation of the ethnic composition of the ECP in 1944–65, which was published in 1966, at the end of the 'thaw' period. According to this study, Estonians were 70–5 per cent of the population at the time, but less than 50 per cent of party members.[67] From the mid-1960s onwards, the share of Estonians was slightly over 50 per cent. The number of ethnic Estonians in the Central Committee also increased after the Stalin era, while the politburo still continued to have a majority of Russians and 'Yestonians'.[68] The majority population thus had a low representation in the party, but the figures do not tell whether this resulted from a want of applications or a want of admissions into the party. The so-called Yestonians were, in this investigation, included among Estonians.

In spite of apparent political suspicions towards the majority population, demonstrated in the tendency to keep them out of strategic economic and political sectors, the central planning authority chose to industrialise the Baltic area more heavily than most other parts of mainland Russia. The decisions were taken in the early years of Soviet occupation – the late 1940s and early 1950s. In this period, deportations and purges took place, but, simultaneously, resources were scarce, and investment in the new republics still exceeded that of Russia by some 50 per cent.[69] In addition to the political and ethnic insecurity in the area, industrialisation meant that raw materials, energy and labour had to be imported. A number of explanations for this puzzling behaviour have been presented. For a final answer, however, the discussions at the central level must be studied in the archives.

One argument for the Baltic area has been the infrastructure assets. In tsarist Russia, the harbours were of primary strategic importance, as well as for the transport system of that period. However, in the Soviet era, trade to the west decreased precipitously, and raw materials, energy and labour were transported into the area mostly from mainland Russia. Due to low raw-material prices, this did not change the investment calculations significantly. Harbours still had important functions for transit to other parts of Russia, but were less crucial than at the beginning of the century. For military reasons (for the Soviet navy) the coastline seems to have been of great value, too. Infrastructural improvements had been undertaken in Estonia in the economic nationalist programmes of the late 1930s. Some railway investments, but mainly electrification and hard-surface roads, belonged to this category.[70]

Secondly, and more specifically, the oil-shale mines of north-east Estonia took on a special importance for the Leningrad area in the 1940s, when energy was in short supply.[71] The mines and the power stations were mostly manned with Russian workers. This production was also the first to be referred to a central level in the *sovnarchozy* period.

Thirdly, closeness to the Leningrad industrial area seems to be a more general way of explaining industrial allocation to the Baltic countries. There is a tradition, albeit short, of industrialisation on the western rim of Russia. Historically, agrarian productivity tended to be higher there, as did educational level. Whether ethnical differences determine the higher education and skill levels, as nationalist historiography sometimes maintains, is, however, debatable.[72]

Fourthly, the allocation can be considered as part of a conscious plan of ethnic integration, the main aim being the immigration of non-Estonians. As a consequence, the working class in Estonia would grow, and supposedly be more inclined to accept socialism than the small-holding peasantry that dominated the period of independence.[73]

NATIONALISM AND DEMISE OF THE SOVIET UNION 1987–1991

As *glasnost* opened the public debate in the Soviet Union, dissent and secessionist tendencies proved to be very strong in all three Baltic republics. Organisations were quickly formed and received massive popular support, mainly along ethnic lines. In the early 1980s, a school reform threatened the position of the Estonian language, which provoked resentment.[74] But the first protest movement in Estonia was of environmental character. A plan for large-scale phosphorite mining in north-eastern Estonia, threatening the water reserves in a large part of the territory, met opposition in the summer of 1987, and was shelved by October. In the autumn, plans for regional economic self-determination in the Estonian Republic began to be discussed in the Estonian press, two years before the fall of the Berlin Wall.[75] In the spring of 1988, a Popular Front for the support of *perestroika*, the first political organisation independent of the Communist Party, was formed in Estonia (it is also said to be the first within the USSR) and was, to a general surprise, accepted by the Soviet regime. Shortly afterwards, demonstrations in Tallinn took on a mass character, and the 'Yestonian' secretary of the ECP was replaced by a 'local' Estonian and friend of Gorbachev.[76] In March 1990, there were elections to the Supreme Soviet of Estonia with independent candidates, and the new body, called the Supreme Council, declared the start of a transition period to the re-establishment of an independent Estonia.[77] The ECP in its majority supported the movement towards independence, but eventually split over the matter. Following the unsuccessful *coup* against Gorbachev in August 1991, a Resolution on National Independence was taken in the Supreme Council, and recognised by Yeltsin and later by the Soviet State Council in September 1991.[78]

The approximately 600,000 non-Estonians reacted by setting up their own organisations. A first pro-Soviet movement, called the Inter-movement, was dismantled because it supported the *coup* against Gorbachev, and was replaced by the Representative Assembly of Russian-speaking Population, which acted according to the Soviet Constitution. The overriding issue since independence has been the citizenship law. In February 1992, Estonian citizens were legally defined as those who were citizens before Soviet occupation and their descendants, thus conspicuously excluding immigrants of the Soviet period. To acquire citizenship, residence in Estonia for three consecutive years and knowledge of the Estonian language is demanded. The latter provision has proved difficult for many Russian-speaking residents. Others protest by not applying for citizenship. Many remain stateless today. For them, new provisions, allowing them to participate in local elections and having a certain cultural autonomy through their own schools and cultural councils, have facilitated life somewhat, but the issue remains crucial in the new state (see figure 18.1).[79]

The legacy of the Soviet Union and its policy of economic development was, first, that industrialisation had been very rapid. The industrialisation that took place was not geared to self-sufficiency; instead, the internal division of labour made independence more difficult. Secondly, the terms of trade in the fixed-price system had been favourable to the Baltic countries with a relative paucity of natural resources and a high level of value added in industry. Trading on the world market, terms of trade turned against the Baltic countries.

A third legacy is a large Russian minority inside the Baltic republics. In Estonia, it is still geographically concentrated in Tallinn and the north-eastern area, and to the factories, which belonged to the all-Union level in the period 1965–85. These factories have known serious problems, but luckily, although many of them partly relied on military production, it seems as if they have been able to change to civilian production, at least to some extent. A large unemployed Russian minority, stateless and depending on a very weak social security system, would obviously be a highly destabilising force. So far, an explosive situation has been avoided, although at a high cost of uneasiness and security for all involved.

CONCLUDING REMARKS

What are the decisive economic aspects of the national question in this part of north-eastern Europe, at the Russian border? It is obvious that, historically, an ethnic division of labour has reigned. The Baltic peoples have been confined to the role of a subdued peasantry, while trade, commerce and entrepreneurship were the lot of their masters. In the first period of independence, this was a problem. Severe nostrification policies and a high level of state intervention in the economy were used to counteract the incomplete class structure. The Soviet era did not exactly reproduce the historical division of labour, but agriculture remained an almost exclusively Baltic occupation, while Estonians were rare to the point of discrimination in leading positions as well as in the most advanced industries, normally related to military needs. Although the level of education is high, the legacy of the Soviet era was not to foster entrepreneurs, traders and commercial talents. To what extent such skills can be quickly learnt in an open economy with international competition is still an open matter.

Estonia has, like most other economies in the European periphery, known state-led industrialisation and economic development inside protected markets. In different forms, and led by different people and nationalities, the state itself has been the main economic actor throughout the twentieth century. The liberal economic policy of the present is, of course, partly due to IMF conditionalities, but endorsed by the elected governments, which have been, by European standards, rather far to the right. There has been a rapid social differentiation in the recent transition period with its losers and its winners, but this differentiation does not seem to be ethnically lopsided. Openness to international investments in the privatisation process has aroused some domestic alarm. Small-scale and growing enterprises are often domestic, while several of the largest producing factories have been bought up, and sometimes also closed down, by international enterprises, often from the Nordic neighbouring countries of Finland and Sweden.

The preservation of the Estonian language, culture and people has been the main aim of nationalist policies. The threat of extinction facing a small and culturally distinctive nation has often enough been real, and should be seen as a backdrop to the harshly nationalist policies of the interwar years, and the treatment of the Russian-speaking minority today. While these reactions might seem somewhat overzealous, there is another problem, which is less discussed today. The combined forces of international mass culture, brain drain and transnational enterprise have swept over the country since independence. State incomes are small and budgetary constraints are rigid. The budget for education and cultural purposes has been severely cut. The open economy, admittedly the only realistic option, might turn out to be another threat to cultural preservation.

NOTES

1 T. Ü. Raun, *Estonia and the Estonians* (Stanford, 1991), p. 72.
2 *Ibid.*, pp. 60–2.
3 M. Hroch, *Social Preconditions of National Revival in Europe* (Cambridge, 1985), p. 77.
4 J. Kahk, 'Peasant movements and national movements in the history of Europe' in A. Loit (ed.), *National Movements in the Baltic Countries during the 19th Century* (Stockholm, 1983), pp. 15–24.
5 E. Jansen, 'Aufklärung und estnische Nationale Bewegung in der zweiten Hälfte des 19. Jahrhunderts' in G. Pistohlkors (ed.), *Aufklärung in den Baltischen Provinzen Russlands* (Vienna, 1996), pp. 57–72 at pp. 59–60.
6 Raun, *Estonia and the Estonians*, p. 77.
7 D. Kirby, *Northern Europe in the Early Modern Period* (London, 1990), vol. I, pp. 83–5.
8 Raun, *Estonia and the Estonians*, pp. 53 and 80.
9 *Ibid.*, p. 55.
10 Hroch, *Social Preconditions*, p. 9.
11 Raun, *Estonia and the Estonians*, p. 61.
12 *Eesti NSV Ajalugu* [History of the Estonian SSR], (Tallinn, 1971), vol. III, pp. 20–1.
13 Raun, *Estonia and the Estonians*, p. 79.
14 E. Jansen, *Carl Robert Jakobsoni 'Sakala'* (Tallinn, 1971), pp. 275–9.
15 A. Köll and J. Valge, *Economic Nationalism and Industrial Growth* (Stockholm, 1998), pp. 32–3.
16 Raun, *Estonia and the Estonians*, p. 59 and T. Ü. Raun, 'The Estonians' in E. C. Thaden *et al.*, *Russification in the Baltic Provinces and Finland* (Princeton, 1981), pp. 287–354.
17 Hroch, *Social Preconditions*, p. 79.
18 Raun, *Estonia and the Estonians*, pp. 83–6 and 102–4.
19 *Ibid.*, p. 104.
20 *Ibid.*, p. 130.
21 *Ibid.*, p. 133.
22 *Ibid.*, p. 72.
23 *Ibid.*, p. 130, based on census data from 1922 and 1934. At independence, border areas with predominantly Russian population were added to the territory.
24 Estimations of the situation in 1945 and 1950 were in *ibid.*, p. 192. In the Second World War, border areas added in 1920 were removed. After 1945, a massive influx of Russian labour took place, not least to supply Leningrad *oblast* with energy from Estonian oil shale.
25 *Eesti NSV rahvamajandus 1970 aastal* [Soviet Estonian economy in 1979], (Tallinn, 1971), p. 29.
26 B. Van Arkadie and M. Karlsson, *Economic Survey of the Baltic States* (London, 1992), p. 20; Raun, *Estonia and the Estonians*, p. 182.

27 T. Myllyntaus, 'Standard of living in Estonia and Finland in the 1930s', *ETA Toimetised, Proceedings of the Estonian Academy of Sciences* 41(3) (1992), 184–91 and M. Herranen and T. Myllyntaus, 'Effects of the First World War on the engineering industries of Estonia and Finland', *Scandinavian Economic History Review 3* (1984), 121–42.

28 A. M. Köll, 'The development gap' in *Emancipation and Interdependence* (Stockholm, 1998), pp. 33–4.

29 Köll and Valge, *Economic Nationalism*, pp. 187ff.

30 *ENSV Ajalugu*, vol. III, p. 214. This official historiography from the Soviet period will evaluate the evidence of Estonian bolshevism higher than would be reasonable, but often the numbers are right.

31 A. M. Köll, *Peasants on the World Market* (Stockholm, 1994), p. 48.

32 *Ibid.*, p. 70.

33 For parallels, see E. Hobsbawm, *The Age of Extremes* (London, 1995), pp. 110–16; the history of the Estonian movement is in R. Marandi, *Must-valge lipu all* [Under the black and white flag], with a summary in German (Stockholm, 1991).

34 Hobsbawm, *The Age of Extremes*, pp. 113–14.

35 Köll and Valge, *Economic Nationalism*, pp. 53–6.

36 *Ibid.*, pp. 78–9.

37 In the archives of the National Finance Committee, April 1937; Estonian National Archives, f. 891/1.

38 Köll and Valge, *Economic Nationalism*, p. 75.

39 I. B. Neumann, *Russia and the Idea of Europe* (London, 1996), p. 1.

40 This part of this chapter does not rely on my own research but, rather, on critical reading of the historiography. Due to the extreme polarisation of nationalist history in exile on the one hand and Soviet-type history on the other, in particular regarding this period and precisely this issue, the task is difficult. It is possible to see an outline of events, but I have been very restrictive in reproducing figures that seem to be gross estimations.

41 Booklet by Harald Runblom, *The Multicultural Baltic Region* (Uppsala, 1994), part I, p. 26.

42 The presentations of Johannes Käbin and Karl Vainu in R. Misiunas and R. Taagepera, *The Baltic States – Years of Dependence* (London, 1983), at pp. 79ff., for instance.

43 S. Sinilind, *Mõningatest rahvuspoliitika aspektidest* [Some aspects of national policies], (Stockholm, 1983), p. 37.

44 Raun, *Estonia and the Estonians*, p. 175 and P. Sandström, *Baltiskt dilemma* (Stockholm, 1991), p. 62.

45 Van Arkadie and Karlsson, *Economic Survey*, p. 8.

46 Misiunas and Taagepera, *The Baltic States*, pp. 285ff.

47 *Ibid.*, p. 108 and Sinilind, *Mõningatest rahvuspoliitika aspektidest*, p. 20. The personnel of the Red Army are excluded.

48 *ENSV Ajalugu*, vol. III, p. 563 and A. Juursoo and R. Pullat, *A Brief History of the Estonian Working Class* (Tallinn, 1981), pp. 106ff.

49 Misiunas and Taagepera, *The Baltic States*, p. 207. This was due to the fact that the immigration did not include peasants.

50 In table 18.2: 1916 and 1922 are based on calculations of the total population, not the active population; 1916 is an estimation, made in *Eesti NSV Ajalugu*, vol. III, pp. 20–1 (the statistical services in the Baltic provinces of tsarist Russia were not very efficient); the data from 1922 are based on a population census; the 1934 data are from *Estonie en chiffres 1920–1935* (Tallinn, 1936), pp. 15–17; 1950 and 1970 data are from *Eesti NSV rahvama-jandus*, p. 237; and 1989 and 1994 data are from *International Labour Statistics* (International Labour Office, Geneva, 1996).

51 Misiunas and Taagepera, *The Baltic States*, pp. 186ff.

52 Van Arkadie and Karlsson, *Economic Survey*, p. 92 and Sandström, *Baltiskt dilemma*, p. 27.

53 Sandström, *Baltiskt dilemma*, p. 92.

54 *Etnilisest ühendusest sotsialistliku rahvuseni* (From ethnic unity to socialist nations], (mimeo, Tartu, 1987), pp. 140–2.

55 The variation in different estimations is dramatic, and they have been done without full access to the local archives. Only local studies have been made since independence. Among them, a Masters thesis from Tartu University by Aigi Rahi estimates the total number at 27,000.

56 Misiunas and Taagepera, *The Baltic States*, pp. 93–9 and Raun, *Estonia and the Estonians*, pp. 176–81.

57 Van Arkadie and Karlsson, *Economic Survey*, p. 99.

58 Misiunas and Taagepera, *The Baltic States*, p. 79 and Raun, *Estonia and the Estonians*, p. 181.

59 For a general discussion of the reform, see A. Nove, *An Economic History of the USSR* (London, 1992), pp. 367–9.

60 Misiunas and Taagepera, *The Baltic States*, pp. 179ff.

61 Sandström, *Baltiskt dilemma*, p. 57ff.

62 *Ibid.*, pp. 26ff and 58; also Misiunas Taagepera, *The Baltic States*, pp. 186ff.

63 Sandström, *Baltiskt dilemma*, p. 58.

64 *Ibid.*, p. 73; Raun, *Estonia and the Estonians*, pp. 198–200.

65 Raun, *Estonia and the Estonians*, p. 233; R. Kionka, 'The Estonians' in G. Smith (ed.), *The Nationalities Question in the Soviet Union* (London, 1990), pp. 40–53 at p. 44.

66 Sandström, *Baltiskt dilemma*, pp. 111ff.

67 A. Panksejev, 'EKP tegevusest partei ridade kasvu reguleerimisel aastad 1944–1965' [Activities of the ECP concerning regulation of party membership in 1944–1965] in *Töid EKP ajaloo alalt* [Works on the history of the ECP], vol. II (Tallinn, 1966), cited in Misiunas and Taagepera, *The Baltic States*, pp. 281–4.

68 Raun, *Estonia and the Estonians*, pp. 190ff and Sinilind, *Mõningatest rahvuspoliitika aspektidest*, p. 75.

69 *ENSV Ajalugu*, p. 571.

70 Van Arkadie and Karlsson, *Economic Survey*, p. 7; Misiunas and Taagepera, *The Baltic States*, p. 104; Köll and Valge, *Economic Nationalism*, app. I.

71 *ENSV Ajalugu*, pp. 573–5; Misiunas and Taagepera, *The Baltic States*, p. 107; Sandström, *Baltiskt dilemma*, p. 62.

72 Van Arkadie and Karlsson, *Economic Survey*, p. 9; Sandström, *Baltiskt dilemma*, p. 85; Sinilind, *Mõningatest rahvuspoliitika aspektidest*, p. 37.

73 Misiumas and Taagepera, *The Baltic States*, p. 107 and Sandström, *Baltiskt dilemma*, p. 85.

74 Raun, *Estonia and the Estonians*, pp. 211ff.

75 *Ibid.*, p. 223; Sandström, *Baltiskt dilemma*, pp. 11 and 20; R. Kionka and R. Vetik, 'Estonia and the Estonians' in G. Smith (ed.), *The Nationalities Question in the Post-Soviet States* (London, 1996), pp. 129–46 at p. 135.

76 Sandström, *Baltiskt dilemma*, pp. 28ff; Kionka and Vetik, 'Estonia and the Estonians', pp. 137ff.

77 Raun, *Estonia and the Estonians*, p. 230; Kionka and Vetik, 'Estonia and the Estonians', p. 138.

78 Kionka and Vetik, 'Estonia and the Estonians', p. 138 and A. Lieven, *The Baltic Revolution* (New Haven, MA, 1994), p. 426.

79 Kionka and Vetik, 'Estonia and the Estonians', pp. 142ff.

CHAPTER 19

Changing structure and organisation of foreign trade in Finland after Russian rule

Riitta Hjerppe and Juha-Antti Lamberg

INTRODUCTION

Finland became independent in December 1917. Separation from Russia and the new European 'economic order' imposed many important changes on the Finnish economy after the First World War. Very notable were the changes in foreign and Russian trade, which were of utmost importance to the Finnish economy – separation virtually ended the considerable trade with Russia. New markets and a reorganisation of trade were needed. Finland's independence was also very significant for many groups in society. The Finns were not a united people with clear goals; rather, there were severely conflicting fronts. There were the rightist/White and leftist/Red fronts, which led to a civil war a few months after independence, the result being a White victory and a politically divided people.

There were also the nationalistic groups whose ideas had been stimulated by the nationalistic movements of the other European countries from the middle of the nineteenth century. It is difficult to determine the goals of the nationalistic movement as they seem to have changed over time and were sometimes even conflicting. On the one hand, an important goal of the nationalistic movement was a better position for the Finnish language, the language of the majority. On the other hand, the aim was a better position for Finland in the Russian Empire.[1] It seems obvious to try to get a better position, but total independence was not, however, a unanimous goal of the nationalistic movement, even if from the 1890s on, the russification programme[2] had antagonised the nationalists. In addition, Swedish-speaking groups also had strong nationalistic aims concerning the autonomous position, or even the independence, of Finland.

But was there a connection between the nationalistic ideas and the economic goals? Did the various groups in the economy take nationalistic views into account in their economic activities? Studies of nationalistic movements characteristically bypass economic questions.[3] An exception is Miroslav Hroch, who briefly mentions one group of economic actors. He claims that the industrialists of a subordinated group generally do not address national questions but rather follow the views of the stronger partner, and that they stress economic questions in their activities.[4]

Traditionally, historians have assumed that major political changes also affect economic development strongly. Sometimes that is clearly the case – for example, the Revolution of 1917 radically modified the whole economic structure of Russia. Still, the problem of the impact of institutional or political changes on economic growth is much more complicated if we adopt the hypothesis of Douglass C. North. He argues that institutional change occurs because of the interaction between the organisations, both formal and informal constraints, in contrast to the traditional assumption that emphasises the importance of the formal constraints. Institutional change means to North that 'yesterday's choices are the initial starting point for today's'. North argues that 'even when revolutions occur they turn out to be far less revolutionary than the initial rhetoric would suggest'.[5]

This chapter takes a pragmatic position and defines Finland's independence as an absolute solution of the national question. Independence is interpreted as an 'historical accident' which was not expected, especially among business circles. Also analysed is how 'revolutionary' were the economic impacts of the First World War, independence and the civil war of 1918 on Finland's foreign trade and trade relations. The chapter also tries to determine whether nationalistic ideas were guiding economic activities or if the economy evolved without being influenced by, or even evolved in contradiction to, nationalistic ideas.

The chapter concentrates on the economic situation and foreign economic ties of Finland during the couple of decades before the First World War, during the war and immediately after it, and finally how the situation was stabilised in independent Finland in the 1920s. The foreign trade relations of Finland are considered, as Finland was a very open economy during the second half of the autonomous period (from the 1860s to 1917). A closer look is taken at what happened to the organisation of foreign trade and how decisions concerning foreign trade relations were made after independence.

Foreign trade as well as macroeconomic development have been studied in the past, particularly by Erkki Pihkala, Per Schybergson, Jorma Ahvenainen and Riitta Hjerppe.[6] Therefore it is not necessary to

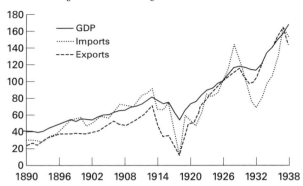

Figure 19.1. The volume indices of GDP, imports and exports of goods, 1890–1938
(1926 = 100)
Source: Riitta Hjerppe, *The Finnish Economy 1860–1985. Growth and Structural Change*
(Helsinki, 1989).

go into detail, but rather explain the main lines of developments from
our point of view. The creation of organisations dealing with foreign
trade policy has not been presented in this way before, and the information has been compiled from the archives of the organisations and the
Ministry of Trade and Commerce as well as from academic literature.

THE ECONOMY

Economic development in Finland 1890–1913

The Finnish economy was undeveloped at the beginning of the
autonomous period, in 1809, and it was mainly based on subsistence
agriculture with a small commercial sector. The first manufacturing
enterprises, using modern technology, found their markets in Russia.
These were aided by Finland's favoured customs position.[7] The Finnish
economy grew gradually, at least from the 1820s on, even if the standard
of living was still very low. Towards the end of the nineteenth century
growth accelerated and the decades before the First World War can
definitely be characterised as a period of industrialisation (see figure
19.1).

From the middle of the nineteenth century Finland experienced rapid
structural changes, particularly significant among which was the
increase in the openness of the economy. The relation of export and
import values to GDP had quickly grown from insignificant levels to

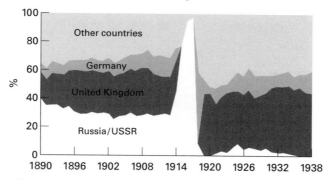

Figure 19.2. The distribution of exports by country, 1890–1938
Source: Kaarina Vattula, *Suomen taloushistoria* III, *Historiallinen tilasto* [Finnish economic history, vol. III, Historical statistics], (Helsinki, 1983).

about a fifth and a quarter respectively. Those were considerable shares in those days.[8] It has been considered that economically Finland had a relatively favourable position as a part of the Russian Empire because of the trade opportunities it opened to the Finns.[9] Russian trade was at its highest in the 1860s, 1870s and 1880s when about half of Finland's imports and exports were with Russia.[10] This share clearly declined by the outbreak of the First World War when more than a quarter of the trade was with Russia. Germany replaced Russia as a major supplier of goods and Great Britain became the largest export country (see figures 19.2 and 19.3).

The structure of trade also changed. During the autonomous period Finnish exports were divided as follows. The Russian market welcomed textiles, other consumer goods and increasing amounts of paper made of wood fibre; relatively unprocessed pig iron and wrought iron were gradually replaced by engineering products.[11] While absorbing relatively few processed products based on timber or cattle rearing, the western market bought diminishing amounts of tar, but rapidly increasing amounts of sawn timber and some butter.[12] During the last years before the First World War, three quarters of exports contained products based on wood, mostly sawn goods, but also paper, pulp and round timber. The export selection actually became more one-sided towards the last decades of the nineteenth century: sawn timber to western markets and paper to Russia.

Exports paid for imports, which for the most part were raw materials and intermediate products, most importantly grain. Finnish grain tariffs had been abolished in the spirit of free trade in the 1860s (Russian grain

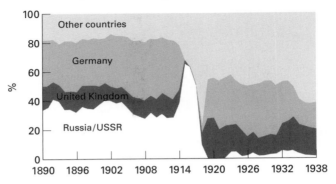

Figure 19.3. The distribution of imports by country, 1890–1938
Source: Vattula, *Suomen taloushistoria* III.

would have come to the country duty free in any case). Other primary import items from Russia were raw sugar and raw tobacco. Finnish self-sufficiency in grain was only about 40 per cent before the First World War. Finland had actually adapted itself well to the world of relatively free trade and was importing materials it was not very fit to produce because of natural conditions (notably grain). It paid for the latter with products better suited to Finnish conditions (cattle products, timber). Raw material imports as a share of total imports was 56 per cent in 1890, which grew to 60 per cent in 1913.

The second important group of imports consisted of consumer goods, partly from Russia, partly from western countries. The third was made up of investment goods, the share of which was still low. In an undeveloped country, the investment ratio was still low, and so was the need of investment goods in trade. About 6 per cent of imports consisted of machinery and equipment in 1890. This share had risen to 9 per cent in 1913. What is significant about imports is that almost no investment goods came from Russia – they came mainly from Germany and the United Kingdom.

Finland also had other lively international relations through migration, through the activity of some foreign entrepreneurs, through financial ties and the gold standard.[13] The Finnish Senate was a borrower on the international financial market, both in St Petersburg and in central European financial centres since the 1860s.[14] Proximity of the large city of St Petersburg was an important factor in the livelihood of the people in the south-eastern border area, the Carelian Isthmus. They could provide the city with food and firewood, for example, and also find work there for longer or shorter periods of time. Finnish companies and private businessmen consistently had lively commercial relations with Russians, for example the sales agencies of the Finnish paper industry. Many Finnish businessmen acted primarily in the Russian markets.

World war years

When the First World War started, the most important effects on the Finnish economy were problems of foreign trade. The largest import item, flour from Germany, and the largest export item, sawn goods to the United Kingdom, plummeted immediately, as all imports from Germany, an enemy country, were prohibited, and Germany also closed the seaway to the United Kingdom. Consequently, many branches of industry faced great difficulties because of lack of imported raw materials or intermediate goods: chemicals for the paper industry, cement for construction, cotton for textile factories, coal for fuel. Some of these were partly replaced by imports from Russia or transit traffic through Sweden, some by transportation via the Arctic Sea. Trade in food had been controlled by Finland's Senate, the government, since 1914, and, at the same time, the first domestic rationing organisations for food distribution were created.[15]

At the outbreak of war, the Russian army sent its orders to Finnish industry. The Finnish engineering industry, as well as the textile, leather and shoe industries, could sell all they could produce. In the metal industry this even led to the expansion of plants.[16] About a quarter of all import and export volumes were lost immediately in 1914, but then volumes remained at about this level in 1915 to 1916.[17] GDP fell by 4 to 5 per cent in 1914 and 1915, but by 1916 the decrease stopped because of increased orders for war supplies from Russia.

The revolutions of 1917 threw the Russian economy into turmoil, and the Finnish economy really started to suffer. Finnish imports and exports dropped by about 40 per cent, GDP by 16 per cent. Exports to Russia continued until the summer, but not all of them were paid for; the unfavourable exchange rates also caused losses for Finnish industrialists. The most dramatic collapse was in the grain trade where imports fell from 378,000 tons in 1916 to 27,000 tons in 1917, when imports ceased altogether early in the year. In addition to food shortages, the chaotic conditions in Russia caused unemployment in Finland. The Russians discontinued fortification works in southern Finland, and industries laid off workers when orders stopped coming in. The end of the small-scale peasant trade in St Petersburg and the disappearance of the Russian vacationers caused economic difficulties for the inhabitants of eastern Finland, particularly those of the Carelian Isthmus.[18]

Independence and the civil war

Finland's declaration of independence in December 1917 in no way changed the economic situation immediately. International recognition of independence took time and so did the political and administrative reorientation. The economic problems were well known, but it was obvious that there were no quick solutions. There was no balance of political power in the new nation, either. Accordingly, the situation soon turned into chaos. For example, there were 40,000 Russian soldiers in the country and the labourers and leftist peasants began to form Red Guards units following the Russian example. On the other side, the middle class and other peasants organised paramilitary groups in all parts of the country and also sent a couple of thousand of their young men to Germany to be trained as soldiers for the expected battle for independence. In addition, just before the outbreak of civil war, Finnish officers who had fought in the Russian army but had returned to Finland started to form the White Army under the leadership of Baron Carl Gustav Emil Mannerheim.

Social and political contrasts led to a civil war in January 1918. Practically the whole of southern Finland was at war. Military operations were, at least at first, more chaotic than organised. However, quite soon the White Army was able to dominate the war and to defeat the Red Army, which was supported by some Russian units. Additionally, German troops came to Finland to help the White Army and they conquered Finland's capital, Helsinki. The last Red units surrendered at the beginning of May 1918.

The civil war and the First World War reduced economic activity still further. In 1918 GDP fell by another 13 per cent, bringing the total fall since 1913 to one third. Many factories were closed for months and the production volume of industry, which had kept its prewar volumes because of Russian demand, dropped by a fifth in 1917 and more than a third in 1918, to about half of the 1913 level. In 1918 foreign trade volumes were only about a tenth of the pre-war level, and only minimal amounts of grain, previously a necessity, were imported. In 1918 imports and exports were hardly possible other than with Sweden, Denmark and Germany. The difficult situation led to unfavourable trade agreements

with Germany, Austria-Hungary, Turkey and Bulgaria, which were subsequently nullified by the Versailles Treaty. New trade partners were
sought, for example in the Ukraine and southern Russia, but that did not
succeed, either.

Foreign trade was strictly controlled by the domestic rationing organisations from January 1918 to the autumn of 1919. Also the Inter Allied
Trade Committee was monitoring trade from February 1919 to the
autumn of that year. Trade with Germany was forbidden. Because of
the unresolved situation regarding political and economic relations,
trade with Soviet Russia required permission from Finland's Ministry of
Trade and Industry until the spring of 1921 – that is, until after the Tarto
peace treaty.[19]

Stabilisation of the economy after the First World War

While Finland's eastern trade virtually ceased and stayed insignificant
during the interwar period, western trade, however, revived relatively
quickly (see figures 19.1, 19.2 and 19.3 for trade details). Looking at the
stabilisation of trade relations both in the short run and in the longer
run, Ahvenainen holds that the most important period in the formation
of postwar trade relations was the period 1918–20.

In the short run, Soviet Russia, because of the civil war, was unable
to deliver goods that were desperately needed in Finland – grain, sugar,
tobacco and other raw materials. The shortage of imported food may
have even contributed to the outbreak of the civil war in Finland.
Regionally, the impact of the separation from Russia affected the
country unevenly. It caused critical difficulties to the population and
businesses of eastern Finland, which had had close connections with the
Russians.[20]

In the longer run, the Tarto peace treaty in late 1920 was not satisfactory from an economic point of view and no trade agreement could be
worked out during the 1920s and 1930s between Finland and the Soviet
Union.[21] Finland, which was very dependent on foreign trade, had to
seize every opportunity to start trade. Finnish producers looked for and
found new markets in the west. Furthermore, products, which had previously been bought from Russia, started to be in ample supply at favourable prices in world markets. Many Finnish agriculturists and forest
owners were unhappy with potential Soviet competition in grain and
round timber and did not want revival of trade.[22] Relatively quickly, the
need for many economic ties between Soviet Russia/the Soviet Union

and Finland disappeared.[23] On the other hand, it is not surprising that Finnish merchants and industrialists were hoping that eastern markets would become accessible. Particularly paper exporters, who had had their major markets there, were eager to continue trade with familiar customers, even if there was uncertainty about the continuance of trade as some of their bills from the revolution year remained unpaid. An important hindrance was the new Soviet bureaucracy, which made direct private trade relations impossible. However, the continuation of old relations would still have been a relief. It is difficult to see any nationalistic motivation in the activities of businessmen, whose motive was to make profits.

Nationalistic ideas were not hindering some new entrepreneurs from entering eastern Finland in the 1920s. They wanted to use the vast natural resources of Soviet Carelia, and built wood-working factories, saw-mills and pulp factories with the aim of buying their round wood from Carelia. The use of imported timber stayed insignificant, however. The overall trade shares with the Soviet Union rose to less than 5 per cent at their highest in the middle of the 1920s.[24]

Western trade routes opened in February 1919. Finnish exports started to rise from 1918 and reached a fivefold increase. Foreign trade regained its important place. The timber and paper industries were the first to reach their prewar levels. In the interwar period, the structure of Finland's exports came to be almost totally dominated by wood, paper and pulp (on average 85 per cent, 1920–38). The commodity structure had changed in the direction it had already begun to take around the turn of the century. In 1919 GDP rose by a fifth, and another 12 per cent in 1920. The growth of GDP in the 1920s and the 1930s developed very favourably (4.7 per cent annual growth, 1920–38). The currency situation stabilised after about two to three years of turbulence, and Finland joined the new gold standard in 1926.

Sawn goods relatively quickly found their old markets in the west. The reconstruction boom caused an enormous demand for timber when the war was over, and prewar volumes of wood and paper were reached or passed in 1920. Some pulp had been sold to the western market since the 1890s and this continued slowly. The bulk of paper had gone to Russia before and during the war, but there was little or no hope of recovering the markets there. The new western buyers were more interested in mechanical and chemical pulp than paper.[25] The relative share of paper as a proportion of total exports fell while that of pulp increased.

Consequently, the result of trading solely with the west was a change of exports to less-processed goods. This pattern persisted for a long time.

The chaos in Russia favoured the Finnish wood-working industry as Russian sellers stayed out of the export markets of timber until the end of the 1920s. Finland was one of the largest sellers of timber in the international markets in the 1920s and 1930s.

The reorientation to western export markets was relatively smooth and was aided by the foundation of producers' cartels after the civil war. As producers of bulky, relatively unprocessed items, the separate sellers were not large enough in the international market. However, with the support of strong central marketing organisations, domestic producers were able to find buyers and stabilise their position in western markets. The most important cartels were created in the pulp, paper and wood-fibre industries. Dairy producers had already created a central sales organisation, Valio, before the First World War. The producers of sawn timber did not, however, centralise their sales except for a short period after 1918. Engineering products and ships as well as consumer goods, which had already been losing significance in trade with Russia, were almost totally without foreign markets. Even on the domestic market, they had to compete hard with western products, which forced the industries that had to compete with imports to seek tariff protection.

The commodity structure of imports soon regained its earlier content: raw materials and intermediate goods dominated. Investment goods actually increased their share as consumption goods relatively declined. By 1922 the main western trade partners had almost secured the shares that they would hold up to the 1930s. In addition to the earlier trade partners – namely the United Kingdom and Germany – Sweden and the United States also came to have significant shares.

FOREIGN TRADE POLICY

Administration of trade during the autonomous period

Finland stayed administratively relatively independent during the period of the Grand Duchy (1809–1917). The bureaucratic machinery developed significantly while economic growth was accelerating. Finnish foreign trade relations were characterised by a lack of their own trade agreements,[26] but, on the other hand, by formal customs autonomy. After 1810 Finland was treated as an independent customs area even in relation to Russia. Consequently, it had its own tariff administration with, for example, its own trade statistics. Nevertheless, Finland had to follow Russian guidelines in foreign trade policy. During the 1850s, 1860s and 1870s, Finland's customs duties became low, especially on food imports. It has been claimed that after 1880, when many countries returned to more protected markets, Finnish politicians and bureaucrats were reluctant to try to raise duties because they were afraid that the Russian government would incorporate Finland more closely into the Russian customs area. However, Finland's tariff policy can be characterised as passive at the beginning of the twentieth century.[27]

Foreign trade administration during the civil war

Since Finland had no military organisation under the Russian regime, the army had to be recruited from volunteers. It is natural that the most competent civilians got the top positions of responsibility in the White Army. The Finnish business elite – factory owners, landlords and professional managers – came to dominate the decision-making and administration, especially regarding economic questions.[28] Already, at the very beginning of the civil war, it was obvious that the financial and material problems had to be solved before any serious military manoeuvres could be started. On these questions, the role of the representatives of industry and banks became crucial. Finnish banks were able to finance military expenses.[29]

There was also a need for quick organisation of the foreign policy administration. Foreign policy, foreign trade policy and military issues were the only sectors in which there was no significant bureaucratic tradition from the prewar period. Two central organisations, the Special Staff of Engineers[30] of the White Army and the Trade and Industry Commission were formed to perform economic policy tasks. The most important administrative and organisational decisions concerning foreign trade were made in these two organisations, which controlled non-food trade during 1918 and 1919: the former controlled foreign trade during the civil war and the latter was created to take over its functions after the war in the spring of 1918. The Trade and Industry Commission was discontinued in 1919 and replaced by more formal and permanent organisations, initially by the Ministry of Trade and Industry.

The Special Staff of Engineers was appointed in January 1918 by the Commander-in-Chief of the White Army with the task of 'learning what stocks of commercial and industrial commodities were already in the country and taking the initiative in both putting them to use and in creating new branches of production'. The control of foreign trade was also the responsibility of the Staff.[31] The Staff was divided into six sub-sections, of which the Section of Economy and Purchases was responsible for foreign trade policy. Regionally, Finland was divided into eight 'Engineering Territories'.[32] At the end of the war there were about 100 'engineers' working at the managerial level.

The higher officers of the Staff were engineers who had previously worked in Finnish industry. The managing director of the Staff was Gustaf Aminoff, who was responsible to Gösta Serlachius, the 'chief of the Equipment Section', owner of a big pulp and paper company, and to Rudolf Walden, the 'manager of the Service Section of the White Army', who later owned the mighty paper and pulp corporation, the United Paper Mills. The officers who had responsibility for the territories also belonged to the small group of key persons in Finnish trade and industry. Worth special mention are Väinö Matti Viljanen and Axel Solitander, who were later recruited as managers for the national pressure groups: Viljanen for the Association of Finnish Industry (AFI) and Solitander for the Central Association of Finnish Woodworking Industries (CAFWI). Walden, Solitander and Viljanen can be described as 'new faces' in the Finnish business elite, as they clearly improved their status during the civil war.[33] These men were businessmen with a strong self-interest and were only loosely connected to the nationalistic movement. Their willingness to join rationing organisations can be analysed as profit-seeking rather than nationalistically motivated behaviour, even though it is obvious that these key people had patriotic motives, too.

The formative period (1918–1919) in foreign trade administration

The Special Staff was planned to take care of military and wartime needs and the leading officers felt that the organisation was unable to take responsibility for postwar non-military issues. When the defeat of the Red Army seemed probable in April 1918, the Staff of Engineers recommended that the Senate of Finland create a civil organisation that would replace the Staff. Aminoff also promised to provide the new organisation with personnel.[34] Consequently, the Senate of Finland decided to create a Trade and Industry Commission (TIC) in April 1918. Its task was to supervise trade and industry, including export and import trade. As the workload of the Commission increased, new subsections were created. The most important of these was the Licence Bureau, which dealt with export and import applications.[35] It was stated in the regulation of its foundation that the chairman and the members of the Commission were to be chosen from 'the leading representatives of industry, trade, banking, agriculture and also of the state administration'.[36] In practice, the highest personnel of the Staff of Engineers moved to the new organisation – for example, Gustaf Aminoff himself and Solitander and Viljanen from the Territorial Section got the top posts.[37]

What must be underlined is the fact that the people who demanded the creation of the Commission, and later changes to the organisation, were themselves members of the Staff of Engineers and later members of the executive committee of the TIC.[38] Consequently, the formative period of the new trade policy institutions/organisations was characterised by the influence of a relatively small group of people who could affect the early trade policy and integrate themselves and the private sector into the political decision-making machinery.

Douglass C. North uses the term 'window of opportunity' to describe a situation where some extraordinary institutional changes are possible. Accordingly, it can be claimed that Finland's civil war and the rationing period were this kind of a 'window', which made it possible for those in economic circles to integrate into the political system. It was at this particular time when persons such as Solitander and Viljanen obtained high positions and acquired the power they were able to hold during the whole interwar period. The Staff of Engineers and the Trade and Industry Commission themselves were only temporary controlling organs that faded when the economic and political system normalised after 1919. But with these organisations, the private sector was permanently drawn into the decision-making process, and this continued in the following decades.

The period of stabilisation in Finnish foreign trade policy (1919–1939)[39]

Finland started to stabilise her foreign trade policy after 1919. The rationing system had to be ended and it was necessary to create a policy and administration that would fit into normal international conditions. Foreign trade policy was to be implemented in a world which had not yet recovered from the shock of the war and was living in an era of economic nationalism. Finland had lost her markets in Russia, the western countries had moved toward protectionism, and the Finnish administrative system was badly unprepared. Among other problems, Finnish prohibition law had irritated the wine-exporting countries and Finland was threatened with the loss of her markets in those countries that had previously taken about 15 per cent of Finnish exports.[40]

The principal questions, which actually came to determine Finland's foreign trade policy in the interwar years, were officially formulated as follows: first, protection of national agriculture and self-sufficiency in essential foodstuffs; secondly, protection of industry working exclusively or mainly for the home market; and thirdly, maintenance and expansion of exports of products based on the natural resources of the country by means of the most-favoured nation (MFN) principle.[41] These questions had a strong rhetorical link with nationalistic ideas. However, rhetoric and nationalistic ideas seldom direct trade policy but they can easily be used to legitimise the profit-seeking motives of interest groups. The reconciliation of these principles, which were in fact at times contradictory, was not easy. The result was that the importance of exports moderated the influence of the first two principles. What is to be pointed out is that protection of agriculture was accepted by all economic interest groups. This can be interpreted as the heritage of the civil war, when Finland had a critical shortage of food, although self-sufficiency was a target in the interwar world elsewhere, too.[42]

The principles of tariff policy were formed in 1919 when the government enforced a 'provisional' tariff, and a year later when the first luxury tariff (for the budget year 1921) was imposed. Finnish tariff policy in the interwar period was characterised by: moderate protectionism; customs duties were an important part of the state revenue; and imports of 'luxuries' were subject to special taxation. In the 1930s the luxury tariff came to be the foremost protectionist weapon against imports, but it was used in trade agreement negotiations, too. The 1919 tariff was preserved until 1938 and parliament renewed the tariff annually as a part of the budgetary process.[43]

The trade agreement policy (1919–39) can be divided into two periods. In the 1920s practically all treaties were based on the MFN clause. Special concessions had to be made for France, Germany, Spain and Estonia, but their economic impact was insignificant. In the 1930s Finland had to adapt itself to international protectionism. The major treaties were made with Germany and Britain in 1933 and 1934. For example, the import quotas Finland had to grant to Britain in 1933 were economically considerable, and also affected the structure of the Finnish foreign trade. On the other hand, Germany lost her share of imports mainly because of her restrictive tariff policy. Accordingly, in the 1920s Finland founded her trade agreement policy and trade agreement nego-tiation machinery. The foreign policy administration was inexperienced in negotiating trade agreements and, consequently, representatives of the private sector came to have an important role in the negotiations. A good example is the 'Flying Trade Commission', which negotiated in the western countries in 1919. The Commission had an official status but there were no representatives from the Foreign Ministry in the group. In the 1930s the trade agreement policy became crucial for the whole economy and, consequently, the economic impact was greater.

The influence of economic pressure groups became a significant feature in the Finnish foreign trade policy in the interwar period.[44] This is in accordance with what, for example, North and the rent-seeking school have described: when the possible pay-off from political action is raised high enough, companies will invest in political action. Accordingly, exercising political pressure is basically seen as an invest-ment decision. As already mentioned, the representatives of the private sector, in practice, dominated the trade agreement negotiations. In tariff policy the situation was more complicated since the decisions were made in parliament. The most important channel of influence for trade and industry was the Finnish corporatist committee system. All the central associations were represented in the Trade Agreement Commission (1919), which controlled foreign trade policy, in the committees planning new tariffs, and in the committees planning state purchases.[45]

However, a traditional rational-choice hypothesis about a situation in which the different groups were competing with each other can only be partially accepted. The heritage of the civil war and anti-socialist atti-tudes were strong among Finnish business circles and, therefore, all the central organisations were able to co-operate. A good example of this is the grain tariff question, in which the various groups co-operated despite their different orientations on the questions of protection or non-pro-tection. Also, as mentioned in earlier studies, both the industries that had to compete with imports and the exporting industries started to finance right-wing parties in the 1930s, purely for political reasons. Obviously, they saw that they were no longer able to manipulate foreign trade policy issues as efficiently as earlier. This kind of evidence does not confirm to the findings of public-choice studies. However, there is no evidence that nationalistic ideas or the language question had any major effect on the political direction of these pressure groups.[46]

Elements both of continuity and discontinuity can be discerned in the formation of organisations, formal institutions and informal institutions in this period. These are presented below in a schematic form.

Elements of continuity

Organisations:	Companies
	Persons
Formal institutions:	Major part of the legislative system
	Property rights
Informal institutions:	Personal networks
	Business traditions
	Power/class structure

Elements of discontinuity / New elements

Organisations:	Foreign trade policy administration[47]
	National cartels[48]
	Central pressure groups
Formal institutions:	Relations with Russia
	Highest authority in Finland
	Trade agreements
	Tariff system[49]
	Adaptation of corporatism
Informal institutions:	Use of 'experts' in formal decision-making (corporatism)
	Anti-socialism
	Consensus (in the 1930s)
	Western orientation in foreign policy

Despite the significant changes, especially on the formal level, the continuity of informal institutions, persons, natural resources and production tended to keep Finland on the pre-independence development path, at least in the interwar period. This is in accordance with North's argument that revolutions (here, political independence) are seldom as revolutionary as their rhetoric would suggest.

DISCUSSION: THE NATIONAL QUESTION AND ECONOMIC CHANGE

Finnish historians have recently continued discussions about the consequences of Finland's connection with Russia. Economic historians generally claim that the connection was not a bad one for the economy. Other points of view tend to stress the autonomous period as a preparation for Finnish independence, Finland having developed nationally, culturally and politically despite Russian rule.[50]

It is obvious that the largest groups of the nationalistic movement, which had started during the middle of the nineteenth century, did not have total independence as a target. A recognised position for the Finnish language has to be seen as one aim. The position of the Finnish language had been improving somewhat since the 1860s. The other relatively clear target was the preservation of Finland's autonomous position in the Russian Empire. Tariff autonomy, self-administration, their own languages (Finnish and Swedish) and currency had raised nationalistic feelings especially among the city bourgeoisie and intellectuals. The cultural contrast between Russia and Finland became more significant when Russia started the 'russification programme' in the 1890s. On the other hand, the russification programme did not seem to affect directly any private business relations. Trade and other economic activities continued as usual. Obviously, no businessmen refused trade relations because of russification. This is in accordance with the ideas of Hroch who, in his studies of attitudes of various groups within society, finds that industrialists are most prone to act in collaboration with the stronger partner and are not affected by nationalistic ideas.

It cannot be claimed that independence was a result of systematic work by the nationalistic movement. Rather, Finland gained its independence because of the chaotic developments in Russia and by using the window of opportunity that suddenly opened. Furthermore, as can be seen above, there had clearly been no systematic planning on how to manage Finland's newly gained independence.

The economic targets of the new government were the revival of the economy – including foreign trade relations – and keeping the population from starvation. The food shortage was a burning question. In the longer run, the target came to be self-sufficiency in food with protected home markets and government support for the agricultural sector, which were also nationalistic targets. These were alleviated by the need to keep strong export markets and export relations, as the trade needs of the country continued to be considerable.

As for the private sector of the economy, targets of the business elite were to open up trade relations and get their businesses going. Nationalist sentiments hardly interfered at all. The Finnish companies who had traditionally exported to Russia were in no way unwilling to continue trade. It also seems that language questions did not arise either; the language of business was still Swedish to a great extent, or alternatively, Finnish and Swedish were used together. Rather, the business elite was hoping that old, well-known business relations could be re-established with the Russians. That turned out to be impossible, mainly because of Russia's new policy orientation. During the first decade of independence, Finnish business continued efforts to buy raw materials from the Soviets. During the New Economic Plan (NEP) period Finnish companies were eager to get concessions to open up economic activities in the Soviet Union.

The economy recovered relatively soon with the help of postwar western demand for supplies from the old customers and the establishment of new trade relations. The structural development of the economy continued in many ways in the same direction it had been taking before the First World War. Foreign trade maintained its relative importance, except for a few critical years during the war. Soviet markets lost their significance and western markets came to dominate. Regarding commodities, western markets demanded less-processed goods, and accordingly the commodity structure of exports came to be almost entirely dominated by timber products, pulp and paper.

A new organisation was needed for foreign trade. As can be seen above, it was created rather painlessly and fairly quickly. The private sector came to have an important role in the public decision-making process through committees, cartels and pressure groups. On the one hand, the new state recruited men who were already experienced for the most influential positions. On the other hand, new talented men, who had come to the fore as a result of the civil war, came to have influence. Generally, the men who dominated foreign trade policy decision-making in 1918 to 1919 were able to maintain their political power in the interwar period. Pressure groups representing the main industries emerged in western European style, and they came to exert power in economic policy decision-making.

Even if there were significant discontinuities in the organisations and formal and informal institutions of the economy, the continuities seem to have outweighed them in the new economic order. Pre-independence personal and business networks, existing legislation and existing property rights formed the foundation for the continuing path of development.

The national question seems to have been insignificant in these developments.

NOTES

1 The Finnish language had been in a subordinate position while the language of administration, higher education and business had been Swedish, generally not known by the lower classes. The position of the Finnish language had improved somewhat since the 1860s. The language quarrel culminated in the 1930s in strikes at the University of Helsinki demanding a better position for the Finnish language in teaching and research. The conflict was solved by legislation that raised the Finnish language to the dominant position, but guaranteed the Swedish-speaking minority a fair position. See Pekka Kalevi Hämäläinen, *Kielitaistelu Suomessa 1917–1939* [Language question 1917–1939], (Porvoo, 1968).

2 The russification programme (1899–1917) aimed at, for example, the gradual integration of the Russian and Finnish postal administrations, joining Finland to Russian military organisations, russification of the Finnish senate (government) and joining Finland to the Russian legislative system. See, for example, Jussi T. Lappalainen, *Itsenäisen Suomen synty* [The emergence of the independent Finland], (Jyväskylä, 1967), p. 19.

3 See E. J. Hobsbawm, *Nations and Nationalism since 1780. Programme, Myth, Reality* (Cambridge, 1994). Hobsbawm does not discuss economic aspects in this book – he discusses political, language and cultural matters.

4 Miroslav Hroch, *Social Preconditions of National Revival in Europe* (Cambridge, 1985).

5 Douglass C. North, 'Where have we been and where are we going?' (published on the internet at http://econwpa.wustl.edu/eprints/eh/papers/9612/9612001.abs), p. 10. See also Douglass C. North, *Institutions, Institutional Change and Economic Performance* (Cambridge, 1994) and Douglass C. North, 'The process of economic change', paper presented at the UNU/Wider Project Meeting on New Models of Provision and Financing of Public Goods, Helsinki, 1997.

6 Erkki Pihkala, 'Suomen ja Venäjän taloudelliset suhtteet I maailmansodan aikana' [The economic relations between Russia and Finland during the First World War], *Historiallinen aikakauskirja* 1 (1980), 29–42; Per Schybergson, 'Finlands industri och den ryska marknaden under autonomins tid (1809–1917), Några synpunkter' [Finnish industry and the Russian market during the autonomuos period], *Turun Historiallinen Arkisto* 41 (1986), 120–35; Jorma Ahvenainen, 'Suomen ja Neuvostoliiton väliset kauppasuhteet 1920-ja 1930-luvulla' [Trade relations between Finland and the Soviet Union in the 1920s and 1930s], *Turun Historiallinen Arkisto* 41 (1986), 168–85; Riitta Hjerppe, *The Finnish Economy 1860–1985, Growth and Structural Change* (Helsinki, 1989).

7 The Finns could export handicrafts and cottage industry products as well as agricultural and forestry products duty free to Russia. Industrial products had relatively high duty-free quotas. Russian products came to Finland duty free except for a group consisting mainly of luxury goods with financial tariffs. See, for example, Schybergson, 'Finlands industri'.

8 Hjerppe, 'The Finnish Economy'.
9 Pihkala, 'Suomen ja Venäjän', p. 29.
10 The Russian trade can be regarded as foreign trade, as Finland had had her own tariff since the early 1810s.
11 In 'Finlands industri', Per Schybergson claims that the Finnish goods were of better quality than the Russian ones and that explains their success. In particular, paper production, based on wood and starting in the late 1860s, grew into a large-scale industry in Finland by selling to the Russian market. According to Schybergson, the customs benefits helped Finnish products to compete in the Russian market. On the other hand, the competitiveness of Finnish industrial products was relatively good, as the Finnish import tariffs had been low since the 1840s, whereas the Russian customs protection had been higher in general. Only a few Russian industrial products drove Finnish goods out of the Finnish markets (namely leather and woollen goods and sail cloth).
12 See Erkki Pihkala, *Suomen ulkomaankauppa 1860–1917* [Finland's foreign trade 1860–1917], (Helsinki, 1969). The favourable price development of sawn timber was also the cause of the considerable improvement of the Finnish terms of trade in the 1870s and again in the 1890s and 1900s, which was very significant for the whole development of industrialisation.
13 As the Finnish mark was pegged to gold in 1878 and the Russian rouble only in the 1890s, this probably emphasised the separateness of Finland from Russia in international matters.
14 See Riitta Hjerppe and Jorma Ahvenainen, 'Foreign enterprises and nationalistic control: the case of Finland since the end of the nineteenth century' in Alice Teichova, Maurice Lévy Leboyer and Helga Nussbaum (eds.), *Multinational Enterprise in Historical Perspective* (Cambridge, 1986).
15 Leo Harmaja, *Maailmansodan vaikutus Suomen taloudelliseen kehitykseen* [The economic consequences of the First World War], (Porvoo, 1940), pp. 352;4 see also Heikki Rantatupa, *Elintarvikehuolto ja säännöstely Suomessa vuosina 1914–1921* [Food supply and rationing in Finland in 1914–1921], (Jyväskylä, 1979).
16 See Timo Herranen and Timo Myllyntaus, 'Effects of the First World War on the engineering industries of Estonia and Finland', *Scandinavian Economic History Review* 3 (1984), 121–4 and Pihkala, 'Suomen ja Venäjän'.
17 Hjerppe, 'The Finnish economy' and Pihkala, 'Suomen ja Venäjän'. Pihkala has estimated the volume of war trade with Russia as if this were not included in the official trade statistics.
18 Pihkala, 'Suomen ja Venäjän', pp. 34–8 and Rantatupa, *Elintarvikehuolto*.
19 Ahvenainen, 'Suomen ja Neuvostoliiton' and Pihkala, 'Suomen ja Venäjän'.
20 Ahvenainen, 'Suomen ja Neuvostoliiton', p. 181.
21 *Ibid.*
22 *Ibid.*
23 *Ibid.*
24 *Ibid.*, and Tapio Hämynen, *Liikkeellä leivän tähden. Raja-Karjalan väestö ja sen*

toimeentulo 1880–1940 [On the move for bread. The population of Border Carelia and its livelihood], (Helsinki, 1993).

25 Kalevi Ahonen, 'Suomen paperinviennin murroskausi' [The critical period of Finland's paper exports], (Jyväskylä, 1972, unpublished) and Jorma Ahvenainen, *Paperitehtaista suuryhtiöiksi. Kymin Osakeyhtiö vuosina 1918–1939* [From a paper mill to a large company. Kymin Ltd 1918–1939], (Kuusankoski, 1972). It has not been adequately clarified why the western market preferred pulp to paper. Some studies have referred, for example, to different marketing and packing techniques of paper, which does not seem an adequate explanation (see Ahonen, 'Suomen paperinviennin murroskausi').

26 In 1887, Finland was mentioned in the Russian–Spanish trade agreement separately, but that does not mean that Finland had any kind of trade agreement policy.

27 See Schybergson, 'Finlands industri'.

28 Rule 8/29, 7.5, D7-30, Archive of the Special Staff of Engineers ('AE'), Finnish Military Archive ('MA').

29 Memorandum of Gustaf Aminoff, 25 February 1918, D7-32, AE, MA; Eino Kuusi, *Kauppapolitiikka* [Trade policy], (Helsinki, 1921), p. 515.

30 In some studies the Special Staff of Engineers has been translated as 'Engineering High Command'.

31 Memorandum of Gustaf Aminoff, 25 February 1918, D7-32, AE, MA.

32 *Ibid.*

33 Memorandum of Gustaf Aminoff, 15 April 1918, D7-30, AE, MA. For personnel, see Jari Eilola, 'Insinööriesikunnan jäsenten sijoittuminen sotien välisellä ajalla' [The career development of the personnel of the Special Staff of Engineers 1918–1939], (Jyväskylä, 1997, unpublished). Solitander, Walden and Viljanen did not start their careers during the civil war, even if they did manage to improve their ranking in business circles. In 1914, both Solitander and Viljanen were teachers at the Technical College of Tempere and Walden worked as a sales agent for Finnish pulp and paper industries in Russia.

34 Aminoff to Senate of Finland, 3 April 1918, D5-1519, AE, MA.

35 Regulation 26, 17 May 1918, Statute Book of Finland 1918; Regulation 50, 6 June 1918, Statute Book of Finland 1918; Harmaja, *Maailmansodan vaikutus Suomen*, p. 82 and Kuusi, *Kauppapolitiikka*, p. 518.

36 Regulation 50, 6 June 1918, Statute Book of Finland 1918.

37 Memorandum of Special Staff of Engineers, HA2, Archive of the Trade and Industry Commission ('ATI'), Finnish National Archive ('NA'); Regulation 50, 6 June 1918, Statute book of Finland, 1918.

38 The Central Chamber of Commerce to the Trade and Industry Commission, April 1918, HA2, ATI, NA; Aminoff to Senate of Finland, 3 April 1918, D5-1519, AE, MA.

39 Some foreign trade restrictions continued until 1921 but *grosso mode*, the 1919 constitutional reform can be thought of as the start of normalisation.

40 Riitta Hjerppe, 'Finnish trade and trade policy in the 20th century', *Scandinavian Journal of History* 1 (1993), 57–76; Erkki Pihkala, *Suomen kauppapolittiikka 1918–1944* [Finnish foreign trade policy 1918–1944], (Keuruu, 1978), pp. 12–18; Henrik Ramsay, 'Det ekonomiska läget' [Economic position], *Ekonomiska Samfundets Tidskrift* (1921); Henrik Ramsay, 'Handelsfördrag och traktatpolitik' [Tariff and trade agreement policy], *Ekonomiska Samfundets Tidskrift* (1923).

41 Memorandum of Väino Voionmaa (manager of the economic department of the Foreign Ministry) for the International Studies Conference, January 1939, in the Collection of Henrik Ramsay, NA; Regulation 32, 29 March 1919, Statute book of Finland 1919. Also see, for example, Hjalmar Procope, 'Vårt tulltariffsystem ur traktatpolitisk synpunkt' [Our tariff policy from the viewpoint of trade agreement policy], *Ekonomiska Samfundets Tidskrift* (1927), and Hjalmar Procope, 'Några randanmarkningar till Finlands handelstraktatpolitik' [Finland's trade agreement policy], *Ekonomiska Samfundets Tidskrift* (1933).

42 Pihkala, *Suomen kauppapolitiikka*; PM of Väino Voionmaa for the International Studies Conference, January 1939, in the Collection of Henrik Ramsay, NA.

43 Regulation 32, 29 March 1919, Statute Book of Finland 1919; Procope, 'Vårt tulltariffsystem'; Pihkala, *Suomen Kauppapolitiikka*.

44 Pressure groups at the national level were founded when the economic interest groups realised that the political independence also made organised political action necessary. Between 1917 and 1921, three such groups were created. These represented agricultural production (the Central Union of Agricultural Producers, CUAP), export industries (the Central Association of Finnish Woodworking Industries, CAFWI, also nicknamed the 'second Foreign Ministry') and import competing industries (the Association of Finnish Industry). See the Annual Report of the CAFWI 1919, protocol of the Central Association of Finnish Industries (CAFI), 28 January 1921, in the Archive of the CAFI; 1918 protocols of the CUAP in the Archive of the CUAP.

45 See, for example, the Annual Reports of the CAFI 1921–31 in the Archive of the CAFI, and the Annual Reports of the CUAP 1918–39 in the Archive of the CUAP. See also Juha-Antti Lamberg, 'Vaalirahoituksen poliittinen taloustiede' [The political economy of campaign funding] in *Uusi institutionaalinen taloushistoria* (Jyväskylä, 1997), pp. 143–70.

46 Lamberg, 'Vaalirahoituksen poliittinen taloustiede'.

47 Except tariff administration.

48 New cartels started in the summer of 1918.

49 The 1919 tariff was remarkably different from the tariff under the Russian regime.

50 *Historiallinen aikakauskirja* 1 (1997), 1–2.

CHAPTER 20

Economic change and the national question in twentieth-century USSR/Russia: the enterprise level

Andrei Yu. Yudanov

The break-up of the USSR brought to a close the history of the state which had been the largest multinational entity in Europe over the preceding three centuries. For a long time to come, historians will probably go on discussing the role the national factor proper had to play in this, the greatest cataclysm of the late twentieth century – notably, the extent to which the peoples within the Soviet Union yearned for independence. After all, in the referendum held democratically some six months before the demise of the USSR, a majority of the population of the country as a whole and of each of the subsequently independent states (apart from the Baltic countries) came out in favour of retaining the Union. However that may be, the ultimate results of the break-up indisputably had a national hue: in place of the polyethnic superpower there emerged some fifteen states organised, in most cases, on the monoethnic principle.

The break-up of the USSR came as a terrible upheaval for the economy of all the successor countries. Nor is it only a matter of the actual consequences of the destruction of the single state, but also of *the kind* of state that went to pieces in this case. The Soviet Union (in contrast, say, to Austria-Hungary, the other multinational Great Power that fell apart in the twentieth century) was based on the so-called *single national economic complex* principle, the implication being that Soviet enterprises were not autonomous organisms, but were parts of a centralised macroeconomic superstructure.

It should be noted that, both in the prehistory and in the very course of these painful adaptation processes, the national factor played a noticeable role, above all because, in virtue of various historical factors, the core of this single national economic complex developed as *the Union-wide web of Russian enterprises* even beyond the boundaries of the age-old Russian lands.

COMMUNITY OF ALL-UNION SUBORDINATED ENTERPRISES,
RUSSIAN FRAMEWORK OF SOVIET ECONOMY

The specific ethnic features in the development of the Soviet economy were determined by two main political factors: first, the officially proclaimed and actually pursued policy of evening out levels of development and equalising living standards among the country's diverse nationalities through the accelerated modernisation of backward USSR republics; and secondly, the principle of priority of all-Union interests over the interests of the republics, which was not officially recognised, but was just as actively applied in practice. The interaction of the two factors resulted on the microeconomic level in the fact that the modernisation of the republics within the USSR went the way of the formation within them of a powerful stratum of enterprises operating not so much for the satisfaction of local requirements as for the fulfilment of all-Union tasks.

Brief survey of ethnic history of all-Union subordinated enterprises

The policy of accelerated creation of industrial enterprises in the backward non-Russian outlying areas of the country was first put into effect in the early years after the revolution. In the dislocation caused by the revolution and the civil war, it amounted not so much to new construction as to the relocation into these areas of enterprises already existing in the centre of the country. From 1922 to 1925, some twenty industrial enterprises were transferred from Russia and the Ukraine to the republics of Central Asia and the Transcaucasus.[1] Since the new sites, as a rule, lacked skilled personnel, the relocation of equipment went hand in hand with a part of the Russian personnel travelling along with it. Thus, a cloth factory began operation in Kustanai (Kazakhstan) in 1923, after the whole of it was transferred to the new place together with the basic personnel from the town of Kolomna, which is near Moscow.

However, the effort to create new industrial enterprises in the 'national republics' (as the non-Slav republics of the USSR used to be called) became massive later, when the implementation of the plan for the country's industrialisation got under way in the late 1920s and in the 1930s. In this period the model mechanism of the creation of new enterprises in the national republics took shape precisely, and it is worthwhile giving a brief description of this mechanism, for it remained in operation throughout the entire USSR period, with insignificant changes here and there.

The mobility of the population required for the construction of plants outside the traditional centres of industry was achieved by means of all-Union political measures known as 'campaigns'. Officially, the campaigns for the construction of plants were not of a coercive nature. A sizeable part of the USSR population viewed these with approval and with enthusiasm, regarding the massive construction effort as a way of overcoming the country's backwardness. But in practice campaigns left the individual with very little opportunity to refuse to travel to distant parts or to return from these before the end of his term.

Campaigns were announced for the construction of the largest enterprises, electric-power plants and railways. These projects were given the status of an 'all-Union shock-work construction project', which implied direct control on the part of the USSR government and the party's Central Committee, making it possible to recruit labour power in all the republics, ensuring priority deliveries of equipment and access to foreign-currency resources and holding out various other benefits.

The centre's control of the largest enterprises also continued after the end of construction, which is why such enterprises were known as 'all-Union subordinated enterprises'. Not only in the national republics, but also in Russia, the giant enterprises were something of a state within the state, subordinate only to the country's top leadership. By contrast, the local authorities were virtually unable to interfere in their activity.

In order to have a clearer view of the overall picture, one should bear in mind the strong propensity of large Soviet enterprises for autarky, or self-sufficiency.[2] Because of the constant shortages of various goods, Soviet enterprises strove to produce everything themselves. They had their own building organisations, their own housing facilities for their workers, their own agricultural production to keep their personnel supplied with foodstuffs, and even their own workshops for the repair of freight cars to make sure that their finished products were delivered in wagons in good repair. And such enterprises, reminiscent of fortresses prepared for a long siege, were independent of the local authorities and were subordinate only to the central authorities.

In underdeveloped republics, all-Union subordinated enterprises were manned by resettlers of various nationalities: Russians, Ukrainians, Belorussians, Jews, Tatars and others. They were usually grouped round those who came from Russia and who were more numerous, and altogether they were regarded by the local population as Russians. That is the basis on which a 'Russian-speaking population' gradually took shape in the national republics. This term was usually used to identify a metaethnic entity of people, membership of which was felt by all new arrivals in each of the republics. Thus, in Latvia, it was not only a Russian, but also an Armenian who felt himself to be Russian or, at any rate, a Russian-speaker; for his part, a Latvian felt himself to be almost Russian in the Transcaucasus.

The next wave of mass relocation of industrial enterprises from the centre of the country to the east (notably, to central Asia and Kazakhstan) that followed upon the industrialisation was caused by their evacuation in the first period of the Second World War, which was most unfortunate for the USSR. By mid-1942, the number of relocated enterprises reached 1,200, with most of these getting down to production at the new site within no more than six months following relocation. Such a rapid commencement of operations was due to the fact that the bulk of the personnel came over together with the enterprises.

After the war, most of the evacuees returned to their homes in Russia, Belorussia and the Ukraine. But not everyone returned. The point is that the equipment taken out to the east was not, in the main, returned to the enterprises of the old industrial centres, but was simply replaced at these enterprises with new equipment. The producer capacities remaining in the east could not be left without skilled personnel, which is why for many Russian-speaking workers the temporary evacuation ended in a permanent resettlement to Kazakhstan or central Asia.

In the postwar period, the development of virgin lands in northern Kazakhstan and the construction of large hydroelectric power stations, mining and processing enterprises, and metallurgical and machine-building plants in virtually all the national republics were carried out in accordance with the campaign scenario described above.

Russian ethnologists V. I. Bushkov and D. V. Mikulsky[3] note that 'the industry created in Central Asia over several decades was provided with manpower mainly through its importation from Russia'. For instance, 'in only 22 years (1950–1971), 235,700 persons were resettled to Tajikistan towns from the European part of the former USSR'. It should be pointed out, by way of comparison, that the entire urban population of Tajikistan in the aforesaid period did not exceed 1 million people.

The distinctions between the campaigns of the postwar period from those of the Stalin epoch amounted mainly to a greater role for money incentives and lesser importance of compulsion in the recruitment of resettlers. What was entirely new in those years was the spread of this process to the Baltic republics, which were highly developed compared with other parts of the USSR. The skill levels of Latvian, Estonian and Lithuanian workers did not require the participation of resettlers in the establishment of new enterprises. Nevertheless, students of the ethnic structure of the population in the Baltic republics note that 'the sharp increase . . . in the numbers of Russians is due to migrations from other republics arranged for the purposes of creating new industrial enterprises'.[4]

Indeed, the proportion of Russians in the entire population of Latvia increased from 1935 to 1989 by 3.9 times (from 8.8 to 34.0 per cent). In the cities – that is, where new enterprises were set up – the proportion of the Russian population went up 6.2 times (from 7.1 to 44.0 per cent), whereas in the rural localities – in the absence of this process – the changes were much weaker (the proportion increased less than twofold – from 9.8 to 18.2 per cent).[5] In Estonia, the proportion of the Russian population increased from 1939 to 1989 from 4.7 to 30.5 per cent.[6]

By the end of the Soviet epoch, all-Union subordinated enterprises played a dominant role in the economy of all the Union republics. In 1989, they employed 51 per cent of all those working in industry in Kazakhstan and Azerbaijan, 54 per cent in Belorussia, 63 per cent in Ukraine, and 71 per cent in Russia.[7]

Causes of stability of Russian character of all-Union subordinated enterprises

The nationalities policy of the Soviet state was not at all aimed at investing all-Union subordinated enterprises with the character of isolated Russian (Russian-speaking) settlements insinuated into an alien local population. On the contrary, from the earliest years of the USSR, the authorities attached much importance to the education and professional training of inhabitants of lagging republics.

The percentage of local personnel in the total number of people employed at industrial enterprises was regarded as a politically important parameter and was under constant party control. The address of builders of the Karaganda Coal Basin (Kazakhstan, 1935) to the workers of Donbass (Ukraine) may serve as a characteristic document of the epoch: 'We are building Karaganda in the conditions of a national republic, a former tsarist colony, in the complete absence of mechanisation, and in harsh housing and everyday conditions. That is why we request you, proletarians of Donbass: send your shock workers to

Karaganda for the purpose of training the former Kazakh nomad in the modern mechanised extraction of coal, for the creation of personnel of skilled miners.'[8]

During the years of the Great Patriotic War (the Second World War), when the cadre workers of industrial enterprises in the Slav republics were mobilised to serve in the Red Army, replenishment of the shortage of manpower in production became an altogether vital necessity. Some 19,000 skilled workers from among local inhabitants were trained at defence enterprises during the years of the war in Kazakhstan alone.[9]

This process went on apace in the postwar years as well. On the whole, impressive and incontestable successes were scored in the field of education and professional training of inhabitants of the national republics during the years of the USSR. Before the revolution, literacy among the adult population (from nine to forty-nine years) in various parts of central Asia and Kazakhstan fluctuated between 2 and 8 per cent, but by the end of the 1950s it went up to 95 to 98 per cent. What is more, in the final decades of the existence of the single state, many once-backward republics even led in the number of skilled specialists employed in the economy. In 1983, for instance, the USSR average was 858 persons with a higher and secondary special education per 10,000 persons in work. But in Kazakhstan, the figure was 859 persons; in Turkmenia, 879; in Georgia, 895; and in Uzbekistan, 899.[10]

Nevertheless, all-Union subordinated enterprises continued to retain their Russian (Russian-speaking) character throughout the entire history of the USSR with amazing stability. This was promoted by a number of factors.

First, the Russian population, which is in principle characterised by a low mobility, after being relocated in the course of campaigns to a new locality, usually again lost its mobility on the spot, because in Russia's conditions movement from town to town was (and still remains) a grave trial for the family. As a result, stable enclaves of Russian (Russian-speaking) population tended to emerge in the places where new enterprises were built. This was also greatly promoted by the gigantic size of the enterprises designed to cater for the requirement of the entire Union. Now and again, the enterprises were so large that the towns in which they were located simply lacked the required number of local inhabitants to service them. Resettlers became the majority section of the population and, in effect, converted their town into a part of Russia, from which there was naturally no good reason to go away.

The Daugavpils Chemical Fibre Works (Latvia) provides one of the outstanding examples of this kind. It was built in the years of the Krushchev seven-year plan and brought about a massive influx of resettlers into what was once a quiet little town. When the construction of the plant was completed, Latvians in Daugavpils became an insignificant national minority. In 1989, it had 16,500 Latvians and 73,900 Russians.[11]

Secondly, despite the efforts of the authorities, they usually failed actually to get the local population to take on jobs at the emerging all-Union subordinated enterprises. Initially, the main reason there, as has been noted above, was the low skill standards among the local workers. Later on, what came to the fore was the unwillingness of the local population to work in industry (especially in heavy industry).

For political reasons, the latter circumstance could not be discussed aloud by Soviet researchers, but it was widely known among the people and often provided the basis for Russian everyday nationalism. On the other hand, western researchers usually explained the unwillingness of non-Slav peoples in the USSR to work at industrial enterprises for the following reasons: either, the pre-industrial mentality of these peoples, notably, the Oriental traditions of working in agriculture, trade or the state apparatus, but not at industrial enterprises; or an urge to obtain high unofficial ('grey' or 'black') earnings.

In industry, especially in heavy industry, all incomes came down to official wages. By contrast, agriculture, trade, services and the state apparatus offered many ways of obtaining semi-legal or illegal earnings, ranging from the growing and private sale of southern fruits and flowers, which in the USSR was an exceptionally profitable occupation, all the way to bribery and theft. Nancy Lubin, for instance, cites data to show that the illegal earnings of a doctor in Uzbekistan in the early 1980s were six times higher than his official salary, and those of a salesman fifty times higher.[12]

It is important to emphasise that the receipt of unofficial earnings in the national republics was much more widespread, and that the authorities took a much more condoning view of these, than in Russia. Western researchers have long been saying that this state of affairs resulted from a compromise between socialist ideology and the traditional Oriental way of life.[13]

Union-wide web of Russian enterprises

The tendency towards the self-isolation of industrial enterprises (notably, large enterprises in heavy industry) from the local surroundings ran through the whole history of such enterprises set up in the national republics. The alien national make-up of job-holders at all-Union subordinated enterprises with respect to local inhabitants has already been mentioned, but it is also important to bear in mind the quantitative aspect of the matter.

Examples of an overwhelming prevalence of Russian (Russian-speaking) personnel may be found in the most different periods in virtually all the national republics. Thus, trade-union statistics show that, in 1931, more than 40 per cent of those employed at industrial enterprises in Azerbaijan were Russians, while in technically intricate industries the numbers of Russian workers (52.1 per cent in the oil industry and 61.1 per cent in machine-building) were altogether many times larger than the numbers of Azerbaijanis working at the enterprises (18.6 and 12.5 per cent respectively).[14]

In Uzbekistan, some 110,000 new jobs were created at large industrial enterprises from 1929 to 1940. However, only 14 per cent of these (15,700 jobs) were held by Uzbeks together with other native nationalities.[15]

In later years, official Soviet sources began to conceal similar information, because it did not accord with the myth of the emergence of a *single Soviet nationality*, and so was politically inconvenient. Nevertheless, western studies confirmed that no fundamental changes had occurred. Lubin, among others, gives the figures of representative polls carried out in the 1970s at seven major machine-building plants in Uzbekistan. On average, Uzbeks at these plants made up less than 20 per cent of the total number of employed, while at the mammoth maker of agricultural hardware Chirchikselmash (15,000 employees), their proportion was altogether under 2 per cent.[16]

In the years of *perestroika*, when national problems were freely dealt with, the 'Russianness' of the implanted industry was noted even by Soviet authors. G. L. Smirnov, for instance, writes about 'the obvious preponderance of other-nationality [that is, Russian-speaking] groups in various lines of industrial production and building (for instance, in Latvia and Estonia – up to 80%)'.[17] This state of affairs was also characteristic for Kazakhstan: 'On the whole, in terms of percentage, employment of non-native groups of the population in industry in 1991 came to 79% of all those employed in industry.'[18]

The isolation of all-Union subordinated enterprises from the local environment was promoted, to no lesser extent than by the Russian-speaking make-up of personnel, by the nature of their production ties: they delivered their products not to enterprises in their own republic and received semi-finished products not from these, but exchanged products with other all-Union subordinated enterprises scattered across the Union.

Thus, the Daugavpils Chemical Fibre Works (Latvia) used only raw materials supplied by other republics, while its finished products were consumed mainly outside Latvia (cord fabric, one of the main products made at this works, was used in the manufacture of automobile tyres, which Latvia did not turn out at all). Such examples of all-Union subordinated enterprises integrating not so much with the local economy as with the all-Union economy are fairly typical. This was promoted by the following factors.

(1) In the urge to obtain economies of scale and scope, a large number of giant enterprises were created in the Soviet Union. The urge for giganticism was obviously hypertrophied, since because of the artificial understatement of the prices of energy, raw materials and transport the projects of even irrationally large enterprises appeared to be quite profitable. Raw materials for these were often hauled from thousands of kilometres away, while the finished products were shipped out across the whole Union. In such conditions, the framework of a single republic appeared to be much too narrow for giant enterprises: simply because of their size, they could function only in an all-Union economic environment, but not in a republican one.

(2) The centralised system of administration of the USSR economy was arranged on the sectoral principle, while territorial connections were weak. Any sectoral ministry (say, ferrous or non-ferrous metallurgy) found it simpler to organise deliveries of raw materials and semi-finished products between *its own* enterprises, no matter how far away from each other these were located, than to be oriented towards *alien* suppliers – that is, those outside their subordination – even where these suppliers were territorially much nearer.

(3) Financially, all-Union subordinated enterprises were also linked with the all-Union budget, and not with the places in which they were situated. Prior to 1980, for instance, the law was such that they did not pay any taxes or other charges into the local budgets at all.

One could say, by way of summing up, that the USSR had a Union-wide web of large enterprises of impressive proportions covering all the Union republics. History has known of empires whose unity was ensured by garrisons of soldiers of the dominant nation erected throughout the territory. The Soviet multinational superpower generated a modern, industrial version of implementation of this principle.

The Union-wide web of all-Union subordinated enterprises was the 'hand of Moscow', which stretched to the most distant parts of the state. And while the Russian resettled-worker, in contrast to the Roman legionnaire, was not an instrument of national coercion and enjoyed virtually no privileges, the network of enterprises – up to 90 or 80 per cent of it manned by Russian or Russian-speaking personnel – constituted a powerful force economically binding together a gigantic multinational country.

FATE OF A FRAGMENTED COMMUNITY OF ENTERPRISES

The break-up of the USSR and the emergence of fifteen nation states in its place was a powerful force, which intervened in the functioning of the Union-wide web of enterprises that had taken place over a period of many years. How did it withstand such intervention?

Disruption of economic ties

The treaty on the establishment of the CIS provided that the twelve former Union republics entering the new organisation would maintain the single economic space. However, history ran a different course. The economic and political situation in each of the newly formed states developed in its own way: there were differences in the state of the budget, credit policy, level of taxation, pace of privatisation and implementation of other reforms. The once single economy was being torn apart by centrifugal forces.

The common currency was the first to succumb. Some time later export and import tariffs and restrictions appeared on the scene. The disintegration was most sharply intensified by the isolationist policy of Russia, the most powerful CIS state. Yegor Gaidar's radical reformist government regarded the other former republics of the USSR as, above all, spongers and hangers-on seeking to obtain Russian oil and gas for next to nothing. The government strove to fence itself off from its former allies, regardless of the losses this was bound to cause to them, and obviously underestimating the damage to its own country.

The maladjustment of the old ties to the new market conditions was yet another highly important factor. Co-operation between enterprises in the various republics – well justified in the USSR's planned economy – in many cases became disadvantageous in a market economy. In other words, many of the ties were not broken off by external forces (the foreign-currency disorders, the customs restrictions and so on), but were abrogated by the enterprises themselves as being no longer useful.

The newly acquired openness of the new countries with respect to the external world likewise operated in the same direction. Many of the goods made by former Soviet enterprises turned out to be altogether uncompetitive when compared with western goods, and for that reason not required by erstwhile consumers in other CIS countries.

All these factors produced a cascading process of foreign-trade shrinkage. Within no more than two or three years, the level of integration attained in the Soviet period between the economies of the CIS countries was reduced many times over (see table 20.1).

It was, of course, the former all-Union subordinated enterprises that suffered most from the disintegration. Since they had operated with many, sometimes with tens and hundreds of, suppliers in the various republics of the former Soviet Union, they were often forced to stop production because of even one broken co-operation tie.

The effects of the shrinkage of marketing outlets were just as disastrous for the former all-Union subordinated enterprises. Many of these enterprises were set up for the *full* satisfaction of all the requirements of the USSR in a given type of product. In machine-building, for instance, 5,120 commodity groups, or 87 per cent of the total number of commodity groups identified for this industry, were manufactured for the whole country by only one producer. In chemicals, the respective figure was 47 per cent, and in metallurgy, 28 per cent.[19] Having lost the possibility of marketing their products outside their own republic, the former all-Union monopolists were confronted with the highly acute problem of low capacity utilisation.

Now and again, capacity utilisation fell to such a low level that production became not just economically unprofitable, but even technologically impossible. The Akrikhin pharmaceutical plant, which is situated at Kupavna near Moscow, was the USSR's largest producer of active substances, from which finished forms of drugs were made at forty-four enterprises operating in various republics of the Union. Following the break-up of the USSR, traditional consumers outside Russia discontinued their purchases. The production of active substances at Akrikhin dropped to a quarter. With that kind of capacity utilisation it became impossible to use chemical reactors. As it was put most bluntly by the workers, 'the stirring rod don't reach, won't do the mixing'.[20]

Apart from the reduction in mutual trade, the exodus of the Russian-speaking population from the national republics became a specific

Table 20.1. *Inter-republic trade as a percentage of foreign-trade operations* of republics (countries) of the USSR and CIS, 1988 and 1995*

Republic (country)	1988	1995	Change
Armenia	89.1	51.9	−37.2
Azerbaijan	85.6	36.8	−48.8
Georgia	86.5	47.4	−39.1
Kazakhstan	86.3	59.9	−26.4
Kirghizia	86.9	65.8	−21.1
Moldavia	87.8	64.7	−23.1
Russia	57.8	21.1	−36.7
Tajikistan	86.3	36.9	−49.4
Turkmenia	79.0	74.6	−4.4
Ukraine	79.0	57.3	−21.7
Uzbekistan	85.8	42.1	−43.7
Belorussia	85.8	65.1	−20.7
USSR/CIS	**71.8**	**32.2**	**−39.6**

Notes:
*For the USSR, the proportion of inter-republic trade turnover in the amount of foreign-trade turnover and inter-republic turnover; for the CIS, the proportion of trade with other CIS countries in the total foreign-trade turnover.
Sources: R. Langhammer and M. Luecke, *Die Handelsbeziehungen der Nachfolgestaaten der Sowjetunion* (Kiel, 1995), p. 4; *Sodruzhestvo nezavisimykh gosudarstv v 1995 godu* [Statistical Yearbook of the CIS] (Moscow, 1996), p. 96.

problem facing all the former all-Union subordinated enterprises. It began back in the late 1980s, on the appearance of the first few acute conflicts on an ethnic basis. However, the return resettlement assumed massive proportions in 1992, that is after the break-up of the Union.

Table 20.2 shows that the migration streams between Russia, Ukraine and Belorussia were sharply reduced after the break-up of the USSR. There was a decline both in arrivals in Russia and in departures from it, something that may be easily explained: in view of the emergence of new frontiers, which cut across the old migration streams, and the sharp decline in living standards in the post-Soviet space, people came to change their place of residence most unwillingly, *unless they were impelled to do so by special causes.*

Against this background, the sharp growth of arrivals in Russia of

Table 20.2. *Migration of population between Russia and former USSR republics, 1980–93 (in thousands)*

Years	Migration streams with Ukraine and Belorussia			Migration streams with other republics		
	Arrivals in Russia	Departures from Russia	Net arrivals in Russia	Arrivals in Russia	Departures from Russia	Net arrivals in Russia
1980	436.2	419.8	16.4	439.9	353.8	86.1
1985	411.1	383.3	27.8	465.7	318.7	147.0
1989	357.1	359.7	−2.6	497.2	332.0	165.2
1991	255.7	326.5	−70.8	436.3	260.7	175.6
1992	235.6	366.9	−131.3	690.2	203.2	487.0
1993	224.1	218.2	5.9	698.8	150.9	547.9

Source: The Demographic Yearbook of Russian Federation 1993 (Moscow, 1994), pp. 380, 382, 400 and 401.

inhabitants of former USSR national republics (from 440,000 in 1980 to almost 700,000 in 1993) provides pertinent evidence that they were impelled to return to their historical motherland by *special* circumstances, notably local nationalism, ranging from infringement of rights to out-right threats to life.

Even more impressive is the over-six-fold growth in net arrivals in Russia (from 86,000 to 548,000 people) from the national republics. Within five years (1990–4), some 14 per cent of the Russians living in the non-Slav republics left them, with the Baltic countries and Kazakhstan each losing 8 per cent of the Russian population, central Asia 21 per cent, and the Transcaucasus 37 per cent.[21]

Accordingly, the former all-Union subordinated enterprises have lost a sizeable part of their skilled personnel.

It is not only Russians who are leaving (for Russia), but also Germans (for Germany), Jews (for Israel), and representatives of other regions of the former USSR (for instance, the northern Caucasus and the Transcaucasus). It is not only representatives of the intelligent profes-sions, such as scientists (including those who had worked all their life in Tajikistan and who make up the cream of Tajik science), that are leaving, but also representatives of workers' professions, mainly those with high skill standards.

This was, for instance, the description given to the situation in Tajikistan by Bushkov and Mikulsky[22] *before* the start of the civil war in that country (and so before the appearance of the main flood of refugees). By 1994, that unfortunate country was abandoned by 42 per cent of the Russians who had lived there.[23]

The scale of the decline in production caused by the disruption of economic ties is impressive. It is well known that the overall drop of the GDP in the CIS countries in 1995, as compared with 1990, came to about 42 per cent, while industrial production shrank even more heavily – by 52 per cent.[24] Researchers come to very different conclusions when assessing the significance of the break-up of the Union for this catastrophe, but all of them cite some very large figures. Ivan Korotchenya,[25] for instance, assumes that the break-up of the USSR caused some 30 to 60 per cent of the overall GDP drop. S. A. Sitoryan and Oleg Bogomolov[26] speak of 30 to 50 per cent, while Arkadi Volsky's[27] assessment may be interpreted as 40 per cent.

Search for ways of adaptation

The present state of the economy does not suit any of the countries that emerged in place of the USSR. Below are considered three outlined ways of adaptation to the new conditions in the context of three countries in which the said trends have been most pronounced.

Russia: between isolationism and reintegration

Russia is the only one of the USSR successor countries that is large enough to be capable of producing, by itself, everything (or almost everything) necessary. That is exactly the route taken by many of Russia's enterprises that were once part of the Union-wide web. At any rate, the history of almost every successfully operating Russian enterprise includes a description of how it took steps, over the course of time, to reorient its economic ties towards Russia, so surviving the break-up of the USSR.

'Our raw-material network was scattered across the USSR: Ukrainian plants, Belorussian plants, the Baltic, Russia – a vast list', says A. V. Rassadnev, Director-General of the Moscow Tyre Works.[28] 'But when the struggle of sovereignties got under way, and the USSR began to break up, we were found to be ready for that, in contrast to many other enterprises. I realised that one should be oriented solely towards Russia . . . Everything, if you recall, began with the Baltic, and there I had [a supplier,] the Daugavpils Chemical Fibre Works. This means the customs and generally a mass of impediments. Accordingly, we turned our attention to the Shchyokino Khimvolokno, which is quite near, in the Tula Region.'

Virtually the same thing is told by V. Konev, Director of the Moscow Electrical Measuring Instruments Works: 'When information was received that, say, we could not obtain something from Belorussia or Moldavia, the designers were set the following task: here is a resistor that is not made in Russia, it has been left in Minsk or Kishinyov. That is why some other resistor needs to replace this one.'[29]

Consequently, in Russia the break-up of the USSR intensified the trend towards autarky, which was even then characteristic of Soviet enterprises. Instead of all-Union co-operation, orders for required parts and components were placed with the nearest enterprises or, wherever possible, these were replaced by items of their own making.

GAZ, one of the largest automobile enterprises in Russia, offers an indicative example. For the manufacture of its new truck model, the GAZel, which is, incidentally, highly successful on the CIS market, it itself manufactured 200 new machine-tools and 12,000 tools for these. Commenting on GAZ's success, the authoritative Russian journal *Expert* said that one of the reasons was the 'company's autarky: it does everything not to be dependent on anyone else'.[30]

But when there arises a possibility to re-establish co-operation ties with enterprises from other CIS countries, many Russian enterprises display great interest in it. Nor is that surprising: the largest part of the 'single national economic complex' of the former USSR remains in Russia, and it may have its gains maximised by the re-establishment of lost ties. Thus, in the first eight months after the creation of the Customs Union of Russia, Belorussia, Kazakhstan and Kirghizia in 1996, the trade turnover between these countries increased by 80 per cent.[31]

There are numerous examples of mutually advantageous re-establishment of co-operation ties between enterprises of the four countries mentioned above, and also of Ukraine (even if to a lesser extent). The Belorussian works Tsentrolit was, for all practical purposes, restored to life after the resumption of deliveries to the Russian enterprises Norilsk Nikel, the Murom and the Maikop Machine-Building Works, while the latter got a supplier of precision cast items required for the normal functioning of their equipment.

In Ukraine, the monopsonistic consumer of large-diametre pipes, Gazprom, a Russian gas concern that is gigantic even by world standards, is building up a multinational enterprise called Trubtrans. The latter is to supply pipes to Gazprom, manufacturing these through in-depth co-operation between Russian and Ukrainian plants, in the course of which semi-finished products of different stages of readiness are to cross the border of the two countries to and fro.

Consequently, the main line of the Russian way of overcoming the crisis caused by the break-up of the single country is to maintain the key enterprises of the historically rooted web of enterprises either through autarkic reliance on one's own forces or by means of re-establishment of lost ties with other post-Soviet countries. This does not mean, of course, that the new Russian community of enterprises will be an exact copy of the erstwhile Union-wide web. In the conditions of the market, the links between enterprises cannot remain such as they were under the planned economy. However, the most important enterprises set up in the Soviet epoch and the technological and economic ties linking them together are to be retained.

The Baltic countries: rejection of Soviet heritage?

Developments in Latvia, Estonia and Lithuania took a fundamentally different turn. The national factor is having a great influence on the future of enterprises in these countries. The former Union-wide web of all-Union subordinated (Russian) enterprises is regarded either as an economic threat to independence or as a chain manacling the Baltic to Russia. That is why the re-establishment of integration ties with former partners is seen as an extremely undesirable prospect. No wonder all three countries refused to join the CIS.

For Estonia and Latvia, almost one half of whose population consists of Russian-speaking inhabitants, the problem has yet another aspect. The national movement in these countries developed under the slogans of struggle against the danger of transformation of the native nation into an ethnic minority on its own territory.

Since the attainment of independence, it has become a policy in the national question in both countries (not recognised officially, but none the less real for all that) to try to make the Russian-speaking population leave the Baltic. This purpose is served by numerous acts of discrimination on the national principle, ranging from infringement of the rights of the Russian-speaking population to take part in privatisation and to own land, to refusal to grant citizenship, which has led, for instance, to such things – inconceivable in modern Europe – as deprivation of Russian-speaking inhabitants of the right to take part in elections, including elections of municipal authorities in the cities in which they make up a majority (such, in particular, are the laws of Latvia).

Guided by the logic of ousting the Russians, the authorities of the Baltic countries, while they may not have striven to increase the growing desolation that gripped the former all-Union subordinated enterprises after the break-up of the USSR, have not done much to prevent it, either. Meanwhile, numerous unofficial statements have expressed the hope that upon the bankruptcy of the enterprises, the Russians employed there would be forced to leave the country. Virtually all the major enterprises of the heavy industry of the Baltic have found themselves in a very grave situation. RAF (Latvia), the Baltic's only automobile works, for example, has ceased to turn out motor cars, has been fragmented into three parts, and is expected, in the long run, to turn out only simple spare parts for western motor cars.

In place of the industry built up in the Soviet period, banking, trade, insurance and the traditionally developed local agriculture were to become the basis of the economy of the Baltic countries. In other words, it was an attempt to reject the Soviet industrial heritage and to create a fundamentally new, post-industrial community of companies.

However, most of the plans described above have turned out to be utopian. A post-industrial society cannot be instantly created in a vacuum. The fact is that the economic ties with Russia and other CIS countries are much too important to be abandoned. Thus, the servicing of the transit of foreign-trade flows between the CIS and western countries across their territory has become the main source of foreign-currency earnings for the Baltic countries. It has been estimated that Estonia, for instance, is getting up to 80 per cent of its foreign-currency revenues and up to 40 per cent of GDP from these services.[32]

As a result, the urge to fence one's country off from Russia has given way to acute competition for the servicing of its foreign trade, which has been joined by the seaports of Riga and Ventspils (Latvia), Tallinn (Estonia) and Klaipeda (Lithuania). Incidentally, very many Russians are employed in the Baltic ports, so that there again developments tend to run counter to the policy of ousting the aliens. The key importance of the Russian market for the marketing of foodstuffs has likewise been demonstrated.

The future will show whether this revival of Russo-Baltic economic ties will also subsequently involve the enterprises once constituting a part of the Union-wide web of all-Union subordinated enterprises.

Uzbekistan: creative nationalism?

The enthusiasm of a whole people for a national idea has on many occasions in world history served as a socio-psychological prerequisite for the economic flourishing of this or that country. In the post-Soviet space, Uzbekistan is the only candidate for the role of a successfully self-asserting nation.

In contrast to other USSR successor nations, Uzbekistan did not opt for a 'shock', but for a slow, 'Chinese' way of reformation of its economy, with the retention of the authoritarian political system and strong state regulation of the economy. Uzbekistan did not live through any sharp decline in production: by 1995, industrial output in the country had not dropped below the 1990 level. Uzbekistan has gradually developed into the incontestably strongest state of central Asia and has even commenced economic expansion into Russia, the former 'metropolitan country'.

In Uzbekistan, the transformation of the former Union-wide web of all-Union subordinated enterprises took the form of their radical modernisation with the aid of foreign capital. The most impressive example of this kind is offered by the automobile enterprise UzDaewooAvto (projected capacity of 200,000 automobiles a year) founded as a joint venture with the South Korean Daewoo corporation.

The UzDaewooAvto enterprise, erected on the site of an old tractor-trailer works in the town of Asaka, is designed not only to satisfy the requirements in automobiles of Uzbekistan itself and of its central Asian neighbours, but also to win the Russian market, on which some 70 per cent of the automobiles are to be sold. Virtually all the machine-building enterprises in the country are being reprofiled for supplying the new giant with parts and components: at first twenty, and, after the automobile maker reaches the planned capacity, over fifty, plants are to deliver their products to the automobile maker, so that the proportion of local-made parts and components is to go up from 30 to 70 per cent.

The signs of national self-assertion are in evidence in all the features of the UzDaewooAvto project beginning from a demonstrative maintenance of super-natural cleanliness on the shop floor (workers operate in white gloves, which they change four times a day), to the proud declaration issued by President Islam Karimov of Uzbekistan at the opening of the works: 'In the past, Russia supplied us with bad cars, which is why the roads were bad; we now have good cars – and the roads will be good.'[33]

The UzDaewooAvto project is not the only one of its kind. The UzBAT tobacco corporation, set up as a joint venture with BAT, is likewise expected to supply the whole of central Asia and, possibly, other countries of the CIS as well. Negotiations are under way with Iveco on a joint venture to manufacture buses, with Daimler-Benz on the manufacture of trucks, and so on.

Inspired by the early successes and constantly rousing the national consciousness with reminiscences of the country's greatness in the Tamerlane epoch, Uzbekistan has been actively transforming the part of the Union-wide web of enterprises that fell to its lot. It will be easily seen, however, that the old ties continue to exert an influence on this process. The marketing outlets and the suppliers of parts and components (for instance, for the UzDaewoodAvto project – enterprises of Russia and Kirghizia), the high-technology facilities persistently maintained despite their loss-making (the Chkalov Aircraft factory in Tashkent), and the economic alliances (apart from the fairly amorphous CIS, there is Uzbekistan's closer alliance with Kirghizia and Kazakhstan) – all these are primarily oriented towards the post-Soviet space.

CONCLUDING REMARKS

John Rothschild, a theorist of ethnopolitics, has expressed the view that in a modernising society the non-ethnicised political forces usually strive to transform the modernisation-caused national contradictions either into a class policy (socialists) or into an ideology of individualism (liberals). But these efforts often end in an explosion of nationalism.[34] Something similar has apparently occurred in the USSR. A country craving political and economic change, while being relatively calm in the sense of interethnic relations, found itself plunged into a series of acute national conflicts after the Russian democrats led by Boris Yeltsin tried to use the national factor in the struggle for power.

The process of transition to a market economy turned out to be an onerous one for all the post-socialist countries. However, the break-up of the multinational Soviet state and of the Union-wide web of enterprises that unified it – *preceding* the start of the transformations – caused a grave crisis in the economy even *before* the emergence of the difficulties caused by the transition itself. The course of reforms in the republics of the former USSR may be proceeding so painfully because the reforms began with the economic disaster generated by the tragic resolution of the national question in the USSR.

However, there is some evidence of a trend towards the regeneration of the historically shaped community of enterprises. The all-Union (Russian) web of enterprises turned out to be stronger than the state that created it, and may well go on determining economic development on the entire post-Soviet space for a long time to come.

NOTES

1 L. A. Brutyan and B. G. Ivanovsky, *Trudoyoe sodruzhestvo sovetskikh narodov. Uchastiye narodov SSSR v sozdanii yedinogo narodnokhozyaistvennogo kompleksa* (Moscow, 1986), p. 27.

2 For details, see A. Yudanov, 'Large enterprises in the USSR: functional disorder' in A. Chandler, F. Amatori and T. Hikino (eds.), *Big Business and the Wealth of Nations* (Cambridge, 1997), pp. 397–432.

3 V. I. Bushkov and D. V. Mikulsky, *Tadzhikskoye obshchestvo na rubezhe tysyacheletiy (etnopoliticheskaya situatsiya v nachale 1990-ykh godov)* (Moscow, 1992), p. 9.

4 O. Ye. Kazmina, 'Dinamika etnicheskoi struktury naseleniya Latvii v XX veke' in M. N. Gubolgo (ed.), *Natsionalnye protsessy v SSSR* (Moscow, 1991), pp. 185–212 at p. 202.

5 *Ibid.*, pp. 199 and 209.

6 A. Kirkh and M. Kirkh, 'Nuzhna li regionalnaya natsionalnaya politika?' in *Natsionalnye protsessy v SSSR*, pp. 138–51 at p. 141.

7 S. A. Sitoryan and O. T. Bogomolov (eds.), *Problemy reintegratsii i formirovaniya ekonomicheskogo soyuza stran SNG* (Moscow, 1994), p. 31.

8 Brutyan and Ivanovsky, *Trudoyoe sodruzhestvo sovetskikh narodov*, p. 57.

9 *Ibid.*, p. 74.

10 *Ibid.*, p. 128.

11 *Latviya v tsifrakh v 1989 godu. Kratkiy statisticheskiy sbornik* (Riga, 1990), pp. 26 and 29.

12 N. Lubin, *Labour and Nationality in Soviet Central Asia: An Uneasy Compromise* (London, 1984), pp. 191 and 192.

13 See, for instance, L. Dienes, *Soviet Asia: Economic Development and National Policy Choices* (London, 1987), pp. 150–5 and 270.

14 *Sotsialisticheskaya industrializatsiy Azerbaidzhana. Dokumenty i materialy* (Baku, 1957), p. 586.

15 Lubin, *Labour and Nationality*, p. 77.

16 *Ibid.*, pp. 87–8.

17 G. A. Smirnov, 'Obrazovaniye SSSR – voploshcheniye leninskoi contseptsii federatsii svobodnykh natsiy' in *Sotsialno-politicheskiye problemy mezhnatsionalnykh otnosheniy v SSSR* (Moscow, 1989), p. 41.

18 Institut razvitiya Kazakhstana, *Mezhnatsionalnye otnosheniya v Kazakhstane: etnicheskiy aspekt kadrovoi politiki* (Almaty, 1994), p. 25.

19 I. M. Korotchenya, *Ekonomicheskiy soyuz suverennykh gosudarstv: strategiya i taktika stanovleniya* (St Petersburg, 1995), p. 58.

20 *Expert* 9 (1995), 39.

21 *Naseleniye Rossii 1995. Tretiy yezhegodnyi demograficheskiy doklad* [3rd demographic report of the Institut narodnokhozyaistvennogo pronozirovaniya RAN] (Moscow, 1996), p. 82.

22 Bushkov and Mikulsky, *Tadzhikskoye obshchestvo na rubezhe tysyacheletiy*, p. 55.

23 *Naseleniye Rossii 1995*, p. 82.

24 *Sodruzhestvo nezavisimykh gosudarstv v 1995 godu* [Statistical Yearbook of the CIS], (Moscow, 1996), pp. 16 and 19.

25 Korotchenya, *Ekonomicheskiy soyuz suverennykh gosudarstv*, p. 60.

26 Sitoryan and Bogomolov, *Problemy reintegratsii i formirovaniya*, p. 12.

27 A. Volsky, 'Stanovleniye obshchesoyuznogo rynka – osnova ekonomicheskogo razvitiya strany', *Ekonomicheskiye nauki* 5 (1991), p. 5.

28 *Expert* 8 (1995), 39.

29 *Expert* 8 (1996), 38.

30 *Expert* 16 (1995), 14 and 18.

31 *Financial Izvestiya*, 3 October 1996.

32 *Expert* 44 (1996), 10.

33 *Kommersant* 46 (1996), 13.

34 J. Rothschild, *Ethnopolitics: A Conceptual Framework* (New York, 1982), p. 3.

Index